NATURAL LAW AND MODERN
MORAL PHILOSOPHY

NATURAL LAW AND MODERN MORAL PHILOSOPHY

Edited by

**Ellen Frankel Paul, Fred D. Miller, Jr.,
and Jeffrey Paul**

CAMBRIDGE
UNIVERSITY PRESS

CAMBRIDGE
UNIVERSITY PRESS

32 Avenue of the Americas, New York NY 10013-2473, USA

Cambridge University Press is part of the University of Cambridge.

It furthers the University's mission by disseminating knowledge in the pursuit of education, learning and research at the highest international levels of excellence.

www.cambridge.org
Information on this title: www.cambridge.org/9780521794602

First published 2001

A catalogue record for this publication is available from the British Library

Library of Congress Cataloguing in Publication data

Natural Law and Modern Philosophy / edited by Ellen Frankel Paul,
Fred D. Miller, Jr., and Jeffrey Paul.   p.   cm.
Includes bibliographical references and index.
ISBN 0-521-79460-9 (pbk.)
1. Ethics. 2. Natural law.
I. Paul, Ellen Frankel.   II. Miller, Fred Dycus, 1944-
III. Paul, Jeffrey.
BJ1012 .N38   2000
171'.2–dc21   00-051921
CIP

ISBN 978-0-521-79460-2 Paperback

Cambridge University Press has no responsibility for the persistence or accuracy of URLs for external or third-party internet websites referred to in this publication, and does not guarantee that any content on such websites is, or will remain, accurate or appropriate.

CONTENTS

INTRODUCTION

Natural law has played an important role in ethics, political philosophy, and legal theory for at least twenty-five hundred years, starting perhaps with Heraclitus's observation that "all human laws are nourished by one divine law." The natural law tradition has included a wide array of philosophers: Plato, Aristotle, Aquinas, Grotius, Hobbes, Locke, Kant, and Hegel, among others. Although natural law beliefs informed the framers of the American Constitution, by the twentieth century interest in natural law had waned in the United States as well as in Western Europe. World War II and its aftermath, however, did much to rekindle interest in natural law, sparked by the desire of the victorious Allies to hold Nazi officials responsible for their crimes. The notion that there is a higher law to which all human laws and rulers must conform in order to be considered legitimate—the essential claim of natural law's adherents—provided the justification for the Nuremberg trials of Nazi war criminals.

In more recent years, lawyers, philosophers of law, and moral philosophers have continued a lively debate over both the coherence of natural law theory and its utility in analyzing policy issues ranging from abortion, to capital punishment, to just war theory. Interest in natural law's relationship to various moral theories, such as virtue ethics and moral realism, has also been hotly debated, as have the relationships between natural law and various theories of rights. The nine essays in this volume address some of the most intriguing questions raised by natural law theory and its implications for law, morality, and public policy. Some of the essays explore the implications that natural law theory has for jurisprudence, asking what natural law suggests about the use of legal devices such as constitutions and precedents. Other essays examine the connections between natural law and natural rights. Others discuss the interaction between natural law and various political concepts, such as citizens' rights and the obligation of citizens to obey their government. Still others analyze the natural law teachings of the tradition's great expositors.

An important general problem for natural law theories concerns the ability to link moral commitments to facts about the natural world; providing a convincing account of such a connection is a difficult task. One prominent way of attempting to link values and nature is presented in this volume's first essay, Larry Arnhart's "Thomistic Natural Law as Darwinian Natural Right." Canvasing the work of several important thinkers, beginning with Thomas Aquinas and ending with contemporary sociobiologist E. O. Wilson, Arnhart traces a lineage of Darwinian ethical naturalism that seems to provide support for a natural law ethics. Hundreds of years before Darwin, Aquinas, relying heavily on the work of

Aristotle before him, noted that man has a natural impulse toward marriage and familial bonding. From this insight, Aquinas was able to assess various forms of sexual mating practices with respect to their ability to serve these ends of human life. This use of natural impulses as a starting point for moral assessments gained favor from later philosophers and scientists. Adam Smith, for example, extended Aquinas's reasoning and showed how the human "moral sentiments" have an impact on economics as well as ethics; for Smith, the natural inclination of "sympathy" toward the interests of others is the touchstone for human moral development. Smith's own views had considerable influence over Charles Darwin, who saw how his own theory of natural selection could yield a scientific account of how a moral sense could arise as a component of human nature. The social theorist Edward Westermarck also played a prominent role in the Thomistic lineage by showing how anthropological and sociological accounts of marriage and family lend empirical support to many of the hypotheses suggested by earlier ethical naturalists. Today, Arnhart says, it is Wilson who is the most prominent advocate of this sort of ethical naturalism. Wilson advocates "consilience," the idea that a small number of natural laws provide the underpinning of all knowledge, scientific as well as philosophical. Drawing heavily on the same sort of discussions of marriage and family that provided support for other ethical naturalists, Wilson posits that human morality is linked to nature through the biologically based "epigenetic rules" of ethics. Like Aquinas, Smith, Darwin, and Westermarck before him, if Wilson is right in connecting morality and nature, then a significant hurdle for much of contemporary natural law theory has been overcome.

Though natural law may be compatible with modern evolutionary biology, it is still an open question how easily natural law can rest alongside various contemporary normative theories. Of particular interest here are theories of natural rights; since natural rights assume an important position in current political thought, any tensions between natural law and these rights may pose a problem for natural law theorists. Tensions of this sort are discussed by Douglas J. Den Uyl and Douglas B. Rasmussen in their essay, "Ethical Individualism, Natural Law, and the Primacy of Rights." Den Uyl and Rasmussen begin by considering the positions of various theorists who either assimilate natural rights into a natural law perspective (e.g., John Finnis and Henry Veatch) or assert that the natural rights perspective simply "accents" certain aspects of natural law thinking (e.g., A. P. d'Entrèves). Den Uyl and Rasmussen argue that both of these approaches are misguided, and that there are in fact significant issues that distinguish natural lawyers from natural rights advocates. In discussing both "new" and "traditional" natural law theories, Den Uyl and Rasmussen suggest that at its root the natural law perspective does not sufficiently take into account the fact that the human good is individualized and agent-relative. Specifically, the stress that the natural law framework places on the common good prevents that framework from adequately dealing with the important interconnection between individual choice and human flourishing. Natural rights, in contrast, do take this interconnection seriously, and as such, Den Uyl and Rasmussen argue, the natural rights perspective is preferable to that offered by natural law. This is not to say that the natural law tradition is entirely wrongheaded; Den Uyl and Rasmussen take pains to point out that this tradition is far more conducive to the natural rights approach than are most other contemporary ethical theories. In particular, the teleological eudaimonism that is generally adopted by natural lawyers is also the ethical position favored by many natural rights advocates. Yet while this similarity has made proponents of natural law and natural rights valued allies in the face of various philosophical challenges, when one is forced to select a normative political philosophy, the two erstwhile allies become distinct rivals.

The next two essays in this volume discuss the roles that consent and natural law play with respect to political obligation. Mark C. Murphy begins his essay, "Natural Law, Consent, and Political Obligation," by noting that contemporary natural law theorists provide accounts of political obligation that consciously avoid giving any important role to the consent of the governed. Under the usual natural law approach to political obligation, the central normative idea is that of the common good; the law, says the natural lawyer, provides a partial specification of what one must do if the common good is to be promoted. Yet this raises a question: why is the law's particular specification of the common good, or of how one should act to promote it, of any special value? Given that there are numerous different reasonable specifications of the common good, which are each better and worse than others in various respects, it is not clear why even those individuals who are committed to promoting the common good should necessarily follow the specifications of it set forth in the law. Murphy notes John Finnis's attempt to respond to this concern. Finnis says that because effective pursuit of the common good in a community of practically reasonable agents requires authority, law is society's best candidate as a tool for this pursuit. On this account, law is seen as a "salient coordinator," and because it is the best possible salient coordinator, it is authoritative. Yet Murphy argues that Finnis has moved a step too far; at best, Murphy claims, Finnis has shown that those who disobey the law are being *unreasonable*. To truly express the idea that law is obligatory, however, one has to show that it is *wrong* not to obey the law. Getting this result from a natural law account of political obligation, Murphy argues, requires that natural law accounts of obligation invoke consent. Law can be obligatory if one is willing, for the sake of practical reasoning, to consent to accepting the law's judgments regarding the common good. If one does this, then choosing not to obey the law would effectively be a violation of one's duty to promote the common good, and would thus be an immoral action. Therefore, once this "acceptance sense" of consent is incorporated into the natural law account of political obligation, one can meaningfully say that it is wrong for someone to break the law: natural law needs consent in order to generate an adequate theory of obligation.

One reason that natural law theorists have tended to avoid using consent when presenting accounts of political obligation is that consent-based obligations have been increasingly under attack. In his "The Natural Basis of Political Obligation," George Klosko mounts just such an attack; he begins by criticizing contemporary conceptions of the individual. Whereas many political theorists seem to view the individual in isolation, Klosko argues that any accurate portrayal of an individual must take into account the fact that he or she receives indispensable benefits from the state. When one considers this in light of the principle of fairness, which states that the receipt of benefits from a system of provision generates obligations to that system, it becomes clear that individuals in fact have political obligations to their government whether or not they have consented to it. Various theorists argue against this conclusion by noting that indispensable public goods can be provided by private provision mechanisms. If this is the case, then it would seem that the state cannot generate obligations to itself merely by providing individuals with benefits. However, Klosko claims that before arguments from alternative provision can be used to reject one's existing obligations, one must present a plausible system of alternative provision. When this requirement is fully appreciated, it seems that truly adequate alternative provision mechanisms will be difficult to find; it is tough to see, for example, how public defense could be provided by a collective scheme other than the state. Yet the problems with alternative supply are not simply practical. Game-theoretic analysis of the provision of public goods has long shown that there are theoretical problems involved in trying to provide such goods in the absence of a strong central authority. Political philosopher Michael Taylor has argued, however, that once we take into account the fact that politics is a continuous process that can yield cooperative outcomes, alternative provision mechanisms seem feasible. Klosko rejects this argument. For public-goods provision to be effective in a society without a central authority, he argues, we need conditions in which it is easy to tell whether others in the society are cooperating with the provision scheme. In large modern states, however, this information requirement simply cannot be met. Given this, the theoretical problems faced by alternative provision mechanisms are not eliminated by the continuous nature of politics. Because alternative supply seems both practically and theoretically implausible, Klosko concludes, it seems clear that citizens will have a difficult time finding a provision mechanism that will allow them to obviate their political obligations to the state.

In legal philosophy, natural law arguments posit that external rules influence what types of laws can be considered legitimate. In this vein,

Michael S. Moore, in "Law as Justice," shows how moral truths are part of the calculus by which one determines whether given propositions of law are true. Natural lawyers, Moore states, argue that because something is legal only if it obligates, and because something obligates only if it is not unjust, then something is legal only if it is not unjust. Natural lawyers use a functionalist approach to establish the first step of this argument. Under this approach, one argues that law has a particular function and that this function can only be realized if law is obligating. One might find it appealing here to suggest that this functionalism argument is all that is needed to establish the natural law conclusion that something can be legal only if it is just. Moore argues, however, that this direct functionalist argument is false; functionalism alone cannot support the natural lawyer's desired conclusion. Moore illustrates this by looking at various things one may categorize as "legal." With respect to the laws of individual cases, for example, it seems clear that the judge's role in deciding a case is not simply to follow the plain meaning of the statute at issue or to simply act in accordance with that statute's purpose; rather, his obligation is to balance the values inherent in following those procedures against all other values that might be implicated by his decision. The judge's obligation to make such all-things-considered judgments cannot be established, however, by mere appeal to the functions of the laws of cases. This means that the natural law view of the laws of cases cannot be established by functionalism alone; some form of independent argumentation is needed to reach the natural lawyer's conclusion. While functionalism does allow for a limited connection between the laws of cases and values, it does so in too weak a way to make sense of judicial obligation. Moore applies similar analysis to common law rules and concludes that the functionalist account of these rules is likewise too weak to generate obligation on the part of individuals. Substantive justice cannot be ensured by a functionalist natural law account, and must seek its substantiation elsewhere, perhaps in some conception of the common good or the good *tout court*.

In his essay, "The 'Laws of Reason' and the Surprise of the Natural Law," Hadley Arkes examines the role of reason in assessing the legitimacy of positive law. The leading minds and jurists among the American Founders often found it necessary to trace their judgments back to the "axioms" or "first principles" of the law. Men like Alexander Hamilton, John Marshall, and James Wilson saw nothing odd then in writing about "the law of nature and reason." But what seems to have vanished from the recognition of lawyers, and even conservative jurists, in our own time, is that the understanding of "natural law" was indeed bound up with "the laws of reason." There is still a disposition to regard natural law as bound up with systems of belief, with no anchor in propositions that are knowably true or even necessary. Even writers friendly to natural law may slip into discussions about "theories" of natural law. But that stance must presuppose that the discussants will finally choose among the theories that seem more or less persuasive, more or less true. What seems to be lost in this perspective, Arkes argues, is that natural law is not to be found anywhere in that inventory of "theories." It is to be found, rather, in those deeper principles of judgment, the principles to which one must finally appeal in making judgments about the validity of those contending theories. Arkes seeks to recall how an earlier generation understood the natural law as bound up with the laws of reason, and he develops the argument through a series of notable cases: Lincoln's opposition to the decision in the *Dred Scott* case; the classic arguments made by James Wilson and John Jay in *Chisholm v. Georgia*; and the attempts by the Supreme Court in recent years to revive the Eleventh Amendment. That project in revival by the Court faces the prospect of being stymied at its foundation by a possibility that seems to run beyond the imagination of the judges: namely, that the Eleventh Amendment is unworkable precisely for the reasons that Wilson and Jay explained in the *Chisholm* case: not only did those first jurists get the matter right, but they were right of necessity, because their judgment was anchored in the axioms of the law.

Our next essayist focuses on the morality of the lawmaker. In his contribution to this volume, "Natural Law as Professional Ethics: A Reading of Fuller," David Luban argues that the work of legal philosopher Lon Fuller can be seen as an example of natural law theory applicable not so much to laws themselves as to lawmakers. A consistent strand in Fuller's work is his claim that 'lawmaker' is a *purposive concept*: labeling someone a lawmaker automatically implies that this person can be judged in reference to his ability to engage in the duties of that occupation. The duties— or, to use Fuller's term, the "role-morality"—of the lawmaker emerge from the choice of law as a tool for governing others. Unlike other methods of governing, such as managerial direction, using law to govern others implies a respect for the autonomy and moral powers of the governed. To fulfill his role-morality, then, a lawmaker must acknowledge these moral characteristics and be successful at managing the resultant relationship between those who govern and those who are governed. On this reading, Luban notes, Fuller is a not a "natural lawyer" in the sense that he asserts a necessary link between legal and moral terms. Rather, Fuller links morality and law by conceiving of law as a discipline whose practitioners can be morally judged on the merits of their performance in their role. Luban argues that seeing Fuller in this way gives Fuller's account of the link between morality and law the resources to deal with some of the strongest arguments of "progressive positivists" like Frederick Schauer, Neil MacCormick, and Robin West. However, Fuller's theory also seems to have a troubling aspect. Even if lawmaking is seen as a purposive activity whose ultimate goal is respecting the moral agency of the governed, it is not at all clear how Fuller's eight "principles of legality"—eight principles that he claims are found in all lawmaking regimes—can prevent the lawmaker from focusing only on respecting the moral agency of particular classes of people. There may be a significant difference between "those whose agency the law respects" and "those who are governed by the law." Luban notes, for example, that the vast majority of legal regimes throughout history have tolerated gender subordination while respecting the eight principles; this suggests that Fuller's account of the moral dictates of lawmaking do not in fact guarantee that the law has the moral content that Fuller ascribes to it.

Though natural law raises numerous interesting theoretical issues, it also has certain implications for public policy. In "Fairness in Holdings: A Natural Law Account of Property and Welfare Rights," Joseph Boyle uses a Catholic natural law perspective to develop an argument for the establishment of welfare rights. Boyle begins by surveying Aquinas's account of property. Aquinas believes that it is morally permissible for humans to possess various things and use them for human benefit. Yet there are two aspects to this concept of possession. When considered as the authority to take care of and distribute things, Aquinas thinks possession of things should be held by individuals; when possession is considered in terms of the actual use of goods, Aquinas says that possession should be in common. Under Aquinas's theory, individual ownership is permitted because it allows for the advantageous use of things, but the discretion that ownership provides is matched by an obligation to give to others that which one does not need. This obligation emerges from a moral norm of neighborly assistance; our obligation to help others begins with those who are close to us, and over time gradually expands outward. This expansion is affected by the technology and social organization in society. The result is that in modern states, our duties of neighborly assistance extend well beyond those whom we meet face-to-face. Carrying out these duties, Boyle argues, requires the sort of social coordination that can only be provided through political action. Unlike voluntary organizations, political society can utilize regulatory power and compel public support in order to help the needy. That aid to the needy is provided through politically established means does not change the fact that the ultimate root of these welfare rights is the prepolitical obligation of individuals to provide neighborly assistance. This implies, in addition, that one's political obligation to help the needy may not exhaust one's moral obligation. Even after one has paid one's taxes and fulfilled other state-imposed commitments, one may still be morally required to help one's neighbors or other needy individuals.

In the volume's final essay, "Natural Law, Natural Rights, and Classical Liberalism: On Montesquieu's Critique of Hobbes," Michael Zuckert analyzes the natural law views that Montesquieu presents in his *The Spirit of the Laws*. In the philosophical wake of Hobbes's *Leviathan*, a diverse array of natural law thinking emerged, and Montesquieu's precise location amid these varying schools of thought is difficult to ascertain. Zuck-

xiv   INTRODUCTION

ert examines three critiques of Hobbes that emerge in *Spirit*, and argues
that Montesquieu's overall project should be seen as an attempt to develop a natural law doctrine based on Cartesian ontology and aimed at
refuting Hobbes's conventionalism. In the first of these critiques, Montesquieu seems to differ with Hobbes over the character of the natural
law, but Zuckert shows that once we fully assess Montesquieu's position
on this issue, the actual differences raised in this critique are minimal. In
contrast, Montesquieu's second critique of Hobbes makes the differences
between the two apparent. Though both Hobbes and Montesquieu agree
in paying significant theoretical attention to the state of nature, the conclusions they reach are very different. Hobbes argued that man develops
society in order to overcome the state of nature; in contrast, Montesquieu
argues that the "laws of nature," his term for the natural forces motivating human action, spur humans to assemble into societies. On Montesquieu's account, only after men enter into societies and lose the feelings
of weakness that they had in the state of nature do they become more
aggressive and enter into a Hobbesian state of war. It is this state of war,
created by social life, that drives men to develop positive laws; these
positive laws, Montesquieu says, are a reassertion of the laws of nature.
In later sections of *Spirit*, Montesquieu's third critique of Hobbes emerges
as Montesquieu presents an account of political right through which positive laws can be judged. Based on natural right, Montesquieu's account
is quite different from that of Hobbes, and is in fact fairly close to the
account presented by Locke. Unlike Locke, however, Montesquieu's standard of good government is simply the ability to provide citizens with the
opinion of security. This emphasis on the *opinion* of security represents
Montesquieu's subjectivization of the criteria of political right. Advocating this subjective criterion leads Montesquieu to favor various political
mechanisms that provide citizens with greater peace of mind. Hence,
unlike many of his contemporaries, Montesquieu advocates an independent judiciary and popular representation.

Natural law theory is of ancient pedigree, yet it has proven to be of
enduring value, providing both valuable insights and alternatives to contemporary ethical, legal, and moral theories. These nine essays—written
by leading legal theorists and philosophers—offer important insights into
the nature and implications of the natural law perspective.

ACKNOWLEDGMENTS

The editors wish to acknowledge several individuals at the Social Philosophy and Policy Center, Bowling Green State University, who provided invaluable assistance in the preparation of this volume. They include Mary Dilsaver, Terrie Weaver, and Carrie-Ann Biondi.

The editors would like to extend special thanks to Publication Specialist Tamara Sharp, for attending to innumerable day-to-day details of the book's preparation; and to Managing Editor Matthew Buckley, for providing dedicated assistance throughout the editorial and production process.

CONTRIBUTORS

Larry Arnhart is Professor of Political Science at Northern Illinois University. He is the author of *Darwinian Natural Right: The Biological Ethics of Human Nature* (1998), *Political Questions: Political Philosophy from Plato to Rawls* (1987), and *Aristotle on Political Reasoning: A Commentary on the "Rhetoric"* (1983). He is currently working on a book on the interrelation of biology and natural law from Thomas Aquinas to Edward O. Wilson.

Douglas J. Den Uyl is Vice-President of Educational Programs at Liberty Fund. His interests are in the areas of social and political philosophy and ethics. He is the author of *The Virtue of Prudence* (1991) and *Power, State, and Freedom: An Interpretation of Spinoza's Political Thought* (1983); he is also a coauthor of *Liberalism Defended: The Challenge of Post-Modernity* (with Douglas B. Rasmussen, 1997) and *Liberty and Nature: An Aristotelian Defense of Liberal Order* (with Douglas B. Rasmussen, 1991).

Douglas B. Rasmussen is Professor of Philosophy at St. John's University. He is a coauthor of *Liberalism Defended: The Challenge of Post-Modernity* (with Douglas J. Den Uyl, 1997) and *Liberty and Nature: An Aristotelian Defense of Liberal Order* (with Douglas J. Den Uyl, 1991); in addition, he is a coeditor of *Liberty for the Twenty-First Century* (with Tibor R. Machan, 1995). He has also published numerous articles on epistemology, ethics, and political philosophy, and he guest-edited the January 1992 issue of *The Monist* on the topic "Teleology and the Foundation of Value."

Mark C. Murphy is Assistant Professor of Philosophy at Georgetown University. He is the author of a number of articles on natural law theory, the theory of political obligation, and the moral and political views of Thomas Hobbes. He is the author of *Natural Law and Practical Rationality* and the editor of *Alasdair MacIntyre*; both titles are forthcoming from Cambridge University Press. His current research interests include natural law political philosophy as well as the nature of divine authority.

George Klosko is Professor of Government and Foreign Affairs at the University of Virginia. His books include *Democratic Procedures and Liberal Consensus* (2000), *The Principle of Fairness and Political Obligation* (1992), and *The Development of Plato's Political Theory* (1986). He is also the author of the two-volume *History of Political Theory: An Introduction* (1993, 1995).

Michael S. Moore is Warren Distinguished Professor of Law at the University of San Diego and Co-Director of the Institute of Law and Philosophy at the University of San Diego. His books include *Educating Oneself in Public: Critical Essays in Jurisprudence* (2000), *Placing Blame: A General Theory of the Criminal Law* (1998), and *Act and Crime: The Philosophy of Action and its Implications for Criminal Law* (1993). He is also the coauthor of *Foundations of Criminal Law* (with Leo Katz and Stephen Morse, 1999).

Hadley Arkes is Edward Ney Professor of Jurisprudence and American Institutions at Amherst College. His books include *The Return of George Sutherland: Restoring a Jurisprudence of Natural Rights* (1994), *Beyond the Constitution* (1990), and *First Things: An Inquiry into the First Principles of Morals and Justice* (1986).

David Luban is Frederick Haas Professor of Law and Philosophy at the Georgetown University Law Center. He has written many articles on law, ethics, and political philosophy. He is also the author of *Legal Modernism* (1994) and *Lawyers and Justice: An Ethical Study* (1988), the editor of *The Ethics of Lawyers* (1994), and the coeditor of *Legal Ethics* (with Deborah L. Rohde; 2d ed., 1995).

Joseph Boyle is Professor of Philosophy at the University of Toronto, and is the Principal of St. Michael's College. He has written in the areas of bioethics, social and political philosophy, and just war theory. He is the coauthor of *Nuclear Deterrence, Morality, and Realism* (with John Finnis and Germain Grisez, 1987), and is the coeditor of *Philosophical Perspectives on Bioethics* (with L. W. Sumner, 1996).

Michael Zuckert is Nancy R. Dreux Professor of Government and International Studies at the University of Notre Dame. He works in the areas of political philosophy, American constitutional theory, and American political thought. He is the author of *The Natural Rights Republic: Studies in the Foundation of the American Political Tradition* (1996) and *Natural Rights and the New Republicanism* (1994).

THOMISTIC NATURAL LAW AS DARWINIAN NATURAL RIGHT*

By Larry Arnhart

I. Introduction

The publication in 1975 of Edward O. Wilson's *Sociobiology* provoked a great controversy, for in that work Wilson claimed that ethics was rooted in human biology. On the first page of the book, he asserted that our deepest intuitions of right and wrong are guided by the emotional control centers of the brain, which evolved via natural selection to help the human animal exploit opportunities and avoid threats in the natural environment.[1] In 1998, the publication of Wilson's *Consilience* renewed the controversy, as he continued to argue for explaining ethics through the biology of the moral sentiments.[2]

Many of Wilson's critics have warned that his reductionistic explanation of human ethics as a mere expression of animal impulses promotes a degrading view of human life. Some of his religious critics have explained the emergence of Wilsonian views of ethics as an inevitable consequence of a scientific naturalism that denies God's moral law as the supernatural ground for our sense of right and wrong. Despite the plausibility of such criticisms, I think Wilson's position is much stronger than it might seem at first glance. The full strength of Wilson's Darwinian ethics becomes clear only when it is seen as an expression of what I have called "Darwinian natural right."[3]

A Darwinian view of human nature can support the natural law reasoning of Thomas Aquinas (1225–1274). The biological character of the natural moral law is suggested by a famous statement by Ulpian (d. 228 A.D.), an ancient Roman jurist: "Natural right is that which nature has taught all animals."[4] (Here the term "natural right" [*ius naturale*] is interchangeable with "natural law" [*lex naturalis*].) To illustrate the natural

* I am grateful to the Earhart Foundation for a research grant that supported the writing of this essay.
[1] Edward O. Wilson, *Sociobiology: The New Synthesis* (Cambridge, MA: Harvard University Press, 1975), 3, 129, 563.
[2] Edward O. Wilson, *Consilience: The Unity of Knowledge* (New York: Alfred A. Knopf, 1998).
[3] Larry Arnhart, *Darwinian Natural Right: The Biological Ethics of Human Nature* (Albany: State University of New York Press, 1998).
[4] "Ius naturale est, quod natura omnia animalia docuit." Justinian, *Justinian's Institutes*, ed. and trans. Peter Birks and Grant McLeod (Ithaca, NY: Cornell University Press, 1987), 1.2.

1

inclinations that human beings share with other animals, Ulpian referred
to the sexual union of male and female and the parental care of offspring
as animal propensities that sustain human marriage and family life in
conformance to natural law. Quoted at the beginning of Justinian's *Institutes* (533 A.D.), Ulpian's remarks entered the medieval tradition of natural law reasoning, and they were cited by Aquinas when he explained
natural law as rooted in "natural inclinations" or "natural instincts" that
human beings share with other intelligent animals.[5]

Adam Smith (1723–1790) continued this tradition of thought by explaining morality as expressing the moral sentiments of human nature.
Influenced by Smith's moral theory, Charles Darwin (1809–1882) explained the moral sentiments as manifesting a moral sense rooted in the
biological nature of human beings as social animals. The sociologist Edward Westermarck (1862–1939), who was influenced by both Smith and
Darwin, defended a view of morality as founded in moral emotions shaped
by natural selection throughout evolutionary history. Wilson recognizes
that his biological theory of the moral sentiments belongs to a tradition of
ethical naturalism that includes Smith, Darwin, and Westermarck. However, he does not recognize the roots of that tradition in the natural law
reasoning of Aquinas.

In this essay, I will develop the common ground that exists between
Aquinas, Smith, Darwin, Westermarck, and Wilson. In doing this, I will
indicate how biological reasoning about human nature can strengthen the
case for natural law by giving it the support of Darwinian science. As
suggested by Ulpian's statement, I will use sexual mating, parental care,
and familial bonding as examples of the biological basis of natural law.

I will use the term *natural law* to refer to the following cluster of ideas:
(1) animals have innate propensities, (2) the normal development of each
kind of animal requires the fulfillment of these propensities, (3) animals
with conscious awareness desire the satisfaction of these propensities,
and (4) human beings use their unique capacity for rational deliberation
to formulate ethical standards as plans of life for the harmonious satisfaction of their natural desires over a complete life. I will argue that
Darwinian biology supports this natural law understanding of ethics by
showing how such inborn desires and cognitive capacities arise as products of human biological nature.

II. Thomas Aquinas

Aquinas's best statement on natural law is in the section on law in his
Summa Theologiae. Within that section, one of the crucial passages is his

---

[5] For the history of Ulpian's remarks in medieval thought, see Michael Bertram Crowe,
The Changing Profile of the Natural Law (The Hague, The Netherlands: Nijhoff, 1977), 43–51,
142–55. Crowe finds Aquinas's use of Ulpian's definition of natural right puzzling, because
Crowe wants to interpret natural law in a Kantian way, as a set of purely rational principles
set apart from animal nature.

explanation of how the primary precepts of natural law conform to the three levels of natural inclinations. The importance of the passage justifies quoting it at length.[6]

> Since good has the idea of an end, and evil the idea of a contrary, hence it is that all those things to which a human being has a natural inclination, reason naturally apprehends as good, and consequently as objects to be pursued, and the contraries of these as evil and to be avoided. Therefore, the order of the precepts of the natural law is according to the order of the natural inclinations. For there is first in a human being an inclination to good according to the nature which he shares with all substances: insofar as every substance seeks the preservation of itself according to its own nature. And according to this inclination, those things through which human life is preserved and threats to life avoided belong to the natural law. Secondly, there is in a human being an inclination to some things more special to him according to the nature that he shares with other animals. And according to this inclination, it is said that those things are of natural law "that nature has taught all animals," such as the joining of male and female, the education of children, and similar things. In a third mode, there is in a human being an inclination to good according to the nature of reason, which is proper to him: thus a human being has a natural inclination to that which knows the truth about God, and to that which lives in society. And according to this inclination, those things that pertain to this kind of inclination belong to natural law: for example, that a human being avoid ignorance, and that he not offend those others with whom he must live, and other such things that pertain to this inclination.[7]

This passage sketches the three levels of human natural inclinations that must be satisfied for the fullest flourishing of human life. In the passage, Aquinas assumes a series of principles that he takes from Aristotle. Aquinas says, for instance, that "the good is the desirable." Although the diverse goods of life are desirable in different ways, there is "one ultimate end" corresponding to the "unity of human nature." Furthermore, "the ultimate end is the ultimate term of desire's natural inclination."[8]

Comparing this passage with Aquinas's other references to natural inclinations, it becomes clear that he is using Aristotle's biological psy-

---

[6] In my translations of Aquinas's Latin, I have tried to be as literal as possible.

[7] Thomas Aquinas, *Summa Theologiae*, I–II, q. 94, a. 2.

[8] Thomas Aquinas, *Commentary on Aristotle's "Nicomachean Ethics,"* secs. 9, 21, 94, 106–7.

chology to distinguish the three kinds of inclination.[9] First, there are the natural tendencies of the body that work automatically, with little or no cognitive awareness. Second, there are the natural tendencies of sensory desires that require the cognitive awareness that human beings share with other animals. Finally, there are the natural tendencies of intellectual desires that require the conceptual cognition that is uniquely human. Thus, for example, at the first level, the human body naturally tends to preserve its healthy functioning in ways that do not depend on conscious awareness. At the second level, human beings share with some other animals the sensory desires for conjugal bonding and parental care of offspring; these desires require the cognitive ability for perceptual judgment that is found only in intelligent animals. Aquinas quotes Ulpian's remarks as applying to this second level of natural law, which human beings share with other animals.[10] At the third level, human beings have intellectual desires for goods such as knowledge and social interaction, which require the cognitive ability for conceptual judgment that is uniquely human. Aquinas does recognize that there is a natural diversity in the desires of human beings that distinguishes one individual from another. For example, although there is a natural tendency to sexual union among most human beings, a few individuals will have a natural temperament that inclines them to celibacy. Consequently, Aquinas sometimes distinguishes the natural human desires as either "generic" (shared with other animals), "specific" (shared with other human beings as rational animals), or "temperamental" (the individually unique traits of a human being).[11] He draws this trichotomy of the human desires from Aristotle's theory of biological inheritance.[12]

Aquinas observes that unlike plants and inanimate entities, human beings and other intelligent animals display reason and desire in their movements.[13] Intelligent animals consciously apprehend the objects of their desires, gather and assess information in their environment relevant to their desires, and then act according to their judgment of how best to satisfy their desires. In doing this, they learn to apprehend physical things and other animals as pleasurable or painful, useful or harmful, friendly or hostile. They act voluntarily in that they initiate acts as guided by some knowledge of their goals. They remember the past and anticipate the future. As social animals, they judge the intentions of other animals and communicate with them to act for common ends. They display and

---

[9] Aquinas, *Summa Theologiae*, I, q. 59, a. 1; I, q. 80, a. 1; I-II, q. 1, a. 2; I-II, q. 6, a. 1-4; I-II, q. 26, a. 1; I-II, q. 35, a. 1; I-II, q. 41, a. 3.

[10] Ibid., I-II, q. 94, a. 2; I-II, q. 95, a. 4, ad 1; II-II, q. 57, a. 3; Aquinas, *Commentary on Aristotle's "Nicomachean Ethics,"* sec. 1019.

[11] Aquinas, *Summa Theologiae*, I-II, q. 46, a. 5; I-II, q. 51, a. 1; I-II, q. 63, a. 1.

[12] Aristotle, *Generation of Animals*, 767b24–769b31.

[13] Aquinas, *Summa Theologiae*, I, q. 78, a. 4; I, q. 80, a. 1; I, q. 83, a. 1; I-II, q. 6, a. 2; I-II, q. 40, a. 3; I-II, q. 58, a. 1; Aquinas, *Commentary on Aristotle's "De Anima,"* secs. 629, 874.

recognize social emotions such as love, hate, and anger; learn from experience; and transmit what they learn to others. Insofar as Aquinas thus recognizes the continuity between human beings and other intelligent animals, he takes a position that is at least compatible with the Darwinian idea that the human species evolved from ancestral species of nonhuman animals.[14]

The biological character of Aquinas's reasoning about natural law as rooted in natural desires is clear in his account of marriage and familial bonding. Citing Ulpian, Aquinas declares that marriage is natural because it satisfies natural desires that human beings share with some animals.[15] He speaks of the human disposition to marriage as a "natural instinct of the human species."[16] On his account, the primary natural end of marriage is to secure the parental care of children; the secondary natural end is to secure the conjugal bonding of male and female for a sexual division of labor in the household. Among some animals, Aquinas observes, the female can care properly for her offspring on her own, and thus there is no natural need for any enduring bond between male and female. For those animals whose offspring do require care from both parents, however, nature implants an inclination for male and female to stay together in order to provide the necessary parental care.[17] Just as is the case for those animals whose offspring could not survive or develop normally without parental care, human offspring depend upon parents for their existence, nourishment, and education. To secure this natural end, then, nature instills in human beings natural desires for sexual coupling and parental care. Even if they do not have children, however, men and women naturally desire marital union because, not being self-sufficient, they seek the conjugal friendship of husband and wife sharing in household life.

Marriage as constituted by customary or legal rules, Aquinas says, is uniquely human, because such rules require a cognitive capacity for conceptual reasoning that no other animals have. Even so, rules of marriage provide formal structure to natural desires that are ultimately rooted in the animal nature of human beings. This is not to say that human nature will lead all human beings to desire marriage: it is beneficial for human communities to have a few people who do not marry, but instead pursue

[14] For a good survey of the evidence in Aquinas's writings that supports this conclusion, see Judith Barad, *Aquinas on the Nature and Treatment of Animals* (San Francisco: International Scholars Publications, 1995). For the argument that Aquinas's view of human nature and natural law is rooted in a "biological paradigm," see Anthony J. Lisska, *Aquinas's Theory of Natural Law: An Analytic Reconstruction* (Oxford: Clarendon Press, 1996), 68, 96–109, 131, 189–91, 198–201, 218–22, 258.

[15] Aquinas, *Summa Theologiae*, II–II, q. 57, a. 3; Suppl., q. 41, a. 1; Aquinas, *Commentary on Aristotle's "Nicomachean Ethics,"* sec. 1019.

[16] Aquinas, *Summa Contra Gentiles*, bk. 3, chap. 123.

[17] Ibid., bk. 3, chaps. 122–23.

contemplative lives for which marriage would be an impediment. A few people will be inclined by their natural temperament to lead such a life.[18]

Aquinas judges every form of sexual mating as natural or unnatural depending on how well it satisfies the two aforementioned natural ends of marriage—parental care and conjugal bonding. Completely promiscuous mating is contrary to nature insofar as it would hinder both parental care and conjugal bonding. Monogamous mating (one husband with one wife) is fully natural because it satisfies both natural ends. Polygynous mating (one husband with multiple wives) is partly natural but partly unnatural.[19] It is natural insofar as it is possible for a polygynous marriage to secure both parental care and conjugal bonding. However, it is partly unnatural: polygyny often impedes conjugal bonding because the jealousy of the co-wives tends to promote conflict in the household. Polyandrous mating (one wife with multiple husbands) is completely unnatural, because the jealousy of the co-husbands would impede both parental care and conjugal bonding. The reason that polygyny and polyandry are "asymmetrical" in terms of fulfilling the natural ends of marriage is that between men and women, it is much more difficult for men to know which children are theirs. Consequently, the uncertainty of paternity in a polyandrous marriage would weaken the inclination of the husbands to care for the wife's children. (Fraternal polyandry—brothers sharing a wife—can mitigate but not eliminate this problem.) In competing for mates, the sexual jealousy of men is typically much more intense than the sexual jealousy of women. As a result of these natural differences between men and women, it is easier for women to share a husband than for men to share a wife.

Aquinas also uses his criteria of mating to assess incest. Because it impedes the natural ends secured by marriage, Aquinas believes that incestuous mating is contrary to natural law. Although it is possible for a father to impregnate his daughter or for a son to impregnate his mother, the sexual bonding that is fitting for husband and wife would contradict the asexual bonding that is fitting for parent and child. Furthermore, from experience we see that children of incestuous matings "cannot thrive."[20]

In developing this reasoning about the natural law of marriage, Aquinas appeals repeatedly to Aristotle's biological studies of animal mating. Following Aristotle, Aquinas observes that complete promiscuity is natural only for animals whose offspring do not require the long-term care of both parents. Many animals practice polygyny. Monogamy is common among some animals, such as birds, for whom monogamy secures the

---

[18] Aquinas, *Summa Theologiae*, Suppl., q. 41, a. 2; Aquinas, *Summa Contra Gentiles*, bk. 3, chap. 123.

[19] Aquinas, *Summa Theologiae*, Suppl., q. 65, a. 1; Aquinas, *Summa Contra Gentiles*, bk. 3, chap. 124.

[20] Aquinas, *Summa Theologiae*, Suppl., q. 54, a. 3; Aquinas, *Summa Contra Gentiles*, bk. 3, chap. 125.

good of offspring that could not survive and develop without intensive care by both parents over long periods of time. Although incest occurs among some animals, other animals, including human beings, show a natural avoidance of it. In comparison with other animals, human beings are strongly monogamous but mildly polygynous. To conform to the natural law of marriage, human laws must satisfy these natural instincts of human biological nature. In regulating marriage, Aquinas explains, "positive laws should proceed from the instinct of nature, if they are human; just as in the demonstrative sciences, also, every human discovery takes its origin from naturally known principles."[21]

Influenced by Aristotle's biology, Aquinas recognizes that every animal species is unique, and that the human species' uniqueness lies in its capacity for conceptual reasoning as mediated by language. This allows human beings to rationally deliberate about the best way to satisfy their natural desires for mating and parenting and then to formulate their conclusions about the proper customary or legal norms for marriage and familial bonding. Like other intelligent animals, human beings are moved by sensory desires to act for reasons, and this requires some cognitive ability to judge opportunities and threats in one's environment. Yet human beings are also unique among animals in being moved by intellectual desires to compare alternative reasons for action in the light of past experience and future expectations; this allows humans to formulate and execute deliberate conceptions of a whole life well-lived.[22]

In employing such biological reasoning, Aquinas was influenced by the work of Albert the Great, his teacher at the University of Paris, who wrote a massive survey of the whole field of zoology, beginning with Aristotle's corpus. Albert's work in biological science was part of his larger project to vindicate the scientific study of natural causal laws through reason, observation, and experimentation; the end result of this work was to establish science as a source of knowledge independent from theology.[23] (It was fitting, therefore, that in 1941, Pope Pius XII proclaimed Albert the patron saint of natural scientists.) Relying on a critical reading of Aristotle's biology, Albert stressed the uniqueness of human beings as the only animals endowed with the powers of intellect and speech. Yet he also observed that other animals, though they lack human levels of reasoning and communicative prowess, are not all equally lacking; various creatures exhibit subtly different levels of sophistication in these areas. We see that "the animals other than the human are not entirely without the power of thought," which shows that nature "progresses gradually through

---

[21] Aquinas, *Summa Contra Gentiles*, bk. 3, chap. 123.

[22] Aquinas, *Commentary on Aristotle's "De Anima,"* secs. 395–98, 631–35, 643–50, 803–4, 812–46.

[23] See James A. Weisheipl, ed., *Albertus Magnus and the Sciences* (Toronto, Canada: Pontifical Institute of Mediaeval Studies, 1980).

many intermediates."[24] Some nonhuman animals, Albert observed, do have "experiential knowledge" that manifests "a sort of prudence" and a "capacity for instruction," which thus shows that these animals have at least "a shadow of reason."[25] Many animals have some "estimative power" by which, while deciding how they should act to satisfy their desires, they judge the intentions of other animals.[26] The most intelligent of the non-human animals are simians—monkeys and apes—and pygmies, which belong to a species that is intermediate between simians and humans. The simians and pygmies, Albert says, show "a human likeness beyond all [other] animals," and "seem to have something like reason."[27]

Albert also observed that as political animals, human beings are like other social animals such as ants, bees, wasps, and cranes. Human sociality is unique, however, insofar as it can be based on formal laws or customary rules formulated deliberately by reason. Similarly, ethics in the strict sense is uniquely human to the extent that it requires some rational deliberation in formulating a plan of how to live. Albert notes, however, that some other animals do exhibit "some natural inclination to a likeness of virtue," because their natural instincts and cognitive capacities incline them to act according to a "plan of life."[28] On each of these points—and on the points involving human and animal capacities to reason and communicate—Albert reiterates a biological teaching of Aristotle that is later adopted by Aquinas.

There is, then, plenty of evidence that Aquinas's natural law is rooted in the natural instincts of human biological nature. Despite this, many of the most influential scholarly commentators on Aquinas give little attention to the biological foundation of Aquinas's understanding of natural law. John Finnis, for example, has led a recent revival of interest in Thomistic natural law, yet he largely ignores the importance of biological reasoning to Aquinas's account. Although Finnis is forced to acknowledge Aquinas's claim that the natural law is similar for human beings and other animals, he quickly dismisses this idea in his restatement of Aquinas. For Finnis, the biological uniqueness of human beings as the only animals capable of conceptual reasoning and language in the strict sense creates an absolute separation between human beings and other animals.[29]

Finnis believes that the precepts of natural law cannot be properly derived from natural human desires, because to do so would commit the "naturalistic fallacy" by moving from natural facts to moral values. Like

[24] Albertus Magnus, *On Animals: A Medieval Summa Zoologica*, trans. Kenneth F. Kitchell, Jr., and Irven Michael Resnick (Baltimore, MD: Johns Hopkins University Press, 1999), 587.
[25] Ibid., 1415–18.
[26] Ibid., 766–73, 1420–25.
[27] Ibid., 1420–21.
[28] Ibid., 58–62, 64–67, 93, 745–47, 1420, 1446–47.
[29] John Finnis, *Natural Law and Natural Rights* (Oxford: Clarendon Press, 1980), 401; John Finnis, *Aquinas: Moral, Political, and Legal Theory* (Oxford: Oxford University Press, 1998), 82, 103, 116, 147–48, 153–54.

Ralph McInerny, however, I do not think that Aquinas separates facts and values in this way.[30] For Aquinas, the good is the desirable. Every purposive human action implicitly involves the judgment that what we seek to accomplish through that action will be desirable in the sense of truly perfecting or fulfilling us. Consequently, the judgment that we *ought* to desire what is *truly* perfective of us is already present in any given desire. There is no purely *factual* desire separated from *prescriptive* desire—hence, there is no fact-value dichotomy.

In contrast to those like Finnis, I believe that the Aristotelian and Thomistic tradition of ethical naturalism is rooted in a biological understanding of human nature.[31] Alasdair MacIntyre has recently taken a similar position despite his earlier demurral. In his remarkably influential book *After Virtue* (1981), MacIntyre tried to defend an Aristotelian and Thomistic view of ethics as founded on the moral and intellectual virtues, but he wanted his ethical view to be independent of Aristotle's "metaphysical biology."[32] Almost twenty years later, in *Dependent Rational Animals*, he has conceded that "I was in error in supposing an ethics independent of biology to be possible."[33] He gives two reasons why he now thinks his previous view was in error. First, we cannot explain how we develop into moral beings unless we explain how our biological nature as animals makes such a form of life possible for us. Second, denying or denigrating our bodily nature as animals obscures our natural vulnerability and dependence. As animals, we are vulnerable to physical and mental ills and disabilities, and this vulnerability makes us dependent on others to secure our survival and flourishing; this dependence is most commonly evident in childhood and old age. Accepting a link between biology and ethics, MacIntyre goes on to state that the Aristotelian and Thomistic understanding of the animal nature of human thought and action is confirmed by modern Darwinian biology.[34] My purpose in this essay is to elaborate some of the arguments that support MacIntyre's change of mind.

III. ADAM SMITH

To understand the significance of Adam Smith's account of natural law, we need to understand the criticisms that faced the Aristotelian and Thomistic account of natural law as rooted in the biology of human

---

[30] Ralph McInerny, *Ethica Thomistica: The Moral Philosophy of Thomas Aquinas* (Washington, DC: Catholic University of America, 1982), 36–38, 56.

[31] See Arnhart, *Darwinian Natural Right*.

[32] Alasdair MacIntyre, *After Virtue: A Study in Moral Theory* (Notre Dame, IN: University of Notre Dame Press, 1981), 56, 139, 152, 166–67, 183, 220.

[33] Alasdair MacIntyre, *Dependent Rational Animals: Why Human Beings Need the Virtues* (Chicago: Open Court, 1999), x.

[34] Ibid., 5–6, 11–12.

nature. The modern break with the Aristotelian and Thomistic account began in the seventeenth century with Thomas Hobbes. Aristotle and Aquinas had claimed that human beings are by nature social and political animals. Hobbes denied this claim and asserted that social and political order is an utterly artificial human construction. For Aristotle and Aquinas, moral and political order was rooted in biological nature. For Hobbes, such order requires that human beings conquer and transcend their animal nature. What Hobbes identified as the "laws of nature" that should govern human conduct were actually "laws of reason" by which human beings contrive by rational artifice to escape the disorder that ensues from following their natural inclinations.[35]

Hobbes assumes a radical separation between animal societies as founded on natural instinct and human societies as founded on social learning. Human beings cannot be political animals by nature, Hobbes believes, because "man is made fit for society not by nature but by education."[36] Against Aristotle and Aquinas, Hobbes argued that this dependence of human social order on artifice and learning meant that human beings were not at all like the naturally social animals (such as bees and ants).[37] Despite the monism of Hobbes's materialism, in which he seems to think that everything is ultimately reducible to matter in motion, his political teaching presupposes a dualistic opposition between animal nature and human will: in creating political order, human beings transcend and conquer nature.[38] This Hobbesian dualism is developed by Immanuel Kant in the eighteenth century when he formulates the modern concept of culture.[39] Culture becomes that uniquely human realm of artifice in which human beings escape their natural animality to express their rational humanity as the only beings who have a "supersensible faculty" for moral will. Through culture, human beings free themselves from the laws of nature.

In opposition to the Hobbesian claim that human beings are naturally asocial and amoral, Francis Hutcheson and other Scottish philosophers of the eighteenth century argued that human beings were endowed with the natural instincts of social animals, and that this natural sociality supported a natural moral law as expressed in the natural moral sense. Hutcheson's theory of the moral sense can thus be seen as a revival of the

---

[35] Thomas Hobbes, *Leviathan*, chaps. 14–15.

[36] Thomas Hobbes, *De Cive*, chap. 1.

[37] Hobbes, *Leviathan*, chap. 17; Hobbes, *De Cive*, chap. 5, par. 5; Thomas Hobbes, *De Homine*, chap. 10.

[38] On Hobbes's dualism, see Leo Strauss, *The Political Philosophy of Hobbes: Its Basis and Its Genesis*, trans. Elsa M. Sinclair (Chicago: University of Chicago Press, 1952), 7–9, 168–70.

[39] Immanuel Kant, "Speculative Beginning of Human History," in Kant, *"Perpetual Peace" and Other Essays*, trans. Ted Humphrey (Indianapolis, IN: Hackett, 1983), 49–60; Immanuel Kant, *Critique of Judgment*, trans. Werner S. Pluhar (Indianapolis, IN: Hackett, 1987), secs. 83–84.

Thomistic conception of natural law as founded in the inclinations or instincts of human nature.[40]

As a student of Hutcheson's at the University of Glasgow, Adam Smith began to develop a similar position, which he later elaborated when he took over Hutcheson's chair as Professor of Moral Philosophy at Glasgow.[41] "Every system of positive law," Smith insists in his *Theory of Moral Sentiments* (1759), "may be regarded as a more or less imperfect attempt towards a system of natural jurisprudence" encompassing "the rules of natural justice."[42] In *The Wealth of Nations* (1776), he presents his theory of economics as a "system of natural liberty."[43] As suggested by his terms—"natural jurisprudence," "natural justice," and "natural liberty"—Smith thinks that the essence of his moral and economic system is conformity to nature.

Smith extends the tradition of natural law by showing how ethics and economics could be rooted in the moral sentiments of human nature and the natural inclination to sympathy. Although human beings are naturally selfish, they are also naturally social in that they are inclined by sympathy to take an interest in the fortunes of others. Sympathy includes pity or compassion—our inclination to share the sorrow of others—but beyond that, Smith uses the term "sympathy" in a broad sense to denote "our fellow-feeling with any passion whatever." Although we can have no direct experience of the feelings of others, we can by sympathy imagine what we would feel in similar circumstances. We take pleasure not only in sharing the feelings of others, but also in knowing that they share our feelings.[44] What Smith says about the nature of sympathy corresponds to what Aristotle and Aquinas identify as the natural inclination of human beings to feel friendship or affiliation with their fellow human beings.[45]

Smith believes that human beings, formed by nature for social life, are endowed with a strong desire to please their fellow human beings and a strong aversion to offending them. From this fundamental premise about human nature, Smith infers that we are inclined to act in a manner that will garner the praise of others. We judge the conduct of others as proper if it harmonizes with what we would do in their circumstances, and likewise we judge our own conduct as proper if it would be approved by others.

---

[40] See Robert A. Greene, "Instinct of Nature: Natural Law, Synderesis, and the Moral Sense," *Journal of the History of Ideas* 58, no. 2 (April 1997): 173–94.

[41] Adam Smith, *The Theory of Moral Sentiments*, ed. D. D. Raphael and A. L. Macfie (Oxford: Clarendon Press, 1976), 300–304, 321–27; Ian Simpson Ross, *The Life of Adam Smith* (Oxford: Clarendon Press, 1995), 48–59, 159–64.

[42] Smith, *Theory of Moral Sentiments*, 340–41.

[43] Adam Smith, *An Inquiry into the Nature and Causes of the Wealth of Nations* (Oxford: Clarendon Press, 1976), 2:687.

[44] Ibid., 9–16.

[45] Aristotle, *Nicomachean Ethics*, 1155a3–b16; Aquinas, *Commentary on Aristotle's "Nicomachean Ethics,"* secs. 1538–50.

We come into the world as children dependent on the care of parents and other adults. To survive and flourish, we must learn to moderate our passions so that we can secure the mutual sympathy that elicits the care we need. We feel pleasure in social approbation and pain in social disapprobation. At some point, however, we discover that we cannot please everyone. We notice that even when we do what well-informed and unbiased observers would judge as proper, our conduct might be considered blameworthy by those whose judgments are distorted by misinformation or personal bias. To protect ourselves from being influenced by such partial judgments, we learn to imagine ourselves acting in view of a perfectly informed and impartial spectator. We then adopt the perspective of this impartial spectator as the internal tribunal or conscience before which our conduct is to be judged. Consequently, we desire not only to be praised, but to be worthy of praise, and we can feel a sense of honor in doing what is worthy of praise from an impartial spectator even when we are not actually praised by anyone.[46]

Although Smith's analysis of moral experience is complex, he summarizes his teaching in this brief passage:

> When we approve of any character or action, the sentiments which we feel, are . . . derived from four sources, which are in some respects different from one another. First, we sympathize with the motives of the agent; secondly, we enter into the gratitude of those who receive the benefit of his actions; thirdly, we observe that his conduct has been agreeable to the general rules by which those two sympathies generally act; and, last of all, when we consider such actions as making a part of a system of behaviour which tends to promote the happiness either of the individual or of the society, they appear to derive a beauty from this utility, not unlike that which we ascribe to any well-contrived machine.[47]

Thus, Smith's moral philosophy explains moral experience as a combination of reason and emotion. The first perceptions of right and wrong are derived from emotion rather than reason, because "nothing can be agreeable or disagreeable for its own sake, which is not rendered such by immediate sense and feeling."[48] From these particular experiences of sentiment and feeling, reason derives general rules or maxims by induction. These rules or maxims enable us to judge that some courses of action tend to be approved and others disapproved. We can then use these general rules to regulate our moral judgments in a steady way that is free from the uncertain fluctuations of immediate feeling. Consequently, Smith

---

[46] Smith, *Theory of Moral Sentiments*, 116–17, 129–30, 145.
[47] Ibid., 326.
[48] Ibid., 320.

states his agreement with Aristotle's teaching that virtue must be in accordance with reason: "As our most solid judgments, therefore, with
regard to right and wrong, are regulated by maxims and ideas derived
from an induction of reason, virtue may very properly be said to consist
in a conformity to reason, and so far this faculty may be considered as the
source and principle of approbation and disapprobation."[49]

Is Smith's theory of moral sentiments compatible with the Aristotelian
and Thomistic account of natural law, as I have suggested? Finnis would
deny this, because he would argue that while Smith (like his friend David
Hume) looks to emotion or sentiment as the primary source of moral
norms, Aquinas would insist that the first principles of natural law are
apprehended by reason rather than emotion. Yet Finnis must concede the
importance of emotion and desire in Aquinas's account of human action.
Aquinas, Finnis writes,

> does not assert that one acts only for reasons, or that one can act
> without the support of one's emotions. . . . Emotions are inherently
> good, natural, and desirable. They *serve* reason and rational will by
> helping to move one to act intelligently and indeed reasonably. . . .
> Any ideal of passionless, unemotional rational action is constantly
> repudiated by Aquinas. . . . In virtuous action, emotions are taken up
> into reason. . . . So by "reason for action" I shall consistently mean a
> reason understood by intelligence and attractive to will.[50]

Here and elsewhere in his writing, Finnis uses the word "attractive" to
denote the emotional or affective inclination that Aquinas sees as necessary for any motivation to action.

Finnis thus acknowledges, but fails to elaborate, Aquinas's understanding of moral action as requiring a union of desire and reason, an idea,
drawn from Aristotle's biological psychology, which is reiterated by Smith.
Aristotle agrees with Smith about the primacy of desire or passion in
motivating human action. "Thought by itself moves nothing," Aristotle
believes, although he says that reason can guide the desires that do move
us.[51] Desire is always what moves us; thought never moves us without
desire. Therefore, Aristotle explains, deliberate choice (*proairesis*) requires
a conjunction of desire and reason into "desiring thought" or "thinking
desire."[52]

Aquinas adopted this position in following Aristotle's biological view
of human action as animal movement.[53] On Aquinas's account, animals

---

[49] Ibid., 270–72, 319–20.
[50] Finnis, *Aquinas*, 62, 74–76, 78.
[51] Aristotle, *Nicomachean Ethics*, 1139a36–b6.
[52] Aristotle, *De Anima*, 433a10–31; Aristotle, *Nicomachean Ethics*, 1139a36–b6.
[53] Aquinas, *Commentary on Aristotle's "De Anima,"* secs. 395–98, 631–35, 643–50, 803–4, 812–46.

act to satisfy their appetitive desires in the light of their sensory appre-
hension of what appears good to them in their immediate circumstances.
Intelligent animals, therefore, can be said to have reasons for action insofar as they act purposefully for ends that they grasp as being good for
them. Human beings act in the same way, but they also have a capacity
for conceptual reasoning in their practical judgments that other animals
lack. Human beings can use conceptual thought to judge present desires
in the light of past experiences and future expectations, which allows
them to plan the fullest satisfaction of their desires over a whole life;
animals that act only through sensory awareness of their present situation
lack this capacity. Aristotle, Aquinas, and Smith agree that conceptual
reasoning allows human beings to exercise moral judgment in a way that
other animals cannot. They also agree that moral judgment serves the
natural desires of the human animal.

The fundamental agreement between Smith and Aquinas is evident, for
example, in their accounts of marriage as conforming to natural human
inclinations. Like Aquinas, Smith argues that marriage is natural because
it is rooted in natural inclinations or instincts that humans share with
other animals. Among all animals, Smith observes, the sexual bonding of
male and female is proportionate to the dependence of the offspring on
parental care.[54] Among those animals whose offspring can survive and
flourish with no parental care or with the care of the female alone, there
is no permanence to the bonding of male and female. In contrast, among
animals whose offspring need the care of both parents, there is an enduring sexual bond that insures that both male and female will provide
parental care. Smith observes that the dependence of the young on long-
term and extensive parental care is greater in the human species than it is
for any other animal. This explains the natural tendency in humans for
the sexual attraction of male and female to become an enduring conjugal
bond in which both individuals feel parental affection for the children.
Moreover, this long period of childhood dependence on parental care
makes it necessary for children to learn to moderate their passions in
response to the praise and blame of their parents: children must learn to
accommodate their will to that of others. This is the beginning of their
moral education, as they become habituated to that reasonable modera-
tion of the passions that becomes the basis for the moral and intellectual
virtues necessary for adulthood.

Smith agrees with Aquinas in defending monogamy as the most natural form of marriage because it secures the natural ends of parental care
and conjugal bonding. Unlike monogamy, Smith argues, polygyny has
"many bad consequences" or "inconveniencies."[55] Like Aquinas, he iden-

---

[54] Smith, *Theory of Moral Sentiments*, 129, 142, 145, 219; Adam Smith, *Lectures on Jurisprudence*, ed. R. L. Meek, D. D. Raphael, and P. G. Stein (Oxford: Clarendon Press, 1978), 141–43,
438.
[55] Smith, *Lectures on Jurisprudence*, 150–60.

tifies the primary problem of polygyny as the jealousy of wives who become rivals because the husband they share must divide his affections: his conjugal affections are divided, as are his paternal affections.

Smith also agrees with Aquinas in condemning incestuous marriage as "shocking and contrary to nature."[56] It is contrary to nature, Smith says, because the natural affections of familial attachment between parents and children or between siblings are contrary to the natural affections of sexual mating between husband and wife. There is, consequently, a natural tendency for most human beings to feel that incest is "shocking and abominable." Yet while the marriage of a parent to a child or of siblings to one another would be universally contrary to nature, the other rules for avoiding incest can vary depending on the variable rules of kinship as determined by custom. For example, prohibiting a man from marrying his deceased wife's sister, because the wife's sister is considered to be the husband's sister, is a rule of custom rather than of nature. On this point, Smith follows the lead of his teacher Hutcheson, who referred to the universal repugnance that human beings feel in reaction to incest as a manifestation of a natural sense of right and wrong. Smith and Hutcheson were thus rejecting the claim of Hobbesian philosophers like Bernard Mandeville, who insisted that the abhorrence of incest was not a product of nature at all, but a purely learned response based only on custom.[57]

While Smith spoke repeatedly of nature as instilling those moral sentiments that would promote the survival and propagation of human beings as social animals, he could not explain exactly how it was that nature could shape the human animal in this way. Such an explanation was later provided by Charles Darwin.

IV. CHARLES DARWIN

Darwin explains how the natural inclinations that lead to the moral sentiments could have been implanted in human nature by natural selection in the course of our evolutionary history. In doing this, Darwin strengthens the tradition of natural law reasoning by deepening its biological foundation.

In 1836, after returning from his voyage on the HMS *Beagle*, Darwin began writing out, in a series of notebooks, the ideas that would eventually be published in *The Origin of Species* (1859), *The Descent of Man* (1871), and other books. These notebooks indicate that from his earliest research, Darwin was striving to find a biological explanation for the human moral sense.[58] The notebooks also indicate that Darwin was much

---

[56] Ibid., 163–66, 446–47.

[57] Bernard Mandeville, *The Fable of the Bees* (Oxford: Clarendon Press, 1924), 1:330.

[58] Charles Darwin, *Charles Darwin's Notebooks, 1836–1844*, ed. Paul H. Barrett et al. (Ithaca, NY: Cornell University Press, 1987), 537–38, 558, 563–64, 587–89, 618–29.

influenced by his reading of James Mackintosh's *Dissertation on the Progress of Ethical Philosophy* (1836), which surveyed the entire history of ethical philosophy and argued for a version of the Scottish theory of the natural moral sense.[59] From Mackintosh's book, Darwin was introduced to Adam Smith; later, in *The Descent of Man*, Darwin would incorporate Smith's theory of sympathy into his own theory of the moral sense.[60]

Darwin goes beyond Smith and Mackintosh by showing how the moral sense could have arisen in human nature as a product of natural selection.[61] Darwin agrees with Kant and other writers "who maintain that of all the differences between man and the lower animals, the moral sense or conscience is by far the most important."[62] Kant wrote about the human sense of duty or "ought" as showing us "man as belonging to two worlds"—the empirical world of natural causes and the transcendent world of moral freedom; in contrast, Darwin suggests that human morality can be studied "exclusively from the side of natural history."[63] In developing his evolutionary theory of morality, Darwin adopts a Smithian naturalism rather than a Kantian dualism. Like Smith, Darwin sees nature as the comprehensive whole of which human beings are a part. Thus, he rejects Kant's dualistic separation between the "phenomenal" realm of causal nature and the "noumenal" realm of human freedom.

Like Aquinas and Smith, Darwin observes that one of the central traits of the human species is the duration and intensity of child care. For that reason alone, human beings must by nature be social animals. The reproductive fitness of human beings requires strong attachments between infants and parents and within kin groups. Darwin believes that this instinctive bonding of parents and children is the foundation of all social bonding and of the moral sense: "The feeling of pleasure from society is probably an extension of the parental or filial affections, since the social instinct seems to be developed by the young remaining for a long time with their parents; and this extension may be attributed in part to habit, but chiefly to natural selection."[64] For Darwin, this supports Smith's claim that the moral emotions of sympathy, arising first within the family and then extending beyond it, are the basis for social cooperation and moral judgment.[65]

Darwin also follows Aquinas and Smith in recognizing the abhorrence of incest as a universal, or nearly universal, trait of human family life.

[59] James Mackintosh, *Dissertation on the Progress of Ethical Philosophy* (Edinburgh, Scotland: Adam and Charles Black, 1836).
[60] Charles Darwin, *The Descent of Man, and Selection in Relation to Sex* (London: John Murray, 1871), 1:81–82.
[61] Ibid., 1:70–106, 2:390–94.
[62] Ibid., 1:70.
[63] Ibid., 1:70–71; Immanuel Kant, *Critique of Practical Reason*, trans. Lewis White Beck (Indianapolis, IN: Bobbs-Merrill, 1956), 90.
[64] Darwin, *Descent of Man*, 1:80.
[65] Ibid., 1:80–86.

Although he does not elaborate his explanation, he suggests that avoiding incest would have the advantage of preventing the bad effects of inter-breeding in the same family.[66] As we shall see, this idea will be developed by Edward Westermarck.

Darwin believes that natural selection favors kinship as well as mutu-ality and reciprocity as grounds for cooperation and morality. Animals with the sociality and the intelligence of human beings recognize that social cooperation can be mutually beneficial for all participants. They can also recognize that being benevolent to others can benefit oneself in the long run if one's benevolence is likely to be reciprocated.[67] Smith sees mutuality and reciprocity as enforced by moral emotions such as grati-tude and resentment.[68] Darwin's theory suggests that the natural incli-nations to feel such moral emotions were favored by natural selection because they contributed to survival and reproductive fitness.

In another parallel with Aquinas and Smith, Darwin believes that hu-man beings are the only truly moral animals because only they have the reflective capacity to judge desires by considering not only present cir-cumstances, but also past experiences and future prospects. Human be-ings can thus judge that some desires are more important or enduring than others when considered as part of a whole plan of life. "Any instinct which is permanently stronger or more enduring than another, gives rise to a feeling which we express by saying it ought to be obeyed."[69] As social animals, humans feel concern for the good of others, and they feel regret when they allow their selfish desires to impede the satisfaction of their social desires.

Darwin develops a theory of how human morality could have emerged through four overlapping stages. First, *social instincts* led early human ancestors to feel sympathy for others in their group, which promoted a tendency to mutual aid. Second, the development of the *intellectual fac-ulties* allowed these human ancestors to perceive the conflicts between instinctive desires, so that they could feel dissatisfaction at having yielded to a momentarily strong desire (like fleeing from injury) in violation of some more enduring social instinct (like defending one's group). Third, the acquisition of *language* permitted the expression of social opinions about good and bad, just and unjust, so that primitive human beings could respond to praise and blame while satisfying their social instincts. Fourth, the capacity for *habit* allowed individuals, through acquired dis-positions, to conduct themselves in conformance with social opinions. Darwin also stressed the role of *tribal warfare* in the development of mo-rality: such contests spurred the development of the intellectual and moral

---

[66] Charles Darwin, *"The Origin of Species" and "The Descent of Man"* (New York: Modern Library, 1936), 485–86, 896.

[67] Darwin, *Descent of Man*, 1:82, 1:93, 1:106, 1:161–66.

[68] Smith, *Theory of Moral Sentiments*, 76–89, 94, 106.

[69] Darwin, *Descent of Man*, 1:70, 1:88–89, 1:391–92, 2:390–92.

capacities that allow individuals to cooperate within groups so as to compete successfully against other groups. "Ultimately our moral sense or conscience becomes a highly complex sentiment—originating in the social instincts, largely guided by the approbation of our fellow-men, ruled by reason, self-interest, and in later times by deep religious feelings, and confirmed by instruction and habit."[70]

As soon as Darwin published his naturalistic theory of morality in *The Descent of Man*, he was attacked by biologist George Jackson Mivart. Mivart insisted on a Kantian separation between nature and morality. Although the human body could be explained as a natural product of biological evolution, Mivart contended, the human soul was a supernatural product of divine creation. As an expression of the soul's transcendence of nature, morality manifested a uniquely human freedom from natural causality.[71]

Thomas Huxley, Darwin's most vigorous proponent, immediately defended Darwin against Mivart's attack. Yet even Huxley moved later in his life—particularly in his famous 1893 lecture on "Evolution and Ethics"—toward Mivart's position of rejecting evolutionary ethics. Huxley adopted the Hobbesian-Kantian view described in Section III, in which the moral improvement of humanity requires a self-abnegating denial of human nature because human beings in their natural state are selfish and asocial. He rejected Darwin's ethical naturalism by denying that ethics could be "applied natural history" because he had adopted the Kantian concept of culture as a uniquely human realm of activity that transcends biology. He interpreted Darwin's "struggle for existence" as a Hobbesian war of all against all; on such an account, there is no natural ground for social cooperation or moral concern. Because of the "moral indifference of nature," one could never derive moral values from natural facts: "The thief and the murderer follow nature just as much as the philanthropist." "Let us understand," Huxley concluded, "that the ethical process of society depends, not on imitating the cosmic process, still less in running away from it, but in combatting it," and thus building "an artificial world within the cosmos."[72]

Although there were many defenders of Darwin's naturalistic ethics, the opposition of Huxley, who otherwise was such a fervent defender of Darwin, has been seen by many scholars as indicative of a fundamental flaw in Darwinian ethics.[73] In recent years, some Darwinian biologists, such as George Williams, have followed Huxley's lead in arguing that

---

[70] Ibid., 1:72, 1:165–66.

[71] George Jackson Mivart, "Darwin's *Descent of Man*," reprinted in David Hull, ed., *Darwin and His Critics* (Cambridge, MA: Harvard University Press, 1973), 354–84.

[72] Thomas Huxley, *Evolution and Ethics, and Other Essays* (New York: D. Appleton, 1894), 31, 44–45, 59, 68, 75–77, 80–85; George Jackson Mivart, "Evolution in Mr. Huxley," *Popular Science Monthly* 44 (May 1893): 319–33.

[73] See Paul Lawrence Farber, *The Temptations of Evolutionary Ethics* (Berkeley: University of California Press, 1994), 58–69.

morality requires a human conquest of nature. Williams hopes that morality as a cultural invention can provide "the humane artifice that can save humanity from human nature."[74]

The opposition to Darwinian ethics from Huxley and those who agree with him rests on a series of dichotomies posed by both Hobbes and Kant: biology versus culture, nature versus nurture, instinct versus learning, emotion versus reason, and facts versus values. Underlying all of these is the fundamental dichotomy between animality and humanity. Human beings, Hobbes and Kant argue, transcend their animal nature by using their unique rationality to construct a cultural world of moral values based on social learning; this world suppresses the biological emotions that would otherwise render human life solitary, poor, nasty, brutish, and short. The proponent of Darwinian ethics must reject all of these dichotomies—and their resultant worldview—as false. Darwin acknowledges the uniqueness of human beings as rational moral agents, but he also believes that even in their uniqueness, human beings are fully integrated within the natural world. Given this, he thinks that the moral nature of humans is rooted in their animal nature. In this way, Darwin's biological reasoning supports the tradition of ethical naturalism begun by Aristotle and continued by Aquinas and Smith. The importance of Darwin's contributions to this tradition of ethical naturalism was made clear in the work of Edward Westermarck.

V. Edward Westermarck

Although he is not well known today, Edward Westermarck was one of the most renowned social theorists of the late nineteenth and early twentieth centuries. In recent years, there has been renewed interest in his work among scholars who recognize him as one of the most able proponents of applying Darwinian naturalism to the social sciences and moral philosophy.[75] In particular, his biological explanation of the "incest taboo" has recently emerged, after many years of neglect, as one of the best examples of how Darwinian social theory can explain human social behavior.[76]

Westermarck first won international recognition with the publication, in 1889, of his *History of Human Marriage*, a massive survey of the subject in which he explains the desires for family life and sexual mating. These

---

[74] George Williams, "A Sociobiological Expansion of *Evolution and Ethics*," in James Paradis and George Williams, eds., *Evolution and Ethics* (Princeton, NJ: Princeton University Press, 1989), 213.

[75] See Timothy Stroup, *Westermarck's Ethics* (Abo, Finland: Abo Akademi, 1982); and Larry Arnhart, "Westermarck's Ethics as Darwinian Natural Right" (paper presented at the International Westermarck Symposium, Helsinki, Finland, November 19–22, 1998).

[76] See Robin Fox, *The Red Lamp of Incest*, 2d ed. (Notre Dame, IN: University of Notre Dame Press, 1983); and Arthur P. Wolf, *Sexual Attraction and Childhood Association: A Chinese Brief for Edward Westermarck* (Stanford, CA: Stanford University Press, 1995).

desires, he argues, were founded in moral emotions that had been shaped
by natural selection as part of the biological nature of human beings. In
later writings such as *The Origin and Development of the Moral Ideas* (1906)
and *Ethical Relativity* (1932), he elaborates a general theory of ethics as an
expression of the moral emotions.[77] Combining ideas from Smith and
Darwin with the comparative data of social behavior as collected by
anthropologists and sociologists, he defends a naturalistic theory of ethics
rooted in the natural moral sentiments. He thus provides an empirically
grounded scientific theory of human nature that supports the Thomistic
understanding of natural law.[78]

Like Aquinas, Smith, and Darwin, Westermarck argues that human
marriage is natural because it satisfies some of the deepest inclinations of
human nature. Against those who believe that primitive human beings
lived in a state of complete promiscuity with no enduring ties between
males and females, Westermarck contends that conjugal bonding has always been a natural instinct for human beings. It attained this status, he
says, because it was favored by natural selection: conjugal bonding provides parental care for offspring that could not survive without such
care.[79] This natural inclination to conjugal bonding gave rise to habits,
customs, and institutions that sanctioned marriage as facilitating an enduring union of parents and children. As social animals with a highly
developed intellect, human beings feel moral indignation toward men
who abandon their wives and children, and this moral emotion of disapproval is expressed in customary and legal rules that enforce the duties
and rights of spouses, parents, and children.

Much of Westermarck's work on human marriage is about the
great variability of marital practices—from monogamy to polygyny to
polyandry—across different societies and different historical periods. Yet
even in this variation, Westermarck sees regularities that manifest the
universal nature of human marital emotions—the same regularities seen
by Aquinas, Smith, and Darwin.[80] Westermarck's work shows that monogamy is practiced in all societies—and that in some it is the only
permissible form of marriage. This, of course, is compatible with the
arguments of Aquinas, Smith, and Darwin that monogamy is the most
fully natural form of mating. Westermarck also confirms Aquinas's and
Smith's analysis of the problem of polygyny: in societies that allow men

[77] Edward Westermarck, *The History of Human Marriage*, 5th ed., 3 vols. (New York: Al-
lerton, 1922); Edward Westermarck, *The Origin and Development of the Moral Ideas*, 2 vols. (London: Macmillan, 1906); Edward Westermarck, *Ethical Relativity* (London: Kegan Paul, Trench,
Trubner and Co., 1932).

[78] For an example of how a Westermarckian anthropological naturalism can support
Thomistic natural law, see Thomas Davitt, *The Basic Values in Law*, rev. ed. (Milwaukee, WI:
Marquette University Press, 1978).

[79] Westermarck, *History of Human Marriage*, 1:22, 1:38, 1:53, 1:71, 3:365.

[80] Ibid., 3:104, 3:107, 3:206, 3:221-22; Westermarck, *Origin and Development of the Moral
Ideas*, 2:387-92.

to have multiple wives, the co-wives do tend to exhibit sexual jealousy, which creates conflicts that are difficult to manage. Polyandry, Westermarck finds, is the rarest form of marriage because the intense jealousy of men makes it almost impossible for them to share a wife. This supports the Thomistic argument on polyandry. When polyandry is practiced, Westermarck notes, it seems to be a response to unusual circumstances, such as a low population of women in proportion to men, or harsh economic conditions that, for example, force brothers to share a wife so that their family's property is not divided.

The most famous part of Westermarck's study of marriage is his theory of the incest taboo.[81] Like Aquinas, Smith, and Darwin, Westermarck notes that incest is almost universally condemned as a morally abhorrent violation of nature. All societies prohibit mothers from marrying their sons and fathers from marrying their daughters. With few exceptions, all societies also prohibit marriages of natural brothers and sisters. Westermarck's Darwinian theory for explaining these phenomena can be stated in three propositions.[82] First, inbreeding tends to produce physical and mental deficiencies in the resultant offspring, which lowers their fitness in the Darwinian struggle for existence. Second, as a result of the deleterious effects of inbreeding, natural selection has favored the mental disposition to feel an aversion toward sexual mating with those whom one has been intimately associated with since early childhood. Third, this natural aversion to incest has inclined human beings to feel moral disapproval of incest, and this moral emotion has been expressed culturally as an incest taboo.

Westermarck's view of incest illustrates his account of ethics as rooted in natural emotions that are shaped by natural selection during human evolutionary history. The avoidance of incest works through an emotional aversion favored by natural selection. Because this emotion tends to be shared by most human beings, it gives rise to moral emotions of disapproval that are expressed in customary and legal rules that prohibit incest. These rules are culturally variable in their specific details, but they are grounded in an emotional propensity of human nature that is universal.

Westermarck's theory of incest was rejected by Sigmund Freud and others who believed that the incest taboo shows how moral rules arise as cultural inventions that suppress human nature by repressing immoral emotions. Freud was a Hobbesian who saw human beings as so naturally selfish in their emotions that they could not live together in civilized societies unless they created cultural rules to subdue their natural inclinations. On this sort of account, human beings must conquer their animal nature through the moral imperatives of human culture, where culture is conceived of as an autonomous realm of human rationality set apart from

[81] Westermarck, *History of Human Marriage*, 2:82–239; Westermarck, *Origin and Development of the Moral Ideas*, 2:364–81.
[82] See Wolf, *Sexual Attraction and Childhood Association*, 506.

nature. Writing in the late 1960s, Claude Lévi-Strauss spoke for the many social scientists who adopt this position when he described the transcendent character of the incest taboo: "Before [the taboo], culture is still non-existent; with it, nature's sovereignty over man is ended. The prohibition of incest is where nature transcends itself."[83] By contrast, Westermarck believes that the incest taboo shows how moral rules arise as cultural practices that *express* human nature by manifesting the moral emotions. Like Aquinas, Smith, and Darwin, he sees human beings as naturally social animals with the natural emotions that fit them for social life.

Westermarck believes that all of the moral sentiments studied by Smith can ultimately be explained in basically the same way that he explains the abhorrence of incest. As animals formed by natural selection for social life, we are inclined to feel resentment toward conduct that we perceive as painful, and kindly emotion toward conduct that we perceive as pleasurable. The mental dispositions to feel such emotions evolved in animals by natural selection because these emotions promote survival and reproductive fitness: resentment helps to remove dangers, and kindly emotion helps to secure benefits. For the more intelligent animals, these dispositions have become conscious desires to punish enemies and reward friends.

Moral disapproval, Westermarck continues, is a form of resentment, and moral approval is a form of kindly emotion. In contrast to the non-moral emotions, however, the moral emotions show apparent impartiality. (Here one can see the influence of Smith's idea of the "impartial spectator.") If I feel anger toward an enemy or gratitude toward a friend, these are private emotions that express my personal interests. In contrast, if I declare some conduct of a friend or enemy to be good or bad, I implicitly assume that the conduct is good or bad regardless of the fact that the person in question is my friend or my enemy. This is because it is assumed that when I call that conduct good or bad, I would apply the same judgment to other people acting the same way in similar circumstances, independently of how it would affect me. This apparent impartiality characterizes the moral emotions, Westermarck says, because "society is the birth-place of the moral consciousness."[84] Moral rules originated as tribal customs that expressed the emotions of an entire society rather than the personal emotions of particular individuals. Thus, moral rules arise as customary generalizations of emotional tendencies to feel approval for conduct that causes pleasure and disapproval for conduct that causes pain.

Although Westermarck stresses the moral emotions as the ultimate motivation for ethics, he also recognizes the importance of reason in ethical judgment. Thus, he follows Aquinas, Smith, and Darwin in argu-

[83] Claude Lévi-Strauss, *The Elementary Structures of Kinship*, trans. James Harle Bell, John Richard von Sturmer, and Rodney Needham (Boston: Beacon Press, 1969), 30–31.
[84] Westermarck, *Ethical Relativity*, 109.

ing that ethical experience combines reason and emotion. "The influence of intellectual considerations upon moral judgments," he indicates, "is certainly immense."[85] Emotions, including the moral emotions, depend upon beliefs, and those beliefs can be either true or false. For example, I might feel the moral emotion of disapproval toward someone because I believe he has injured his friends, but if I discover by reflection that the injury was accidental and not intentional, or that his action did not actually cause any injury at all, my emotion of disapproval vanishes. Moreover, since our moral judgments are generalizations of emotional tendencies, these judgments depend upon the inductive use of human reason in reflecting on our emotional experience.

Westermarck's emphasis on the variability, relativity, and subjectivity of ethical experience has provoked some critics to complain that he does not recognize any enduring or universal standards of ethical conduct. It seems to these critics that Westermarck's ethics is radically arbitrary. Yet Westermarck clearly relies on the uniformity of human nature as a ground for universal ethical principles. Despite radical differences in ethical judgments, "the general uniformity of human nature accounts for the great similarities which characterize the moral ideas of mankind."[86] Such uniformity must exist, he argues, because despite individual and social variation, human beings belong to the same animal species and therefore display similarities in their mental constitution. Thus, Westermarck's ethical theory does not promote nihilism or irrationalism, for he sees the moral emotions that constitute the basis for his ethics as manifesting the natural propensities of a universal human nature. This appeal to the natural human inclinations makes his account of ethics a restatement of natural law reasoning, but one with a more solid foundation in an empirical Darwinian science of human nature.

If Westermarck's ethical theory really is founded on an empirical science of human nature, as he suggests, then it should be subject to empirical confirmation or falsification. The debate over his theory of the incest taboo illustrates how his claims might be tested by scientific research. Critics from Freud onward have dismissed Westermarck's theory with two criticisms. First, the occurrence of incest in all societies seems to indicate that there is no natural resistance to it. Second, if the taboo were natural, there would seem to be no need for cultural rules enforcing the taboo.[87] Both of these criticisms, however, assume a simple dichotomy between fixed instinct and flexible culture that Westermarck denies. According to Westermarck, the instinctive propensity to incest-avoidance is

[85] Westermarck, *Origin and Development of the Moral Ideas*, 1:10.
[86] Ibid., 2:742.
[87] See Richard C. Lewontin, Steven Rose, and Leon J. Kamin, *Not in Our Genes: Biology, Ideology, and Human Nature* (New York: Pantheon, 1984), 137; and Philip Kitcher, *Vaulting Ambition: Sociobiology and the Quest for Human Nature* (Cambridge, MA: MIT Press, 1985), 280, 348.

a tendency to learn sexual aversion when certain conditions are satisfied: most human beings are inclined to feel sexual aversion toward those with whom they have been intimately associated since early infancy. Westermark predicts, therefore, that most human beings raised in the familial environment typical for human beings will feel a strong aversion to incestuous relationships. But he also predicts that in some circumstances, some human beings will not acquire this aversion. For example, he thinks father-daughter incest is more likely to occur when fathers have been separated from their daughters during early rearing. Furthermore, he predicts that because of the natural variability in human emotional temperaments, a few human beings will not show the aversion to incest that is normal for most people, and these deviant individuals will provoke a deep disgust from others. Because of this temperamental variability, human communities will develop cultural practices to enforce an incest taboo that expresses the general feelings of the community by condemning those few who are inclined to commit incest.[88]

Anthropologist Arthur Wolf has recently indicated, in his survey of the scientific study of incest, that some of Westermarck's predictions seem to have been confirmed by the empirical evidence.[89] Wolf's special contribution to this research is his study of marriage in China. In parts of China, there were once three forms of marriage. In the "major" form of marriage, the bride went to live with her husband's family on the day of the wedding. In the "minor" form, a girl would, in infancy, join the family of her future husband as a *sim-pua*, or "little daughter-in-law," but they would not be married until she reached sexual maturity years later. In the "uxorilocal" form, the husband would submit to the authority of his fatherin-law. From his meticulous study of marriage records in Taiwan, Wolf concluded that people in minor marriages showed far more sexual dissatisfaction than did those in the two other forms of marriage. Minor marriages tended to produce more divorces, more adultery, and fewer children. Wolf argued that this observable behavior showed that these spouses, having been reared together in the same family from early infancy (age three or earlier), felt the sort of sexual aversion to one another that is predicted by Westermarck's hypothesis. Although not genetically related as brother and sister, they displayed the same emotional discomfort with sexual union that brothers and sisters typically feel toward one another. Natural selection has endowed us with a natural instinct to learn an emotional aversion to sexual mating with those whom we have been intimately associated with during our early years of rearing; in evolutionary history, this aversion helped us avoid the deleterious consequences of breeding with close kin. This same natural propensity will

---

[88] Westermarck, *History of Human Marriage*, 2:82, 2:88, 2:192, 2:201–3.
[89] Wolf, *Sexual Attraction and Childhood Association*, 497–515.

produce such an aversion even when the people with whom we have been reared are not our genetic kin.

The experience of the Israeli *kibbutzim* shows the same pattern.[90] In *kibbutzim* with collective child-rearing, children from different families grow up together from earliest infancy. Although not biologically related, they live with one another as if they were siblings. Biologically unrelated children are permitted to marry, but they never do, because they feel no sexual attraction to one another. As predicted by Westermarck, early childhood association inhibits sexual attraction.

Freud and other critics of Westermarck assumed that human beings were the only animals that avoid incest, and thus that the incest taboo must be a cultural invention by which human beings subdue their animal emotions. However, primatologists have recently provided us with evidence that monkeys and apes show a tendency to avoid incest that is similar to that displayed by human beings.[91] Incest does occur among these other primates, but it is unusual, and it seems to arise only among exceptional individuals with abnormal temperaments. Since the chimpanzee, which is genetically closer to human beings than is any other living species, displays incest-avoidance as humans do, it is likely that incest-avoidance arises from a genetic propensity derived from a common ancestor.

Westermarck surveyed the biological research of his time and suggested that inbreeding tends to produce high rates of infant mortality and of mental and physical defects. Modern genetic research confirms this conclusion. Inbreeding increases the probability that deleterious recessive alleles (alternative forms of a gene) in a population will be expressed and result in a genetically defective offspring. This is because members of the same family have a similar genetic makeup, including similar patterns of recessive alleles. A recessive allele is more likely to cause a problem for offspring when it is inherited from both the paternal and maternal lines of a genealogy. Thus, the probability of producing genetically defective offspring increases in direct proportion to the closeness of the genetic relationship between two inbreeding individuals.[92]

The evidence for Westermarck's theory of the incest taboo comes from a variety of intellectual disciplines—sociology, anthropology, primatology, genetics, and evolutionary biology. For this reason, the incest taboo provides Edward Wilson with one of his best examples of what he calls "consilience," the idea that nature is governed by a seamless web of causal laws that cross the traditional disciplines of study.

[90] Ibid., 435–38.
[91] Ibid., 388–422.
[92] See William H. Durham, *Coevolution: Genes, Culture, and Human Diversity* (Stanford, CA: Stanford University Press, 1991), 293–309.

VI. EDWARD O. WILSON

Wilson advocates the notion of "consilience" because he believes that
all knowledge can ultimately be unified in a small number of natural laws
that explain how the world works. He is against the modern trend of
fragmentating knowledge into apparently unrelated domains. He argues,
instead, for linking the natural sciences, the social sciences, and the humanities in the common effort to explain everything through the universal laws of nature. This quest for unified knowledge, which was begun by
the ancient Greek philosophers and renewed by the thinkers of the Eu-
ropean Enlightenment, continues, he believes, to provide the deepest
motivation for scientific inquiry.[93]
Wilson shares with Albert the Great and Thomas Aquinas the belief
that nature is a rational order of causal regularities that can be understood
by human observation and reasoning. He also shares with them the belief
that human morality can be understood as part of this rational order of
nature. Just as Albert and Aquinas sought to explain the natural moral
law as rooted in human nature, Wilson wants to explain the natural moral
sentiments as part of a comprehensive science of nature. Wilson's quest
for "consilience" shows how the tradition of natural law reasoning can be
extended and deepened through a modern science of human nature.
Human nature, Wilson insists, is not a product of genes alone or of
culture alone. Rather, human nature is constituted by "the epigenetic
rules, the hereditary regularities of mental development that bias cultural
evolution in one direction as opposed to another, and thus connect the
genes to culture."[94] For example, the rules of human language are not
strictly determined by either genes alone or culture alone, but instead
arise from the interaction of genetic mechanisms and cultural learning.
Genes initiate a process of development that endows the human brain
with neural mechanisms for acquiring language, so that in normal circumstances, a typical human child is prepared to learn whatever language is spoken in his or her social environment. Despite the diversity of
human languages as shaped by diverse cultural traditions, there is a
natural pattern of regularities: all normal human beings are prepared to
learn a language, and the languages that they learn have universal traits
that reflect the human brain's adaptation for learning language.[95] Such
regularities of gene-culture interaction are what Wilson means by "epigenetic rules."
Since morality is ultimately rooted in the moral sentiments of human
nature, a natural science of morality requires a biology of the moral

---

[93] Wilson, *Consilience*, 3–13.
[94] Ibid., 164.
[95] Edward O. Wilson, *On Human Nature* (Cambridge, MA: Harvard University Press,
1978), 63–64; Wilson, *Consilience*, 132–33, 161–63.

sentiments, Wilson argues.[96] Human biology is the study of the "epigenetic rules" that constitute human nature, and the biology of the moral sentiments is the study of the "epigenetic rules" of moral experience. Although Wilson concedes that we are a long way from achieving such a biology, he has repeatedly throughout his writings used Westermarck's Darwinian theory of the incest taboo as the prime example of how biology can explain the moral sentiments.[97] Westermarck's theory is, so far, the best example of this sort of explanation.

As developed by Westermarck, the incest taboo illustrates the "epigenetic rules" of morality. Despite the diversity in how cultures interpret the incest taboo, there is a pattern to the taboo that manifests itself in all human cultures. The evidence surveyed by Wolf and others, Wilson concludes, confirms Westermarck's argument that human beings, as shaped by natural selection, are naturally inclined to learn an aversion to incest because they are naturally inclined to feel an emotional aversion to sexual relations with their childhood intimates. This natural emotional abhorrence of incest is shared by practically all human beings and is expressed in all cultures as an incest taboo.

Wilson suggests that all moral rules might ultimately be explained in the same way that Westermarck explains the incest taboo. Morality, at the deepest level, depends on gut feelings that some things are right and others are wrong. The precise content of these feelings depends on what human beings learn through social experience, and this experience varies greatly across different cultural traditions. Yet the regularities in these moral feelings manifest the natural inclinations of a universal human nature that is prepared to learn some things more easily than others.

Wilson argues that social cooperation was advantageous for survival and reproduction during the evolutionary history of intelligent social animals like human beings. Natural selection favored those genetically heritable dispositions that promoted cooperative behavior, which included innate propensities to social emotions such as sympathy, love, guilt, shame, and indignation. Eventually, the highly developed intellectual faculties of human beings allowed them to formulate customary rules of conduct that expressed these social emotions of approval and disapproval. For example, the natural dependence of children on adults favored the emotional attachment of parent-child bonding. This dependence came to be expressed as social rules approving of parental care and disapproving of parental neglect. Similarly, the benefits of cooperating for

[96] Wilson, *Consilience*, 238–56.
[97] Wilson, *On Human Nature*, 37–39, 68–69, 229; Charles J. Lumsden and Edward O. Wilson, *Genes, Mind, and Culture: The Coevolutionary Process* (Cambridge, MA: Harvard University Press, 1981), 37, 71, 85–86, 147–58, 238, 357; Charles J. Lumsden and Edward O. Wilson, *Promethean Fire: Reflections on the Origin of Mind* (Cambridge, MA: Harvard University Press, 1983), 64–65, 115, 119, 124–27, 133–38, 175–80; Michael Ruse and Edward O. Wilson, "Moral Philosophy as Applied Science," *Philosophy* 61, no. 236 (April 1986): 173–92; Wilson, *Consilience*, 173–80.

mutual advantage in evolutionary history favored dispositions that enforce reciprocity—emotional approval of fairness and emotional disapproval of cheating. The innate disposition to learn such emotions would
then be expressed as social rules that rewarded cooperators and punished
cheaters.

Citing the research of neurologists like Antonio Damasio, Wilson infers
that the innate propensity to experience moral emotions, which has been
shaped by natural selection, is etched into the neural circuitry of the
human brain.[98] To live successfully as social animals, human beings must
make practical decisions guided by the emotional control centers of their
brains. Our brains incline us to feel sympathy and concern for the pleasures and pains of others, to feel love and gratitude toward those who
help us, to feel anger and indignation toward those who harm us, to feel
guilt and shame when we have betrayed our family and friends, and to
feel pride and honor when others recognize our good deeds. Insofar as
these moral emotions are felt generally across a society, they support
social rules of love, loyalty, honesty, and justice. It might be, however, that
a few human beings suffer from abnormal circuitry in their brains that
prevents them from feeling, or feeling very strongly, the moral emotions
that sustain morality. This seems to be the case for psychopaths, who feel
no obligation to obey moral rules because they apparently do not feel the
moral emotions that support such rules. If so, then we must treat such
people as moral strangers.[99]

Once Wilson's biology of moral sentiments is understood as an out-
growth of the natural law tradition, we can envision a recrudescence of
interest in the study of natural law rooted in natural science. We might
realize that much (if not all) of what Aquinas said about the natural
inclinations supporting natural law would be confirmed by modern biological research. For example, we might conclude that the biological study
of the social bonding between male and female and between parents and
children provides a modern, scientific way of understanding what Aquinas identifies as the natural inclinations toward conjugal bonding and
parental care. Aquinas's reasoning about marriage—that monogamy is
completely natural, polygyny only partly natural, and polyandry completely unnatural—makes sense in the light of modern biological theories
of human mating and parenting.[100] As we have seen, Aquinas explained
the natural inclinations by appealing to Aristotle's biological account of
human nature compared to the natures of other animals. Wilson's biology
of the moral sentiments continues in that same tradition of Aristotelian
biological naturalism.

---

[98] Wilson, *Consilience*, 112-15; Antonio Damasio, *Descartes' Error: Emotion, Reason, and the Human Brain* (New York: G.P. Putnam, 1994).

[99] On psychopaths as moral strangers, see Arnhart, *Darwinian Natural Right*, 211-30.

[100] For surveys of some of the biological research on human mating and parenting, see ibid., 89-160.

I realize, however, that in linking Wilson and Aquinas in this way, I am likely to provoke at least two objections. First, it might be claimed that Wilson's entire project of "consilience" assumes a crudely reductionistic materialism that contradicts Aquinas's view of the irreducible complexity of nature. Second, it might be argued that the link I see between Wilson and Aquinas is clearly spurious because Wilson himself rejects Aquinas's teachings about natural law on the ground that they constitute a "transcendentalist" view of ethics.

My response to the first objection is that Wilson's position is fundamentally ambiguous because he adopts two opposing views of "consilience." Sometimes he identifies "consilience" as a strong form of reductionism, which seems implausible to me and contrary to Aquinas's view. At other times, Wilson identifies "consilience" as "emergent complexity," which seems more plausible to me and consistent with Aquinas's view. Under "consilience" as strong reductionism, all phenomena would have to be explained by reduction to the laws of physics. Even as Wilson affirms this position, however, he concedes that it could be wrong and that it surely is an oversimplification. Complete reduction to the laws of physics cannot work, Wilson indicates, because at each higher level of natural organization, phenomena emerge that cannot be explained or predicted by the laws that govern the lower levels of organization. For example, the laws of physics, for all they can tell us about atomic and subatomic particles, cannot provide a complete account of the interactions between complex molecules—developing such an account requires study of the laws of chemistry. Wilson's rejection of strong reductionism conflicts with those instances where he seems to support that position, and this tension runs throughout *Consilience*.[101]

Wilson could be more consistent and plausible if he adhered strictly to a notion of "consilience" as "emergent complexity." On this account, the laws of each level of natural organization must be consistent with the laws of the lower levels, although the laws of the lower levels are not sufficient to predict or explain the phenomena observed at higher levels. "Consilience" as "emergent complexity" is implicit in what Wilson says about the "epigenetic rules" of ethics. The laws of physics are necessary but not sufficient to explain these biologically based rules for human moral development; these rules, as biological propensities for learning some things more easily than others, are necessary but not sufficient to explain the moral experience of particular societies and particular individuals. As Wilson indicates, explaining the biology of the moral sentiments would require research at many levels, including the social histories of ethical systems and the individual histories of people living in a variety

---

[101] For instances of this ambiguity, see Wilson, *Consilience*, 55, 67–68, 70–71, 83–86, 109, 162–65, 167, 172–73, 240, 255, 263, 266, 276–77, 297–98.

of cultures.[102] The "epigenetic rules" of human biology shape the broad patterns of incest rules that are universal propensities across all human societies. Yet within these broad patterns, the specific content of incest rules will be determined by social customs that are peculiar to particular human groups. Given these circumstances, thinking that we could reduce our knowledge of the incest rules of particular human groups to knowledge of the laws of physics seems naive.

We should expect ethics to display both the universality of human nature and the particularity of human history. Wilson relies on the idea that ethics is ultimately an expression of natural moral sentiments. As we have seen, this idea belongs to a tradition of ethical naturalism that stretches from Aristotle and Aquinas to Smith, Darwin, and Westermarck. An important insight of that tradition is that although ethics is rooted in the universal propensities of human nature, the determination of what is right for particular people in particular circumstances depends on "prudence," the practical wisdom of those with a shrewd grasp of concrete cases and historical contingencies.

While Wilson recognizes that he belongs to a tradition of thought that includes Aristotle, Smith, Darwin, and Westermarck, he explicitly rejects Aquinas's views. Against the Thomistic "transcendentalist" claim that ethics is rooted in absolute standards that exist outside of humanity, Wilson argues for the "empiricist" claim that ethics is rooted in natural human inclinations. This leads Wilson to dismiss Aquinas's natural law reasoning on the ground that it seems to assume absolute moral values as derived from God's will.[103] It is this rejection of Aquinas that gives rise to the second objection that I note above.

Wilson is certainly right in thinking that Aquinas regards the natural law as ultimately an expression of God's will: this position follows necessarily from Aquinas's belief in God as the creator of nature. However, Wilson is wrong in thinking that Aquinas must therefore be an ethical "transcendentalist" who believes that moral knowledge comes only from some supernatural source beyond the natural experience of human beings. After all, Aquinas distinguishes the natural law, as known by the human mind's grasp of the natural inclinations, from the divine law, as known by God's revelation of his will through the Bible. Natural law conforms to the natural ends of human beings as directed toward earthly happiness. Divine law, in contrast, conforms to their supernatural ends as directed toward eternal happiness.[104]

Aquinas contends that the "moral precepts" of the Mosaic law—such as the rules against murder, theft, and adultery—belong to natural law, and, consequently, that they can be known by natural experience even

---

[102] Ibid., 255.
[103] Ibid., 238–39, 248, 251.
[104] Aquinas, *Summa Theologiae*, I–II, q. 91, a. 4.

without being revealed as divine commandments. These precepts belong to natural law, Aquinas says, because they derive their force from "natural instinct."[105] The Mosaic law incorporates natural law insofar as it secures the conditions for satisfying the natural human desires for life, sexuality, familial bonding, and social order generally. Unlike the moral precepts, the "judicial" and "ceremonial" precepts of Mosaic law—such as the Jewish dietary restrictions and procedures of worship—could not have been known if they had not been revealed as divine law.[106] These precepts derive their force from being instituted for the people of Israel. Before they were instituted, it was arbitrary whether the matters covered by these precepts were arranged in one way rather than another.

The contrast between Aquinas's "empiricist" view of natural law and his "transcendentalist" view of divine law is clear in his account of marriage. As we have seen, Aquinas believes that marriage belongs to natural law insofar as it serves two natural ends—the parental care of children and conjugal bonding. A Darwinian scientist like Wilson can accept this moral claim because it depends upon the observable nature of human beings. Aquinas believes, however, that marriage also serves a supernatural end that goes beyond natural experience. As a sacrament of the Catholic Church, marriage symbolizes the supernatural mystery of Christ's union with the Church.[107] If this religious doctrine strengthens the marital commitment of those who believe it, then it reinforces the natural moral sense associated with marital bonding and thereby promotes the earthly happiness of human beings. Yet the sacred meaning of the doctrine points beyond nature to the eternal happiness that Aquinas believes to be the final end of human longing. Thus, the sacred meaning of marriage comes from a divine law that transcends human understanding and is beyond the realm of natural science. However, the secular meaning of marriage comes from a natural law that can be known by natural experience and is open to scientific study. This secular meaning is compatible with Wilson's "empiricist" view of morality.

It might seem that in my eagerness to establish the common ground between Wilson and Aquinas, I have distorted Aquinas's position by setting aside the "transcendentalist" elements of his teachings. One might wonder whether my account of Aquinas really adds anything essential to my argument for Darwinian natural right. I would stress, in response, that Aquinas himself distinguishes the "divine law," which depends on religious faith, from the "natural law," which can be known by natural reason alone. Given this distinction, Aquinas believes that the Christian believer and the Aristotelian philosopher can both look to the laws of nature as the basis for a shared understanding of the world. Similarly, I

[105] Ibid., I–II, q. 100, a. 11.
[106] Ibid., I–II, q. 100, a. 1.
[107] Ibid., III, q. 60, a. 2; Suppl., q. 42.

would argue that today the religious believer and the Darwinian scientist, differing as they do in their worldviews, can each look to the laws of nature as a ground of common human experience that can be known by natural reason alone.

Recognizing Wilson's biological explanation of morality as a form of natural law reasoning should promote a fruitful cooperation between Darwinian scientists and Thomistic philosophers. Scientists who want to explain the biological nature of human morality could give their research philosophic depth by linking it to the tradition of natural law. Philosophers who want to defend a view of morality as rooted in human nature could find scientific support for their work in the biological study of human behavior.

VII. CONCLUSION

I have argued that Aquinas's view of natural law and Wilson's view of human biology belong to the same intellectual tradition of ethical naturalism, one that also includes Smith, Darwin, and Westermarck. Aquinas explains that natural law is rooted in the natural instincts of human beings as rational and political animals. Smith says that morality is an expression of the natural moral sentiments of human beings as social animals that feel natural desires for social approval and natural aversions to social disapproval. Darwin describes the natural moral sense of human beings as being shaped by the biological mechanism of natural selection; it is this mechanism, he says, that makes humans the unique kind of animal that they are. Westermarck treats the moral ideas of humanity as a manifestation of the moral emotions that have allowed the human animal to survive and reproduce in evolutionary history. As the latest link in this historical progression, Wilson explains the moral rules of human societies in terms of the "epigenetic rules" of gene-culture interaction that are formed by Darwinian evolution.

The common ground for all of these thinkers is the claim that morality is ultimately an expression of natural human propensities that can be understood by a science of human nature. This common ground is illustrated by the group's shared view of marriage and familial bonding as satisfying the natural human desires for parental care and conjugal union. This common ground is also evident in their rejection of the Hobbesian-Kantian view of morality as an artificial contrivance of reason that attempts to transcend human nature.

We can anticipate that the future will bring wondrous advances in the scientific study of human nature. These advances will come from many fields of biology, such as genetics, neurobiology, developmental biology, evolutionary theory, and the study of animal behavior. Yet unless it is combined with knowledge from the social sciences and the humanities, this new knowledge from the natural sciences will not illuminate our understanding of human morality. To achieve such an understanding, we will need a unification of knowledge across all these previously separated disciplines of study. Linking the scientific tradition of Darwinian biology and the philosophic tradition of Thomistic natural law could help to support such a unification of knowledge, and hence help to support a comprehensive study of human nature. This prospect is exhilarating, because the final goal would be nothing less than a complete understanding of humanity's place in nature.

Political Science, Northern Illinois University

ETHICAL INDIVIDUALISM, NATURAL LAW, AND THE PRIMACY OF NATURAL RIGHTS*

By Douglas J. Den Uyl and Douglas B. Rasmussen

> Through a shift of emphasis from natural duties or obligations to natural rights, the individual, the ego, had become the center and origin of the moral world, since man—as distinguished from man's end—had become that center or origin.
>
> —Leo Strauss, *Natural Right and History*[1]

I. Introduction

Whether or not Strauss's observation is historically accurate,[2] it does suggest two sets of questions for philosophical examination. (1) Is Strauss correct to view natural duties and natural rights as the same type of ethical concept? Do they serve the same function? Do they work on the same level, and are they necessarily in competition with each other? (2) Does saying that the individual human being is the center of the moral world require that one reject the idea of a human end, or *telos*? Does accepting the ethical centrality of a human *telos* require that one reject ethical individualism? Are they mutually exclusive?[3]

---

* For criticism, we are grateful to the other contributors to this volume and to its editors, as well as Paul Gaffney.

[1] Leo Strauss, *Natural Right and History* (Chicago: University of Chicago Press, 1953), 248.

[2] There is a wide-ranging controversy surrounding the issue of when so-called "modern," as opposed to "classic," natural right first appears on the intellectual or conceptual landscape. For the most part, we shall be avoiding this historical debate, but the following distinctions are important to keep in mind. According to Strauss and others, there are two types of "natural right." On the one hand, there is "classic" natural right or natural duty (also called "objective" right), which focuses on what is right (or obligatory) as determined by a living thing's nature. This is regarded as an exclusively ancient or medieval concept. On the other hand, there is "modern" natural right or natural rights (also called "subjective" or individual rights), which focuses on the importance of the individual *qua* individual. This concept is considered a unique product of modernity. These historical claims have been challenged most recently in two different works: Brian Tierney, *The Idea of Natural Rights* (Atlanta, GA: Scholars Press, 1997); and Fred D. Miller, Jr., *Nature, Justice, and Rights in Aristotle's "Politics"* (Oxford: Clarendon Press, 1995).

[3] Putting this second set of questions a little differently, does ethical individualism require that one accept nominalism, mechanism, hedonism, or some other doctrine traditionally opposed to the idea of a human *telos*? Alternatively, do essentialism, teleology, and eudaimonism each require the rejection of individualism? That is to say, does accepting essentialism, teleology, or eudaimonism require one to accept a Platonistic interpretation of the human *telos* and banish individuating considerations from one's moral deliberations? See also notes 5 and 6.

Regarding the first set of questions, we do not believe that natural duties and natural rights serve the same function. Though we do uphold making natural (or individual) rights *politically* primary, we do not think that arguing for such rights requires that one reject the human *telos* as the standard for morality. As we shall explain later, duties and rights are different types of ethical principles. Each is primary in its own order.

In order to defend the idea that natural duties and natural rights are different types of moral principles and are not in competition with each other, it shall be necessary to show that the human *telos*, while objective, is, among other things, both individualized and agent-relative. To do this, however, we must reject the dichotomy implied by the second set of questions. Strauss's dichotomy betrays a disturbing tendency among proponents of both natural duties and natural law to reify the human *telos* and thus make it some good that competes with the good of individual human beings. This is an error. There is no such thing as the flourishing of "man"; there is only the flourishing of individual human beings.

Furthermore, we think that the modern emphasis on the ethical importance of the individual and the role of natural rights in political theory is perfectly compatible with natural teleology[4] and moderate realism.[5] Indeed, it is our contention that natural rights can be an extension of the natural law tradition—not a complete rejection of it. Natural rights are

---

[4] We have argued that there is a place for natural teleology in the modern world, if an account of natural ends is limited and if science is not held to be militantly reductionistic. See Douglas B. Rasmussen and Douglas J. Den Uyl, *Liberty and Nature* (La Salle, IL: Open Court, 1991); and Douglas B. Rasmussen, "Human Flourishing and the Appeal to Human Nature," *Social Philosophy and Policy* 16, no. 1 (Winter 1999): 1–43. See also note 6.

[5] *Moderate realism* is one of three basic positions taken in regard to "the problem of universals"; the other two positions are *realism* and *nominalism*. The problem may be expressed by considering two interrelated questions. First, can our concepts be grounded in reality if it is the case that universals do not exist in some manner in cognition-independent reality? Second, can the nature of the entities in cognition-independent reality be thoroughly individualized if it is true that our conceptual classifications reflect something real? Realism says "no" to the first question; nominalism says "no" to the second. Moderate realism, in contrast, answers both questions affirmatively.

Moderate realism holds that universals only exist through our mode of cognition—reality is always and necessarily individualized—but that we can, through our cognition (via a type of mental focus usually called "abstraction without precision"), discern a basis for our predications. There is, for example, a basis in reality for assigning the predicate "man" to Socrates, but not to Fido. Yet the universal under consideration here, the abstraction "man," does not exist in cognition-independent reality. Thus, for the moderate realist, individuals are natured, and natures are individualized.

Accordingly, there is no problem in speaking of right that results from considerations of an individual's nature *and* from considerations of individuality. To speak in Strauss's terms, "classic" natural right (or natural duties) can be based on considerations of human nature, and "modern" natural right can be based on considerations of human individuality; they do not necessarily conflict with each other. Rather, they can, as we will argue in this essay, complement each other. Indeed, Brian Tierney has recently observed that "the metaphysical 'moderate realism' of Aristotle and Aquinas affirmed the primary existence of individual entities in the external world, in opposition to the Platonic theory of ideal forms. There is no reason why such a metaphysics should be incongruous with an emphasis on individual rights." Tierney, *The Idea of Natural Rights*, 34.

also, however, a correction of that tradition, specifically its tendency to reify the human *telos* and ignore individuating features of a person.

We shall take up this last contention when we consider the failure of both new and traditional natural law theorists to understand and appreciate the role of natural rights in political philosophy. We shall see this when we consider the concept of the common good of the political community. Before doing this, however, we will first evaluate the ways in which natural rights have been traditionally thought to be an extension of natural law. This discussion will also include some mention of the ways in which advocates of natural rights have failed to appreciate this connection or have directly undermined it. Since our project is largely conceptual rather than historical, we shall concentrate on principles as they apply to both sides of the debate over whether the connection in fact exists. To sum up our conclusions on these matters here: the main problem with traditional natural law theory is its failure to understand the individual character of the good; the main problem with most modern natural rights theories is their rejection of teleological eudaimonism in ethics.[6]

Finally, a few comments about our own views should be made before we begin this examination of these various positions. We hold that there is a contemporary account of natural-end ethics[7] that can be used to support a version of natural rights classical liberalism. This ethical view holds that *phronêsis* (or practical wisdom) is the central intellectual virtue of the flourishing or self-perfecting human life and that the human good is not monistic and simple, but plural and complex. Human flourishing cannot be achieved or maintained without paying very close attention to its individuality, but it is, at the same time, profoundly social in character. Succinctly stated, then, human flourishing is objective, inclusive, individualized, agent-relative, self-directed, and social.

We have argued in other places,[8] and we will do so again in Section V of this essay, that the foregoing conception of human flourishing gener-

---

[6] *Teleological eudaimonism* holds that human flourishing is the natural end or *telos* of human life, that it is the moral standard by which human conduct is evaluated. Humans may choose not to hold flourishing as their moral standard, but they cannot choose not to be human or not to have the overall potentiality *for* human flourishing. Accordingly, human choice or self-direction is not radically free; it functions for the sake of the human good. Self-direction does not create its own potentiality for human flourishing. Yet self-direction is the central, necessary element in the actualization of this potentiality—that is, in the discovery, implementation, integration, and enjoyment of the goods that constitute human flourishing. A contemporary account of this view is explained in Douglas B. Rasmussen, "Perfectionism," in Ruth Chadwick, ed., *Encyclopedia of Applied Ethics* (San Diego, CA: Academic Press, 1997), 3:473–80. See also the sources in note 7.

[7] See Rasmussen, "Human Flourishing and the Appeal to Human Nature"; and Douglas J. Den Uyl, *The Virtue of Prudence* (New York: Peter Lang, 1991).

[8] Douglas J. Den Uyl and Douglas B. Rasmussen, "'Rights' as MetaNormative Principles," in Tibor R. Machan and Douglas B. Rasmussen, eds., *Liberty for the Twenty-First Century* (Lanham, MD: Rowman and Littlefield, 1995), 59–75; Douglas B. Rasmussen and Douglas J. Den Uyl, *Liberalism Defended: The Challenge of Post-Modernity* (Cheltenham, UK: Edward Elgar, 1997); and Rasmussen and Den Uyl, *Liberty and Nature*.

ates a need for a concept of rights that has an irreducible function. Rights are for us an ethical concept, but they are different from other such concepts. Rights are not directly concerned with human flourishing, virtue, or even moral obligation; rather, they are concerned with context-setting, that is, with providing guidance in creating, interpreting, and evaluating political/legal systems. Their aim is to solve a problem that results when one tries to establish a political/legal order that, in principle, will not require that one form of human flourishing be preferred to any other.[9] In other words, rights aim to reconcile the individualized and social character of human flourishing. We shall return to this idea after we consider other views of rights and human flourishing.

II. Natural Rights as an Extension of Natural Law

One way of seeing natural rights as not being in conflict with natural law is to assimilate the former to the latter. One does this by thinking of natural rights as simply principles of natural law expressed through an individual.[10] An extreme version of this position is taken by legal philosopher Heinrich Rommen. On his account, rights are conflated with what is right such that rights are "the sphere of right that is 'given' with the nature of a person."[11] We see how this is cashed out when Rommen cites favorably Thomas P. Neill's view that each natural right is "founded on a corresponding duty on the part of its possessor. The right to freedom of religion, for example, is based on the duty to worship God, just as the right to work is based on the duty of self-preservation and self-perfection."[12] We have, then, only rights to that which we are duty-bound to pursue. On this view, rights do little more than reiterate the notion that obligations are held by individuals; the concept of rights does no new substantive work.

Natural law views that give more status to the concept of rights, such as those of philosophers John Finnis and Henry Veatch, also have a similar problem in the end. On Finnis's account, rights are ways of expressing principles of justice. For him, the natural law tradition is incomplete without the language of rights, because the language of rights is a more precise linguistic tool for describing obligations of justice than is the language of traditional natural law.[13] It is not clear, however, why the language of duties could not be adapted to do the same work, however

[9] In Section V we call this *liberalism's problem* and explain how it results from the individualized, agent-relative, and social character of human flourishing.

[10] Even the individuality is in doubt here. Heinrich Rommen speaks of the importance of "personality" in natural law, but personality is itself a kind of generic category of ends to which individuals must adhere. There is little that is genuinely individual about it. Heinrich A. Rommen, *The Natural Law*, trans. Thomas R. Hanley (Indianapolis, IN: Liberty Fund, 1998), 206.

[11] Ibid.

[12] Thomas P. Neill, *Weapons for Peace* (Milwaukee, WI: Bruce Publishing Co., 1945), 155, quoted in Rommen, *The Natural Law*, 216.

[13] John Finnis, *Natural Law and Natural Rights* (Oxford: Clarendon Press, 1980), 205 ff.

much rights-talk has evolved as the preferred mode of discourse. Perhaps the argument is that to speak of someone's rights (or what they have a right to in a certain situation) is more *economical* than alternative modes of expression. It is, in other words, a good deal easier to say that Mary has a right to X than to spell out the extent and scope of her duties. But this sort of account leads one to suspect that the substantive moral work is being done by the principles of justice, with rights serving as a way of conveying a meaning determined elsewhere. Our suspicions on this point are supported by the following:

> But when we come to explain the requirements of justice, which we do by referring to the needs of the common good at its various levels, then we find that there is reason for treating the concept of duty, obligation, or moral requirement as having a more strategic explanatory role than the concept of rights.[14]

Rights are important, says Finnis, because the individual is the one who benefits from and acts in accord with the obligations implied by rights. Although this point does correctly note the necessary connection between rights and individuals, it fails to identify the nature or significance of this connection. For Finnis, individuals are vehicles for translating obligations into practice, but are not significant to defining the nature of the obligations themselves. Moreover, what Finnis says about individuals with respect to obligations is said in the same way that he discusses individuals with respect to duties or benefits, thereby marking out no new territory for rights other than, again, advantages gained through an economy of language. The idea that individualism is somehow morally central to the very nature of rights is not present here. Consequently, Finnis's position with respect to rights is an assimilationist position; he simply sees natural rights as an extension of natural law.

The assimilationist position is also advanced in the theory of rights put forward by Henry Veatch.[15] In an effort to avoid having to ground rights on deontological theories[16] or interest-based theories—ethical frameworks that he (rightly) rejects—Veatch has posed a novel "third way" of grounding natural rights. On his account, natural rights are not derivative of natural duties we owe to others, nor are they the results either of social contracts or of interests manifested through calculations of personal or social advantage. Instead, natural rights are derived from duties one

---

[14] Ibid., 210.

[15] Henry B. Veatch, *Human Rights: Fact or Fancy?* (Baton Rouge: Louisiana State University Press, 1985), 160–96. The following paragraphs criticizing Veatch's theory are from material in Rasmussen and Den Uyl, *Liberty and Nature*, chap. 3; and Den Uyl, *The Virtue of Prudence*, chap. 9.

[16] A *deontological theory* is any theory in normative ethics that holds "duty" and "right" to be basic and defines the morally good in terms of them. Such theories attempt to determine obligations apart from a consideration of what promotes or expresses the good. For Kantians, this is accomplished primarily by a universalizability test.

naturally owes to oneself.[17] The argument runs something like this: Since we all by nature have obligations or duties of self-perfection (given by an Aristotelian ethic), each of us is required by nature to fulfill these obligations. To prevent or interfere with a person's efforts to fulfill his natural obligations deprives that person of what he and others recognize he ought to do. Therefore, our duty to self-perfection generates the right not to have the pursuit of our end impeded.

We believe that two important features of this argument should be accepted. First, it is true that no one has the right to interfere with another's pursuit of self-perfection. Second, Veatch's "third way" is the correct one in the following senses: (1) it appeals to self-perfection rather than to interest or formal deontic duties;[18] (2) it understands self-perfection in such a way that an individual's own pursuit of it is at least of structurally equivalent value to anyone else's pursuit of it; and (3) the argument provides a naturalistic and morally informed basis for saying that whatever rights exist will be universalized across all individuals. Nevertheless, some problems arise from Veatch's basic failure to distinguish between a right and what is right. In the foregoing summary of Veatch's argument, for example, it is evident that one possesses the right to freedom from interference only so long as one is pursuing one's self-perfection. Suppose, however, that one is not doing this; suppose an individual's self-perfection lies in writing philosophical treatises, but he is instead pursuing a life of sloth, hedonism, or simply sport. Do others have the right to interfere with this person's path of degradation? We think not. But there is nothing in Veatch's argument that gives one the right to deviate from the path of virtue.

Veatch's argument, of course, does not say that others *would* have the right to interfere with this person; if they do not, however, it cannot be because they would be violating this person's rights. Veatch has correctly seen that having a right is connected to liberty, yet he has failed to see that having a right has a broader extension than doing (or being in pursuit of) what is right. Our rights are not based upon any actual pursuit or achievement of what is right, but upon protecting the possibility of such achievement in society. Let us label the failure to distinguish clearly between having a right and doing what is right—which we have witnessed with Rommen and Finnis as well—the *moralist fallacy.*

But suppose we ignore the moralist fallacy for a moment. It still seems to us that Veatch's argument would, in any case, contain a non sequitur. If an individual has a duty of self-perfection, why are others duty-bound to refrain from interfering with his pursuit of it? Granted, if they interfere, the individual will be prevented from doing something he is obligated to do, something that others recognize that he is obligated to do. However, saying this is some distance away from saying that others are thereby

[17] Veatch, *Human Rights,* 160–66.
[18] See note 16.

obligated *themselves* not to interfere, for the individual's obligation does not necessarily give others a reason to refrain from interference. Something is surely missing, then, from Veatch's argument. One approach to this problem might be to claim that by preventing you from achieving your self-perfection, an individual is doing something that prevents him from achieving his own. However, this is neither always nor necessarily the case, for one person's good is not necessarily the same as another's. Moreover, to use the situation described above, an individual who prevents you from degrading yourself may actually *enhance* his own self-perfection, since he has contributed something to another's well-being, which may in turn reflect upon his own virtuous character. He surely can keep you from degrading yourself by violating your rights. Therefore, unless one can show without begging the question that a violation of another's rights is always a denial of one's own obligation to self-perfection, this attempt to give people a reason not to interfere with others will not work.

It would also seem to follow from Veatch's theory that if I prevent or interfere with *my own* achievement of self-perfection (e.g., by willfully turning away from the good), then it would be the case that I have violated my own rights. On Veatch's theory, rights are generated out of the pursuit of an obligation, and an interference with such a pursuit constitutes a rights violation. Veatch draws no distinctions based on who is doing the interfering; Rommen and Finnis fail to do so as well. Surely, however, while it can be said that someone may have rights and either exercise them or fail to exercise them, it is absurd to speak of someone violating his own rights. What is correct, of course, is to say that someone has failed in his obligations. Unlike "obligations" (or at least "obligations" under natural law ethics), "rights" is a relational concept that applies only with respect to other persons.

It should be evident by now that Veatch's argument fails because he, like Rommen and Finnis, assumes that the duty expressed by a right is similar in nature to other moral duties that one might have, however more or less important some of those duties might be in relation to others. In other words, he believes in duties to self and that there is an objective right, but he does not believe that individual human beings have rights in any irreducible sense. In fact, Veatch is quite explicit about this, saying that "on a natural law theory of ethics . . . a person's rights are strictly conditioned upon that individual's life, liberty, and property being the necessary means of his living wisely and responsibly and of his becoming and being the person that a human being ought to be."[19]

Regarding the individual who engages in nonperfecting conduct, Veatch states:

---

[19] Veatch, *Human Rights*, 205.

The actions that he takes and the conduct that he pursues are then no longer right at all; nor can his natural rights to life, liberty, and property be said to entitle him so to live in the way he has foolishly and unwisely chosen to do. In other words, that one should abuse one's rights [viz., engage in nonperfecting conduct] must not itself be taken to be right, or even one's right in any strict sense.[20]

Clearly, then, when Veatch speaks of a person's right to X-ing, this is but a shorthand for saying two other things. First, Veatch means that it is right that the person Xs, or that X-ing is necessary to something else that is itself right for the person to do. Second, he means that it is in virtue of the rightness of X-ing, or in virtue of X-ing being the means necessary to do something else that is itself right, that others (somehow) have the duty not to interfere with a person's X-ing. The concept of natural rights on Veatch's account really is, then, superfluous; the only concepts his account needs are that of what is right and that of the duty of persons to do what is right.

In the end, what Veatch's "third way" really establishes is that the recognition of our own obligation to self-perfection is coupled to a recognition that others have an obligation to their own self-perfection, and that the obligation to self-perfection takes very different forms in very different people. Therefore, when we attempt to consider this obligation from a social perspective, we need to set aside how we are different and find the common critical element that runs through all pursuits of self-perfection. This is why we said above that Veatch's argument is correct to the extent that it establishes the appropriate model of universalization. But if one goes further, as Veatch does, and conflates rights with what is right, one not only leaves the concept of rights with no work to do that cannot be done by duty or obligation, but, more importantly, pluralism and individualism are threatened. The more closely that rights are identified with what is right, the more likely it is that a particular form of self-perfection will be structurally incorporated into the principles of rights, to the prejudice of other forms. Furthermore, if one does not want one's principles of rights to be vacuous, some answer to the question of what is right must be given. Yet in a social context where all individuals must be addressed, this answer must always be put in universal form—and it is precisely this universal form that is so problematic, even contradictory, to the individualized nature of any positive account of self-perfection.

The issue, then, is not only finding some work for the concept of natural rights to do, but also finding a role for the individual as something more than a mere repository of interchangeable obligations. We will return to this issue later. In any case, as a strategy for claiming that there is compatibility between the natural law and the natural rights tradition, the

[20] Ibid.

assimilationist approach of Rommen, Finnis, and Veatch succeeds by effectively removing natural rights. Since this seems to be no solution, we must be mindful of the possibility that our own position does the reverse—namely, that it effectively removes natural law by assimilating it into a natural rights position. This possibility raises the question of whether the two traditions can be distinct without being antithetical in some fundamental way. The recent work of philosopher Fred D. Miller, Jr., and intellectual historian Brian Tierney might be considered as efforts to indicate how the two traditions might be compatible yet still distinct.[21] For our purposes, Tierney is more relevant here, since he deals with the late-medieval/early-modern period when natural rights begin to evolve from natural law.

We must first note that much of Tierney's discussion is devoted to showing that natural rights (also called "subjective" or "individual" rights) were developed in conjunction with traditional natural law teaching. This thesis counters the view that natural rights are strictly the invention of modern nominalist political theory. However interesting this thesis may be, it shows historical coincidence rather than doctrinal consistency. That two doctrines developed together over time does not imply consistency between them. Joint development may even represent a split or tension within a school of thought or an ambiguity about the nature of a certain concept.

Does Tierney's account provide us with a more philosophical understanding of the compatibility between natural law and natural rights? To answer this question, we must distinguish between two doctrines not being incompatible and two doctrines being compatible. Two doctrines are not incompatible when there is no ostensible contradiction between them. In discussing Ockham and Aquinas, for example, Tierney notes that Ockham's doctrine of "subjective" rights does not directly contradict Aquinas's doctrine of natural law.[22] However, this does not mean that there is any structural or other significant relationship between the two doctrines. Presumably, if two doctrines are compatible, then they work together in some direct way or share some central principle or principles. The best argument we could find Tierney making for why natural law is compatible with natural rights might be called the *moral capacity solution*. Tierney mentions it in connection with Christian Wolff—an eighteenth-century philosopher who followed Leibniz but incorporated Aquinas into his thought as well:

> Natural law, law inherent in the rational nature of man, obliges each person to seek human flourishing. But the fulfillment of moral obligation requires a certain freedom of action; and Wolff declared, "This faculty or moral power of acting is called a right (*ius*)." Carrying the

---

[21] Miller, *Nature, Justice, and Rights in Aristotle's "Politics"*; Tierney, *The Idea of Natural Rights*.
[22] Tierney, *The Idea of Natural Rights*, 286.

argument further, Wolff explained that "What the law of nature obliges to as an end, *ius* gives as a means."[23]

Natural rights, then, refer to those spheres of freedom that individuals must have in order to fulfill their moral obligations. These spheres of freedom of action are distinct from the principle upon which action is based—that is, the obligation to seek human flourishing—so there is a distinction here between natural rights and natural law. Yet on this account, natural rights and natural law are dependent upon each other and hence function in necessary relation to each other. In addition, both could be called "natural" because the foundations of the moral principles are derived from man's rational nature, or because it is within the very nature of the meaning of moral action to include both elements.[24] Either way, compatibility is achieved.

The problem with the moral capacity argument is that it is not clear why we need to designate a special term (i.e., "natural rights") for the spheres of free action. These could easily be subsumed under what we mean by moral obligation itself. There are perhaps practical reasons for distinguishing between moral obligation and the spheres of free action. But why are the spheres of action anything other than the scope of the applicability of moral obligation, and if they are just that, why not simply consider them as part of what we mean by moral obligation? Moreover, the spheres of free action seem delimited by moral obligation, rather than the reverse; hence, the significant work here is done by moral obligation, not the spheres of free action. It seems, then, that the moral capacity argument does not truly give an independent role to the realm of natural rights. It might be argued, however, that what would really make rights distinctive is how they determine obligations by delimiting spheres of freedom. Consequently, although the moral capacity argument is superior to the assimilationist position, it is still unclear whether it can ultimately preserve an independent role for both natural law and natural rights. Thus, it may, in the end, simply be a modified form of assimilationism.

Given that Tierney's position ends up looking assimilationist, we are still left with the problem of understanding how natural law and natural rights can be distinct yet compatible. There is another account that attempts to do this. On this account, the natural rights perspective "accents" certain features of the natural law tradition. This process of "accenting" gives the natural rights approach a rather different look than that of the natural law approach, but the roots of natural rights can still be traced back to natural law. One exponent of this position is A. P. d'Entrèves. He argues that although the natural rights perspective is quite

---

[23] Ibid., 51; Christian Wolff, *Institutiones Juris Naturae et Gentium*, ed. M. Thommann, in Wolfe, *Gesammelte Werke*, ed. Jean Ecole (Hildesheim, Germany: Olms, 1968–83), 26: 1.1.46, 24.

[24] We mean that these could be alternative meanings in general, not within Christian Wolff's doctrine.

different from that of natural law, its basic elements are to be found in the natural law tradition.[25] For d'Entrèves, the natural rights tradition is characterized by rationalism, individualism, and radicalism (radicalism here referring to political and social reform). The importance of reason and the basic worth of the individual, ideas found in the natural law tradition, are thus "accented" in the natural rights tradition and transformed to radicalism by a move from what *is* right to what the individual has a right *to*—in d'Entrèves's terms, a move from "objective" right to "subjective" right. Though it is less than fully clear in d'Entrèves, the move from objective to subjective right that brings about the radicalism may itself be the result of an increased emphasis upon the individual. In any case, the primacy of reason and the importance of the individual were central to traditional natural law, but what was later done with such ideas was not.

> There was nothing new in the notion that man is born free and equal to all other men; in the idea of an original state of nature; in the quest for an explanation of the change which had come about with the rise of social and political institutions. It is only a shifting of accent on these commonplaces of natural law theory which can explain why all of a sudden we are faced with a doctrine which purposely sets out to construe civil society as the result of a deliberate act of will on the part of its components. The shifting of accent is the same that we have analyzed in the transformation of natural law into a purely rational and secular principle. The accent is now on the individual.[26]

Apart from confirming our interpretation of d'Entrèves's argument, this passage raises the issue of where to draw the line between an "accent" and a change of principle or doctrine. Is social contract theory just the result of giving more attention to the centrality of the individual, or does it represent a significant shift away from something fundamental to the natural law tradition? In part, the answer to this question comes from how one interprets what was central in the traditional natural law approach.

Perhaps in light of contemporary communitarian critiques of liberal individualism,[27] d'Entrèves's claim seems somewhat incredible. What-

[25] A. P. d'Entrèves, *Natural Law: An Introduction to Legal Philosophy* (London: Hutchinson University Library, 1970), esp. chap. 4.

[26] Ibid., 58.

[27] Charles Taylor, *Sources of the Self* (Cambridge, MA: Harvard University Press, 1989); Charles Taylor, *Philosophy and the Human Sciences* (Cambridge: Cambridge University Press, 1985); Charles Taylor, *The Ethics of Authenticity* (Cambridge, MA: Harvard University Press, 1991); Alasdair MacIntyre, *After Virtue*, 2d ed. (Notre Dame, IN: Notre Dame University Press, 1984); Alasdair MacIntyre, *Whose Justice? Which Rationality?* (Notre Dame, IN: Notre Dame University Press, 1988); Alasdair MacIntyre, *Three Rival Versions of Moral Enquiry* (Notre Dame, IN: Notre Dame University Press, 1990); Michael J. Sandel, *Liberalism and the Limits of Justice* (Cambridge: Cambridge University Press, 1982); Michael J. Sandel, ed., *Liberalism and Its Critics* (Oxford: Blackwell, 1984); Michael Walzer, *Spheres of Justice* (New York: Basic Books, 1983).

ever other complaints one might have about natural law theory, no one has ever accused it of lacking a sense of community or of being atomistic. Yet the individualism connected to the natural rights tradition has certainly called forth such criticism. It also seems probable that the early exponents of natural rights would not have conceived of their project as one of "accenting" parts of the natural law tradition.

Before we get too carried away with this line of criticism, it should be noted that such new natural law theorists as Finnis, Germain Grisez, and Robert George provide the very "accents" d'Entrèves describes as being present in natural rights.[28] For these theorists, the individual is said to be squarely at the center of natural law theory. Moreover, if we consider the uses to which natural law theory is put against certain contemporary trends and practices, it seems that social reform is part of the theory as well.[29] Finally, reason is also central to the new natural law theories; they actively criticize contemporary forms of reasoning for having too much of a secular thrust. Natural rights, therefore, insofar as they are legitimate at all, would be a way of accenting what is already in the natural law perspective. On the surface then, d'Entrèves appears to have a case when we look at contemporary theory: natural law and natural rights seem distinct, yet compatible.

It is our position that there are more significant differences between natural law and natural rights than d'Entrèves's position would indicate. In some cases, most notably with respect to individualism, the natural rights approach is different from—and superior to—the natural law approach. This is not a matter of accent, but of alteration. In offering an alternative to the natural law tradition, however, the natural rights approach may have lost sight of what was valuable in that tradition. Here we believe d'Entrèves has an important insight to offer. D'Entrèves cites the following from the twentieth-century Aristotelian philosopher John Wild:

> All genuine natural law philosophy . . . must be unreservedly onto-logical in character. It must be concerned with the nature of existence in general, for it is only in the light of such basic analysis that the moral structure of human life can be more clearly understood.[30]

In addition, d'Entrèves cites Rommen in the same connection:

> The idea of natural law obtains general acceptance only in the periods where metaphysics, queen of the sciences, is dominant. It recedes

---

[28] Aspects of their position are examined in Section III of this essay.

[29] This again depends on how one looks at the individual. There is some question as to whether the social criticism of the new natural law theorists is done in the name of individual freedom as classical natural rights criticism was.

[30] John Wild, *Plato's Modern Enemies and the Theory of Natural Law* (Chicago: University of Chicago Press, 1953), 172, quoted in d'Entrèves, *Natural Law*, 152.

or suffers an eclipse, on the other hand, when being . . . and ought-
ness, morality and law, are separated, when the essence of things and
their ontological order are viewed as unknowable.[31]

This basic insight is one with which we are in accord. Early natural rights
theorists provided a more broadly based ontological and metaphysical
framework from which to understand natural rights, and in this way
connected themselves to the natural law tradition described in the foregoing passages. Recall the opening parts of Hobbes's *Leviathan*, Locke's
First Treatise, or Rousseau's *Discourses*. At least with respect to philosophical anthropology, the study of what it is to be human, the concept of
"nature" remains in both the natural law and early natural rights perspectives. That is to say, in these perspectives, one's theory about nature,
or human nature in particular, is central and significant to the moral and
political positions that one takes.

A few pages after presenting the passages quoted above, d'Entrèves
criticizes the natural law tradition for being too ontological, which is to
say for being too objective and thus closing itself off to the subjective
orientation of the natural rights approach.[32] However, d'Entrèves fails to
ask and answer the basic questions, namely, whether the ontology that
the natural rights advocates do provide is in any significant way similar
to what is found in traditional natural law, and, if not, whether the ontology of the natural rights tradition has something significant to say
about why that tradition is different. There is another question as well:
namely, whether the sort of ontology found in the natural law tradition
could be adapted to the natural rights approach.

We cannot engage here in a lengthy discussion of the first two questions. It seems, however, somewhat safe to say that the teleological perspective of classical natural law metaphysics was something that was not
a part of the philosophical anthropology of the early modern era. Indeed,
it is likely that these early moderns were looking for a metaphysical
framework that accorded with what they took to be the demands of
modern science and realism in political theory—something that classical
metaphysical doctrines did not do. Indeed, it is not implausible to argue
that theories of natural rights may have looked the way that they did
precisely because of this self-conscious endeavor to deviate from the classical metaphysical tradition. For us, however, the question is the opposite:
can a theory of natural rights get a foothold within a metaphysical perspective that is more akin to that of classical teleological eudaimonism? In
essence, what we are attempting to do here, and have attempted to do
elsewhere, is to draw this connection.[33]

---

[31] Rommen, *The Natural Law*, 141, quoted in d'Entrèves, *Natural Law*, 152.

[32] D'Entrèves, *Natural Law*, 157 ff.

[33] See Rasmussen and Den Uyl, *Liberty and Nature*; Rasmussen and Den Uyl, *Liberalism Defended*; and Den Uyl and Rasmussen, " 'Rights' as MetaNormative Principles."

We agree with those who argue that a wider metaphysical perspective is ultimately necessary for any complete account of rights in a political theory. This desire for the wider perspective runs counter to the attitudes of most political theorists today, at least in philosophy, but again the matter is too extensive for treatment here. At best we can provide a small indication of how natural rights might retain some of the key elements of the classical teleological perspective.

The problem with d'Entrèves's argument as it stands is that it is not clear why the movement from the objective right to the subjective right was such a good thing. The best we can make out is that a shift *has* taken place and that a theory would be somehow out of step not to take account of this shift. It is possible that the natural rights position gives the individual more pride of place than traditional natural law theory does, and that d'Entrèves believes that this is a good thing. We would concur with this, but other than sentiment about the value of individuals, it is not obvious what is so valuable about the "subjective" emphasis. Furthermore, in light of communitarian criticisms of atomism in modern political and social theory, some might even argue that the turn toward the subjective was for the worse! D'Entrèves comes out of a post–World War II framework in which collectivist doctrines abounded and where individuality seemed especially vulnerable. Today, some critics claim we are awash in individualism.

Our position, then, is relatively simple, and one we have stated earlier. We wish to take a classical teleological eudaimonistic approach to ethics and a moderate realist approach to metaphysics and epistemology and use these as a foundation for a modern-looking political theory, that is, one that emphasizes the liberty of the individual. With respect to the particulars of this essay, our claim is that the natural law approach as we find it today is not sufficiently attentive to the individual, and thus we prefer the natural rights approach. However, the natural law tradition, by emphasizing a teleological eudaimonistic framework, is closer than are other ethical frameworks to having the correct foundation for natural rights. Thus, although we would not go so far as to say the two traditions are opposed, we see real differences that go beyond mere accenting.

III. HUMAN FLOURISHING ACCORDING TO NEW AND TRADITIONAL NATURAL LAW

By "new natural law theorists"[34] (hereafter NNLT), we mean those thinkers who regard ethics as independent of philosophical anthropology,

---

[34] For examples of this position, see John Finnis, *Natural Law and Natural Rights*; Germain Grisez, *The Way of the Lord Jesus*, vol. 1, *Christian Moral Principles* (Chicago: Franciscan Herald Press, 1983); and Robert P. George, *Making Men Moral* (Oxford: Clarendon Press, 1993).

natural philosophy, and metaphysics.[35] By "traditional natural law theorists" (hereafter TNLT), we mean those thinkers who regard a philosophical anthropology, natural philosophy, and metaphysics as necessary for
any justification, explanation, or account of the human good and ethics.[36]
It is our contention that both sets of theorists fail to appreciate sufficiently
the individualized and agent-relative character of the human good. Consequently, they fail to realize one of the chief bases for an irreducible
concept of natural rights. In this section, we shall examine both approaches to natural law.

NNLT reject any attempt to base an "ought" on an "is." They hold, on the
contrary, that there is a logical gap between a truth (that is, what is the case)
and the motivating force that produces an action (that is, what one ought to
do). On this account, then, no theoretical truth can be, by itself, the basis for
a practical truth. Thus, Aquinas's first principle of practical reason, "good
is to be done and pursued, and evil is to be avoided,"[37] is not dependent in
any sense upon metaphysical or philosophical anthropological theory.
Rather, it and the primary principles of practical reason that express various components of human flourishing (that is, the basic human goods) are
self-evident.[38] No mediating premises are required to grasp the truth of these
principles; they are not deduced or inferred from any is-statement.

NNLT also contend that human flourishing is not a single dominant end
that makes all other goods merely instrumental goods. Rather, they argue
that human flourishing is comprised of basic goods that are valuable in
themselves. These basic goods are all equally fundamental, and none can
be reduced to being an aspect of the others. They are, as such, incommensurable,[39] for each helps to define what it is for a human being to flourish.[40]

[35] Philosophical anthropology, as noted above, asks the question, What is it to be human?
Natural philosophy and metaphysics traditionally ask, respectively, What are the funda-
mental principles of nature? and What is it to be?
[36] For examples of this view, see Russell Hittinger, *A Critique of the New Natural Law Theory*
(Notre Dame, IN: University of Notre Dame Press, 1987); Benedict M. Ashley, "What Is the
End of the Human Person? The Vision of God and Integral Human Fulfillment," in Luke
Gormally, ed., *Moral Truth and Moral Tradition* (Dublin, Ireland: Four Courts Press, 1994),
68–96; Ralph McInerny, *Ethica Thomistica: The Moral Philosophy of Thomas Aquinas* (Washington, DC: Catholic University of America, 1982); Henry B. Veatch, *For an Ontology of Morals*
(Evanston, IL: Northwestern University Press, 1971); and Veatch, *Human Rights*.
[37] Aquinas, *Summa Theologiae*, I-II, q. 94, a. 2.
[38] It is argued that in the case of such a basic good as knowledge, any attempt to question
seriously its desirability is operationally self-refuting. That knowledge is a good to be
pursued is presupposed by all serious assertions, including the assertion that knowledge is
not a good. See Finnis, *Natural Law and Natural Rights*, 73–75.
[39] Ibid., 112.
[40] As Robert George states at *Making Men Moral*, 13–14:

> Thus, the complete human good—integral human well-being and fullfillment—is in-
> trinsically variegated. There are many irreducible, incommensurable, and thus basic
> human goods. And the basic goods are fundamental aspects of the well-being and
> fulfillment of flesh and blood human beings. They are not Platonic forms that some-
> how transcend, or are in any sense extrinsic to, the persons in whom they are instan-
> tiated. Nor are they *means* to human flourishing considered as a psychological or other
> state of being independent of the basic human goods that provide reasons for action.
> Rather, they are *constitutive* aspects of the persons whom they fulfill.

Though they do not claim that their catalog of basic goods is exhaustive, the NNLT list seven: life, knowledge, play, aesthetic experience, sociability, practical reasonableness, and religion.[41] These goods are not extrinsic to persons; they are not merely things that persons have.[42] Instead, they are that by which persons flourish. Together these basic goods constitute aspects of an individual's human flourishing, or what the NNLT sometimes call "complete, integral fulfillment."

The NNLT formulate their first principle of morality as follows: "In voluntarily acting for human goods and avoiding what is opposed to them, one ought to choose and otherwise will those and only those possibilities whose willing is compatible with integral human fulfillment."[43] They regard this abstract principle as, however, too general to guide morally significant choice, and so they develop "requirements of practical reasoning" or "modes of responsibility" that provide guidance that is more specific. These principles of practical reasonableness are supposed to be a more determinate guide for human conduct than is the Aristotelian doctrine of the mean. They are a response to the various ways that passions and feelings can deflect one from choosing in accord with the first principle of morality.

It is not necessary, for our purposes, to examine all of these principles.[44] We can instead focus on the contention that practical reasonableness requires (1) that there be no arbitrary preferences among basic forms of the good; (2) that there be no arbitrary preferences among persons; and (3) that one maintain a certain detachment from all specific and limited projects one undertakes. We shall examine each of these positions.

(1) That human flourishing is something objective and not simply a matter of opinion is clear. Thus, one ought neither ignore any of the basic goods nor arbitrarily discount or exaggerate them. That is to say, one should not value or weigh any one of the basic goods to such an extent that one treats the other goods as being of no account. Furthermore, one should not treat any instrumental or derivative good as if it were a basic good. One must instead find a way to participate in each of the basic goods to some extent, and never mistake a means to these ends with the ends themselves.[45] Proscribing arbitrary valuation of basic goods is, then, certainly a requirement of practical reasonableness.

What is not clear, however, is the role of the individual in this process. The NNLT describe, for example, the proscription against arbitrary valuations as a matter of regarding basic goods or life-plans "impartially."[46] Yet if we accept this description, we ignore what individuals bring to

[41] Finnis adds "reality versus appearance" to this list in his *The Fundamentals of Ethics* (Washington, DC: Georgetown University Press, 1983), 75.

[42] Grisez, *Christian Moral Principles*, 121.

[43] Ibid., 184.

[44] See Finnis, *Natural Law and Natural Rights*, 100–133, for a fuller examination.

[45] Ibid., 106.

[46] Ibid., 107–8. See also Grisez, *Christian Moral Principles*, 189.

moral considerations and confuse a theoretical insight with one that is practical.

Practical reasonableness does not require that persons be impartial in their valuations of basic goods. Rather, the excellent use of practical reason requires that individuals discover how a basic good, along with the other basic goods, is to be coherently achieved. This process requires that individuals not value these basic goods equally; they must be given different valuations or weightings. The value or weight that a basic good is accorded in an individual's life is crucially dependent on the circumstances, talents, endowments, interests, beliefs, and histories that descriptively characterize that individual—we call this characterization an individual's *nexus*.

Certainly, each of the basic goods, when considered as such and apart from the particular individuals whose goods they are, is of no more importance than any other. Each is equally necessary in defining the very character of human flourishing. This is an important theoretical point. Yet these goods are only real, determinate, and valuable when they are given particular form by the choices of flesh and blood persons. In reality, the importance or value of these goods is dependent on factors that are unique to each person, namely, each person's nexus. This is an important practical point. If the theoretical perspective is confused with the practical perspective, then the role of the individual in moral reasoning becomes irrelevant.

The NNLT admit that in choosing any coherent or harmonious life-plan, there will be a degree of concentration on one or some of the basic goods at the expense of others. Further, they admit that this degree of concentration is based on a consideration of factors that pertain to the individual. As John Finnis states:

> Each of us has a subjective order of priority amongst the basic values; this ranking is no doubt partly shifting and partly stable, but is in any case essential if we are to act at all to some purpose. But one's reasons for choosing the particular ranking that one does are reasons that properly relate to one's temperament, upbringing, capacities and opportunities, not to differences of rank of intrinsic value between the basic values.[47]

What are we to make, however, of Finnis's description of the order of priority as "subjective"? How are we to understand his reference to any "differences of rank" between the intrinsic goods that comprise human flourishing? Regardless of Finnis's intent, we contend that one should not take "subjective" here to mean that any ordering of basic goods that results from a consideration of one's nexus is as morally valid as the next.

[47] Finnis, *Natural Law and Natural Rights*, 93–94.

Nor should we assume that basic goods are somehow real, determinate, or valuable apart from their relation to the lives and choices of individual human beings.

The NNLT do reject a Platonistic vision of the human good and admit that human flourishing is always related to individuals, but they do not explicitly consider whether this relationship is essential to what human flourishing is. As already noted, they even acknowledge that basic goods are not extrinsically related to individuals. They do not develop, however, the implications of this insight. Is human flourishing something that is inherently related or unrelated to individual human beings? Is it agent-relative[48] or agent-neutral?[49] What content does the individual bring to our understanding of human flourishing? These questions are never explicitly addressed by the NNLT.

Finnis states that "every human being is a locus of human flourishing."[50] Robert George describes persons as "loci of human goods."[51] These remarks do not capture the individualized and agent-relative character of the human good. In fact, they show a profound failure to understand this individualized and agent-relative character. We should not imagine the basic goods that comprise human flourishing as existing or having value apart from the individuals whose goods they are. Further, we should not imagine individuals as mere placeholders or loci in which these goods are instantiated. Individuals are not metaphysical pincushions in which these basic goods are "stuck," and individuals do more than locate these basic goods in space. It is only through their practical choices that individuals make these goods determinate, real, and valuable.

The point here is both crucial and fundamental, and it bears repeating. Flourishing does not merely occur within an individual's life, as if an individual were simply a placeholder. Instead, the relationship between flourishing and an individual's life is much closer. The status of human flourishing as the ultimate value arises and obtains only in relationship to some individual's life. Moreover, the value of human flourishing is found and expended in those activities of an individual that constitute his or her flourishing. Human flourishing is thus neither some value-at-large nor a *tertium quid* (third thing). In other words, part of the description of flour-

---

[48] Human flourishing, G, for a person, P, is *agent-relative* if and only if its distinctive presence in world W_1 is a basis for P ranking W_1 over some other world W_2, even though G may not be the basis for *any other* persons ranking W_1 over W_2.

[49] An ethical theory is *impersonal* when all ultimately morally salient values, reasons, and rankings are *agent-neutral*, and these are agent-neutral when they do *not* involve as part of their description an essential reference to the person for whom the value or reason exists or for whom the ranking is correct. "For any value, reason or ranking V, if a person P_1 is justified in holding V, then so are P_2-P_n under appropriately similar conditions.... On an agent-neutral conception it is impossible to weight more heavily or at all, V, simply because it is one's own value." Den Uyl, *The Virtue of Prudence*, 27. Accordingly, under agent-neutrality, when it comes to describing a value, reason, or ranking, it does not ethically matter whose value, reason, or ranking it is.

[50] Finnis, *Natural Law and Natural Rights*, 221.

[51] George, *Making Men Moral*, 39.

ishing involves an essential reference to the individual for whom it is good. Strictly speaking, we should not say that a human being is a locus of human flourishing or that flourishing occurs in an individual. Rather, we should say that a human being is a flourisher or that an individual is flourishing.

Furthermore, since our humanity is not some amorphous, undifferentiated universal, neither is human flourishing. Instead, it is determinate and particular. Flourishing is not simply achieved and enjoyed by individuals; it is itself individualized. There are individuative as well as generic potentialities, and this makes human flourishing unique for each person.

Properly conceived, then, an ethics of human flourishing is a version of moral pluralism. There are many *summa bona*. However, this does not require that human flourishing be subjective in either the sense that it consists in merely satisfying favorable feelings or in the sense that its value is conferred upon it simply by someone's preferences. This individualized account of human flourishing offers diversity without subjectivism.

The NNLT tend to confuse the objectivity of human flourishing with impartiality or agent-neutrality. They do this because they think that if human flourishing is something objective, it cannot have, as part of its description, an essential reference to the person for whom it is good. It is, however, quite possible for human flourishing to be objective while also being both agent-relative and individualized. Simply because something is only valuable relative to some individual (or simply because something is individualized) does not necessarily make its value merely a matter of that individual's attitude toward it or, indeed, make its value merely something that is desired, wanted, or chosen. An old question is crucial here: relative to what? Human flourishing is agent-relative in the sense that it is essentially related to some individual or other. Yet a natural-end ethics of the kind we are advancing regards an individual human being as more than a bundle of passions and desires. There are real potentialities, needs, and circumstances that characterize both *what* and *who* an individual is. Thus, simply because an individual is interested in or has a desire for something does not necessarily mean that the thing is good *for* him. The agent-relative and individualized nature of human flourishing is therefore compatible with its being objective.[52]

(2) That one should not be selfish, apply moral principles in a biased fashion, or indulge in various forms of special pleading is not controversial. However, it is questionable whether these proscriptions are best characterized by a general rule that one should be impartial toward all human subjects. Finnis argues that one should be impartial toward all

[52] These themes are developed in greater detail in Rasmussen, "Human Flourishing and the Appeal to Human Nature"; and Den Uyl, *The Virtue of Prudence.*

human subjects who are or who may be partakers of the basic goods because "intelligence and reasonableness can find no basis in the mere fact that A is A and is not B (that I am I and am not you) for evaluating his (our) well-being differently."[53] Furthermore, Finnis says, the only reason for me to prefer my own well-being (which includes the well-being of my family and friends) is that "it is through *my* self-determined and self-realizing participation that I can do what reasonableness suggests and requires, viz., favour and realize the forms of human good indicated in the first principles of practical reason."[54] Finally, Finnis endorses the claim that the basis for treating everyone impartially is the principle of universalizability.[55]

The points Finnis makes here are problematic. If human flourishing is always essentially related to persons as particular individuals, then contrary to Finnis's first point above, practical reason does require that when one is deciding how to act, one must consider whose good may be affected. Individuals are not simply placeholders and may not be substituted for one another, because it *is* ethically relevant whose good one's actions affect. For example, that some activity is good for someone else's children but is not good for one's own is not something to which one ought to be indifferent. Furthermore, if the human good is agent-relative, then Finnis is mistaken to claim that the only reason to prefer one's own well-being is that it is a means for achieving basic goods. Basic goods are for the sake of the fulfillment of individual human beings; individuals are not for the sake of achieving basic goods.

Finally, it is not necessary to reject an agent-relative conception of human flourishing or discount its individualized character in order to avoid selfishness and various forms of special pleading. Nor is agent-relativity incompatible with the principle of universalizability.[56] We will explain these claims in turn.[57]

First, to say that human flourishing is agent-relative does not mean or imply that human flourishing cannot involve concern for others, or that acting for the welfare of another cannot be a value or a reason for one's conduct. Acting for the sake of a given person can be good for you even if others would not find it good to perform the same acts for that person themselves. Friends helping and nurturing one another and parents sacrificing for their own children are among the many examples of how

---

[53] Finnis, *Natural Law and Natural Rights*, 107.

[54] Ibid.

[55] Ibid., 107–8.

[56] Finnis also implies that agent-neutrality is required if one is to follow the demands of justice. However, this claim confuses the virtue of justice, which does not necessarily require impartiality, with the justice that is rendered by a political/legal system, which does. See our discussion of this very issue in Den Uyl and Rasmussen, " 'Rights' as MetaNormative Principles," 68–71.

[57] The next two paragraphs are adapted from Rasmussen, "Human Flourishing and the Appeal to Human Nature," 10, 22–23.

flourishing can be agent-relative and nonetheless involve authentic concern for others. Even in situations that are not regarded as instances of flourishing, we find agent-relativity compatible with concern for others, as in the case of soldiers risking their lives for their own comrades during battle. Therefore, agent-relativity and egoism should be distinguished.

Second, to say that human flourishing is agent-relative does not preclude it from being universalized. Universalizability does not require an agent-neutral view, for it is possible to hold a moral theory that claims that a person's good is agent-relative and nevertheless be able to universalize the maxims of actions based on that theory. Let us say that human flourishing, G_1, for a person, P_1, is agent-relative if and only if its distinctive presence in world W_1 is a basis for P_1 ranking W_1 over some other world W_2, even though G_1 may not be the basis for any other persons ranking W_1 over W_2. Let us also say that the same holds true of goods G_2-G_n for persons P_2-P_n, respectively. Conduct based on such agent-relative goods can be universalized as follows: Just as the production of P_1's good is a reason for P_1 to act, so too the production of P_2's good is a reason for P_2 to act. P_1 cannot claim that G_1 provides him with a legitimate reason to act without acknowledging that G_2 provides P_2 with a legitimate reason to act. In other words, if one knows that attaining one's good provides one with a legitimate reason to act, *because it is one's good*, then one also knows that another person's attaining his or her good provides that person with a legitimate reason to act. The italicized phrase represents the knowledge that a person's attaining his or her good provides a person with a legitimate reason to act; this claim is what is universalized. That this is universalized, however, does not mean that human flourishing is not always essentially related to some person. Thus, agent-relative values can be universalized. Contrary to what Finnis suggests, being agent-neutral is not necessary for universalization.[58]

(3) Finnis states that "there is no good reason to take up an attitude to any of one's particular objectives such that if one's project failed and one's objective eluded one, one would consider one's life drained of meaning."[59] If one fails to succeed, one should not give up trying. One should, then, practice a certain detachment regarding one's projects. Certainly, this is good advice. It would be irrational to assume that one's life *must* be drained of meaning if one's project fails, for there are usually other ways to achieve the basic goods that flourishing requires. Moreover, persons are not static. A project that is crucial for achieving basic goods at

---

[58] It should also be noted here that the ability of a value to be the basis for universalizable conduct is not sufficient to establish common values or a reason for other-regarding conduct among persons. This is so because the universalization of agent-relative goods does not show P_1's good to be P_2's good (or vice versa), nor does it show that the production of P_2's good provides P_1 with a reason for action (or vice versa). Thus, if P_1's good should conflict with P_2's, universalizability would not provide a way out of this conflict.

[59] Finnis, *Natural Law and Natural Rights*, 110.

one time might not be so at another time. However, none of this precludes the possibility that some projects are so important that without them one has lost all chance of flourishing. There might be persons constituted such that only a very limited number of projects will allow them to achieve basic goods. There might also be projects for which nothing else will suffice, and moments and situations that are crucial for flourishing but will only come once.

Finnis is certainly correct to reject fanaticism, but the truth is simply that what is fanatical for one person can, for another, be nothing more than a principled commitment to a particular life-plan. What the NNLT consistently fail to consider is that the appropriate weightings that different individuals accord the basic goods in their life-plans may vary radically. There are various forms of human flourishing, and accordingly there are various forms of moral failings and moral tragedies. Certain projects might be crucial for some people and unimportant for others. Only by ignoring the individualized and agent-relative character of human flourishing could one think otherwise.

After considering these three positions of the NNLT, it should be clear that the NNLT fail to appreciate sufficiently the role of the individual in any account of human flourishing. If we investigate their views further, we find this made even more evident. As noted above, the NNLT often describe human flourishing as "integral human fulfillment." They claim that this is neither individualistic fulfillment nor the fulfillment of some greater good apart from the basic goods. Instead, it is the complete fulfillment, in terms of achieving basic human goods, of all persons and communities.[60] Germain Grisez, for example, says that "[t]he ideal of integral human fulfillment is that of a single system in which all the goods of human persons would contribute to the fulfillment of the whole community of persons."[61] Understanding this conception of human flourishing requires, then, that we consider how the NNLT understand the common good of the political community. We shall do this in the next section. The remainder of this section shall consider TNLT.

TNLT argue that any account of human flourishing and moral obligation cannot be adequately defended or explained without a supporting philosophical anthropology. This is true. The NNLT claim that the basic goods that comprise human flourishing are self-evident, but this does not show that they are not based on human nature.[62] The issue is not whether these goods are deduced or inferred from human nature; rather, it is whether these goods are recognized to be goods *for* individual human beings. If human flourishing is agent-relative, then it is because of what individual human beings *are* that these goods are known to be good. By

---

[60] George, *Making Men Moral*, 15–16.

[61] Grisez, *Christian Moral Principles*, 185.

[62] Self-evidence here need not involve mere analyticity; it can also refer to that which is evident from reflection on reality.

not acknowledging that the basic goods are grounded in the nature of individual human beings, the NNLT, despite their protestations to the contrary, treat these goods as if they had value and reality independent and apart from the choices of individual human beings.

The TNLT are, for the most part, clear that the basic goods are goods *for* individual human beings. Thus, we accept their initial insight. However, we do not accept the subsequent claim of the TNLT that an analysis of human nature reveals a particular valuation or weighting of the basic goods that is proper for any individual.[63]

There are three problems with this claim. First, an analysis of human nature cannot reveal any relative valuations or weightings of the basic goods, much less one that is proper for all individuals. Analysis of human nature can provide, at best, a cluster concept that lists the basic goods, and this could support the claim that no one can flourish without having these basic goods in some form. Yet an analysis of human nature does not show, for example, how friendship should be valued relative to knowledge; human nature as such does not provide this information. There is, then, no recipe for flourishing that human nature can provide the individual.

Second, even if it is the case that some basic goods are ontologically more fundamental than others, this does not mean that a particular individual's valuation or weighting of basic goods should reflect this dependency. For example, it might be the case that one cannot enjoy any other basic good unless one also has the good of knowledge, but this does not mean that the life of a philosopher or scientist is the best life for everyone. Nor does it mean that one should spend more time and effort pursuing knowledge than one does pursuing leisure or developing relationships with family and friends.[64] The importance or value of a basic good for some person cannot be determined apart from a consideration of that person's nexus.[65]

Certainly, an individual should not disvalue or give no weight to a basic good, particularly those that are ontologically more fundamental than other basic goods. If, continuing from the previous example, knowledge is more ontologically fundamental than other basic goods, then gaining and developing knowledge must be accorded some importance and value in every person's life. Yet this does not show that every individual should value or weigh a more ontologically fundamental good more highly than other basic goods. This no more follows than the claim that the view from the basement of one's house should be valued more than the view from one's balcony.

Third, an understanding of human flourishing *as such* does not specify the individual forms of flourishing, but not specifying these forms is not

[63] See Hittinger, *A Critique of the New Natural Law Theory*; and Ashley, "What Is the End of the Human Person?"

[64] The alternative here need not be friendship or leisure; it could be any other basic good.

[65] As noted earlier, a person's nexus is that set of circumstances, talents, endowments, interests, beliefs, and histories that descriptively characterize him.

to deny their existence. In fact, such an abstract consideration[66] of human flourishing requires that flourishing exist in some particular way or manner. It requires that in reality there exist *many* individualized forms of human flourishing, and it is an individual's nexus that determines which form, which way or manner, of flourishing is appropriate for that individual. As noted above, human flourishing is neither some *tertium quid* nor some value-at-large.

To reiterate, knowledge of the proper form of flourishing for a particular individual cannot be achieved by a theoretical or speculative account of human nature alone. What one needs is knowledge of those particularities of an individual's life that are essential to giving the components of human flourishing reality, determinacy, and value; only practical wisdom can provide this sort of knowledge.

It is of course necessary to have theoretical or speculative knowledge, for it is important to be able to consider things in the abstract. Nevertheless, this does not mean that such theoretical insight should replace practical insight when it comes to the valuation or weighting of the basic goods that constitute human flourishing. The TNLT expect too much of theoretical or speculative knowledge and not enough of practical wisdom, and hence they fail to appreciate sufficiently the individualized and agent-relative character of human flourishing.

Both the NNLT and the TNLT, then, fail to grasp sufficiently the importance of the individualized and agent-relative character of the human good. As we shall see, this leads them to conceptions of the common good of the political community that are problematic, and to an inability to see the true importance of natural or individual rights.

IV. NATURAL LAW AND THE COMMON GOOD OF THE POLITICAL COMMUNITY

One way of looking at the common good is as Finnis does. Finnis considers the common good to be the procurement of those conditions that will foster the attainment, by individuals, of "a whole ensemble of material and other conditions that tend to favour the realization, by each individual in the community, of his or her personal development."[67] Finnis's definition logically allows for the possibility that securing these conditions will not require that particular people be provided with particular things, or indeed with anything at all. It is conceivable that the common good could be obtained by insuring conditions that, while allowing individuals to act for their own development, do not provide benefits to particular individuals or respond to individuals' claims for particular goods or services. Therefore, to hold a belief in the common

---

[66] Aquinas called this type of abstraction "abstraction without precision." See note 5 above and also Rasmussen, "Human Flourishing and the Appeal to Human Nature," 22.

[67] Finnis, *Natural Law and Natural Rights*, 154.

good does not commit one to a position that *necessarily* requires the state to be active in securing goods and services for its citizens. It is possible to assume that a minimally active state would do all that is necessary to provide for the common good, that is, to secure the conditions necessary to help individuals achieve the goods they need to flourish.

Yet even if we assume that adhering to a notion of the common good does not commit one to any particular political ideology of state intervention, it still seems to be the case that we can ask why the notion of the common good implies anything at all about political action. One might answer that the province of politics is the province of that which is common to us all; we believe, however, that this response makes some arguable assumptions. The fact that something is common to us all does not necessarily imply the need for political concern or action involving that thing. This is especially true if what is at issue, as it is here, is just what the role of politics should be. For example, we would argue that the political is properly concerned only with securing conditions that make it *possible* for individuals to pursue their own self-perfection among other individuals (as opposed to securing those conditions that tend to encourage the development of self-perfection, or to securing self-perfection for individuals outright). If one takes this position, it does not follow at all that politics is necessarily concerned with everything that might qualify as a "common good" (that is, those things that are good for all individuals). Politics, in other words, may be concerned with what is common, but what is common is not necessarily the province of the political.

If politics were *necessarily* concerned with all that is common, then we could not separate, for political purposes, the conditions necessary for the possibility of self-perfection among others from the conditions necessary for the achievement of self-perfection. Yet we can certainly do this. It may very well be, as we believe it is, that the conditions for making any sort of flourishing possible are less robust in character than the conditions that tend to promote individual flourishing directly. Perhaps any individual's flourishing can be optimally encouraged by giving him an income above the current national median, but a social order that redistributes to give everyone an income over that level is certainly different from one that simply allows anyone who achieves that level of income to keep it. It should be noted here that we are generally skeptical that there are "common goods" except in the most generic sense, and this generic sense is misleading in its own way; we discuss this problem elsewhere.[68] Here, for the sake of argument, we shall ignore it and grant that general conditions for promoting flourishing can be discussed meaningfully. If they can, then the issue at hand is not so much about the nature of the common good, but rather about the nature of politics and its connection with the common good. Our point is that even if we grant that X will contribute to the general prospects of flourishing among members of a society, it cannot be

[68] See Rasmussen and Den Uyl, *Liberty and Nature*, chap. 4.

assumed that X should be provided as a matter of political action or that political activity is called for if ~X obtains.

This leads us to the question of whether the conditions for the possibility of flourishing among others should take precedence over conditions that tend to promote flourishing more directly.[69] A full answer to this question cannot, of course, be provided here, though the fact one can raise the question sensibly indicates that we cannot simply assume that claims about what would encourage flourishing have any particular political priority. The question of the appropriate role of political activity with respect to goods promotive of flourishing leads us, however, to another issue. Is the flourishing exhibited by individuals a function of the conditions that tend to encourage it, or are these conditions themselves the result of individual actions in pursuit or maintenance of flourishing activities? Putting the matter another way, do individuals through their own actions and relationships with others simply embody goods that precede these actions and relationships, or do goods—whatever their nature and commonality—arise and continue as a result of individual actions, whether performed singly or in coordination with others? We call the first and second alternatives expressed in these questions the *conditionalist thesis* and the *individualist thesis*, respectively.

Before one tries to answer the preceding questions by saying that something of both positions is true, it must be noted that we are raising the issue behind those questions in a fundamental sense. Saying that both positions are true is perhaps correct in some sense, but not in a fundamental one, because this response does not speak to where we should orient our efforts as we try to bring about flourishing. If individuals' actions secure, maintain, or otherwise give form to the goods connected to flourishing, then it is these *actions* that must become the focus of our efforts; on this account, focusing on the goods themselves would be misguided, for they are simply derivative of those actions. If actions are the focus of our efforts, and we allow for a plurality of ends and a diversity of approaches to them, then we will tend to concentrate on allowing for freedom of action. However, if flourishing is a function of having conditions available such that individuals can enjoy the goods that flourishing requires, then we should concentrate our efforts on establishing the right conditions rather than on the actions themselves. On this account, actions are seen as the product of prior conditions, as opposed to conditions being seen as the product of individual action.

Finnis might object that some goods, such as friendship, are essentially actions (or actions in a relationship of a certain sort), and that therefore the distinction posed above is not a good one. Finnis likes to speak of how goods such as friendship are not exhausted by anyone's enjoyment of

---

[69] In our more optimistic moments, we tend to think that a real securing of the conditions for the possibility of flourishing among other individuals would generally have the effect of creating the conditions that encourage flourishing more directly, but our argument does not hang on this connection.

them, suggesting both that these goods somehow preexist the actions that characterize them and yet somehow only find expression through individual actions.[70] It is difficult, however, to imagine exactly what good preexists the actions or relationships produced in something like a friendship, let alone what politics could do to move people toward the enjoyment of this good. It seems likely that the more a good is defined in nonmaterial terms of individual action, the less it is suited to political purposes. In contrast, material conditions (money, for example) are more promising as objects of political action, because we can identify them and measure the extent to which individuals have them. But if we look for nonmaterial *ends* of political action, it would seem that freedom of association would be the condition that comes to mind for goods like community and friendship.

In some of these cases, such as that of freedom of association, the "condition" obtained could easily square with our prescription that politics stick to securing and maintaining the conditions for the *possibility* of flourishing among others. Since freedom of association does not guarantee friendship, or even community—if by "community" one means something more than nonviolent coexistence—freedom of association falls within the purview of things securing only the possibility for flourishing. It is not so easy to imagine, however, what else can be said if freedom of association is meant to foster a tendency toward friendship more directly. What we would expect to see under attempts to promote friendship more directly is that certain types and modes of friendship could be fostered, but only at the expense of other types or modes of friendship. More specifically, if those creating the friendship-fostering conditions could not imagine a particular sort of friendship, or thought a particular sort of friendship would be difficult to encourage, then that sort of friendship would most likely be frustrated by whatever conditions were implemented.

Our point is not, however, to bicker about what will or will not be more likely to promote a certain end, but first to raise the issue of orientation toward the common good. It seems to us that if someone allows for the possibility of a plurality of modes of flourishing, agent-relativity of value, and the derivative character of material conditions, then one is more likely to look to procedural approaches to the common good than to a notion of the common good that seeks to realize a certain state of affairs or material conditions. Our second point is that by accepting the individualist thesis, we can speak meaningfully of both the conditions *and* individual action. In contrast, the conditionalist thesis, to the degree one takes it seriously, seems to make individuality disappear. The more directly that conditions C produce states of flourishing F, the less that individual I matters to the connection between C and F. At one extreme we might

[70] Finnis, *Natural Law and Natural Rights*, 141-56.

imagine C invariably producing F for I,[71] while at the other extreme we might imagine C being necessary for, but in no way directly productive of, F. The latter position, of course, would be, in practical terms, close to our own position, for at that end of the spectrum it seems difficult to speak of anything being "produced" or "encouraged" between C and F.

Most of those who advocate conditionalism yet want to allow for some degree of individuality will not take either of these extreme positions; they will place themselves somewhere in the middle. Yet this middle ground is endlessly contentious: there are no clear criteria for successfully producing F, and no clear criteria for the degree to which C can be altered. Any political program trying to rest on such a middle ground will have to be systematically interventionist, because there is no guarantee that a given level of C will encourage F the same way from one time to the next. Consequently, either because one is on the invariability end of the spectrum or because of the inevitable contentiousness of securing the appropriate conditions, individuals count for very little. Either they do not count because the right conditions produce the right effect through them whether they will it or not, or they do not count because one's lack of confidence in the causal connection between C and F forces one to think in terms of aggregates and reasoning that is "for the most part." In either case, "collective" action will supplant individual action.

If one accepts the individualist thesis, however, then both C and F—and the relationship between them—are functions of I. Hence, on the individualist thesis, we need not sacrifice talk of conditions that encourage flourishing, nor give up talk of individual actions. For it is quite possible, within a political program that seeks only to secure the conditions for the possibility of flourishing among others, that people will jointly aspire to produce conditions favorable to flourishing. Once those conditions are themselves seen to be the product of individual action, there is no contradiction or tension between individual action on the one hand and the establishment of common conditions on the other. Furthermore, one cannot argue that the individualist thesis eliminates the role of conditions in the same way that the conditionalist thesis eliminates the role of individuals. The conditions do not progressively disappear as we look more and more to individuals, because the goods in question that constitute the preferred conditions are just the aspirations of individuals. What *would* be threatened by such an approach would be goods that are the aspiration of some collective entity rather than any individual. But we know of no natural law theorists who wish to be seen as collectivists.

The traditional natural law theory's account of the common good is not so different from the account Finnis provides. Henry Veatch, for example,

---

[71] Since this is a political issue, it must be "I_n" in the sense of any individual rather than "I" in the sense of a particular one, because we can imagine C as being invariable for one person but not another and thus not invariably producing F for all.

defines the common good as "a social system or social organization or social order designed and disposed so as to make various of the goods of life available to the individuals who make up the community."[72] This appears to have less to do with flourishing than does Finnis's account, but Veatch's fuller discussion leaves no doubt that flourishing is the driving force of his theory. Veatch's definition of the common good shows that he, like Finnis, is a conditionalist when it comes to the common good; he thinks goods are to be provided so as to promote flourishing among individuals. Yet Veatch is less concerned to argue about the character of the conditions that he thinks should obtain than he is to discuss the very nature of the common good in the face of what he calls the "hyper-individualist" position. Veatch wants to show two things: that there is a good that is the good of anyone and everyone rather than the good of an individual, and that this good is a necessary feature of any community or political organization and can take precedence over the good of an individual in cases of conflict.

Veatch wants us to imagine a situation where we come to recognize that to have a community at all, we need rules and procedures that individuals must adhere to even if doing so does not enhance their own good. These rules and procedures are good for everyone collectively, for it allows them to reap the benefits of living in community. Of course, these rules and procedures that are good for everyone collectively are also good for each individual. Veatch's point here is that this common good is somehow different from one that refers to individuals alone. Once one accepts that there can be a good that is not defined in terms of individuals alone, then a wedge has been introduced for giving the common good a status that cannot be displaced by talk of individuals. Indeed, it seems fair to say that this notion of the common good is of fundamental importance to both camps of the natural law tradition.

One cannot help but wonder at times whether some of the arguments that natural law theorists present in defending the concept of the common good conflate a person's overall good with a person's more immediate interest. Descriptions of the nature of the common good are often given in examples involving clubs, enterprises, organizations, and the like, and such examples lend themselves to this obfuscation. In all sorts of common enterprises, a person's more immediate interest clearly may have to be subordinated to the "good" of the whole; when we are part of a group, it is not so difficult to recognize times when our own preferences may have to be set aside or compromised so that the group might flourish. Indeed, at an abstract level it might be said—and surely this is accepted by those who believe in objective goodness—that what is good for one in general is not necessarily the same as what might be in one's interest at a given time. Indeed, one feature favoring the classical ethical tradition is that it

---

[72] Veatch, *Human Rights*, 127.

seems to align these apparently distinct items. Perhaps the desire of classical theorists to unify the two explains the conflation. It does not, however, remove the distinction. Even if the distinction was not glossed over, it does not follow from the fact that X is good for one that therefore it must necessarily trump an interest one has in ~X when considered in the political arena where force may be used to secure actions or outcomes. The value of some goods, for example, may be integrally dependent upon one's self-realization of their value. If someone does not recognize the value of such a thing, trying to force him to recognize its value may antagonize that person and lead to an increased desire on his part to resist outside direction involving that thing's value. This antagonism, of course, will prevent the sort of self-realization needed to properly value the good in question.[73]

If Veatch were to examine our own position, he would argue that the conditions for the possibility of flourishing among others are our theory's "common good"—the good that trumps any individual good contrary to it, and which is distinct from the good of any individual. Presumably, his point would be that at some level in any theory, individual rights can be overridden by appeals to the common good, for those rights are themselves predicated upon establishing the conditions for their exercise. This is supposed to show that individual rights are conceptually derivative of the common good. Furthermore, it means that in any case of conflict between an individual right and the common order that gives rise to and sustains it, the order must prevail. One presumably cannot respond by saying the common good is nothing other than that state of affairs where individual rights are protected, because that state of affairs is itself a condition that supercedes the individual rights that jointly compose it.

However, the foregoing argument moves too fast. Conditions of any sort, including our conditions for the possibility of flourishing among others, are not self-maintaining. Individual action must sustain them. But here again, Veatch would notice a difference. The individual action that matters when one is sustaining these conditions is action that looks to the *common* order rather than to the individual himself. Consequently, while individuals must act to sustain the values of a common order, that order is still distinct from actions directed at attaining their own personal values. Yet our point, one already made with respect to Finnis, is that whatever good one is considering—whether it be the common good or a good of one's own—is a good only because of the acts of choice that make it so for the individuals who are to realize the good. If one claims that those choices are themselves a product of the conditions that produce them, we can repeat another point we made in our discussion of Finnis: conditions

---

[73] We are well aware of the issues concerning habituation and the like. Our point here is simply that it does not follow from the fact that X is good for P that P's interest in ~X must be diverted in some way.

are themselves the product of individual choice and action, and are thus derivative of such choices and action.

Moreover, the good of the whole is only inherently at odds with the good of the individual if one forgets that individuals have concerns about the conditions they live in among others. In this, we agree with the natural law tradition that we are social beings whose fulfillment must come in the company of others. Given our position on this, we have some skepticism about asocial "state of nature" modes of analysis. Yet saying that in no way alters the fact that whether a good be a common one or not, its goodness lies in its chosen character. Because of this point, our view is that only a position which advocates securing the conditions for the possibility of flourishing among others can respect common and individual goods equally, because only this sort of position respects what is actually common to both types of goods—namely, individual choice. The "condition" spoken of in this context is not a condition that tends to promote the good of individual choice; rather, it *is* that good, socially considered. Since individual choice is not in itself necessarily promotive of other goods of flourishing, it cannot be said that it provides a condition for flourishing in the same sense that the natural law tradition would like the common good to do. In this respect, it aligns with the natural rights tradition in making rights fundamental. That tradition not only focuses upon the individual, but it also has lowered expectations about what politics can accomplish with respect to the promotion of flourishing. The conditions it seeks are largely negative ones of noninterference, because these are most in accord with the centrality of individual choice. The natural rights tradition's main defect, as noted, is that it forgets that we have rights because we are social beings, not because we are atomized in a state of nature.

In summary, the perspective that political society is essentially like other common enterprises, with a good that can override the goods of individuals when the two conflict, is essentially defective. It fails to appreciate at the most fundamental level the connection between individual choice and goodness, and it fails to grasp the role of individual choice in obtaining and preserving the very goods that natural law theorists put forward as necessary for flourishing. The conditionalist conception of the common good also seems to beg a number of questions about the role of politics, including what the purpose of politics is. Finally, the natural law tradition seems largely united in its placing of the "common good" at the center of the theory. The superiority of the natural rights tradition, in our view, is its inherent compatibility with what is central to the nature of goodness itself.

V. THE POLITICAL PRIMACY OF NATURAL RIGHTS

Both the NNLT and the TNLT are correct to hold that human flourishing is not atomistic. To think that human beings can flourish independently of and apart from others is to commit the fallacy of reification (that is, of treating abstractions as realities) just as much as one does if one thinks that human nature or society can exist independently of and apart from individuals. Being asocial is not a policy consistent with human flourishing, and therefore individuals ought to be concerned with the nature of and conditions for social life.

Moreover, NNLT and TNLT are correct to hold that individuals cannot flourish or morally mature without societies and communities in which there are shared values. People need to live and work with others in accordance with some common set of values. Of course, it is also true that these values should be truly good for the individual rather than blindly accepted. The need for community life does not necessarily mean that individuals must accept the status quo; persons may need to leave or change their community. Yet this cannot be done if sociality is only possible with those with whom one currently shares common values. It must be possible, then, for persons to have relationships with others with whom there is only a potential for shared values. That is to say, it must be possible to have relationships with others when all one knows is that one is dealing with another human being.

Furthermore, though human sociality is always manifested in some particular family, group, community, culture, and society, it is not thereby limited to those particular manifestations. It is not confined to some select group or pool of humans, but is, in principle, open to *any* human. There is no *a priori* limitation regarding with whom one may have a relationship. To claim, then, that one's flourishing or moral maturation is impossible without sharing values with others is not to claim that sociality is confined to only those currently existing relationships and sets of values. Human sociality allows for openness toward human beings in general, including strangers. Indeed, human flourishing is possible only if people can be open to relationships with individuals with whom one shares no values *as of yet*.

When interpersonal or social life is understood as concerned with relationships with *any* human being, and when the individualized and agent-relative character of human flourishing is grasped, then the need for a different type of ethical norm is recognized. What is needed is a norm that is concerned *not* with the guidance of individual conduct in moral activity, but with the regulation of conduct such that conditions might be obtained whereby morally significant action can take place. The open-ended character of our natural sociality creates the need for a principle that will allow for the possibility that individuals in different communities and cultures might, without creating moral conflict, flourish in different ways. That is to say, there needs to be a principled answer to the following questions: How do we make potential relationships among humans, each of whom has a unique form of human flourishing, ethically compossible? How do we find a standard concerned with the creation, interpretation, and evaluation of a political/legal context that in principle will not require that the human flourishing of any person or group be preferred to that of others?

These questions are definitive of the liberal approach to political philosophy, and hence we call them *liberalism's problem*. It is precisely the need for an answer to these questions that creates the conceptual space for an ethical concept that is concerned not with the conditions for flourishing, but with the conditions for the *possibility* of flourishing *in society*. It is crucial to grasp this distinction, for it is the key to understanding the function of natural rights. Natural rights do not aim at directly or positively promoting (or maximizing) human flourishing; rather, they only aim at solving liberalism's problem. Natural rights classical liberalism, then, recognizes at its very root the problem of reconciling the individualized and agent-relative character of human flourishing with the open-ended nature of human sociality. This explains why natural rights classical liberalism is a political improvement on the natural law tradition; it is better able to provide a principled answer to liberalism's problem.

When viewed in light of liberalism's problem, natural rights can be understood as norms that regulate conditions under which moral conduct can take place—that is, they are *metanorms*. As metanorms, natural rights deal with the open-ended nature of social life and do not assume a shared set of values or commitments. Hence, their context is as universal as possible. They are only concerned with making potential relationships among humans, each of whom has a unique form of human flourishing, ethically compossible. The type of moral requirement that is imposed for establishing this context must be both something everyone's form of flourishing requires and something that everyone can in principle fulfill. Natural rights so understood (which could also be called "metanormative justice") are not a matter of personal flourishing, but a matter of creating, interpreting, and evaluating the political/legal conditions for civil order. Their fundamental importance is grounded in both the social and individual character of human flourishing.

Since human flourishing is individualized and agent-relative, one cannot establish an ethical basis for a political/legal context on some abstract understanding of human flourishing.[74] The ethical basis supporting such a context must be something that is common and peculiar to every act of human flourishing and something in which each and every person has a necessary stake. Otherwise, the pluralistic dimension of human flourishing will not be given its due, and liberalism's problem will not be addressed.

This brings us, then, to the self-directed nature of human flourishing. Human flourishing is not only an actuality; it is an activity. It is an activity

[74] One might assert here that knowledge of the basic goods could be derived from abstract considerations of flourishing, and that this knowledge might be able to form an ethical basis of the type discussed here. This is incorrect. Basic goods are valueless apart from the virtue of practical wisdom. They become valuable—that is, their proper combination, pattern, or weighting is achieved—only in relation to and because of the efforts of individual human beings.

in accordance with virtue, and the central virtue of human flourishing is practical wisdom. Yet practical wisdom is not passive. It is fundamentally, at its very core, a self-directed activity. Regardless of one's level of learning or degree of ability, the functioning of one's reason or intelligence is not something that occurs automatically. It requires individual effort.

Self-direction is both central and necessary to the very nature of human flourishing. It is the only feature of human flourishing that is common to all acts of human flourishing and peculiar to each. It is thus the one and only feature of human flourishing that everyone needs to have protected in the concrete situation, the one and only feature whose protection is compatible with each and every person having any possibility of flourishing. Self-directedness is thus the key to solving liberalism's problem.[75] Self-directedness is not amoral,[76] and its protection is something that, in principle, everyone can fulfill. Furthermore, since self-directedness is not only common to, but required by, all forms of human flourishing (or its pursuit), it can be used to create a political/legal order that will not require that the flourishing of any person or group be sacrificed to any other.

Yet self-direction cannot exist when some people use others without their consent. Moreover, since the initiation of physical force is the single most basic and threatening encroachment upon self-directedness, the aim of the natural right to liberty is to ban legally such activity in all its forms. The natural right to liberty allows each person a sphere of freedom in which self-directed activities can be exercised without the interference of others. This freedom must be compossible, meaning that the exercise of self-directed activity by one person must not encroach upon or diminish that of another. This freedom must also be equal, in the sense that it must allow for the possibility of diverse modes of flourishing, and therefore must not be structurally biased in favor of some forms of flourishing over others. The natural right of liberty, then, translates socially into a principle of maximum compossible and equal freedom for all. Thus, a theory of rights that protects persons' self-directedness can be used to create a political/legal order that will not necessarily require that the flourishing of any person or group is sacrificed to any other.

By protecting the possibility of self-directedness, the right to liberty serves human flourishing, not in the sense of directly and positively

---

[75] It is important to realize that by "self-directedness" in this context, we do not mean full-blown Millian autonomy or the directedness of the perfected self where one is fully rational. Instead, we mean simply the use of reason and judgment upon the world in an effort to understand one's surroundings and make plans to act within or upon them. The actions of the most self-perfected of individuals are certainly "self-directed" in this sense, but nothing in our description of self-directedness requires or implies any reference to such individuals, or even to successful conduct. The protection of self-direction in this sense does not favor one form of human flourishing over any other, because it is the act of exercising practical reason that is being protected, not the achievement of its object.

[76] Before ever addressing questions about what one should think about, or how one should conduct oneself, it is the case that one should think and act for oneself—that is to say, one should be self-directed. See Douglas J. Den Uyl and Douglas B. Rasmussen, "Reply to Critics," *Reason Papers* 18 (Fall 1993): 120–21.

promoting it, but rather by preventing encroachments upon the condition under which human flourishing can exist. The aim of the right to liberty is to secure the possibility of human flourishing, but it does so in a very specific way: it seeks to protect the possibility of self-directedness. In this way, the right to liberty is justified by an appeal to the nature of human flourishing, and a solution to liberalism's problem is provided.

According to our understanding of human flourishing, all ethical principles are based on the human good, but they are not all reducible to the same basic type or function. Thus, it is possible for there to be a difference between ethical principles that provide guidance to people in achieving the good and doing right—"normative" principles—and ethical principles that are used to create, interpret, and evaluate a political/legal order or context in which people try to achieve good and do right—"metanormative" principles. The right to liberty, then, is a metanormative principle, and we can thus understand why natural rights are a political improvement on the natural law approach to politics. The natural law approach, in both traditional and new forms, tries to ignore the implications of the realization that an ethics of human flourishing is a version of moral pluralism. It therefore fails to even recognize liberalism's problem. The natural rights approach, in contrast, explicitly addresses liberalism's problem and provides us with an answer—or, at least, with the best answer to date.[77]

VI. CONCLUSION

The natural law and natural rights traditions have been uneasy bedfellows. Both have stood fast against movements of historicism, conventionalism, and relativism that have pervaded modern political and social theory.[78] Both have appealed, if not to nature directly, then at least to an independent ontological order in grounding their respective approaches. Natural law theory has, however, always had a measured-to-distant connection to classical liberalism, whereas the natural rights tradition spawned it directly. Furthermore, the natural law tradition has been uncomfortable with the perceived individualism of the natural rights tradition. In this respect, we have taken the side of the natural rights tradition. However,

[77] The argument in this section is developed more fully in Den Uyl and Rasmussen, " 'Rights' as MetaNormative Principles"; Rasmussen and Den Uyl, *Liberalism Defended*; Rasmussen and Den Uyl, *Liberty and Nature*; and Rasmussen, "Community versus Liberty?" in Machan and Rasmussen, eds., *Liberty for the Twenty-First Century*, 259–87.

[78] *Historicism* is the view that truth is limited to and determined by particular historical periods. *Conventionalism* suggests that conventions alone determine what people regard as true; it is like historicism because conventions are found within historical periods. *Relativism* is the broadest of the three terms and holds generally that there are no truths independent of our perception or understanding of them. Each of these positions is a reaction against the idea that truth can be transpersonal, transcultural, and transhistorical. See Douglas B. Rasmussen, "Ideology, Objectivity, and Political Theory," in J. K. Roth and R. C. Whittemore, eds., *Ideology and the American Experience* (Washington, DC: Washington Institute for Values in Public Policy, 1986), 45–71.

we have also sought to ally ourselves with the moderate realist aspects of at least the traditional natural law position. We have, therefore, sought to relieve some of the tension between the two traditions. In doing so, however, we may have brought ourselves into tension with other doctrines, specifically those that give politics a central role in moral life. Since our own position does not give politics a role to play in the development or perfection of moral life, we may stand outside both of the traditions we have discussed here.

However successful our efforts in this essay have been, we believe we have raised interesting questions: namely, what are the sources of tension between the natural law and natural rights traditions, and what, if anything, can be offered to reconcile them? These questions stand on their own, and we have tried to give some indication of our answers by noting some of the similar and dissimilar elements in the two traditions. We have also suggested that if any reconciliation is possible, it will come through a modified Aristotelianism—one that embraces moderate realism *and* values moral individualism.

Philosophy, Liberty Fund
Philosophy, St. John's University

NATURAL LAW, CONSENT, AND POLITICAL OBLIGATION*

By Mark C. Murphy

I. Introduction

There is a story about the connection between the rise of consent theories of political obligation and the fall of natural law theories of political
obligation that is popular among political philosophers but nevertheless
false. The story is, to put it crudely, that the rise of consent theory in the
modern period coincided with, and came as a result of, the fall of the
natural law theory that dominated during the medieval period. Neat
though it is, the story errs doubly, for it supposes both that consent did
not play a key role in natural law theories of political authority offered in
the medieval period (a supposition falsified by close inspection of the
view of Aquinas, perhaps the paradigmatic natural law theorist[1]) and
that natural law theory did not play a key role in the consent theories of
political authority offered in the modern period (a supposition falsified
by close inspection of the views of Hobbes and Locke, perhaps the paradigmatic consent theorists[2]).

It is bad history to set up natural law and consent theories of political
authority as unqualifiedly antagonistic to each other. But it is not an
unfair description of the accounts of political authority offered by recent
natural law theorists—I have in mind in particular philosophers Yves
Simon and John Finnis—to say that these accounts were developed in
self-conscious opposition to voluntaristic accounts of political obligation
and that their formulations rule out as normatively unnecessary a citizen's consent to adhere to the dictates of the civil law. If we are blinded
by the bad history, we might think it altogether natural or obvious that a
contemporary natural law view would eschew any basic appeal to consent. But the fact that a number of predecessor natural law theorists saw
no inconsistency in grounding their accounts of political obligation both
in the natural law and in consent should give us pause, and provides us

* I owe thanks to Pat Kain, Paul Weithman, Bob Roberts, and Henry Richardson for
instructive criticisms. John Hare was particularly helpful both in criticism and in conversation. I was supported by a fellowship from the Erasmus Institute while this essay was
drafted.
    [1] See my "Consent, Custom, and the Common Good in Aquinas's Theory of Political
Authority," *Review of Politics* 59, no. 2 (Spring 1997): 323–50.
    [2] See my "Was Hobbes a Legal Positivist?" *Ethics* 105, no. 4 (July 1995): 846–73, for a
discussion of Hobbes's natural law view.

with some motivation to inquire further into whether the rejection of consent within a natural law account of political obligation is the most plausible line for the natural law theorist to take.

The appeal to consent as part of the most defensible account of political authority might be rejected by the natural law theorist on two grounds. First, the natural law theorist wants to say that the natural law account just does not *need* consent: its premises about the place of the common good and justice in the reasonable person's deliberation, along with the need for authority to coordinate action justly for the common good, provides on its own an account of the obligation to adhere to the civil law; any appeal to consent would be either superfluous or inconsistent with the main thrust of this account. Second, the natural law theorist might simply point to the consensus that seems to have developed against consent theories of political obligation: those writers that have recently turned their attention to the problem of political obligation on the whole agree that in any sense in which 'consent' names a sort of act capable of generating moral requirements, there is very little consent within political communities as presently constituted. If an appeal to consent turns out to be a necessary feature of the natural law account of political authority, then, that would be bad news for the natural law theorist, at least for the natural law theorist whose aim is not to debunk the existence of political obligation but to provide a positive account of it.

My aim in this essay, then, is to respond to these two arguments for the rejection of consent: that a natural law account of political obligation does not need consent; and that an appeal to consent would be damaging to the plausibility of such an account. First, I want to show that there is a gap in the natural law account of political obligation, that the recently formulated natural law view that tries to get by without an appeal to consent in explaining political obligation is unsuccessful. Second, I want to show how a natural law theory of political obligation that imbeds a consent account within it closes this gap, and closes it in a way that leaves the view relatively invulnerable to criticisms leveled against other versions of consent theory.

II. The Natural Law Account of Political Obligation

The account of political obligation characteristic in the natural law tradition takes as its central normative concept the idea of the common good. (This is unsurprising: almost *every* natural law account of *any* aspect of the political order takes the common good as its central normative concept.) The basic idea is that the moral requirement to obey the law is grounded upon the moral requirement to promote the common good of one's political community.

Since my concern in this essay is to adjudicate between natural law accounts of political authority that appeal to consent and those that do not, I will not spend much time here dealing with two related, vexing questions: one concerns the precise nature of the common good; and the other concerns the formulation and defense of the practical requirement to pursue it. There is, no doubt, a great deal of disagreement within the natural law tradition concerning the content of the common good. Some, like Aquinas and Simon, take it to be the distinctive good of the political community as a whole, though its realization is something that perfects each and every member of the political community.[3] Others, like Finnis, understand the common good instrumentally, as those conditions the obtaining of which assists each and every member of the political community in realizing his or her good.[4] I prefer an aggregative conception on which the common good is that complex state of affairs constituted by the realization of the good of each and every member of the political community.[5] While any complete natural law account of the political order would have to fix on one understanding of the common good to the exclusion or subordination of the others, we can say a great deal about the natural law account of political authority by appealing to features of the common good likely to appear in any of these three conceptions.

Turning to the other vexing question, that of the formulation and defense of the practical requirement to promote the common good of one's political community, there is no doubt reason to wonder about the strength of this principle, why it has the agent-relative cast that it does, and how it is to be defended. But since I am engaged in an intramural dispute about the proper formulation of the natural law account of political obligation, rather than a defense of the natural law view against skeptics, I will put these questions to the side as well. Before moving on, however, one point is worth noting: providing a defense of such a principle with this agent-relative cast is key to the natural law theorist's approach to the *particularity* requirement on theories of political obligation.[6] An account of political obligation must, that is, explain the presence of a special tie to one's own laws and one's own government, not just to those of any political community, or any minimally just political community. The reason that one is bound to adhere to these laws, and not to those in some other political community, is that one is bound to promote the common good of one's own political community in a way that one is not bound to promote

---

[3] For relevant Thomistic texts, see Thomas Aquinas, *Summa Theologiae*, trans. Fathers of the English Dominican Province (New York: Benziger Bros., 1947), I–II, q. 19, a. 10; II–II, q. 26, a. 3; II–II, q. 26, a. 4, ad 3; II–II, q. 31, a. 3, ad 2; II–II, q. 47, a. 10. For Simon's view, see Yves R. Simon, *A General Theory of Authority* (Notre Dame, IN: University of Notre Dame Press, 1980), 23–79.

[4] See John Finnis, "Public Good: The Specifically Political Common Good in Aquinas," in Robert George, ed., *Natural Law and Moral Inquiry: Ethics, Metaphysics, and Politics in the Work of Germain Grisez* (Washington, DC: Georgetown University Press, 1998), 174–209.

[5] See my "Natural Law, the Common Good, and the Political Order," forthcoming.

[6] See Leslie Green, *The Authority of the State* (New York: Oxford University Press, 1988), 227–28; and A. John Simmons, *Moral Principles and Political Obligations* (Princeton, NJ: Princeton University Press, 1979), 30–35.

the common good of other political communities. Just as one has a special responsibility to *this* community's common good, one has a special responsibility to adhere to *this* community's set of laws. We cannot, consistent with the main thrust of the natural law account, forgo a principle of promotion of the common good with an agent-relative cast in favor of a similar principle with a more agent-neutral cast, for that would leave the natural law view without a way to satisfy the particularity desideratum.

Each person in a political community is bound to promote the common good of that community. Since it is possible that sound practical thinking may recognize limits on how far an agent must extend him- or herself in seeking the common good, we may say, without begging any questions, that this principle can also be stated in the following way: *each person is bound to do his or her share in promoting the common good*. I will call this practical principle, upon which the natural law account of political obligation is based, the *common good principle*. What, then, is the relationship between a citizen's being bound by the common good principle and that citizen's being bound to adhere to the civil law of his or her political community? The connection is this: that adherence to the law is a constituent of doing one's share in promoting the common good, such that (a) in adhering to the demands of the law, one is to some extent fulfilling the moral requirement to do one's share in promoting the common good; and (b) if one does not adhere to the demands of the law, one is *ipso facto* failing to do one's share in promoting the common good. The natural law theorist is not claiming that every reason to promote the common good is exhausted by the content of the civil law, or even that what is a matter of strict duty with respect to promoting the common good is exhausted by the law. The claim is that at least part of the strict duty to promoting the common good is that one adhere to the dictates of the civil law. One likely is under duties with respect to promoting the common good that go beyond the demands of the law, but one will invariably go afoul of the common good principle if one fails to obey the law.[7]

Now, one might think that such an account of the obligation to obey the law is bound to be a nonstarter, due to the tight structural similarities between this sort of account of the obligation to obey the law and utilitarian 'public interest' accounts that have been roundly criticized. Suppose that one were to affirm a crude act utilitarian account of political obligation by asserting that each act should promote the public happiness and that obedience to law is required because it is necessary to promoting the public happiness. Now, some have responded to such accounts by noting that there are clear cases in which obedience to law does not promote the public interest, and so the act utilitarian account fails because

---

[7] There may be good reasons for the law to fail to require something that duty requires toward the promotion of the common good. For example, some particular law of this sort may be burdensome, unjust to enforce, etc. On this point, see, for example, Aquinas, *Summa Theologiae*, I–II, q. 96, a. 2.

it establishes only an obligation to obey the law when such obedience is optimific.[8] This criticism is, I think, wrongheaded, because there is no reason to suppose that an account of political obligation cannot be limited in some way—that citizens are bound to obey all laws that are not unjust, for example.[9] The more important point, which the defectively formulated criticism suggests but does not make explicit, is that in the act utilitarian account no normative weight is carried by the existence of the law. The act utilitarian account of the obligation to obey the law has this problematic feature for two reasons. First, it appeals to an end, the public interest, that can be characterized independently of anyone's decisions, and which is such that various states of affairs can be ranked with respect to the extent that they realize this end. Second, the account holds that what counts as one's share in promoting this end is similarly independently characterizable, as simply whatever one can do to realize a state of affairs that best approximates the public interest. Thus, what the law says (or assumes) about the content of the common good, and what one should do to help realize it, is normatively impotent.

But whatever the vices of the natural law account, they do not include the law's normative impotence. Theories of the common good in natural law accounts are, as I noted above, various, but they tend to reject the notion that the content of the common good and the contours of the duty to promote it can be specified apart from agents' decisions. The result is that on these accounts, the law can make a genuine difference, normatively speaking. The natural law view puts forward the common good as an ideal, one that is impossible to realize in practice. The proximate object of political action, the common good that can be reasonably hoped for, is a specification of the common good ideally conceived. Candidate specifications of the common good cannot be readily ranked, though, as approximations to the common good ideally conceived, and thus must be fixed upon partly by moral norms other than those of maximization and partly by acts of sheer discretion or free choice. Furthermore, the natural law view holds that what counts as doing one's share in promoting the common good, even assuming a particular specification of the common good, is itself something that requires specification.[10] What justice re-

[8] See Simmons, *Moral Principles*, 47–49; and M. B. E. Smith, "Is There a Prima Facie Obligation to Obey the Law?" *Yale Law Journal* 82, no. 5 (April 1973): 964–65.
[9] I discuss this point in my "Surrender of Judgment and the Consent Theory of Political Authority," *Law and Philosophy* 16, no. 2 (March 1997): 134; and in my "Moral Legitimacy and Political Obligation," *APA Newsletter on Law and Philosophy* 99, no. 1 (Fall 1999): 77–80.
[10] My discussion of specification of moral principles is inspired by and draws from the work of my colleague Henry Richardson. See his "Specifying Norms as a Way to Resolve Concrete Ethical Problems," *Philosophy and Public Affairs* 19, no. 4 (Fall 1990): 279–310. One difference in our discussions is that Richardson focuses on the need for specification as arising from *conflict* between moral principles, while I focus on the need for specification as arising from the initial *vagueness* of a moral principle. In recent work, Richardson distinguishes between *specifying* moral norms and *sharpening* them: one carrying out the former process assumes that the extension of a particular norm is determinate, and then proceeds

quires one to do in promoting the proximate common good may be specified in a number of incompatible ways, each with its own distinctive merits (so that the specification decision is not arbitrary, or at least not arbitrary through indifference). Thus, the distinctive merits of each do not entail a uniquely correct solution. There is an openness in the common good principle that makes room for the law to carry some weight in how one is to act in doing one's share to promote the common good, and that is why the law in the natural law account need not suffer from the normative impotence from which the law suffers in the act utilitarian account.

The natural law account of political obligation holds, then, that the law provides an authoritative partial specification of what one is to do in fulfilling the common good principle. The idea of political obligation as specificatory is, I think, extremely important. It is widely acknowledged that political obligation must display a certain content-independence,[11] so that within a certain range of otherwise eligible proposals for action, when the law picks out a certain one, this determines the one to act on. The most natural way to explain content-independence is to provide an account on which the mere fact that an act is prescribed by law invariably adds normative weight to the performance of that act. But if we explain content-independence in this way, we leave ourselves open to an argument that philosopher Joseph Raz levels against the very idea of political obligation. Raz claims that if there were an obligation to obey the law, then it would follow that the duty not to murder is stricter and weightier if the law proscribes it than if it does not. But since the duty not to murder is not made stricter and weightier by the existence of law, there is no such obligation.[12] One might quibble with Raz over whether this implication is counterintuitive, but I agree with Raz on that point; what I deny is that the content-independence of political obligation entails that normative weight is added with every law. The point of the law's authority, on a natural law view that appeals to the common good principle, is to fix some of the content of that principle, to settle, in part, how agents are to act on it. If, then, there are some acts the performance of which or the refraining from which are simply *entailed* by the common good principle, then no extra normative weight need be added to their performance or nonperformance by the existence of a law prescribing or proscribing them: they are part of any minimally acceptable specification of the common good principle. If, as I think, acts of murder, rape, torture, assault, and fraud are all, in themselves, failures to do one's share in promoting the

---

to qualify it; one carrying out the latter assumes that the extension of a particular norm is indeterminate, and then proceeds to make it more determinate. See Henry Richardson, "Specifying, Balancing, and Interpreting Bioethical Principles," *Journal of Medicine and Philosophy* 25, no. 3 (June 2000): 288–91.

[11] See Green, *The Authority of the State*, 36–59.

[12] See Joseph Raz, "The Obligation to Obey: Revision and Tradition," *Notre Dame Journal of Law, Ethics, and Public Policy* 1, no. 1 (1984): 142.

common good, there is no need for law to specify that the common good principle includes refraining from these acts. The law does not set aside these acts as not to be done; the common good principle already does this on its own.[13] So Raz's objection fails against specificationist understandings of the obligation to obey the law. But content-independence—at least, any version of content-independence worth wanting—is preserved: within the range of reasonable potential specifications of the common good and citizens' shares in promoting the common good, it is the law that settles, at least in part, which specification will count as doing one's just share in promoting the common good.

This emphasis—on the role of the law in partially specifying the requirement to do one's share in promoting the common good—makes clear both how the natural law view differs from utilitarian 'public interest' accounts and how certain worries about the content-independence of the requirement to obey the law can be handled. But it also brings into relief the central problem that confronts natural law accounts of political obligation. The requirement to adhere to the demands of the law is supposed to be based somehow in the requirement to do one's share in promoting the common good. But both *the common good* and *one's share in promoting it* are in need of specification. That leaves unanswered a crucial question, though: why does the law have the privileged place in rendering specifications of the common good and of the citizen's share in promoting it? Think of it this way: imagine a citizen confronted by a law. The citizen asks, conscientiously, why he is bound to adhere to this law. The answer comes back: because you are bound to do your share in promoting the common good, and the law tells you what must be done in order for you to do your share. The citizen grants the principle but asks for a demonstration from the principle to the conclusion that this law must be followed. What this citizen will want to know is why he must act on the particular specifications of the common good, and of justice in promoting it, rendered by the civil law. Even if he were to allow the necessity of acting on *some* specification of the common good and of his just share in promoting it, he needs an account of why acting on his own specifications of the common good principle, or on a friend's, or on anyone's besides the law's would constitute a failure to live up to the demands of the common good principle.

This is, I believe, the central difficulty for the natural law account. What is at issue is, first of all, how *any* particular (nonentailed) specification of a general normative principle can become authoritative for an agent, so that the agent is failing with respect to that general normative principle if

---

[13] So Aquinas, in distinguishing (a) civil laws that are derived from the natural law simply by way of logical deduction from the natural law and the given features of a situation (derivation by *deduction*), and (b) those that are derived from it by a free decision (derivation by *determination*), says that the former get their force from the natural law, while the force of the latter comes from the civil law alone. Aquinas, *Summa Theologiae*, I–II, q. 95, a. 2.

he or she fails to act on that specification, and second, why it is the *law's* specifications of the general principle to do one's share in promoting the common good that are authoritative for the agent. Some natural law theorists want to say that the authoritativeness of the law's specifications can be accounted for simply by the fact that the law possesses a certain *salience* with respect to the coordination problem that citizens face in trying to promote the common good through unified action. I will examine such an account in the next section. I will argue there that such views do not account for the authoritativeness of the law's specifications, though they give an account of the pressures exerted by practical reasonableness toward the establishment of an authoritative system of law. In short, the natural law account of political authority that eschews an appeal to consent explains the need for political authority, and explains why citizens would be bound to establish an authoritative institution; it does not show that such institutions are in fact authoritative.

III. THE 'LAW AS SALIENT COORDINATOR' ACCOUNT

Natural law theorists who purport to account for political obligation without appeal to consent, or any other voluntary act, rely on two premises: (a) that even in a political community composed entirely of practically reasonable agents there is a need for an authority to coordinate action for the common good, and (b) that the law is the salient candidate to fill this role. Given these premises, the defenders of this view hold that in any political community in which there is a legal system that issues directives toward the achievement of the common good, those under this legal system are bound to adhere to its directives.

The most well-elaborated version of this argument has been offered by Finnis. His basic contention is that the existence of a genuine political authority is something that is needed within a political community. Some person, group of persons, or set of rules must serve as authoritative in order to coordinate action for the common good by establishing prescriptions that make a normative difference. Political authority is necessary because the common good is variegated, and different reasonable citizens may settle on different specifications of the common good and of each citizen's proper role in promoting that good.[14] Citizens may, with equal reasonableness, appeal to the common good and justice in promoting it as the source of their specifications; but since these specifications are, though constrained by practical reasonableness, also the product of free, discretionary choice, different citizens' specifications will be incompatible with each other, and cannot serve as bases for common action. Practically reasonable agents will see, then, that it would be a good thing if they were

[14] John Finnis, *Natural Law and Natural Rights* (Oxford: Oxford University Press, 1980), 231–32.

to have reasons for adhering to some common standard for conduct, if there were an authoritative standard for their action to promote the common good. After all, given any realistically realizable specification of the common good that might be put forward as a proximate aim of common action, that specification can be better promoted by practically reasonable citizens in a community where authority exists than it could in one where authority is lacking.

The existence of a common good to be pursued and the availability of a number of ways of reasonably promoting it in common gives rise to a coordination problem, which is in some ways analogous to coordination problems as defined technically within game theory. In game theory, coordination problems are "situations of interdependent decision by two or more agents in which coincidence of interest predominates and in which there are two or more coordination equilibria," where a coordination equilibrium is a situation in which the combination of the players' actions is such that no one would be better off if any single player acted differently.[15] The classic example is Hume's: two people want to get from one side of a river to the other by rowing; they can only get across if both row in tandem; there are a number of different rowing 'patterns' that they can establish. The main point is that they just need to settle on one: it does not particularly matter which. Crucial, then, is the identification of a particular one of the available solutions as salient, either by agreement or by noting features of a solution that exist prior to agreement. If a solution is salient, then a player can expect that others will act on it, and thus, by the definition of a coordination equilibrium, no player will have reason to depart from that standard. To reconsider Hume's case: an agreement between the two rowers can easily make a certain pattern of rowing salient. But a pattern might be salient even in the absence of an agreement. If the two rowers cannot communicate with each other, but can see (and can know that the other sees) a large metronome, mounted to the rowboat and ticking away, there is an obvious pattern of rowing to which to conform.

Now, in attempting to make a similar argument for the law's status as salient coordinator, I of course am not suggesting that everyone's actual purposes are such that adherence to law is a coordination equilibrium. This would be clearly false, given the existence of persons who are uninterested in the realization of the common good. The appropriate restriction to place is to concern ourselves entirely with those practically reasonable persons who are intent on acting on the common good principle. These persons share an end: the realization of the common good. Given that they share an end, and that the law offers a salient point of coordinated action, can we not say that those acting on the common good principle are bound in reason to adhere to the law?

[15] David Lewis, *Convention: A Philosophical Study* (Cambridge, MA: Harvard University Press, 1969), 24, 14.

Even with this constraint placed on the ends of the citizens, the fact that the common good admits of multiple reasonable specifications, each better than another eligible specification in some respects but worse than it in some other relevant respects, undercuts the possibility that the law's mere salience can underwrite an account of the obligation to obey it. For if the common good is subject to multiple specifications, it seems hardly likely that any eligible specification of it must be such that, even if everyone else acts for its sake, there could not be some other eligible conception of the good that would be more closely approximated by an agent's departing from the common standard. To make this more concrete, imagine again a practically reasonable citizen confronted by a law. She asks for an argument from the common good principle to the conclusion that this particular law must be obeyed. Perhaps the law in this citizen's political community dictates that each citizen must pay 10 percent of his or her income in taxes, and of the collected income tax one-third will be spent on defense, one-third on welfare, and one-third on promotion of the arts. Suppose that everyone else in that political community is willing to go along with the tax scheme, and that the distribution of the tax monies is guaranteed to follow the designated pattern. Our practically reasonable citizen, though, would prefer a different specification of the common good, one that emphasized welfare over defense and the arts. She thinks that the common good would be better achieved if she withheld her tax and spent it directly on contributions to homeless shelters, soup kitchens, and the like. Why, this citizen might ask, should the existence of the law's rival specification of the common good be dispositive of what she must do in order to act on the common good principle? It seems clear that there is, in this best-case compliance scenario, rational motivation for unilateral departure from the common standard, even for a practically reasonable citizen concerned for the common good. This sort of salient coordinator view lacks an account of the authoritativeness of the law's specification of the common good, given the presence of rival eligible specifications that can make unilateral defection reasonable.

Finnis insists—contrary to the views of those who suppose that coordination arguments go a long way toward accounting for any authority that the law possesses—that the fact that the common good might be reasonably specified in various ways undermines most coordination arguments. Yet he labels his own natural law view a coordination account. His view is distinguished from the type of coordination argument that he criticizes by the type of salience that the law is held to possess. In the coordination problems of game theory, the salience of the standard consists merely in its being unique in some way, and in fact the solution "does not have to be uniquely good; indeed, it could be uniquely bad."[16] The law, by contrast, has its salience not simply in virtue of its standing

[16] Ibid., 35.

out, its 'catching the eye', so to speak, but in virtue of its superior capacity
to carry out in a reasonable way the specification that must be made. Here
is Finnis's key passage:

> The law presents itself as a seamless web. Its subjects are not per-
> mitted to pick and choose among the law's prescriptions and stipu-
> lations. It links together, in a privileged way, all the persons, and all
> the transactions, bearing on [one's] present and immediate future
> situation. It also links all the people and transactions which have
> borne on [one's] well-being or interests in the past. And finally, it
> links too all the people and transactions that may bear on [one's]
> future interests and well-being as [one] moves into other occupa-
> tions, into retirement, old-age, illness, and death.[17]

Raz is unable to see Finnis's discussion here of the seamlessness of the
law as anything other than question-begging: "For [Finnis], if this is how
the law presents itself, then this is how we ought to take it. To be sure, if
we have an obligation to obey the law, then the conclusion does indeed
follow. But one cannot presuppose that we have such an obligation in
order to provide the reason . . . for claiming that we have an obligation to
obey. This would be a vicious circle indeed."[18] This, I think, misses the
thrust of Finnis's argument. What Finnis is arguing for is the law's normative salience with respect to filling the need for an authoritative standard in pursuing the common good. Law's salience consists in its capacity,
as a result of its terrific scope, to deal with the problems of justice that
invariably attend the pursuit of as massive an end as the common good.
We are all, so the natural law view holds, bound to pursue and promote
the common good, to do our share in helping to realize it. In acting to
promote it, we will need some common specification of it. But in fixing on
a common specification of the common good in a reasonable way, we will
have to keep in mind that the benefits and burdens constituted by or
attendant upon the realization of the common good will have to be justly
distributed. This too is a problem for specification: we will need to render
specifications of distributive principles in order to settle on a specification
of the common good. Now, we will also have to decide what each person's just share in promoting the common good is. But surely if we are to
reach in a reasonable way specifications about what each person's share
is, this will have to be related both to the benefits that one will receive in
the realization of the common good as well as the burdens that will be
laid on one's fellow participants in the action toward the common good.
And once again, this will require specification. We need to keep in mind,

---

[17] John Finnis, "The Authority of Law in the Predicament of Contemporary Social Theory,"
Notre Dame Journal of Law, Ethics, and Public Policy 1, no. 1 (1984): 120.
[18] Raz, "The Obligation to Obey," 150.

further, that how a person is benefited and burdened at a particular time is not dispositive of the justice or injustice of the scheme; we will have to look at how these burdens and benefits are distributed over an entire life, so that no one is required to shoulder excessive burdens at a particular stage of life, and so that over the course of one's whole life the benefits and burdens are equitable. And, finally, we need to realize that the law promises a particularly salient way of solving the coordination problem inasmuch as we may be concerned not only that the standard for common action be eligible with respect to its intrinsic features, but also with respect to the way that it was put into place. A scheme of cooperation that is in itself just can be rejected on the grounds that (a) even though eligible, it is not the scheme that one would have preferred, and (b) the way that it was put into place was itself unfair or discriminatory. But a well-functioning legal system, nondiscriminatory and working in accordance with the rule of law, removes any reasonable ground for complaint on that score.

It is not, then, that the law presents itself as a seamless web, and therefore that is how we should take it. Rather, the very comprehensiveness of the law and the method by which it is put into place makes it peculiarly appropriate to specifying the requirement to do one's share in promoting the common good. The law regulates the whole life of the community, and this makes the law normatively salient to fill the role of authoritative specifier of the common good principle. There may be, no doubt, other candidates: systems of customary rules, perhaps. In simpler societies, a system of customary rules may be able to perform this function quite well. But in a society of any complexity, the need to make adjustments in how the common good is specified and promoted picks out the law—with its "prospect of combining speed and clarity in generating practical solutions to constantly emerging and changing coordination problems, and in suggesting devices by which such solutions can be generated"[19]—as peculiarly appropriate to serve as the practical authority by which the common good is pursued.

Finnis's view, then, is this. Authority is needed for the promotion of the common good, or else practically reasonable agents will be at loggerheads, rendering incompatible specifications of the common good. Due to its capacity to render specifications over the broad range of human life necessary for reasonable determination of the common good principle, the law is particularly well-suited to serve as a practical authority with respect to the common good. Since there is a need for authority in promoting the common good, and a system of law is the normatively salient institution for guiding the promotion of that good, where there exists a legal system that is willing and able to promote the common good by rendering at least minimally reasonable specifications of the common

[19] Finnis, "The Authority of Law," 136.

good principle, then in acting on that principle one is bound to adhere to those of its specifications that are at least minimally reasonable.

There is much in Finnis's view, I think, that any natural law account of political obligation should accept. The natural law theorist should agree, I think, on the need for authority in coordinating practically reasonable agents to act for the common good. Since each agent has a duty to do his share to promote the common good, each agent should do his share in putting into place such an authority. Further, the natural law theorist should agree with Finnis about the normative salience of law as the candidate to fill this role as practical authority. The key question, though, is whether the acknowledgment of the need for a genuinely authoritative institution to guide action to the common good, together with a strong argument that the law is uniquely suited to serve this function, is sufficient to show that where the law exists citizens are under a moral requirement to adhere to it.

I say that it is not. For an institution to be authoritative is for it to have a certain normative power, the power to generate (exclusionary) reasons to ϕ by dictating that agents ϕ. It would be a good thing for a political community to have a practical authority to guide action toward the common good, for otherwise members of that community will (reasonably) act on their conflicting specifications of the common good and justice in promoting it. The presence of such an authority would give members of that community reasons to act on a common specification, and not to act on their own specifications, or what they would render as their own specifications. And the law is the best thing to make practically authoritative. But that authority is needed and that the law is the best candidate does not actually make the law authoritative. It does not show that citizens act wrongly by failing to act in accordance with the law's dictates. At most, it shows that if citizens fail to do their part to make the institution authoritative—perhaps by consenting to it, or something of that sort— then they are acting unreasonably. This is a very important conclusion, but it is *not* the conclusion that there is an obligation to obey the law. There still exists a gap that is not crossed. That it would be a good thing for the law to be authoritative does not mean that the law is in fact authoritative.[20]

---

[20] I thus reach the same conclusion about Finnis's version of the natural law account of political obligation that I reached concerning Jeremy Waldron's 'natural duty of justice' account. Waldron argues that we are all bound to promote justice, and that justice cannot be secured unless institutions function to ensure that the principles of justice are satisfied. Since those institutions will not function well unless those to whom those institutions apply accept the supervision of those institutions, those to whom such institutions apply are bound to comply with them. See Jeremy Waldron, "Special Ties and Natural Duties," *Philosophy and Public Affairs* 22, no. 1 (Winter 1993): 3–30. In response, I argued, a bit too tentatively, that it is unclear whether Waldron's premises implied that justice demands that we adhere to the law, or that justice demands that we make the law authoritative over us. See my "Acceptance of Authority and the Requirement to Comply with Just Institutions: A

Now, one might respond: given what has been granted so far—that practically reasonable citizens will do their share in bringing authoritative institutions into existence to guide action toward the common good, and that our imagined objector is a practically reasonable citizen (among other practically reasonable citizens)—the situation as described may be impossible. For if this citizen is practically reasonable, and the other citizens are practically reasonable as well, they will have put into place a practical authority, and will be obligated to adhere to its specifications. But that can be conceded without lessening the force of the objection to Finnis's view. The fact that a community of practically reasonable citizens will be under an obligation to obey the law does not show that the obligation to obey the law is independent of consent, or some other voluntary obligation-generating act. Rather, it might show that practical reasonableness requires one to submit to a political authority by performing some relevant obligation-generating act, and since practical reasonableness requires this, it follows that a community of practically reasonable citizens in sufficiently promising political conditions will have performed just such acts. And this is, I think, the case. The 'law as (normatively) salient coordinator' view does not close the gap; it does not show that the mere presence of law is enough to render authoritative the law's specifications of the common good principle.

IV. Consent and the Natural Law Account of Political Obligation

The 'law as salient coordinator' account of political obligation offered by Finnis does not explain why the law's specification of the common good principle is authoritative for a particular agent, however well it explains why it would be a good thing for the law to be authoritative over the citizens within a political community. I want to argue for the importance of a particular kind of consent in making the civil law authoritative. But in order to set the stage for the consent account, we need first to deal with a problem that is more fundamental than that of how the law's specification of the common good principle can be made authoritative for an agent. That problem is: how can *any* specification of *any* moral principle become authoritative for an agent, including the agent's own specifications? If one takes oneself (correctly) to be bound by a particular moral principle, specifies it in a certain way, yet fails to act in accordance with that specification, is that sufficient to constitute a violation of that moral principle?

Comment on Waldron," *Philosophy and Public Affairs* 23, no. 3 (Summer 1994): 271-77. I now think that it shows *at most* the latter, just as Finnis's view shows at most that the common good demands that we make the law authoritative over us.

Any attempt to show that one could ever violate a moral principle M simply by failing to act on one's own (nonentailed) specification of M seems bound to founder against the following argument. Let A and B be minimally acceptable, incompatible specifications of M, and let ϕ-ing be the act dictated in A, and ψ-ing the act dictated in B. Suppose that one renders A as the specification of M, yet ψ-s instead of ϕ-ing. How could the agent have violated M by ψ-ing, since ψ-ing is the act dictated by B, which is also a minimally acceptable specification of M?

One might offer a solution along the following lines: one could firmly resolve to act on A as a specification of M, and since one ought to keep one's firm resolutions, one would be acting wrongly with respect to the fulfillment of M by acting in accordance with B rather than A. But this is to equivocate: even if we grant that one would be acting wrongly with respect to the fulfillment of M, that does not mean that one is violating M; rather, one is acting wrongly with respect to the fulfillment of M because one is violating the requirement to keep one's firm resolutions, the content of one of which refers to the fulfilling of M, and *not* because one is violating M itself. And so it may seem that any attempt to make a specification of M an *authoritative* specification of M will do so not by making it the case that one will violate M by acting on any other specification than that one, but rather by making it the case that one will violate some other moral requirement by acting on a different specification of M.

So long as we proceed on the assumption that the only way to violate a moral principle M is to act in a way that is incompatible with the content of M, the conclusion is inescapable that no one of a range of minimally acceptable specifications of M can ever become privileged with respect to the fulfillment of M. But there may be other ways to violate a moral principle besides that of acting in a way incompatible with its content. What I have in mind is that one might act in a way vis-à-vis M that is incompatible with its status as a practical principle, as something that is to guide conduct. While this papers over a dispute, especially relevant with respect to some consequentialist positions, on how moral principles should figure in the deliberation of a reasonable agent, I want to say that a reasonable response to certain moral principles requires not just that one's conduct be consistent with the principle but that one act on the principle, so that one is flouting it by failing to have one's course of deliberation shaped by it. It seems to me that it is this sort of flouting of a moral principle that takes place by failing to act in accordance with one's specification of that moral principle.

To specify a moral principle is to decide, more specifically, how one is going to have one's course of action shaped by that moral principle. When one specifies a moral principle in a certain way and then fails to act on it, what one is doing is refusing to allow that moral principle to guide one's deliberation: in specifying the moral principle in a certain way, one has decided that if the moral principle is to guide one's conduct, it will be through this particular specification, and if one fails to act on that specification, one is thus not allowing that moral principle to govern one's deliberation. Even if, then, the action that one performs is not inconsistent with the content of the general moral principle at stake, the failure to act on the specification will constitute a flouting of the principle.

Let's take an example. Consider an ordinary moral rule and a particular specification of it that one might offer. Take the moral rule (if there is such a moral rule) that one should not consume alcohol to the point of intoxication. I think that there is a lot to be said in favor of this moral rule, that there are a variety of reasons that go into giving this moral rule the formulation that I have given it. People are often jerks when they are drunk. They lose control of their rational faculties and do idiotic things. They become unable to drive safely. But a little wine can be a good thing: there is little objectionable about drinking to the point of cheerfulness and conviviality, where one is loosened up a bit and able to engage socially with others. Now, one who acknowledges this moral rule and aims to live by it will have to come up with a particular specification of that rule, especially with respect to the relevant understanding of 'intoxication'. The relevant understanding is, of course, not a lexicographical issue, but a matter of being sensitive to the core concept, the reasons that push toward the expansion of the concept, and the reasons that push toward its contraction.

Now, it strikes me as highly unlikely that sound practical thinking will reach a determinate interpretation of this moral rule. In fixing on a particular interpretation of 'drinking to the point of intoxication', what occurs is a *decision* from a range of options picked out by practical judgment as eligible. Nevertheless, if my action is going to be governed by the rule in particular circumstances, it cannot simply be left vague. In deciding whether to go for the fifth drink within a two-hour span, I have to make a decision, and it is undeniable that the principle concerning drinking to the point of intoxication is relevant, regardless of whether it allows or forbids the next drink. If I go for one specification of the moral rule rather than another, then it seems to me that this decision settles the question for me, in that if I fail to act on it I am not only acting against that specification but the general rule of which it is a specification. If I specify the moral rule as, in part, 'not having more than four drinks within a two-hour span', and then an occasion occurs on which I feel like having a fifth (a fifth drink, not a fifth *simpliciter*), I am not honoring the principle if I simply flout my decision and have the drink. I may reconsider my decision, thinking that (for example) I did not take into account the difference between drinking on a full stomach and on an empty one, and thus that the rule should be modified. But without such a modification, I act unreasonably in failing to act in accordance with my reasonable specification of the moral rule on intoxication.

In making the claim that the status of a practical principle as action-guiding can cause one's own particular specification of that principle to be authoritative, I am not denying that one might have sufficient reason to alter the specification that one has made. What needs to be made clear, I think, are the different sorts of rationales required: (a) for rendering a specification of a principle, (b) for altering the specification of a principle that one has previously rendered, and (c) for acting in accordance with the specification one has rendered. With respect to (a), the reason to render a specification of a general moral principle is just so that one's actions can be guided by it in particular circumstances where the principle is undoubtedly relevant but where without specification the principle's requirements would be unclear. So, the reason that I have to specify the principle about not drinking to the point of intoxication is just that the principle is undoubtedly relevant in all cases in which I have the opportunity to drink, but it is not clear how much it is reasonable for me to drink. With respect to (b), the reason to preserve the specification that one has rendered is, strictly speaking, not resultant from the character of the moral principle specified, but from the rational unseemliness of changing one's mind without adequate reason for doing so. In rational agents, decisions stand until some inadequacy in the deliberation leading to the decision is detected: some fact was overlooked, some circumstance upon which one has relied changes, some value was under- or over-appreciated. Less strictly speaking, if one constantly alters one's specifications of a moral principle, one has a basis to suspect oneself of not truly acting on the principle, but rather of letting one's particular commitment to that principle be swayed by extraneous factors. If I have a strong urge for a fifth drink after having reasonably specified the no-intoxication principle to limit myself to four drinks, and I just say 'Well, I'll just place the bar at five instead of four,' I have reason to suspect that my specification of the no-intoxication principle is being governed by considerations that are irrelevant, even if the specification newly settled upon is at least minimally acceptable. With respect to (c), the reason for acting on the specification of the principle, as I said, is just that by specifying a principle in a certain way one has decided that this is the way that one will act on this principle, and so if one does not act in this way, then one is not acting on the principle at all. If the principle is one that can be flouted by failing to act on it—and not just by acting in a way that is incompatible with its content—then one is bound to act in accordance with one's specification of the principle.[21]

---

[21] This discussion is meant to supercede my account in "Surrender of Judgment" of the requirement to act on one's specifications of moral principles. I am dissatisfied with the account presented in that paper for two reasons. First, I think that the argument for the principle is a bit ad hoc, taking for itself a premise it probably is not entitled to take. Second, I think that at most the argument would establish a requirement like the 'requirement' to keep one's resolutions, and so would not explain at all why failing to act on one's specification of a moral principle would count as a violation of *that principle*.

Everyone, so the natural law account of political obligation supposes, is bound to do one's share to promote the common good. This principle, if it is to guide our action, is in need of specification, and by rendering a specification of this principle each of us places him- or herself in a position such that one flouts the common good principle by failing to act in accordance with that specification. But none of this tells us, yet, how the *law's* specifications of the common good principle might become authoritative over the citizens under that law, so that they will violate the common good principle by violating the law. What I want to say, though, is this: the law's specifications of the common good principle become authoritative for an agent insofar as those specifications come to fill the same deliberative role as the agent's own specifications would. They come to fill this deliberative role by the agent's accepting the specifications proposed by the law as his or her own for the sake of practical reasoning: the agent allows for a kind of substitution of decision with respect to the specification of the common good principle. And it seems to me that this state of acceptance—where an agent allows the decisions of another to take the place of his or her own with respect to a sphere of action—can, not misleadingly, be called a case of *consent*.

What is this 'acceptance'? Think of it this way: in rendering a specification, one brings to bear relevant considerations, rules out certain alternatives, and then, from the alternatives remaining, settles on one by an act of discretion. This settles the way that the moral principle will govern one's conduct. In accepting another's decision as one's own, one is disposed to take as one's own specification whatever is decided by some other party—or (more likely and more reasonably) whatever, within a certain range and with respect to a certain sphere of conduct, is decided by some other party. Thus there is, in a way, a bypassing of choice. But this need not be unreasonable, if one can have reasonable trust that the considerations that would have to be duly considered in one's own choice have been duly considered by the other (or at least as well as one could do it oneself). And while we can grant that making one's own decisions in a certain matter is a good, it is surely one good among others, and there may be good reason to surrender one's decision in certain cases.

When one accepts the specifications of a moral principle M issued by another as one's own for the sake of practical reasoning, then one cannot act contrary to those specifications without violating M. Because (a) one violates M by failing to act on one's own specification of M, and (b) in accepting another's specifications, those specifications fill precisely the same role that one's own would, one violates M by failing to act on the specifications of M issued by a party whose specifications one accepts. I say, then, that consent in this acceptance sense is a way for the law's specifications of the common good principle to become authoritative for citizens within a political community. If those citizens consent, in the acceptance sense, to the law with respect to the specification of the com-

mon good principle, then they are bound, by way of the common good
principle, to adhere to the specification of that principle as it appears in
the law. Those who consent yet fail to obey the law are flouting the
principle that each ought to do his or her share to promote the common
good of the political community.

What this argument shows, if it is successful, is that if we accept what
is correct in the Finnis account—that it would be a good thing for the law
to be a genuine practical authority with respect to guiding action toward
the common good, and that each citizen is bound to do his or her share
to make the law such a genuine practical authority—then we can describe
a way for each citizen to do his or her part, that is, by consenting to the
law in the acceptance sense. But this leaves two important questions as
yet unanswered. First, is there any reason to suppose that consent in the
acceptance sense is in any way special, a peculiarly appropriate way of
making the law authoritative? Second, even if consent is peculiarly appropriate as a way of making the law authoritative, do we have any
reason to suppose that this consent account succeeds any further in explaining the presence of political obligation than does the standard consent account, which appeals to consent as a speech-act?

With respect to the first question, what makes consent in the acceptance
sense a peculiarly appropriate way to make the law authoritative is that,
unlike other ways of making the law authoritative, the moral principle at
work is the common good principle itself, not some other principle. And
this, to me, seems like an immediate point in its favor: the goodness of
political authority is its capacity to direct citizens to the common good,
and an account of its authority that links it most directly to the normative
force of the common good seems preferable to one that does not.

Another point in favor of consent in the acceptance sense is that it does
better than other accounts with respect to the avoidance of practical conflict. Suppose we make the comparison more particular, and ask, Why go
the route of consent in the acceptance sense, rather than, say, that of
promise? The defender of promise as the best way, or an equally good
way, to generate political authority might agree that political authority is
needed and that the law should serve this role, and might suggest that
something like a promise is a practically reasonable way to institute the
law as authoritative. Well, what would the relevant promise be? The
promise might be: to do what the law says to do, within the limits set by
the common good principle. This would ensure that no requirement that
one finds oneself with as a result of this promise goes afoul of the common good principle; whatever one is bound to do is assured to be congruent with some minimally acceptable specification of the common good
principle. But it does not seem clear to me that a promise of this form
would be a reasonable way to establish the law as authoritative. Here is
why: In putting into place a practical authority, we should also be concerned about the possibility of practical dilemmas, that is, we should aim

to avoid placing ourselves in situations in which we will find ourselves under conflicting practical requirements. If one makes such a promise and then goes on to render one's own specifications of the common good principle, one may find oneself in just such cases of practical conflict: one may be bound both to honor the promise and to act in accordance with one's own specification of the common good principle. Since there are a plurality of reasonable specifications of the common good principle, it would be sheer coincidence for the specifications rendered by the citizen and by the law to coincide. One is therefore bound to end up in practical dilemmas: bound to adhere to one's own specification, and bound to adhere to the law's.

This does not show, of course, that promising is inferior to consent in the acceptance sense as a way to make the law authoritative. Perhaps we have focused on the wrong content for the relevant promise. Instead of promising merely to *act on* the law's dictates, perhaps the promise that should be made is a promise to *accept* the law's specifications. The practical conflicts resultant upon rendering one's own specifications while being bound to act on those rendered by another would be ruled out, at least for those that adhere to their promise. But what now needs to be asked is whether the inclusion of acceptance of specifications within the content of the promise has not made the act of promising nugatory. For the promise is a reason to accept a specification, and once the specification is accepted, one is bound to act on it because it is one's own minimally acceptable specification of a correct moral principle. But we already have reasons to accept specifications, that is, that each person ought to do his or her just share in putting into place an authority that can guide agents toward the common good. And once the specification is accepted, the reason to act on it is that which is put forward in the consent-in-the-acceptance-sense account.

While these arguments are aimed at two particular alternatives to consent in the acceptance sense, I think that they point to a dilemma for any proposal that puts forward a mode of establishing authority other than consent in the acceptance sense: it will either be more prone to generating practical conflicts or it will be redundant. No doubt certain methods of generating content-independent obligations may be useful in addition to consent in the acceptance sense, but nothing can take the place of that form of consent.

The second question, which many writers seem to treat as the only real question, is about the extent to which the consent account succeeds in showing that citizens are actually bound to obey the law. I will not attempt to show that this consent view solves what Leslie Green takes to be *the* political obligation thesis: that all citizens are bound to all of the laws within the political community.[22] It seems to me that while the consent

---

[22] Green, *The Authority of the State*, 225, 228–29; and Leslie Green, "Who Believes in Political Obligation?" in John T. Sanders and Jan Narveson, eds., *For and Against the State* (Lanham, MD: Rowman and Littlefield, 1996), 8.

view I have defended has resources to provide an account of actual political obligation that goes beyond rival consent accounts, it surely does not approach the universality needed to satisfy the political obligation thesis. But it seems to me that even without establishing the political obligation thesis, the natural law/consent view that I have defended would justify a very powerful normative conclusion: that either a citizen is bound to obey the law of his or her political community, *or* that citizen acts unreasonably, *or* the legal system of that political community is an unreasonable one. Let me conclude, then, by discussing the scope of actual political obligation on the natural law/consent view and by considering this modified version of the political obligation thesis.

We may say, first, that consent in the acceptance sense is at least not on a par with consent in the speech-act sense, in that the absence of consent in the speech-act sense does seem to be a brute, easily empirically verifiable fact.[23] More positively, it seems to me that there is an argument that can be made that consent in the acceptance sense to the law as specifier of the common good principle is fairly widespread. Whether consent in the acceptance sense is a widespread phenomenon or not depends on the state of citizens' deliberative dispositions (on how they are disposed to reason practically), for consent in the acceptance sense is a disposition to accept another's specification of a moral principle as one's own for the purposes of practical reasoning. The main reason to suppose that consent in the acceptance sense is a fairly widespread phenomenon is that the law *does* figure so centrally in citizens' deliberations. Folks do tend to treat the law's determinations on matters of public interest as authoritative. Witness, for example, drunk-driving laws, and the seriousness with which folks take the particular specification of the blood alcohol level that counts as determining legal intoxication. Now, those worried about the theory of political obligation seem to think that either (a) we can provide some argument that the law is authoritative, and thus that this particular drunk-driving law should be obeyed, or (b) we must concede that the acceptance of the drunk-driving law is groundless. But the account that I have offered shows this dilemma to be a false one. There are good reasons to accept the law's specification in drunk-driving matters: driving while intoxicated is a matter that bears on the common good, and part of doing our share in promoting the common good is to refrain from driving while overly impaired by alcohol. But we do not need an argument from the

[23] Mark Hall has told me, though, that there is some statistical evidence that a very large percentage of U.S. citizens has at one point or another taken an oath to obey the law. When we put together naturalized citizens, members of the military, public officials, voters in states where something like a loyalty oath is part of one's voter's registration form, and so on, it may appear that many more folks than we might have originally supposed have performed acts of consent to be governed. Of course, we would still need to examine more closely the content and context of these oaths. But Hall's conjecture is, I think, a nice counterweight to the views of those who hold that express consent is obviously not to be had.

law's prior authority to show that a stance of deliberative acceptance of the law's standard is reasonable: what makes the acceptance reasonable is that there is need for such a standard and that the law is the salient provider of such a standard. Those who accept the law's standard, then — and I think that there are many — are bound to adhere to it in virtue of their acceptance.

What is true with respect to driving under the influence is also true in many other areas. What is more difficult is to show that citizens' acceptance of the law's specifications in these matters is acceptance of the right sort. If the common good principle is to provide the basis for political obligation, it must be that as a result of one's acceptance of the law, one flouts the common good principle when one flouts the law. But this will be the case only if one accepts the law *qua* specifier of the common good principle. Not mindlessly; not simply and only to be like one's neighbor; not as a rule of thumb to avoid jail. It may seem naive to hold that people accept the law in some way as specifier of the common good principle. But I think not. As Tom Tyler's recent study suggests, there is a good deal of evidence that willingness to go along with the law has a great deal to do with whether the law appears to be even-handed and just. Willingness to comply correlates more closely with perceived fairness than with favorable personal outcomes.[24] It does not seem to me at all naive, then, to think that citizens' acceptance of the law is in part acceptance of the law as marking out fair solutions to the problem of how the common good is to be promoted through unified action.

The natural law/consent account explains to a nonnegligible extent the actual political obligations that citizens are under. I do not claim that it provides a plausible defense of the thesis that all citizens are bound to obey the law within their political communities, even if those political communities are reasonably just. But one might suppose that since the natural law/consent account falls short of establishing the political obligation thesis, it is therefore of little interest. But there is more to this natural law account than an account of how far citizens are obligated to obey the law, and in what way. The natural law view begins with an account of the requirement to promote the common good and with an argument that citizens ought to do their share in putting into place a practical authority that can govern action toward the common good. If there exists a legal system that is at least minimally reasonable in its procedures for generating specifications of the common good principle, then those that heed the requirements of that principle will consent to its authority, and thus make it authoritative over the way that they pursue the common good. This is an important result, especially in the face of the charge that the natural law/consent account is a failure if it does not

[24] See Tom R. Tyler, *Why People Obey the Law* (New Haven, CT: Yale University Press, 1990).

establish the political obligation thesis. If consent in the acceptance sense is not a widespread phenomenon, it could be the case that there are very few citizens who are tied by bonds of political obligation. For those citizens, disobedience to law is not as such practically unreasonable. But this consent theory would have more to say than this: it would also offer information—although not totally unambiguous—about the citizens of a political community in which political obligation is almost wholly absent, or about the nature of the de facto political authority within that community. With respect to the character of the citizenry, the absence of political obligation could mean that the community is full of unreasonableness, and that it is a community in which citizens fail to submit themselves to authority for the sake of the common good. Alternatively, the absence of political obligation might testify not to the unreasonableness of the citizenry but rather to the serious inadequacy of the political institutions. They might be merely ineffective at promoting the common good or they might lack the discernment or resolution to render a reasonable specification of that good. In other words, these institutions might not merit the consent of the citizenry, either in a wholesale way or with respect to some aspect of the common good. It is possible, then, for the defender of the natural law view to agree in substance with those philosophical anarchists[25] who hold that most of us are not in fact required to obey the laws of our political communities—but who add, in order to complete the account, 'so much the worse for us.'

V. Conclusion

In rejecting an alliance with consent theorists, the natural law theorist takes him- or herself to be refusing help that he or she does not need and that at any rate consent theorists are unable to provide. I have argued that the natural law theorist underestimates the help that consent theory can offer and that the natural law theorist *drastically* underestimates the help that his or her view needs from consent theory. The natural law directs reasonable beings toward authority, not by placing them under it, but by mandating its creation through their own consent.

Philosophy, Georgetown University

---

[25] For a general discussion of philosophical anarchism, see A. John Simmons, "Philosophical Anarchism," in Sanders and Narveson, eds., *For and Against the State*, 19–40. Included in the class of philosophical anarchists are Simmons, Raz, Green, and Smith.

THE NATURAL BASIS OF POLITICAL OBLIGATION*

By George Klosko

I. Introduction

Though questions of political obligation have long been central to liberal political theory, discussion has generally focused on voluntaristic aspects of the individual's relationship to the state, as opposed to other factors through which the state is able to ground compliance with its laws. The individual has been conceptualized as naturally without political ties, whether or not formally in a state of nature, and questions of political obligation have centered on accounting for political bonds.

Within the liberal tradition,[1] the main arguments for political obligations have been based on individual consent, as epitomized in Locke's *Second Treatise* and the Declaration of Independence.[2] However, consent theory has long been criticized on the ground that adequate numbers of citizens cannot be shown to have consented expressly to their governments. Since Hume's essay, "Of the Original Contract" (1748), it has been clear that adequate numbers have not consented tacitly either.[3] Although the idea that political obligation rests on consent still has an important role to play in liberal theory—especially in the form of "hypothetical" consent[4]—I believe that consent theory has left a generally unhelpful

* For helpful comments on and discussion of earlier drafts of this paper, I am grateful to the other contributors to this volume, the editors of *Social Philosophy and Policy*, Colin Bird, Richard Dagger, Joshua Dienstag, Charles Kromkowski, David Mapel, Debra Morris, John Simmons, Vivian Thomson, and Steven Wall.

[1] To avoid unnecessary complexity, I discuss liberal theory on a general level and am not concerned with questions of precise definition. As I use the term, the liberal tradition has at its center the individual and his rights, more or less regardless of how these rights are established and regardless of whether they extend beyond the essentially negative rights of classical liberalism to encompass economic and other welfare rights. Thus, in addition to Locke, Montesquieu, and Mill, this view includes Hobhouse and both Rawls and Nozick.

[2] John Locke, *The Second Treatise of Government*, in Locke, *Two Treatises of Government*, ed. Peter Laslett (Cambridge: Cambridge University Press, 1988); "Declaration of Independence," reprinted in Alexander Hamilton, John Jay, and James Madison, *The Federalist* (New York: Modern Library, n.d.), 619–22.

[3] David Hume, "Of the Original Contract," in Hume, *Essays, Moral, Political, and Literary*, ed. Eugene Miller, rev. ed. (Indianapolis, IN: Liberty Classics, 1985). See also the important discussion of A. John Simmons, *Moral Principles and Political Obligations* (Princeton, NJ: Princeton University Press, 1979), chaps. 3 and 4.

[4] See Hannah Pitkin, "Obligation and Consent," *American Political Science Review* 59, no. 4 (December 1965): 990–99; Jeremy Waldron, "Theoretical Foundations of Liberalism," *Philosophical Quarterly* 37, no. 147 (April 1987): 127–50; and Immanuel Kant, "On the Common Saying: 'This May Be True in Theory, but It Does Not Apply in Practice,'" in Kant, *Kant's Political Writings*, ed. Hans Reiss (Cambridge: Cambridge University Press, 1970).

residue. In concentrating attention on the "isolated individual" and his decision whether or not to commit to political society, consent theory and this underlying view of the individual have deflected attention away from other aspects of the individual's relationship to the state that are more promising grounds for political obligation. To the extent that consent theory is central to the natural law tradition, problems with consent can be viewed as shortcomings of natural law theory as well.

In this essay, I criticize the isolated individual as this conceptualization bears on questions of political obligation. I focus on one particular aspect of the individual's relationship to the state: the claim that the state must provide the individual benefits or services that are necessary for an acceptable life. If we grant this claim, then the baseline position on questions of obligation should not be the isolated individual in the state of nature, but the individual as recipient of indispensable state benefits; adopting the latter baseline makes political obligations far easier to justify. I will concentrate on a theory of political obligation rooted in the principle of fairness; this principle, I shall argue, is able to account for essential state services and their role in political obligations.[5]

An argument along these lines leaves open the counterargument that the state is not necessary to supply the benefits in question. According to political philosopher A. John Simmons, if people would prefer to receive through other means those services provided by a given political body, then they do not incur obligations to that body under the principle of fairness.[6] Accordingly, I will examine the claim that alternative means of supply can obviate obligations people would otherwise have.

My main contention is that, at minimum, alternative provision mechanisms must meet a standard of reasonable plausibility if they are to dissolve any political obligations. Because a certain range of state services is necessary for satisfactory lives, people can avoid obligations to the state only if they can convincingly maintain that they can obtain these benefits through other means.[7] The nature of this plausibility requirement is discussed below. I will examine the possibility of alternative supply, as well as the conditions that must hold if different conceivable mechanisms are

[5] A full exposition of fairness theory, on which I will draw here, can be found in George Klosko, *The Principle of Fairness and Political Obligation* (Savage, MD: Rowman and Littlefield, 1992). Other grounds of political obligation that do not involve voluntary commitment include gratitude, a natural duty of justice, and consequentialism. For an additional possibility, reciprocity, see Mark Hall and George Klosko, "Political Obligation and the United States Supreme Court," *Journal of Politics* 60, no. 2 (May 1998): 466–68.

[6] A. John Simmons, *On the Edge of Anarchy* (Princeton, NJ: Princeton University Press, 1993), 256–60.

[7] It is possible to deny the need for the services in question altogether, which would make it easier to defeat arguments for political obligations. Such an approach, however, would take one beyond the parameters of liberal theory. In this essay, I confine my attention to liberal theory, and so do not discuss this approach. In addition, although the specific benefits discussed in this essay are those of a modern industrial society, my arguments could easily be recast to be made applicable to other kinds of societies.

to meet the requirement. Although I do not claim that alternative supply is impossible, consideration of various mechanisms will indicate that they do not meet it. As we will see, the plausibility requirement is necessary because, while advocating alternative supply, a given individual, Smith, receives essential services from the state and will continue to do so unless her alternative means are likely to work. To return to the point made at the opening of this essay, while Smith may conceive of herself as an isolated individual and resist attempts to subordinate her to the state, indispensable state benefits render her by nature (as Aristotle would say) a member of society.

In contemporary political theory, criticisms of the atomistic individual are not uncommon, nor are claims that the individual is, in some essential sense, a member of society. These are, of course, common themes in communitarianism.[8] In this essay, I set aside common communitarian concerns about the nature of individual identity and how this nature is discovered. These problems can be avoided here because the aspects of community membership on which I focus are minimal and subject to little controversy. For the sake of this essay's argument, the community can be viewed simply as individuals jointly providing and receiving important benefits. I do not contend that this conception exhausts the essence of community, or make claims about its centrality to the notion of community. Perhaps other aspects of the relationship between individual and community remain controversial, but there can be little doubt about those invoked by the conception here. As we shall see, even this modest view of the community supports the plausibility requirement and its accompanying implications for political obligation.

My discussion will proceed in four parts. In Section II, I outline a theory of political obligation rooted in fairness and describe the role that essential state benefits play in this theory. Section III examines Simmons's criticisms of this theory and considers alternative supply. Since alternative mechanisms are a central concern in game-theoretic analysis, Section IV considers possibilities from this perspective. Section V draws out some implications and presents a brief conclusion.

II. Fairness Obligations

The principle of fairness was first clearly formulated by H. L. A. Hart in 1955:

[W]hen a number of persons conduct any joint enterprise according to rules and thus restrict their liberty, those who have submitted to

---

[8] See especially Michael Sandel, *Liberalism and the Limits of Justice*, 2d ed. (Cambridge: Cambridge University Press, 1998); and Charles Taylor, "Atomism," in Taylor, *Philosophy and the Human Sciences* (Cambridge: Cambridge University Press, 1985).

these restrictions when required have a right to a similar submission
from those who have benefited by their submission.[9]

The moral basis of the principle is fair distribution of benefits and burdens.
Under certain conditions, the sacrifices made by members of a cooperative scheme in order to produce benefits also benefit noncooperators, who
do not make similar sacrifices. According to the principle, this situation is
unfair unless there are morally relevant differences between the noncooperators and the members of the scheme. The principle, then, is intended
to justify the obligations of noncooperators.[10]

The principle of fairness operates clearly in certain cases. If we assume
that three neighbors cooperate in order to dig a well, a fourth who refuses
to share their labors but later goes to the well for fresh water is subject to
condemnation by the cooperators. Roughly and briefly, when a person
takes steps to procure benefits generated by the ongoing cooperative
labor of others, he incurs an obligation to share the labor through which
the benefits are provided.[11] In regard to questions of political obligation,
however, things are more complicated. Because of their nature, the benefits that are of greatest interest cannot be procured, or even accepted.
These benefits are important public goods produced by the cooperative
efforts of large numbers of people coordinated by government. The clear-
est examples are public goods bearing on physical security, most notably
military defense, law and order, and important provisions concerning
public health and protection from a hostile environment.[12] Because public
goods such as these are nonexcludable, they must be made available to a
wider population (or the entire population of some territory) if they are
to be supplied to certain members. This presents an immediate problem:
explaining how individuals who have not accepted these goods incur
obligations. Given the voluntaristic orientation of liberal theory, many
scholars argue that because these public goods are not accepted, they
cannot generate political obligations under the principle of fairness.[13]

The most celebrated presentation of this line of argument is that made
by Robert Nozick in *Anarchy, State, and Utopia*. Nozick puts forth a series

[9] H. L. A. Hart, "Are There Any Natural Rights?" *Philosophical Review* 64, no. 2 (April
1955): 185. Some of the language used below in describing the workings of the principle is
from Klosko, *Principle of Fairness*.

[10] David Lyons, *Forms and Limits of Utilitarianism* (Oxford: Oxford University Press, 1965),
164; John Rawls, *A Theory of Justice* (Cambridge, MA: Harvard University Press, 1971), 112.
The underlying moral principle is analyzed by Richard Arneson, "The Principle of Fairness
and Free-Rider Problems," *Ethics* 92, no. 4 (July 1982): 616–33.

[11] For discussion, see Klosko, *Principle of Fairness*, chap. 2.

[12] Though I will not discuss other possible members of this class, I do not rule out that
others may exist.

[13] The dependence of political obligation on accepting benefits is noted in Rawls, *Theory
of Justice*, 113–16; as well as Robert Nozick, *Anarchy, State, and Utopia* (New York: Basic
Books, 1974), 95; and Ronald Dworkin, *Law's Empire* (Cambridge, MA: Harvard University
Press, 1986), 192–93.

of hypothetical situations. For instance, suppose a group of neighbors bands together to institute a public-address system in order to provide their neighborhood with entertainment and other broadcasting. If there are 364 other neighbors and each runs the system for one day, is Smith obligated to take over the broadcasts when her day comes? Nozick assumes that Smith has benefited from the scheme by listening to the broadcasts, but that she nevertheless would prefer not to give up a day.[14] If the neighbors form a street-sweeping association, must Jones sweep the street when his turn comes, even if he does not care a great deal about clean streets? If he refuses to sweep, must he "imagine dirt" when he goes outside, so as not to benefit as a free rider?[15] Nozick believes that Smith and Jones do not have obligations in cases of this sort: "One cannot, whatever one's purposes, just act so as to give people benefits and then demand (or seize) payment. Nor can a group of persons do this." According to Nozick, the principle of fairness does not "serve to obviate the need for other persons' *consenting* to cooperate and limit their own activities."[16]

According to Nozick, then, individuals cannot have obligations imposed on them through the receipt of particular benefits unless they *agree* to the obligations. In essence, Nozick leaves us with a version of consent theory, the individual having to accept his political bonds. The force of Nozick's argument, however, is blunted by examination of the specific benefits discussed in his examples. It is striking that these benefits are of relatively low value. Thus, we must see what happens if we consider schemes that provide more substantial benefits.

As I have argued elsewhere, I believe that when three main conditions are met, the principle of fairness is able to generate powerful obligations under which individuals should contribute to cooperative schemes that provide nonexcludable benefits. These conditions are met when the public goods supplied (1) are worth the costs required for their provision, (2) are indispensable for satisfactory lives, and (3) have benefits and burdens that are fairly distributed.[17]

For our purposes here, the most important condition is (2). My main contention is that when this condition is satisfied, voluntaristic aspects of

[14] Nozick, *Anarchy, State, and Utopia*, 93–94.

[15] Ibid., 94.

[16] Ibid., 95.

[17] Throughout this essay, I generally use the terms "nonexcludable goods" and "public goods" interchangeably. As the term is commonly used, public goods are not only nonexcludable, but are also characterized by "nonrival consumption," that is, A's consumption of the good does not affect the amount available for consumption by other individuals. This aspect of public goods is not of immediate concern here. On public goods, see John G. Head, *Public Goods and Public Welfare* (Durham, NC: Duke University Press, 1974).

Returning to the three conditions, it should be noted that for condition (2) to be satisfied, the public goods in question must be worth their costs for *all* recipients, including those who would prefer not to cooperate rather than to have the costs imposed on them. For reasons of space, I discuss only condition (2) in this essay. Throughout, I assume that conditions (1) and (3) are met, and so do not examine them in detail. For discussion of these and other important aspects of the principle of fairness, see Klosko, *Principle of Fairness*.

political obligations lose much of their purchase. Roughly and briefly, if something is indispensable to Jones's welfare, then we can assume that he benefits from the mechanisms that provide it, even if he has not sought out their services. This is especially important in the case of public goods bearing on security, for one receives these goods without having to pursue them. Because of the importance of such goods, unusual circumstances must obtain for Jones not to benefit from receiving them. Though the class of indispensable public goods is perhaps small, it undoubtedly encompasses those crucial goods mentioned above as being necessary for physical security. That we all need these public goods regardless of whatever else we need is a fundamental assumption of liberal political theory. Liberal theorists generally view providing them as a central purpose of the state, and as we will see, even theorists who argue for alternative supply do not question the need for them.

Let us imagine that Green receives indispensable public goods from cooperative scheme X. Does the fact that Green cannot accept these public goods mean that he does not incur any political obligations as a result of receiving them? Suppose that X provides military defense, which is not only nonexcludable but unavoidable for inhabitants of the territory covered by X. A strong argument can be made that Green does incur obligations in this situation. Because military defense is an unavoidable good, Green receives it whether or not he pursues it, and in fact could not pursue it even if he wished to. Given that the benefits of defense are indispensable, we can presume that he *would* pursue them (and bear the associated costs) if this were necessary for their receipt. If we imagine an artificial choice situation analogous to a state of nature, it seems clear that under almost all circumstances, Green would choose to receive the benefits at the prescribed cost if he had the choice.[18] Because defense is indispensable, it would not be rational for him to choose otherwise. In the case under consideration, however, Green's obligation to the members of X does not stem from hypothetical consent—that he would consent to receive the benefits under some circumstances—but from the fact that he actually receives them.[19] Therefore, the element of choice or consent is of relatively little importance here. Its main function, in the form of hypothetical consent, is to help formulate a check, to make sure that unusual features of a particular situation do not cancel out the strong presumption that Green does incur an obligation.[20]

---

[18] The main exceptions would be circumstances under which the benefits were not worth their costs. For example, in hopeless circumstances, military defense will not be worth the costs needed to secure it. See Klosko, *Principle of Fairness*, 55–56.

[19] The discussion here draws on Klosko, *Principle of Fairness*, chap. 2, where I also consider and counter other possible arguments against obligations in such cases.

[20] Because the benefits supplied by the state are indispensable, the principle of fairness is able to generate obligations even when compliance with them is costly. Theories with other bases—in particular, those based on a natural duty of justice—are able to generate only weak obligations; see George Klosko, "Political Obligation and the Natural Duties of Jus-

Indispensable goods other than defense include, once again, law and order, public health measures, and protection from a hostile environment. In regard to law and order, under which I include the full benefits of the legal order, it is important to note that these benefits go beyond bare physical security. Law and order also make possible an overall framework of ordered liberty that is necessary if we are to carry on sustained activities in a stable, predictable environment. Included in this framework is the coordination of the numerous complex systems necessary for a functioning economy and all that such an economy entails. Given the highly integrated nature of life in modern industrial societies, virtually everyone in these societies benefits constantly—and at extremely high levels—from the legal order.[21]

III. ALTERNATIVE SUPPLY AND THE PLAUSIBILITY REQUIREMENT

As noted above, Simmons argues that the principle of fairness does not generate political obligations.[22] In *On the Edge of Anarchy*, he defends a Lockean theory of political society, which he characterizes as "probably the single most influential" theory on that topic in the history of political thought.[23] Locke, of course, places the individual in the state of nature and claims that free consent is a necessary condition for legitimate political relationships.[24] As Simmons notes, consent is an intuitively clear and forceful basis for political obligations.[25] However, even if we grant that consent is a sufficient condition for political obligations, it remains to be shown that other bases are not adequate. I am concerned in this essay with what Simmons describes as "benefit/reciprocation" theories,[26] and will therefore examine his reasons for rejecting one such theory that is based on the principle of fairness.

---

tice," *Philosophy and Public Affairs* 23, no. 3 (Summer 1994): 251–70. On the role of indispensability in fixing the content of political obligations, see George Klosko, "Fixed Content of Political Obligation," *Political Studies* 46, no. 1 (March 1998): 53–67.

[21] For our purposes, it is not necessary to distinguish law and order from the legal order. The benefits from both can be considered together under the designation "law and order." The highly integrated character of modern society and the role of authority in overseeing this integration are well discussed by John Finnis in his *Natural Law and Natural Rights* (Oxford: Oxford University Press, 1980), chap. 9. An eloquent account of the value of stable background conditions is given by Edmund Burke in his November 1789 letter to Charles Depont, reprinted in Burke, *The Selected Letters of Edmund Burke*, ed. Harvey Mansfield (Chicago: University of Chicago Press, 1984), 256–58.

[22] For Simmons's other criticisms of the principle of fairness, see Simmons, *Moral Principles*, chap. 5; and A. John Simmons, "The Anarchist Position: A Reply to Klosko and Senor," *Philosophy and Public Affairs* 16, no. 3 (Summer 1987): 260–68. I respond to these arguments in Klosko, *Principle of Fairness*.

[23] Simmons, *On the Edge of Anarchy*, 5.

[24] Locke, *Second Treatise*, sec. 95. In his most recent work, Simmons describes "the natural freedom of persons" as "a basic and plausible Lockean premise." A. John Simmons, "Justification and Legitimacy," *Ethics* 109, no. 4 (July 1999): 752.

[25] Simmons, *On the Edge of Anarchy*, 72–79.

[26] Ibid., 76.

Simmons's main objection to a nonvoluntaristic account of the principle of fairness, such as the one presented in Section II, is that it could lead to the imposition of obligations on an individual "who genuinely does not want the goods some cooperative scheme is providing or who would genuinely prefer to do without those goods rather than pay the price demanded for them."[27] Simmons's argument can be countered. Because the benefits discussed in Section II are indispensable, we can set aside the possibility that Jones would really prefer to do without them.[28] More troubling is the possibility that he would prefer not to receive these benefits at the required price. Since one necessary condition for the generation of fairness obligations is that the relevant goods must be worth their costs,[29] I will concentrate on cases in which Jones would prefer not to pay the requisite price. I quote Simmons:

> [T]here are no public goods produced by cooperative schemes that are needed or indispensable *simpliciter*, and so there is no product of a cooperative scheme that can be said to be on balance a benefit (presumptively beneficial) for anyone without further qualification. Goods are only benefits to persons on balance if their costs and the manner in which they are provided are not sufficiently disvalued by those persons. Even a good like physical security . . . may be reasonably regarded by an individual as on balance a burden if it is provided at a prohibitive cost . . . or in a manner that is unnecessary and objectionable.[30]

Because, again, indispensable goods are necessary for acceptable lives and would appear to be worth their costs (as assessed ordinarily), the most interesting cases, for our purposes, concern the provision of these goods in "objectionable" fashion, that is, cases in which individuals would prefer to have them provided through something other than the scheme currently providing them. Simmons notes that "many public goods supplied by the state can be provided by alternative, private means, often at a lower cost and without the imposition of oppressive or restrictive conditions." Someone "who prefers to try to provide [some indispensable] good privately, can hardly be accused of unfairly taking advantage of a

[27] Ibid., 256.

[28] The means through which the imposition of obligations on Jones can be justified are discussed in Klosko, *Principle of Fairness*, chap. 2; for reasons of space, I do not repeat that material here. We should note, however, that in all cases, ceteris paribus principles hold in regard to conditions. The obligations in question are prima facie and so hold in the absence of strong countervailing considerations; for a brief discussion of prima facie obligations, see Klosko, *Principle of Fairness*, 12–14.

[29] As argued in Klosko, *Principle of Fairness*, 48–49, the burden of proof here is on proponents of a given cooperative scheme. Given the great value of indispensable goods, however, it should be possible for them to meet this in many cases.

[30] Simmons, *On the Edge of Anarchy*, 258.

group that unilaterally foists that good upon her on their own terms."[31]
Accordingly, this objection to nonvoluntaristic obligations under the principle of fairness turns on people's preferring that the indispensable goods that a given scheme supplies be provided through other means.[32]

In order properly to assess Simmons's objection, we must have a clear idea of what alternative supply of public goods will be like. There are numerous issues here that Simmons does not explore, but which nevertheless need to be examined. In inquiring whether Jones's preference for alternative supply of some public good exempts him from a requirement to cooperate in the scheme that provides it, I wish to avoid "impossibility arguments." Rather than ask whether alternative mechanisms are possible, we will concentrate on whether they are plausible. In particular, as noted above, we will focus on whether these mechanisms can meet a standard of reasonable plausibility.

Although the plausibility condition is necessarily somewhat vague, it can be filled in to some extent.[33] We can identify at least three basic requirements that an acceptable alternative arrangement must meet. The first and most important requirement involves what we can call *feasibility*. The mechanism must be able to provide necessary services in recognizably effective ways. For instance, any satisfactory military establishment will have to have effective modern armaments. It will not be enough to rely on loosely organized citizen-soldiers and their hunting rifles.[34] The second requirement, which is closely related to the first, is that the mechanism must involve reasonable *background* conditions. In order not to be obviously utopian, the mechanism should not rely on improbable, large-scale changes in the human condition. The anarchistic end-state described by Lenin in *State and Revolution*, for example, would require enormous changes in conditions: it "presupposes not the present productivity of

---

[31] Both quotations are from ibid.

[32] Simmons's argument here represents a departure from his position in *Moral Principles*. In that work, he is within the liberal tradition, as he does not question state supply of indispensable benefits. The essence of his argument for "philosophical anarchism" is that, without questioning state supply, none of the basic arguments for political obligations survives scrutiny. In *On the Edge of Anarchy*, in contrast, Simmons departs from mainstream liberalism and is in effect an anarchist in a more conventional sense, in that he is committed to the nonliberal factual claim that voluntary association can provide important benefits we require.

[33] I am grateful to Colin Bird for discussion on this point.

[34] It could be argued that from a Lockean perspective, the individual himself should be the judge of feasibility. Although I agree that there is a presumption in favor of the individual's judgment, this does not hold without limits; some external standard of plausible feasibility should be appealed to here as well. Although this claim is necessarily somewhat vague—and no doubt controversial—on an abstract level, it becomes less so as it is employed in particular cases. As Richard Arneson argues, the fact that someone believes that "national defense is manna from heaven" does not free that individual from obligations he would otherwise have. In a case such as this, the individual has an obligation to acquaint himself with the morally relevant facts of the situation. Arneson, "Principle of Fairness," 632. When the individual's alternative measures do not satisfy a plausible standard of feasibility, the presumption that he should judge for himself is overruled.

labour and *not the present* ordinary run of people."[35] The main role of the background provision is to restrict the range of mechanisms that can be put forth as feasible.

The final requirement of the plausibility condition bears on the *transition* from existing to alternative mechanisms. An alternative mechanism will not be acceptable unless it can be constructed without significant violations of rights.[36] There must be a critical mass of people committed to the new mechanism, or at least the possibility of interesting sufficient numbers of people in the mechanism without resorting to unacceptable means. These people must not have to be "forced to be free."

A great deal more could be said on the question of what constitutes plausible alternative mechanisms. In order to avoid controversy, however, we can confine discussion to these points, which strike me as uncontroversial and seem in combination to comprise a minimal threshold of acceptable plausibility.

The reason for a plausibility requirement is straightforward. Jones should not be absolved of obligations generated by state supply of essential goods unless he does not need them. Because these goods are indispensable, Jones's obligations can be obviated only if he does not need them *from the state*, a condition that can be satisfied only if an alternative provision mechanism works. If no such mechanism works, Jones will continue to receive state benefits, and so should continue to have obligations on that basis. A strong case can be made that if a given alternative mechanism *is* able to provide Jones's indispensable goods, then he should not have obligations to the state. But things are more complicated if an acceptable alternative mechanism has not yet been set up. It would seem unfair not to allow it a reasonable opportunity to begin to work. Until the mechanism is up and running, however, its proponents must provide good reasons that it is likely to work before obligations they would otherwise have are waived.

Under certain conditions, a proposed alternative mechanism will satisfy the plausibility requirement, and it will therefore seem reasonable to allow Jones to pursue some benefit through the mechanism rather than the state. In order to shed some light on the factors at work in such cases,

---

[35] Vladimir I. Lenin, *The State and Revolution*, in Lenin, *The Lenin Anthology*, ed. Robert C. Tucker (New York: Norton, 1975), 380.

[36] Although not discussed in this essay, a set of acceptable rights is presupposed by fairness theory. A principle of political obligation is only a single moral requirement, which must exist in the context of—and be consistent with—a network of other acceptable principles. For discussion of how considerations along these lines limit political obligations under fairness theory, see Klosko, *Principle of Fairness*, 122–25. Defining the boundary between acceptable and unacceptable violations of rights raises complex issues that cannot be discussed here. At the very least, for an alternative mechanism to meet this transition requirement, the transition from existing society cannot cause *greater* violations of rights than would be alleviated by the development of the alternative mechanism. For discussion of this point, I am grateful to David Brink.

I will consider a number of schemes that provide public goods. Consider state services bearing on sanitation:

> Case 1: As things stand, services bearing on sanitation are provided by the government. However, Jones and his neighbors are willing to pick up trash and otherwise provide for acceptable sanitation on their street.[37]

In this case, there seems to be little reason—barring strong countervailing arguments from the state—not to allow Jones and his neighbors to provide these services in place of some state agency. To the extent that garbage collection is necessary for public health, it is a public good and requirements that people dispose of their garbage can be justified. However, the wide range of options through which people can do this would make it difficult for the state to demand the exclusive right to perform this service. Various neighborhood systems could readily satisfy the feasibility, background, and transition requirements discussed above.

Things become more interesting if greater coordination is needed to produce the relevant public good.

> Case 2: As things stand, services bearing on the safety of the water supply are provided by the government. However, Jones and his neighbors are willing to take measures necessary to ensure acceptable sanitation of their water supply.

Consideration of Cases 1 and 2 shows the importance of what we can call *exclusivity*, a condition that applies when provision of a good must be by a single agency if such provision is to satisfy the feasibility requirement. As noted, for goods like garbage collection, it will be difficult to argue that provision through a single agency is necessary. Clearly, the entity claiming exclusive provision of some benefit must support its contention with convincing empirical or factual considerations to the effect that unless provision of the given benefit is exclusive, it is not feasible. Because individual liberty is an important value, there are strong reasons to allow Jones and his neighbors to provide their own benefits—public goods and otherwise—when the need for exclusive state supply cannot be demonstrated.

---

[37] It could be argued that trash collection is of little importance and is not a public good. However, brief reflection indicates that an acceptable means of dealing with trash is a necessary public health measure, and that some combination of this and other such measures constitutes an indispensable public good. For discussion of how to determine the form in which an essential public good should be provided, see Klosko, *Principle of Fairness*, 80–81.

Consider an additional example:

> Case 3: As things stand, educational or entertainment broadcasts are provided by the government. However, Jones and his neighbors are willing to set up an alternative system of broadcasting along the lines of that discussed by Nozick.

The benefits involved in this case are public goods. Yet as long as the broadcast spectrum can handle more than one channel, the need for exclusive supply of these goods cannot be demonstrated. In cases such as this, in which nonexclusive or multiple supply is obviously feasible, there seems to be little justification for thwarting those parties who wish to establish their own provision mechanisms rather than use those administered by the state.

Exclusivity, of course, is not the only factor that goes into considerations of whether provision of a particular public good generates political obligations; Case 3 provides an illustration of this point. As we saw in the previous section, generating obligations from the provision of neighborhood broadcasting is difficult because this public good is of relatively low value. If Jones could easily do without a given benefit altogether, there seems to be little justification for preventing him and like-minded others from banding together to provide that benefit in a manner that accords with their own preferences. The factor of relative value, then, must be considered alongside exclusivity when we assess the role that various public goods play in delineating political obligations.

When Simmons argues that alternative provision mechanisms can obviate political obligations, he does not provide examples of the alternative mechanisms that he has in mind. It seems likely, however, that they are similar to those in Cases 1 and 3, either requiring little coordination or providing a benefit that is not of great value. When such factors apply, alternative mechanisms can be defended. However, the benefits that are most relevant to discussion of political obligation are essential public goods: these goods are of great value, and as we will see, they can only be provided through highly coordinated mechanisms. Case 2, involving water quality, is therefore more apropos for our purposes. If we stipulate that clean water is essential for acceptable lives, it should be possible to argue that Jones is required to contribute to some mechanism that provides this benefit. The question of whether he should be required to contribute to the specific mechanism controlled by the state would turn on factual questions concerning production. One would need to know whether provision of sanitary water is feasible only if done through a single mechanism, and, if so, whether this mechanism must be the state.

As one can imagine, while it might be possible to argue that state supply of clean water is the only feasible means of providing it, a stronger case can be made for state supply of other essential goods. This is especially true for those goods discussed at the end of the previous section. Although the argument for state supply—and, consequently, for fairness obligations—is strongest with respect to military defense, it is also strong when one considers the goods of law and order, public health measures, and environmental protection. As noted above, "law and order" here encompasses more than physical security. It also includes the wider benefits of the legal order, namely, the coordination of the integrated systems of a modern society and the maintenance of the stable, predictable environment necessary for long-range planning. Clearly, all these benefits are essential, and therefore they must be supplied. I believe that feasible supply of each must be exclusive, and that in practice, all must be supplied by the same entity, the state. Though I cannot provide a knockdown defense of these claims, there are strong considerations in their favor. According to the standard, Weberian definition, the state is an agency that claims a *monopoly* of legitimate force within a given territory.[38] The difficulties occasioned when multiple agencies have the right to use force in a territory are central to the justification for political authority that Locke provides in the *Second Treatise*. These factors support exclusive supply of law and order.[39] At the same time, the degree of coordination necessary for the stable functioning of a modern industrial democracy implies a single controlling authority or, if there is more than one, some sophisticated means of coordinating their activities. Additional services must also be provided by the state. Although I will not discuss these matters in detail, I believe that effective public health measures and environmental protection must be supported by coercive authority, and hence must be supplied by the state. This holds for such public health measures as mandatory vaccination and quarantine, and for environmental challenges such as ensuring acceptably clean air and water. As for military defense, it is overwhelmingly clear that protection against external aggression must be exclusively controlled. It is hard even to imagine how

[38] Max Weber, "Politics as a Vocation," in Weber, *From Max Weber: Essays in Sociology*, ed. and trans. H. H. Gerth and C. Wright Mills (Oxford: Oxford University Press, 1946), 78.

[39] Libertarian anarchists have described several reasonably plausible arrangements for immediate physical protection; these arrangements have been based on voluntary protective associations. See David Friedman, *The Machinery of Freedom* (New York: Harper and Row, 1973); David Friedman, "Anarchy and Efficient Law," in John Sanders and Jan Narveson, eds., *For and Against the State* (Savage, MD: Rowman and Littlefield, 1996), 235–54; Bruce Benson, *The Enterprise of Law* (San Francisco, CA: Pacific Research Institute for Public Policy, 1990); and Murray Rothbard, *For a New Liberty* (New York: Macmillan, 1978). Central to these proposals is the idea that many aspects of protection are excludable goods and thus are subject to market forces. As Friedman points out, in existing societies, significant percentages of security expenditures and security personnel are private. Friedman, *Machinery of Freedom*, 219; see also Benson, *Enterprise of Law*. Detailed examination of these anarchist proposals is not possible in this essay. However, even if protection could be provided through voluntary associations, theorists have not shown how such associations can provide other essential public goods.

appropriate provision of military defense in a given territory could be done through more than one agency.[40]

One will note that the preceding paragraphs contain references to providing essential public goods *in a given territory*. My assumption is that, as a factual matter, these central public goods must be provided exclusively in individual territories. I will not argue for territorial exclusivity at length, as it seems quite obvious, especially in regard to defense and law and order. Because this claim is a fundamental assumption of liberal theory, a scholar who argues against it should be required to present an acceptable account of the nonterritorial provision of central public goods. As is the case with alternative provision mechanisms generally, the standard here is not what is merely possible. Instead, the proponent of nonterritorial provision must provide an account of how it would satisfy the plausibility requirement.[41]

The territorial component of the exclusivity claim has significant implications. Unlike other public goods that can be provided by alternative private means *within a given territory*, the essential public goods of military defense, law and order, and environmental protection require territorial control. Accordingly, if Jones and his associates wish to opt out of government provision of these benefits, their alternative mechanism will not be acceptably plausible unless it is able to exercise exclusive control over their territory or some alternative.

Attaining a suitable territory in an acceptable way will raise enormous problems for proponents of alternative supply. I will not dwell on questions concerning the size that a territory must have in order to be viable. It is likely that both direct physical protection and the benefits of a legal order can be provided in a small community. However, with respect to military defense and environmental protection, problems of size are more formidable and could well render alternative supply impossible.[42] Setting this issue aside, we confront formidable difficulties in explaining how Jones and his associates are to gain exclusive control over a territory, whether it be their own or some other. Up to this point I have invoked only feasibility concerns, but in this context, questions of transition cause

[40] Friedman characterizes provision of defense as "the hard problem"; his suggestions here are highly speculative (Friedman, *Machinery of Freedom*, chap. 34). Rothbard's suggestions are similarly improbable (Rothbard, *For a New Liberty*, 237–41 and chap. 14). Benson concedes the need for state provision of defense (Benson, *Enterprise of Law*, 373). Game-theoretic explanations of alternative provision also have problems with respect to defense; see note 63 below.

[41] That the territorial basis of state services is a problem for consent theory is seen in Harry Beran, *The Consent Theory of Political Obligation* (London: Croom Helm, 1987); for discussion, see Allen Buchanan, *Secession: The Morality of Political Divorce* (Boulder, CO: Westview Press, 1991), 70–73.

[42] Small territories like Monaco or Lichtenstein are sheltered by the protective umbrella provided by the great powers, and therefore arguably have political obligations to those countries. For brief discussion, see Klosko, "Political Obligation and the Natural Duties of Justice," 260 n. 18.

additional difficulties. Plans for alternative supply generally raise issues of secession. One of the many problems encountered here is that, as stated above, the transition requirement rules out significant violations of rights. The need to respect rights is reinforced by the voluntaristic premises of Simmons's position. Thus, inhabitants of a territory who do not wish to join Jones and his associates must not be forced to do so.[43] If these inhabitants wish to remain citizens of the existing polity, and hence under existing authorities, constructing an alternative mechanism in the territory will contravene the exclusivity claim. In other words, not only must Jones and his associates control a territory, but all (or virtually all) inhabitants of that territory must agree with them on how its public goods should be supplied. In view of all these problems, it is unlikely that any alternative mechanism for the provision of military defense, law and order, and environmental protection could be plausible.[44]

Throughout any efforts Jones makes to establish an alternative mechanism, he will be receiving essential public goods from cooperative scheme X. One could ask here why Jones has obligations to X rather than to the alternative mechanism he wishes to establish. After all, examination of the historical record indicates the likelihood that existing governments achieved their positions through acts of military conquest or other injustices.[45] In other words, they were established in ways that fail to satisfy the transition requirement. If we assume that the establishment of X failed to satisfy the transition requirement, then why must Jones support X? There is a ready reply. Jones has obligations to X because he receives benefits from it that are necessary for an acceptable life. Other things being equal, as long as X provides the benefits in question and meets other necessary conditions (e.g., it distributes benefits and burdens fairly, provides democratic decision-making institutions, respects the rights of its citizens, etc.), questions of origins are largely irrelevant.[46]

Jones could well complain about being required to comply with X when he would greatly prefer that its benefits be supplied through other means. According to the principle of fairness, the obligations a given individual incurs as a result of receiving public goods are obviated if

---

[43] See note 36 above.

[44] Though I will not go into depth on the matter, I should note here that the plausibility condition's background requirement plays an important role, both here and in the next section, in ruling out changes in conditions that would make organized coercive mechanisms unnecessary. For example, a proponent of some alternative mechanism who is faced with the objections to alternative supply presented in this section could not respond to these objections by saying that his mechanism would work if large-scale changes in human wants and desires could be brought about.

[45] I quote Hume: "Almost all the governments, which exist at present, or of which there remains any record in story, have been founded originally, either on usurpation or conquest, or both, without any pretence of a fair consent of voluntary subjection of the people." Hume, "Of the Original Contract," 471.

[46] The moral context and additional requirements of fairness theory are discussed throughout Klosko, *Principle of Fairness*; see also note 36 above.

there are morally relevant differences between the individual and the people whose cooperation produces the goods.[47] The question, then, is whether Jones's preferences constitute an adequate morally relevant difference. I believe they do not. In a diverse community, it is likely that people have a wide range of preferences concerning the provision of essential goods. For instance, some might prefer that military defense be provided by a standing army, while others might prefer a draft. Some might prefer reliance on nuclear weapons, even as others support a policy of "no first use." According to the exclusivity claim, however, the provision of defense in a given territory must take on one single form; therefore, some of those who disagree over the proper means of providing defense will have to be disappointed. The principle of fairness holds that decisions concerning provision of essential goods must be made through democratic means—that is, through reasonably fair democratic procedures.[48] Part of the costs involved in providing essential public goods is the need to accede to the preferences of the majority as to how these goods should be provided. In view of the likelihood that many individuals would prefer that a given good be provided through some other means, the fact that Jones would prefer alternative provision does not constitute a morally relevant difference between him and other citizens of X.[49]

In summary, because Jones needs the goods that X produces in order to pursue a satisfactory life, the fact that he receives them generates an obligation for him to cooperate in their provision. He can obviate this obligation only if he can indicate alternative provision mechanisms that satisfy the plausibility requirements; as I have shown, however, finding such mechanisms is a difficult enterprise.

IV. GAME-THEORETIC ALTERNATIVES

Simmons is not alone in upholding alternative provision of public goods. Many scholars argue along similar lines using game-theoretic

[47] In cases where there are such morally relevant differences, one might wonder whether the differences (1) cause the dissolution of existent political obligations, or (2) prevent any such obligations from being constituted in the first place. Though I will not discuss the matter here, I believe the latter option is more likely.

[48] See Klosko, *Principle of Fairness*, chap. 3. For discussion of the attitudes in modern liberal states toward democratic institutions and democracy as a value, see George Klosko, *Democratic Procedures and Liberal Consensus* (Oxford: Oxford University Press, 2000), chap. 5.

[49] This fact would perhaps constitute a morally relevant difference if Jones's alternative preferences were so strong as to raise questions of conscience, in which case imposing majority decisions on him would represent an injustice. Though I cannot discuss here the complex issues concerning pacifists and conscientious objectors, I do believe that their situations involve this sort of strong alternative preference. In such cases, however, the recognition that the individual still has some obligations is seen in provisions for alternative service. For discussion of conscientious-objection practices in some two dozen countries, see Charles C. Moskos and John Whiteclay Chambers, eds., *The New Conscientious Objection* (Oxford: Oxford University Press, 1993).

approaches.[50] A central theme in the work of these scholars is criticism of one important justification for state authority. It is widely argued that the state is necessary for the provision of important public goods because nonstate arrangements have an incentive structure that prevents these goods from being provided. The scholars I am concerned with here argue that private cooperation can in fact provide the relevant goods. These theorists do not generally question the need for central public goods such as law and order and national defense. Rather, the thrust of their arguments is that state mechanisms are not necessary for the provision of these goods.

Game-theoretic analysis of public goods constitutes a large literature, much of which cannot be considered in this context. I will focus here on political philosopher Michael Taylor's recent, sophisticated argument for the feasibility of alternative provision, which I will interpret in the light of the plausibility requirements outlined in the previous section. I believe Taylor's argument is representative of both the strengths and the weaknesses of game theory. If the argument is successful, then one could contend, along with Simmons, that the possibility of alternative supply could obviate obligations otherwise incurred under the principle of fairness.

From a game-theoretic perspective, in many cases individual incentives in regard to public goods have the structure of N-person prisoners' dilemmas (PDs). Although Smith would be better off having good G than not having it, even at the cost of contributing to its provision, she would be even better off if she received the good without having to cooperate. There are two possible scenarios. If enough other people are going to cooperate to ensure G's provision, then Smith's contribution is unnecessary, and it is in her interest not to cooperate. If there are not enough other people cooperating, then it is certainly not in Smith's interest to do so, unless her individual contribution would determine whether or not G would be provided. In a large society (on which, more below), Smith's cooperation would be decisive only under rare circumstances. Considering both possible scenarios, then, we can see that it is not in Smith's interest to contribute, no matter what others do. Because we can assume that other people's incentive structures are similar to Smith's, we can predict that if they reason as she does, they too will not cooperate. This will lead to G not being provided, leaving everyone worse off than they would have been had they all contributed.

If provision of indispensable public goods is construed along these lines, then the need for the state is clear. By using its coercive power to

[50] See Michael Taylor, *The Possibility of Cooperation* (Cambridge: Cambridge University Press, 1987), discussed below. Similar views are advanced by many additional scholars; the contributors to Sanders and Narveson's *For and Against the State* constitute a representative sample.

compel general cooperation—"mutual coercion mutually agreed upon," in ecologist Garrett Hardin's famous formulation[51]—the state leaves everyone better off than they would have been had they been left to their own devices. Taylor refers to this conclusion as the "most persuasive justification of the state."[52] Other scholars agree: according to political philosopher Jon Elster, "politics is the study of ways of transcending the Prisoners' Dilemma."[53]

Theorists have worked out different methods of avoiding this conclusion. Taylor argues that the PD formulation above is inadequate. Under many conditions, he claims, we should interpret public-goods provision as a *supergame*, that is, as an *iterated* PD game.[54] Taylor maintains that traditional analysis of public-goods incentives is flawed because it is "entirely static." He notes, for example, that in economist Mancur Olson's classic analysis of these incentives, "the individual is supposed in effect to make just one choice, once and for all, of how much to contribute to the public good."[55] But the fact that political relationships are continuous opens the way for conditional cooperation. In a continuous relationship, Smith can realize the advantage of a strategy of conditional cooperation, in which she cooperates only if Jones does so as well. Because Jones should reason similarly, it is possible that Smith and Jones could find their way to joint cooperation. It is conceivable that one of the pair could adopt a strategy of unconditional noncooperation, that is, refusing to cooperate regardless of what the other player does. But since mutual cooperation is in each player's interest, this would not be rational. Conditional cooperation is frequently referred to as "tit-for-tat." Knowing that joint cooperation is in Jones's interest as well as her own, Smith can rationally take the first step by cooperating. If Jones takes advantage of her by not cooperating in response, he will gain in this single transaction. However, by acting this way, Jones risks leading Smith and himself toward practicing joint noncooperation in subsequent transactions, an outcome providing a lower payoff than would joint cooperation. Therefore, Jones should forgo the immediate advantage of noncooperation in favor of cooperation, to which Smith will respond by cooperating further, and so forth.[56] Extending this logic to an N-person PD game could result in a situation in which each person cooperates conditionally. Because general coopera-

---

[51] Garrett Hardin, "The Tragedy of the Commons," *Science* 162, no. 13 (December 1968): 1247.

[52] Taylor, *Possibility of Cooperation*, 1.

[53] Jon Elster, quoted in Taylor, *Possibility of Cooperation*, 19.

[54] Under other conditions, a correct construal of the situation would posit it as a game of chicken rather than as a prisoners' dilemma; see note 62 below.

[55] Taylor, *Possibility of Cooperation*, 12.

[56] See ibid., chap. 3, for discussion of this process, including the complexities concerning discounts on future payoffs, a factor I have omitted here.

tion is preferable to general noncooperation, conditional cooperation could result in the production of desired public goods.[57]

In one sense, this argument is convincing. Political interaction is not a one-shot process. But closer examination reveals that there are significant problems in moving from the two-person model to the N-person model. Though problems of transition (once again, the need to gain control of a given territory) could well be formidable here, I will set these aside and instead focus on feasibility considerations. As Taylor recognizes, successful conditional cooperation depends on each participant knowing about the behavior of other participants in each previous stage of the game.[58] This condition is satisfied far more easily in the two-person scenario than it is in the N-person scenario. Olson notes that solutions to PD problems become increasingly difficult as the group in question increases in size.[59] One reason for this is relevant here. To use Olson's term, a group can be described as "large" if the burdens of any one person's contributions are not affected by whether another individual does or does not contribute.[60] In a modern nation-state, this is true in regard to many requirements. For example, whether or not Jones pays his taxes will not detectably affect the payments required of other people, nor will it detectably affect the federal budget deficit (or surplus).[61]

As a society becomes increasingly large, feasibility considerations become increasingly problematic. In particular, the information requirements of conditional cooperation become more difficult to satisfy. In large societies, it is likely that other people will not know whether or not Jones has contributed, that is, whether he has paid his taxes, cooperated in some environmental conservation policy, signed up for military service, etc. This is especially true if there are no state agencies to monitor compliance. Yet if others cannot ascertain whether or not Jones has contributed, then the connection between his cooperation and general cooperation is broken. The traditional logic of the N-person PD will be in effect, and it will not pay for Jones to cooperate.

---

[57] Anthony de Jasay, for one, argues that treating large-number games as supergames solves the difficulties that they present. See Anthony de Jasay, *Against Politics* (London: Routledge, 1997), 206–8, 215–16. However, he deals only with performance and nonperformance of contracts, as opposed to wider forms of noncompliance, including noncontribution to necessary public goods. In the context of contributing toward these goods, noncompliance can be far more difficult to detect (as discussed below), and raises problems that de Jasay's argument does not address. For example, in many public-goods cases, a given individual's incentives to enforce another individual's compliance are significantly different from the incentives he would have in a contract situation. In a typical public-goods case, Jones's defection causes no detectable damage and so does not harm Smith or affect the costs associated with Smith's compliance.

[58] Taylor, *Possibility of Cooperation*, 61.

[59] Mancur Olson, *The Logic of Collective Action* (Cambridge, MA: Harvard University Press, 1965), 36, 48.

[60] Ibid., 12.

[61] For complexities here, see Klosko, *Principle of Fairness*, appendix 2.

Given these considerations, one must conclude that the iterated prisoners' dilemma is unlikely to yield satisfactory solutions to problems of alternative provision.[62] Complex variations on this approach can produce solutions in the highly artificial frameworks of two-person interaction and small group interaction. However, if we increase the number of people or factor in other real-world impediments, it is unlikely that such constructions would satisfy the feasibility requirement.[63]

Empirical evidence supporting this analysis is supplied by political scientist Elinor Ostrom.[64] Ostrom examines long-lasting associations in which participants are able to cooperate in the use of "common-pool resources" without authoritative interference. In these arrangements, cooperation is maintained through what Ostrom describes as "self-organized and self-governed enterprises."[65] Examples of such enterprises can be found governing, among other things, the use of high-mountain meadows in Switzerland, the use of common land in rural Japanese villages, and the irrigation practices of Valencia, Spain. The successful avoidance of free-riding in these and other instances could be thought to give the lie to the traditional logic of collective action as described above. However, Ostrom carefully delineates the special conditions that allow these arrangements to succeed.

A central fact about the successful cases is that in each one of them, "individuals repeatedly communicate and interact with one another in localized physical settings."[66] Repeated interaction reduces crucial problems of accumulating information and monitoring compliance with association norms. Among the conditions Ostrom identifies as making for successful cooperation are that groups are "relatively small and stable" and that participants "face relatively low information, transformation and enforcement costs."[67] The problem, of course, is that associations able to provide the essential public goods discussed throughout this essay will

---

[62] These problems cannot be overcome by analyzing public-goods provision with the model of the game of chicken; see Taylor, *Possibility of Cooperation*, chap. 2. In a chicken scenario, different individuals or subgroups must be able to supply the relevant goods without outside assistance. However, in a large society, this condition will not ordinarily hold for the public goods that interest us. In addition, one must explain the incentives of individuals in these subgroups; these incentives appear to conform to those found in an N-person PD.

[63] The problems with game theory are epitomized by its inability to deal with providing defense. For instance, in *Against Politics*, de Jasay gives the problem extremely scant attention and offers no solution. See de Jasay, *Against Politics*, 208. In Sanders and Narveson's *For and Against the State*, a collection in which the practical and moral necessity of the state is assessed from a variety of game-theoretic perspectives, the problem of defense receives no serious attention.

[64] Elinor Ostrom, *Governing the Commons: The Evolution of Institutions for Collective Action* (Cambridge: Cambridge University Press, 1990). Conclusions similar to Ostrom's are also presented in Robert Ellickson, *Order Without Law* (Cambridge, MA: Harvard University Press, 1991).

[65] Ostrom, *Governing the Commons*, 25.

[66] Ibid., 183–84.

[67] Ibid., 211.

not possess these attributes. Ostrom notes that "[w]hen individuals who have high discount rates and little mutual trust act independently, without the capacity to communicate, to enter into binding agreements, and to arrange for monitoring and enforcing mechanisms," they are unlikely to choose cooperative strategies.[68] Once again, the burden of proof falls on proponents of alternative supply to show that their arrangements are feasible when the conditions that Ostrom identifies as being conducive to successful cooperation are not in evidence.[69]

It could be argued that in regard to game-theoretic analysis, the plausibility standard might represent too severe a test. It is not always clear that theorists who use game-theoretic approaches intend for their analyses to apply under real-world conditions. For instance, Taylor describes his main purpose as follows: "I have merely tried to show that, even if we accept the pessimistic assumption . . . that individual preferences have the structure of a Prisoners' Dilemma at any point in time, mutual [c]ooperation over time may nevertheless take place."[70] Taylor says that in criticizing PD logic, he "make[s] no attempt to provide a positive theory of anarchy or even an indication of how people might best provide themselves with public goods."[71] But of course, unless game theorists are able to argue for the plausibility of their preferred mechanisms under real conditions, they will continue to receive essential benefits from the state and so will continue to incur obligations under the principle of fairness.

V. Conclusion

Game-theoretic analysis suffers from difficulties similar to those encountered in Simmons's extreme Lockeanism. On both accounts, the individual is conceptualized apart from society, deciding how best to satisfy her needs. Neither account considers the fact that this individual is currently receiving essential benefits from the state.

Because the views we have discussed overlook the entanglements of existing societies, they are subject to criticism. In this sense, a communitarian critique of liberal premises—a critique that, at least in spirit, goes back to Robert Filmer—is accurate. The fact that we *constantly* receive enormous benefits from the cooperative efforts of our fellows generates moral requirements for us to share their burdens. State of nature analysis is misleading because it implies that the baseline position for questions of

---

[68] Ibid., 183.
[69] The experimental evidence supporting nonstate solutions to PD problems suffers from severe flaws. Specifically, the experiments that provided this evidence involved small groups of subjects and assigned artificially low values to the costs and benefits of cooperation. See Howard Harriott, "Games, Anarchy, and the Nonnecessity of the State," in Sanders and Narveson, eds., *For and Against the State*, 131-34.
[70] Taylor, *Possibility of Cooperation*, 105-6.
[71] Ibid., 105.

political obligation is that of an absence of obligations. On this account, if individuals do not consent or otherwise commit themselves to political bodies, then they do not have obligations. However, the fact that individuals are members of societies, conceived of as joint producers and consumers of essential benefits, entails a different starting point. As long as individuals do not commit themselves to *other* mechanisms, they have obligations to the existing arrangements from which they benefit.[72]

Because we receive essential goods from existing mechanisms, the burden of proof lies with those who would reject their obligations. To be freed of the political obligations she would otherwise have under the principle of fairness, Smith must defend one of two problematic claims. She can assert that she does not require indispensable goods, a thesis that seems to be implausible on its face. The alternative, however, is that Smith will have to show that these indispensable goods can be provided to her through alternative mechanisms that satisfy a standard of reasonable plausibility. As we have seen, this will be a significant undertaking. Neither of Smith's options is particularly promising.

Government, University of Virginia

---

[72] For discussion of other specific moral requirements generated by membership in communities, see Richard Dagger, *Civic Virtues* (Oxford: Oxford University Press, 1997), chap. 4.

LAW AS JUSTICE

By Michael S. Moore

I. Natural Law's Relational Thesis

A perennial question of jurisprudence has been whether there is a relationship between law and morality. Those who believe that there is no such relationship are known as "legal positivists," while those who hold that some such relationship exists are usually tagged with the label "natural lawyers." Unfortunately, the latter phrase has been used in quite divergent senses. Sometimes it is used to designate any objectivist position about morality; as often, it labels the view that human nature determines what is objectively good or right; and perhaps as often, it labels the view that some natural facts other than facts about human nature determine what is objectively good or right; and sometimes the label presupposes some divine origins to both morality and human law.

In light of these differences in what is meant by "natural law," both in ancient as well as contemporary literature, I shall begin by stipulating the usage that I have found convenient for some time.[1] By "natural law" in legal theory, I understand one to mean the claims that: (1) there are objective moral truths; and (2) those moral truths are at least partly constitutive of the truth conditions for propositions of law. I have called the first claim the *metaethical thesis of natural law* and the second claim the *relational thesis of natural law*. In this essay I am concerned solely with the relational thesis.[2]

The relational thesis asserts there to be some relation between human law and the laws of morality. In an earlier paper, I took some pains to clarify this thesis.[3] The bottom line of that analysis was the following construal of the natural lawyer's relational thesis: the nature of law is such that necessarily, if some institution is sufficiently unjust, it is not a *legal* institution. Legality, in other words, necessarily partakes of morality.

Legality is an attribute of four different sorts of institutions. Most generally, it can be an attribute of some kind of system within society. When

---

[1] Michael Moore, "Law as a Functional Kind," in Robert George, ed., *Natural Law Theories* (Oxford: Oxford University Press, 1992), reprinted as chap. 9 of Michael Moore, *Educating Oneself in Public: Critical Essays in Jurisprudence* (Oxford: Oxford University Press, 2000).

[2] My views on the metaethical thesis are presented in Michael Moore, "Moral Reality," *Wisconsin Law Review* 1982, no. 6 (November/December 1982): 1061–156; Michael Moore, "Moral Reality Revisited," *Michigan Law Review* 90, no. 8 (August 1992): 2424–533; and Michael Moore, "Good without God," in Robert George, ed., *Natural Law, Liberalism, and Morality* (Oxford: Oxford University Press, 1995).

[3] Moore, "Law as a Functional Kind."

115

we ask, "Does this island society have law?" we are inquiring as to whether the essential attributes of a *legal system* are in place.[4] By contrast, when we speak of law within some particular system that we acknowledge to be a legal system, we are often asking about *laws*. For example, we may wonder whether the custom that the public have access to ocean beaches is a law. In such cases, we are inquiring about the legality of some individual rule or other kind of discrete, individuated standard.[5] The third possible venue for legality judgments has to do with classes of rules. Here we ask whether rules of a certain sort are *legal* rules or not. For example, one might urge, as did Bentham, that rules made by courts as they decided cases were not law, and that the idea of a common law of decided cases was wholly illusory.[6] The fourth item calling for some judgment of legality has to do with what lawyers call the "law of the case."[7] Such law consists of singular propositions of law, such as "This contract is valid." These propositions apply only to the particular facts of a given legal dispute, but on those facts they are dispositive; they declare the legal rights and legal duties of particular parties in particular situations.

There is even a fifth sort of judgment we make that is closely related to these four. This is the judgment we make about *areas* of law. That is, admitting that we are in a *legal* system and that some rule or other institution is *legal* in character, we may nevertheless be puzzled about whether this rule or institution is part of one area of law rather than another.[8] The sort of judgments I have in mind include whether punitive-damages rules are part of criminal law or of tort law and whether rules for construing leases are part of contract law or property law. In such cases, doubt is not felt about the legality of the rules, but rather about what *kind* of law the rules are.

The relational thesis of natural law may be asserted at any of these five levels. That is, a natural lawyer may assert: (a) that a social system is a legal system only if it exceeds some threshold of justice in its overall operation; (b) that a rule is a law only if in content or in its operation it is not too unjust; (c) that a class of rules is part of the law only if as a class the rules serve some overall good; (d) that some actual (or predicted)

---

[4] These attributes are the concern of H. L. A. Hart, *The Concept of Law* (Oxford: Clarendon Press, 1961); and Joseph Raz, *The Concept of a Legal System* (Oxford: Clarendon Press, 1970).

[5] Herbert Hart nicely distinguished this concern about laws from more general concerns about legal systems, in his "Positivism and the Separation of Law and Morality," *Harvard Law Review* 71, no. 4 (February 1958): 593–629.

[6] On Bentham's distaste for the common law, see A. W. B. Simpson, "The Common Law and Legal Theory," in A. W. B. Simpson, ed., *Oxford Essays in Jurisprudence*, 2d ser. (Oxford: Oxford University Press, 1973); and Gerald Postema, *Bentham and the Common Law Tradition* (Oxford: Clarendon Press, 1984).

[7] When Michael Detmold urges the unity of *law* and morality, this is what he seems to have in mind. See M. J. Detmold, *The Unity of Law and Morality* (London: Routledge and Kegan Paul, 1987).

[8] On areas of law, see Michael Moore, "A Theory of Criminal Law Theories," in Dan Friedmann, ed., *Tel Aviv University Studies in Law*, vol. 8 (Tel Aviv, Israel: Tel Aviv University Press, 1990), revised and reprinted as chap. 1 of Moore, *Placing Blame: A General Theory of the Criminal Law* (Oxford: Clarendon Press, 1997).

judicial order is the law of the case for which it is (or will be) made only if that order is not too unjust; or (e) that an individual law is part of some discrete area of law only if this individual law serves the value(s) distinctive of that area of law. The natural lawyer who interests me asserts all five of these varieties of the relational thesis. I shall not in this essay attempt to analyze the natural law position with respect to all five of these varieties. Rather, I shall focus on the second and fourth, that is, on laws and laws of cases. My hope is that the problems and solutions explored in these more particular areas can be broadened to the more general topics of law (as legal system), kinds of law, and areas of law.

Before turning to the relational thesis with respect to laws and laws of cases, I shall explore some preliminary matters in the immediately succeeding sections. In Section II, I lay out the traditional argument for the natural lawyer's relational thesis, an argument that focuses on the idea of legal obligation. In Section III, I explore the typical way that natural lawyers have argued for law's necessarily obligating force, a mode of argument based on a functional analysis of law, laws, laws of cases, etc. In Section IV, I deal with two rather general objections to the functionalist program outlined in Section III, objections that cut across all five of the varieties of the natural lawyer's relational thesis. After these general preliminaries, I then turn to the relational thesis for laws of cases (Section V) and for laws (Section VI).

II. The Traditional Argument for the Relational Thesis

The dominant mode of arguing for the relational thesis (at all levels of generality) has centered on the idea of obligation, an idea thought to be crucial to legality. The idea is that law must be distinct from the order of a gunman writ large (to paraphrase Augustine[9]) and that what makes law distinct from mere force lies in the ability of law to obligate obedience rather than merely coerce it. Let us call this step one of the natural lawyer's argument for the relational thesis. As Aquinas summarized this step: law necessarily binds the conscience.[10]

The second step of the argument is to assert that only that which is morally just (or at least "good enough for government work") can bind the conscience. The first idea here is that there is only one kind of obligation, and that is moral obligation.[11] It is not that we cannot give sense

[9] Augustine, *De Libero Arbitrio*, I.v.11.

[10] Thomas Aquinas, *Summa Theologiae*, I–II, q. 90, a. 4, in Anton C. Pegis, *Basic Writings of Saint Thomas Aquinas* (New York: Random House, 1945), 2:746–47.

[11] We can contrast this position with the legal positivism of Austin and Bentham, for whom there were two kinds of obligations: moral obligations and legal obligations. For them, legal obligations were not a kind of moral obligation; legal obligations were simply liability to legal sanctions. This is a very Pickwickian sense of "obligation," because in no real sense is one obligated by threats of painful consequences. As Hart put it, one may be *obliged* to yield to such threats without being *obligated* to yield to them. See Hart, *The Concept of Law*.

to the idea of a legal obligation. A legal obligation, on this view, just is a moral obligation with respect to some legal institution. This makes legal obligation a kind of moral obligation, rather than something distinct from moral obligation. The second idea here, one that is more central, is that legal obligations—moral obligations created by man-made rules—can exist only if those rules are not too unjust in content. The plausible thought is that no one can be morally obligated by morally evil rules.

The two-step argument to the natural lawyer's conclusion is thus:

(1) Something is legal only if it obligates.
(2) Something obligates only if it is not unjust.
(3) Therefore, something is legal only if it is not unjust.

There are other routes to establishing the natural lawyer's conclusion. One might urge a conventionalist semantic thesis by purporting to discover in the usages of "law," "droit," "recht," etc. a common criterion of correct usage that is moral in character.[12] Alternatively, one might view law as an "interpretive concept," and then urge that the best interpretation of that concept is one linking law to morality.[13] One might also do a cosmopolitan sociology, abstracting from social practices the world over those universally treated as *legal* practices in their respective cultures, and discover that practices are treated as legal only if such practices are also moral.[14]

The traditional argument of the natural lawyer as I have reconstructed it above is different than these semantic, interpretive, or sociological modes of argument. In contrast to all of these, the traditional argument is refreshingly *practical*. In its first step, it treats law as something of practical relevance—law changes what we have reason to do.[15] If the argument's first premise is correct, then theorizing about law's nature will not be an academic pursuit in any pejorative sense, for what such theorizing seeks is the nature of one of the things that obligate us as rational and moral people. There is no "academic chalk dust" involved in such an approach, as there easily can be when one uses the semantic, interpretive, and sociological approaches sketched above.

Our practical interest in the traditional argument will be maintained no matter *who* it is that is necessarily obligated by law. There are two pos-

---

[12] John Austin argues against a natural law position by using this sort of semantic analysis to analyze the meaning of "law." John Austin, *The Province of Jurisprudence Determined*, ed. H. L. A. Hart (New York: Noonday Press, 1954).

[13] See, for example, Ronald Dworkin, *Law's Empire* (Cambridge, MA: Harvard University Press, 1986).

[14] This is Hart's method in *The Concept of Law*.

[15] In contemporary jurisprudence, this approach is most closely associated with Joseph Raz. See particularly Raz, *Practical Reason and Norms* (Oxford: Oxford University Press, 1975).

sibilities worth distinguishing here:[16] we might think that law *qua* law obligates everyone in the system, citizens to whom the law is applied as well as the judges who do the application of law to citizens. Alternatively, we might think that law necessarily obligates only judges; citizens, on this weaker view, might be obligated by various laws, but such items could be laws even if they did not obligate citizens to obey them. In either case, the nature of law would be of practical interest to us. If the stronger view is true, of course, the law is of practical interest because we have an interest in knowing what we are obligated to do. Even on the weaker view, we would all have prudential reasons for wanting to know what judges are obligated to do, for even though few of us are judges, it is judges who sanction our behavior.

III. The Functionalist Argument for Law's Binding Force

It is the argument for the first premise in the traditional argument above that interests me here. Specifically, my focus is on what I shall call the *functionalist argument*. This is the argument used by natural lawyers to establish that something can be law only if it obligates someone, citizens or (at least) judges.

The general form of the functionalist argument is best displayed as having three premises:

(1) Some thing X is law only if it serves the distinctive function(s) of law.
(2) The distinctive function(s) of law is Y.
(3) Y is served only if X obligates.
(4) Therefore, something is law only if it obligates.

In more colloquial English, the first premise asserts that law is a *functional kind*, that is, a kind whose essence is to be found in the value(s) it serves more than by the unique structural features it may possess. This functionalist premise applies to the various aspects of law; consider, for example, legal systems. Just like a human heart may have quite diverse structural realizations and still be a heart because it performs the function distinctive of hearts (i.e., pumping blood), so legal systems may be realized through quite different institutions and still be legal systems because they perform the function(s) distinctive of such systems.

One can carry the functionalist premise down to laws, kinds of law, the laws of cases, and areas of law. The premise would hold, for example, that

---

[16] These two roles are worth distinguishing for purposes of argument even if one accepts Heidi Hurd's thesis that the obligation of judge and of citizen correspond with one another. Heidi Hurd, *Moral Combat* (Cambridge: Cambridge University Press, 1999). There are expository advantages served if we separate the roles because in various instances the tugs of intuition are different for the two roles.

one decides if some rule is a law by examining the purpose such a rule serves (that is, its value or function) rather than the rule's structural features, such as its exact wording in some statute or precedent court's opinion. Analogously, rules used by courts to decide cases make up a distinctive kind of law ("common law") because they serve a common function or value. A law governing the rights and duties of particular parties in some particular case is what it is by virtue of the value(s) it serves, not in virtue of, say, the fact that it was stated by some judge at a certain point in proceedings involving the parties. Finally, an individual law is part of criminal law, for example, if the law serves the function distinctive of criminal law, irrespective of whether the law is called "criminal" and irrespective of things like the sanction attached to the law.

The second premise involves specification of the value that makes something into a legal system, a law, a certain kind of law, a law of a case, or an area of law. About legal systems, for example, one might claim that the function of law as such is, among other possibilities, the preservation of order;[17] the coordination of individual goods into the common good;[18] the furtherance of community made possible by an "integrated" treatment of all citizens;[19] or the enhancement of liberty made possible by clear, prospective rules.[20] About laws, the values served may be as diverse as the legitimate ends of legislation. The functionalist claim about a statute forbidding vehicles in a park, for example, might be that the application of such a rule is to be guided by the promotion of pedestrian safety more than by the literal meaning of the terms of such a statute—in which case, "what the law is" depends more on the values served by the statute in question than on its formal features.[21] About kinds of law, the values served are less various. With respect to common law, for example, the functionalist claim might be that such law serves the value of equality sloganized in the principle of formal justice that "like cases are to be treated alike."[22] We find more diversity of values when we consider areas of law. The functionalist claim here could be that criminal law, for example, serves a distinctive kind of justice, retributive justice,[23] whereas tort law serves another kind of justice, corrective justice, etc. When we finally consider the laws of a case, the values served may be even more various.

---

[17] See, for example, Thomas Hobbes, *Leviathan* (Oxford: Clarendon Press, 1909).

[18] See Aquinas, *Summa Theologiae*; and John Finnis, *Natural Law and Natural Rights* (Oxford: Clarendon Press, 1980).

[19] See Dworkin, *Law's Empire*.

[20] See Lon Fuller, *The Morality of Law*, 2d ed. (New Haven, CT: Yale University Press, 1969).

[21] This is the example used in the Hart/Fuller debate. Hart, "Positivism and the Separation of Law and Morality"; Lon Fuller, "Positivism and Fidelity to Law—A Reply to Professor Hart," *Harvard Law Review* 71, no. 4 (February 1958): 630–72.

[22] See Michael Moore, "Precedent, Induction, and Ethical Generalization," in Laurence Goldstein, ed., *Precedent in Law* (Oxford: Oxford University Press, 1988).

[23] See Moore, "A Theory of Criminal Law Theories."

Indeed, as I shall argue, any value whatsoever may be the value served by the law of a particular case.

The third premise asserts the truth of an instrumental calculation, a calculation about the means needed in order for law to serve its distinctive function. Specifically, the assertion is that the various goods of legal systems, laws, kinds of laws, areas of law, and laws of cases are served only if these items obligate obedience.

IV. Two General Problems with the Functionalist Argument for Natural Law

A. The alleged lack of any role for the obligatoriness of law in the functionalist argument for natural law

It may seem that a functionalist view of law is sufficient for the natural lawyer's conclusion, and that it therefore renders unnecessary the claim that something is legal only if it obligates. The idea here is that if law is a functional kind, then something must serve the values of law in order to be law, that is, only good law can be law at all.[24] This, it is urged, is the natural law conclusion, achieved without need of some intermediate premise of law's necessary obligatoriness.

There is this much truth to the charge: if law is a functional kind, then law must be of *some* value to be law at all. Yet that law is necessarily of some value is a very weak natural law thesis. Meticulous Nazis who dutifully observed the procedural niceties associated with the rule of law would create a system having *some* value, even though the content of their rules would be horribly unjust. If one identified the function of law as securing the procedural values of the rule of law, then one could say that such Nazis would have law. Yet any natural law worth talking about should resist being satisfied with this conclusion, and should deny that the system these Nazis would create is a legal system. An acceptable natural law theory should maintain that there is law only if the overall justice of a system reaches a level that obligates at least judges within the system, and this will require that the natural lawyer depend on a premise involving law's obligatoriness.

One might well think that there is some life to the objection, even conceding this reply. Suppose some function for law is discovered that does guarantee that if something is law, it is sufficiently just so as to obligate obedience. In such a case, the obligatoriness of law would do no work in the natural lawyer's argument. That is, the functionalist would have shown that law and morality are necessarily connected because

---

[24] Ruth Gavison suggests this objection. Ruth Gavison, "Natural Law, Positivism, and the Limits of Jurisprudence: A Modern Round," *Yale Law Journal* 91, no. 6 (May 1982): 1266–67. See also Daniel Robinson, "Antigone's Defense: A Critical Study of *Natural Law Theory: Contemporary Essays*," *Review of Metaphysics* 45, no. 2 (December 1991): 382.

anything, to be law, must be strongly moral. Because anything strongly moral is also plausibly thought to be obligatory, the functionalist would have therefore shown that law is obligatory. But the claim that something is legal only if it obligates would be logically epiphenomenal to the natural law conclusion, not a necessary step in the argument for that conclusion.

What this amended objection reveals is that the functionalist approach to natural law could proceed in a manner analogous to the semantic, interpretive, or sociological approaches mentioned earlier. Such a direct functionalist approach to jurisprudence would dispense with the traditional natural law argument and cut straight to its conclusion upon the discovery of a functionalist essence to law. This would occur in much the same way that the semantic, interpretive, and sociological approaches proceed directly to the natural lawyer's conclusion from, respectively, certain linguistic facts about usage of "law," the discoveries that law is an interpretive concept and that "law as integrity" is the best interpretation of it, or some social facts about law in all cultures.

Like these other approaches, a direct functionalist approach to the essence of law is certainly possible. However, like those other approaches, the direct functionalist approach does not include a role for legal obligation and therefore does not show that law has practical relevance. The virtue of the traditional argument's focus on someone's (judge or citizen) obligation is that this focus does give law such relevance. This relevance, in turn, gives us argumentative tools that we lack if we adopt the more abstract, direct approaches. The philosopher Joel Feinberg once confessed that he was at a loss in considering how to establish the natural lawyer's relational thesis if one left aside the obligations of some role, such as a judge.[25] While this may be too strong, Feinberg nicely captures the argumentative advantage provided by the traditional argument's focus on legal obligation, particularly the legal obligations of judges.

B. The alleged incompatibility between law's necessary obligating character and its functionalist nature

In contrast to the previous objection, which construed the functionalist approach to be so *strong* that it begged the question of law's nature as value-laden, another objection regards the approach as necessarily too *weak*. According to this objection, no system can actually obligate obedience unless it is in the service of all the values there are. One can see this objection most clearly by adverting to the third premise in the function-

---

[25] Joel Feinberg, "The Dilemmas of Judges Who Must Interpret 'Immoral Laws,'" in Joel Feinberg and Jules Coleman, eds., *Philosophy of Law*, 6th ed. (Belmont, CA: Wordsworth/ Thomson Learning, 2000), 108–29.

alist argument. This premise not only says that obligation is a *necessary* condition of something serving law's distinctive value(s); it equivalently says that something serving law's distinctive value(s) is a *sufficient* condition for that thing to be obligatory. Yet how can this be? After all, it is highly implausible to think that there is some one value that is so good that it outweighs all other values when they conflict, and less plausible still to think that this dominant value is *the* value served by law. What anyone is actually obligated to do is plausibly a function of all the values there are, so if the values law necessarily serves are limited in the way functionalism asserts, how could law always be obligating?

The only way the functionalist argument can go through in the face of this objection is if the distinctive value(s) that makes an institution legal is connected to all the values there are in such a way that to serve law's value is to serve all values. Then legality could plausibly be sufficient for obligation in the way asserted by the functionalist's argument. The history of post–World War II natural law jurisprudence can be seen as the search for just such a value. Lon Fuller, for example, held that law has a procedural goal as its essential function.[26] For Fuller, the function of all law is the exercise of social control through general rules. If rules are prospective, clear, general, consistently applied, possible to comply with, stable, public, etc., then citizens know what is expected of them, the administration of justice is not ad hoc and arbitrary, and law is efficiently self-executing for properly motivated citizens.

Considering Fuller's account, Herbert Hart put forth a version of the objection we are considering here, claiming that the procedural goal of law could be attained by a regime whose laws were nevertheless ruthlessly evil in their content.[27] In such a "Hell where due process was meticulously observed,"[28] there would be no obligation of citizens to obey the edicts of the regime, nor would even judges have an obligation to enforce them.

Fuller's response to Hart's version of the objection reveals clearly what the natural lawyer needs here. Fuller's faith was that if people "do things the right way" (i.e., fulfill law's procedural goals), then they will "do the right things" (i.e., have laws that are substantively just).[29] Few have shared Fuller's faith in the power of good procedure to make for good substance, but his answer illustrates clearly the problem facing a functionalist natural lawyer. The problem is to derive obligation (of citizens or even judges)

[26] Fuller, *The Morality of Law*.
[27] H. L. A. Hart, "Book Review—*The Morality of Law*," *Harvard Law Review* 78, no. 6 (April 1965): 1281–96.
[28] Grant Gilmore's nice paraphrase of Hart's point. Grant Gilmore, *The Ages of American Law* (New Haven, CT: Yale University Press, 1974), 111.
[29] Lon Fuller, "What the Law Schools Can Contribute to the Making of Lawyers," *Journal of Legal Education* 1, no. 2 (Winter 1948): 204; Fuller, *The Morality of Law*, 152–86, 223–24; Fuller, "Fidelity to Law," 636, 643, 661; and Lon Fuller, "A Reply to Professors Cohen and Dworkin," *Villanova Law Review* 10, no. 4 (Summer 1965): 661–66.

out of the limited values thought to be law's essential function; for when those limited values conflict with the many other values that exist, why are citizens or even judges obligated by only those values giving law its point?

One sees the same problem driving John Finnis in his resuscitation of Aquinas's view that the function of human law is to serve the common good.[30] The common good occupies a special place in Finnis's theory of value. It is not one of the seven basic goods that Finnis believes exist. Rather, the common good is that set of conditions that enables members of political communities to attain for themselves the seven basic goods, not just individually but through coordinated activities; these conditions also enable individuals to enjoy the good of cooperating with others generally, which is itself part of the common good.[31] Importantly, Finnis seeks to link this goal of law to the seven basic goods: "There is a 'common good' for human beings, inasmuch as life, knowledge, play, aesthetic experience, friendship, religion, and freedom in practical reasonableness are good for any and every person. And each of these human values is itself a 'common good'."[32] If this is right, then to serve the goal of law—the common good—is to serve something good for its own sake—human cooperation—which is also good because it serves all the values there are. This is both a plausible basis for obligation and a strong version of natural law.

As a last example, consider Ronald Dworkin's attempt to show that all law serves the function of "integrity."[33] Integrity is not one of the four political goods that Dworkin posits (these goods, he says, are distributive justice, fairness, procedural fairness, and fraternity). Rather, integrity is the good of a political community speaking with one voice. It is a mode of promoting the four political goods, a mode that is distinctively that of law. Integrity is thus served only when all political goods are served, and for the law to serve integrity will be for it to serve such goods. If this is true, then again, law exists only when it strongly serves the good, and law can plausibly be supposed to obligate (necessarily) both citizen obedience and judicial enforcement.

It is not my purpose here to assess the adequacy of these three contemporary functionalist natural law accounts, nor even to consider whether any such general account of law can succeed. Rather, I shall pursue the functionalist strategy at a much lower level of generality. In the succeeding sections, I shall deal with the laws of cases and with laws, suggesting as I go how one might generalize what we learn there to legal systems, kinds of law, or areas of law.

---

[30] Finnis, *Natural Law and Natural Rights*.
[31] Ibid., 154–55.
[32] Ibid.
[33] Dworkin, *Law's Empire*.

V. The Functionalist Account of the Laws of Cases

One may plausibly suppose that the law of a case before a formal decision in that case is rendered by a judge differs from the law of a case after such a decision. I shall therefore divide my discussion along this temporal dimension.

A. The law of the case prior to decision

Here we are met at the outset with the claim that there is no law of the case until the judge in that case decides it. According to this claim, there may be "predicted law" or "probable law," but there is no "actual law" until a judicial order is entered.[34] This view of law is analogous to the view of a baseball umpire whose slogan is "They ain't nothing 'til I call 'em." Even Hart held this view at one time; this was when he was under the sway of J. L. Austin's developing views of "performative utterances."[35] Hart urged that singular propositions of law, such as "This contract is valid," have no truth value until the requisite performance by a judge makes them true by assertion.[36]

Yet this old legal realist view of the law of cases cannot be sustained. Judges do not (always and necessarily) create legal rights and legal duties at the time of adjudication; in some cases, at least, they discover the antecedently existing rights and duties of the parties, rights and duties that existed when the parties acted prior to adjudication. In these cases, then, the parties had legal obligations with respect to each other prior to any judicial pronouncement, and the judge's obligation is to describe accurately what those citizens' obligations were.

One could, of course, drive a wedge between citizen/judicial obligation, on the one hand, and law, on the other. That is, one could insist that there is no law for a particular case until a judge makes some, even while conceding that citizens are obligated as if there is law and judges are obligated to *make* law consistent with such citizen obligations. But what would be the point of such insistence? If citizens are obligated by some standards, and if judges in their role as judges are obligated to decide against those breaking these obligations, then why should we refuse to call such standards law? With such refusal, theorizing about law's nature would lose the practical significance discussed earlier, and such theorizing would become a pejoratively academic enterprise.

Let us assume, then, that there are laws of cases prior to judicial decisions. We next need to flesh out the functionalist account of such laws.

---

[34] This is the view of Jerome Frank, *Law and the Modern Mind* (New York: Brentano's, 1930).

[35] J. L. Austin, "A Plea for Excuses," *Proceedings of the Aristotelian Society* 57 (1957): 1–30.

[36] H. L. A. Hart, "The Ascription of Responsibility and Rights," *Proceedings of the Aristotelian Society* 49 (1949): 171–94.

Consider the law of a case arising under a statute. In such cases, whether the singular proposition of law that decides the case is law wholly depends on a valid interpretation of the statute. If valid interpretations of statutes always involve values, then so do the laws of cases arising under such statutes.

We need an example; consider one presented by Fuller.[37] Two citizens are arrested under a city ordinance forbidding anyone to "sleep in the train station." The first defendant is a ticketed passenger waiting for his train; he nodded off while he was seated. The second defendant is a homeless person ("bum," in Fuller's day) who had spread out his belongings on the floor of the station and lain down, but was arrested before he had actually fallen asleep.

The first defendant presents what Aquinas would call a tension between the "letter" and the "spirit" of the city ordinance.[38] The letter of the ordinance is its literal meaning; literally, defendant one was asleep, so the letter of the ordinance would require his conviction. The spirit of the ordinance is the function or value it serves; if that function is to prevent the use of the railroad station for overnight accommodations, defendant one's conviction would not serve the spirit of the ordinance. Aquinas persuasively argues that in cases where the letter and spirit of a statute conflict, the spirit should prevail. The correct law of the case here is thus, "Defendant one is not guilty of sleeping in the train station."

Much ink has been spilt defending and attacking Aquinas's theory of interpretation.[39] By my lights, its defenders have the better case and have carried the day with most judges in most legal systems. "Purposive interpretation" is now a staple of American jurisprudence. The result is that in our legal system, the truth value of the singular legal proposition, "Defendant one is not guilty of sleeping in the train station," depends as much on a matter of value (what this statute is good for) as on matters of value-neutral fact (such as the historical fact that such an ordinance was passed, or the semantic fact that "sleep" in ordinary English covers what defendant one did but not what defendant two did).

If Aquinas is both correct and generally followed by our judges, then some connection between law and morality has been made out. The singular propositions that decide concrete cases are propositions of *law* only insofar as they further the value behind certain general propositions of law (such as that supplied by the ordinance in the above example).

Legal positivists have three routes open to them to deny this connection between law and morality. One is to deny that the spirit of a statute

---

[37] Fuller, "Fidelity to Law."

[38] Aquinas, *Summa Theologiae*, I–II, q. 96, a. 6.

[39] On Aquinas's side, see Fuller, "Fidelity to Law"; and Max Radin, "Statutory Interpretation," *Harvard Law Review* 43, no. 6 (April 1930): 863–90. On the other side, see, e.g., Frank Easterbrook, "Statute's Domains," *University of Chicago Law Review* 50, no. 2 (Spring 1983): 533–52.

should trump the letter of that statute. Although Fuller thought Hart advocated such a "plain meaning" approach,[40] clearer examples of this sort of positivism are to be found elsewhere. Particularly with the Reagan/Bush appointments to the federal bench in America, one increasingly encounters the view that the law of some case under a statute is a function exclusively of the historical facts surrounding a statute's passage and of the semantic facts giving the words of a statute their normal meaning. Under this view, when a statute's meaning is plain, judges should not hesitate to flout the purpose of the statute if it conflicts with this meaning; when the meaning is not plain, there is no law of cases brought up under that statute until judges make some law for those cases through their orders.[41]

Fortunately, this plain meaning route (also called "literalism" or "strict constructionism") is mouthed more than it is actually applied. Few judges can actually stomach applying a statute so as to fulfill its literal meaning while frustrating its purpose.[42] Justice Oliver Wendell Holmes lampooned this sort of statutory application, noting that judges who engaged in it would in effect be saying to the legislature, "I see what you are driving at but you have not said it so we shall go on as before."[43]

A second route for the legal positivist here is to deny that the function or purpose of a statute is a value. On this view, the purpose of a statute is just another value-neutral fact of history—it is what the legislature intended to achieve in passing the statute. If judges decide the laws of cases under statutes by referring to this factual criteria, then nothing in these decisions depends on a connection between law and morality.[44]

The problems with this "originalist" kind of positivism are legion and well known.[45] It is unclear what sense can be given to the idea of a legislature's intention. If fictionalized, it loses its status as merely a historical fact.[46] If reduced to the intentions held by a majority of individual legislators, it rarely exists and has little normative appeal because the legislature's job in passing a statute is not to have a "moment of shared intention," but to express, in some shared language, whatever mix of

[40] Fuller, "Fidelity to Law."

[41] See, e.g., Easterbrook, "Statute's Domains."

[42] Compare Easterbrook's preaching in "Statute's Domains" with his practice in *In re Erickson*, 815 F.2d 1090 (7th Cir. 1987).

[43] Oliver Wendell Holmes, Jr., quoted in Learned Hand, *The Bill of Rights* (Cambridge, MA: Harvard University Press, 1958), 18.

[44] See, e.g., Joseph Raz, "Authority and Consent," *Virginia Law Review* 67, no. 1 (February 1981): 103–31.

[45] For one of many critiques, see Michael Moore, "The Semantics of Judging," *Southern California Law Review* 54, no. 2 (January 1981): 256–70.

[46] Dworkin stresses this point in his "The Forum of Principle," *New York University Law Review* 56, nos. 2–3 (May/June 1981): 469–518, reprinted in *A Matter of Principle* (Cambridge, MA: Harvard University Press, 1985). See also Moore, "The Semantics of Judging."

different intentions there might be.[47] In addition, even if one can make complete sense of a normatively attractive model of legislative intent, such intent would not prevent the laws of cases under statutes from having a connection to values. Suppose, for example, the town council's intent in passing the no-sleeping ordinance described above was to avoid the annoyance, overcrowding, and danger that would be created were the train station to become a de facto shelter for the homeless. This could give a judge the line of march in applying the ordinance, but it does not tell her how far to go in this direction. Achieving the ordinance's end has to be balanced against the costs (to other values) of such achievement. It is not obvious, for example, that a judge should prevent the station from being used as a shelter in cases where people are dazed or injured in the aftermath of a train wreck or other disaster. As a second example, consider defendant two in Fuller's hypothetical. Although his conviction would serve the purpose of the ordinance, he was not literally asleep and the heightened importance we attach to notice in criminal cases might well prevent his conviction.

Hart charted a third route to denying the connection of laws of cases to morality. This was based on the observation that even putting the best possible moral face on a thoroughly iniquitous statute could result in very unjust applications of that statute.[48] For example, a judge could attribute the best possible purpose to the antebellum fugitive slave laws in America and still end up applying such laws in a way that involves little justice.[49]

Both Hart's objection and the previous objection reveal something touched on earlier: they both show how weakly connected law may be to morality under the functionalist approach to natural law. According to these objections, that the law of some case serves *some* good (i.e., the function of that law) does not generate much confidence that this law of a case serves *the* good in any comprehensive sense. The point here is a perfectly general one about functional kinds. It is plausible to suppose that mousetraps have a function (namely, catching mice), and that the service of this function is what makes something a mousetrap. Even so, the best mousetrap may not be the device that is best at catching mice, for other values may intrude when one is judging whether a mousetrap is good enough for service.[50] For example, a safety-catch that decreases some-

[47] See Radin, "Statutory Interpretation"; Moore, "The Semantics of Judging"; and Antonin Scalia, *A Matter of Interpretation*, ed. Amy Gutmann (Princeton, NJ: Princeton University Press, 1997), 17.

[48] Hart made this point against both Fuller and Dworkin. Hart, "Book Review—*The Morality of Law*"; Hart, "Comment," in Ruth Gavison, ed., *Issues in Contemporary Legal Philosophy* (Oxford: Oxford University Press, 1987).

[49] This is one of Dworkin's favorite examples. Compare Dworkin, "Review of Cover's *Justice Accused*," *Times Literary Supplement*, December 5, 1975, with J. L. Mackie, "The Third Theory of Law," *Philosophy and Public Affairs* 7, no. 1 (Autumn 1977): 3–16; and with Joel Feinberg, "The Dilemmas of Judges Who Must Interpret 'Immoral Laws.'"

[50] This example is Kenneth Stern's, from his "Either-or or Neither-nor," in Sidney Hook, ed., *Law and Philosophy* (New York: New York University Press, 1963), 249–50.

thing's efficiency of mouse-catching but increases the safety of humans who use it may make the thing in question a better mousetrap. The unsafe mousetrap *is* a mousetrap, because it serves the function distinctive of mousetraps; yet this does not guarantee that it is good enough to use.

At the level of legal systems, as we have seen, contemporary theorists have sought to connect the attainment of law's general function to the service of all the values there are. With regard to mousetraps, this move would be analogous to asserting that a mousetrap good at catching mice could not be unsafe for human use (because, e.g., even if it were some-what less safe than other mousetraps, its greater effectiveness would lead to it being used less frequently, and hence to overall safer mouse-catching). For the laws of cases, however, such a move is implausible. The value served by the law of a particular case is too discrete to permit one to have much confidence that the law of a particular case respects all of the values there are.

Consider, in this regard, the case of *Kirby v. United States.*[51] In *Kirby*, the defendant had stopped a steamboat in order to detain a federal mail carrier. The defendant was accordingly arrested and convicted of the federal crime of "obstructing or retarding the passage of the U.S. Mail." He was convicted despite the fact that he was a sheriff and despite the fact that he stopped the steamboat in order to arrest the mail carrier for murder under a valid state bench warrant.

By my lights, the defendant sheriff satisfied the literal meaning of the words used in the federal statute—literally, he did obstruct and retard the passage of the U.S. mail. In addition, his conviction would serve the seeming purpose of the federal statute, which was to secure the passage of federal mail in a federal system made up of independent state author-ities. Nonetheless, the law of the case that the judge was obligated to apply was that the defendant did not obstruct or retard the passage of the U.S. mail. Another value intrudes here, namely, the value of getting mur-derers off the street (or, as it happened, the river). This value easily trumps the slightly increased speed in the passage of the mail that is attainable if murderous mail carriers are considered immune to state arrest while carrying the mail. Moreover, this intruding value can in no sense be encapsulated within the purpose of the obstruction statute. Mak-ing certain that murderers get their just deserts is a real good, as is making sure they are not free to murder again. However, these are not the goods that are the function of the obstruction statute; they are extraneous to that statute's purpose and for that reason I call judgments using such extraneous values "safety-valve judgments."

The functionalist approach to the laws of cases is thus unable to gen-erate a natural law view of such laws without some external support. The functionalist approach connects the laws of cases to values, but only

---

[51] *Kirby v. United States*, 74 U.S. (7 Wall.) 482 (1869).

weakly so, and too weakly to make the laws of cases congruent with judicial obligation. Cases like *Kirby* make explicit that the obligation of a judge in a particular case is to balance (1) the political values that are served by adhering to the ordinary semantic meaning of words used in the relevant statute, (2) the function this statute should be seen to serve, and (3) all values impacted by a provisional interpretation of the statute that is based solely on that statute's semantics or function.[52] The outcome of this balance of values constitutes the law of the case: it is a judge's obligation to find this law, and a citizen's obligation to obey it. This is a natural law conclusion about the laws of cases, a conclusion that functionalism by itself cannot generate.

This conclusion seems to be established instead by some nonfunctionalist argument for the first step of the traditional argument for natural law, namely, the claim that something needs to obligate to be law. Aquinas himself attempts to establish the necessary obligatoriness of law with some dubious etymology of *"ligare,"* the Latin word for law.[53] Even if his etymology were correct, however, such a semantic approach to the question could not establish the point.

The point is better supported by three different observations. First, at least when dealing with the laws of cases within some legal system, law should be a concept holding our practical interest. One possibility here is that our concept of the laws of cases should answer to a citizen's purely prudential interest in avoiding legal sanctions. Such a prudential interest easily generates Holmes's famous predictive theory of the laws of cases: the law is a prediction of judicial force.[54] As is well known, however, such a prudentially oriented notion of law is wholly inadequate for judges or other legal officials, for it is not plausible to suppose that they are engaged in the task of predicting either their own decisions or the decisions of those with power to discipline them.[55]

A concept of law of practical interest to both judges and citizens will therefore be tied to what judges *should* do in some cases, not to what they *will* do. For law to be practically interesting, then, it must generate reasons for action for at least some actors within a legal system. This poses a problem for legal positivists, for if law is not obligatory in nature, as they argue, then it is hard to see how law could provide reasons and therefore be practically interesting. Legal positivists who see this problem respond by claiming that they can remain unengaged (or "detached"[56]) in

---

[52] I defend this view of statutory interpretation at length in Michael Moore, "A Natural Law Theory of Interpretation," *Southern California Law Review* 58, no. 2 (January 1985): 277-398.

[53] Aquinas, *Summa Theologiae*, I–II, q. 90, a. 1.

[54] Oliver Wendell Holmes, "The Path of the Law," *Harvard Law Review* 10, no. 8 (March 1897): 457-68.

[55] See, e.g., Hart, *The Concept of Law*.

[56] This is Raz's term. Joseph Raz, *The Authority of Law* (Oxford: Oxford University Press, 1979).

their jurisprudence. Such positivists argue that the law must "claim" to create reasons for action for certain people,[57] or that certain actors must believe or "accept" that law creates such reasons for action, without such positivists themselves asserting that law does actually create reasons for action.[58]

This detachment might be possible when one does jurisprudence externally, that is, outside any particular legal system.[59] When dealing with singular propositions of law from inside a legal system, however, we cannot remain so detached. If, for example, an American citizen or judge wishes to apply the positivists' concept of law in general to American law, he will have to drop the detachment. This is because these "unengaged" positivist concepts of law require us to believe that if some singular proposition is one of law, then we must believe that this proposition *describes* a reason for us to act. If we believe this, however, then we must believe that the proposition actually *gives* us a reason to act. That is, we are committed to the proposition in fact giving us a reason for action because it is a proposition *of law*. The upshot at this point is that if one wishes to have a notion of law that is of practical interest, but wants to avoid the Holmesian identification of the laws of cases with predicted judicial force, then one is committed to the view that if a singular proposition is part of the law of one's jurisdiction, then that proposition necessarily gives someone a reason for action.

The second point suggesting that laws of cases are obligatory has to do with the kind of reason for action that law generates. Law will hold some practical interest for us if it simply generates *a* reason for someone within our legal system to act in one way rather than another. Yet law will hold much more practical interest for us if it generates not only *a* reason for action, but a *conclusive* (or nearly conclusive) reason for such action, the kind of reason we commonly call an obligation. If law generates this kind of reason, then the question of whether some proposition is one of law grabs our attention in the way that the question of whether we promised to do something grabs our attention: answers to each of these questions often tell us what we ought to do.

Perhaps one can derive this obligatoriness of the laws of cases from the function of law in general. Consider, again, the analogy of promises. One argument for why promises create an obligation to do the promised act, as opposed to merely creating a reason to do that act, stems from a functionalist view of promising. Suppose the practice of promise-making has as its function the good of social cooperation, both for its own sake and for the further good such cooperation makes possible. The function-

---

[57] Ibid.

[58] This is Hart's view in *The Concept of Law*.

[59] I defend the possibility of this kind of external jurisprudence against Dworkin and others in Michael Moore, "Hart's Concluding Scientific Postscript," *Legal Theory* 4, no. 3 (September 1998): 301–27; and in Moore, *Educating Oneself in Public*, chaps. 1, 3.

alist argument would be that social cooperation is only possible if the parties to a promise believe that promises create obligations, a belief the parties can sustain only if promises do in fact create obligations. The good that gives promising its point justifies regarding promises as obligation-creating acts and not merely reason-creating acts. Analogously, one might think that law in general has the function of serving the common good or of making social cooperation possible, and that for this good to be served, the laws of cases must be regarded as obligatory, and therefore must actually be obligatory.

Putting aside this very general functionalist argument, which proceeds from some controversial views of law's general function, let us consider, as a kind of *reductio* argument, the alternative to identifying singular propositions of law with someone's obligation. Suppose in a case like *Kirby*, we identify the singular proposition of law for that case as the singular proposition that is logically derivable from that general proposition consisting of the plain meaning of the federal obstruction statute. On a literal reading of "obstruction," Sheriff Kirby literally obstructed the passage of the U.S. mail when he arrested the murderous mail carrier; thus, the singular proposition of law in this case would be "Kirby is guilty of obstructing the passage of the U.S. mail." Now suppose that we divorce the law from judicial obligation by saying that Kirby is guilty according to the law, but that Kirby's legal obligation was to do just what he did and that the trial judge's legal obligation according to the law is to hold Kirby not guilty of obstructing the passage of the U.S. mail. This view is one held by some positivists, including, notably, legal philosopher Andrei Marmor.[60]

It is pretty clear that what motivates views such as Marmor's is the desire to keep singular propositions of law free from the contamination of value judgments, specifically, those value judgments needed to assess a statute's "spirit" and the "all-things-considered safety-valve judgments" mentioned earlier. Yet Marmor, like others, is unwilling to stomach the preposterous results reached if one truly follows a plain meaning interpretive theory. So he cleaves judicial obligation from the law, and the judge is therefore obligated—*qua* judge, *legally* obligated—to decide contrary to law!

Surely we do not want to do this to our concept of law. If one identifies the law of the case in *Kirby* as the exclusive dictate of the ordinary meaning of "obstruct" in the relevant statute, then the "law" created only *a* reason for Kirby to act in one way, and *a* reason for a judge to sanction him if he acted the other way. Stronger reasons *not* of the law's creation urged Kirby not to act as the law dictated, and those same non-law-created reasons urged the judge not to sanction Kirby for violating the law. What the law is, on this view of law, simply is not a very interesting

---

[60] Andrei Marmor, *Interpretation and Legal Theory* (Oxford: Oxford University Press, 1992).

question. The law, on this view of it, is simply a bit player in the balance of reasons justifying both citizen and judicial behavior. Indeed, one would be hard-pressed to make much sense of the ideal of the "rule of law" because in no sense would law (so conceived) rule anyone's behavior.

The third point in favor of the obligatoriness of laws of cases has to do with who it is that is necessarily obligated by law. The traditional jurisprudential answer, common to both natural lawyers and legal positivists, has been *judges*: the law necessarily obligates judges to decide in accordance with it. Even Hart, who was openly critical of American jurisprudence for its "obsession" with judges,[61] himself created a general theory of law in which the obligations (real or perceived) of judges are central.[62]

Whether the real or perceived obligations of judges are indeed central to there being a legal system is an interesting question, but it is not our question here. Whatever one thinks of judicial obligation as the touchstone of the legality of whole social systems, surely *judicial* obligation is intuitively most closely connected to the legality of singular propositions. If the law of the *Kirby* case was that Kirby was not guilty of obstructing the passage of the U.S. mail, then surely the judge's obligation was to find just that.[63]

In summary, then, I take the traditional argument for a natural law view of those singular legal propositions derived from statutes to be quite strong. This is because I find both steps of the natural lawyer's argument (which I reverse in order here in order to correspond with the argument of this section) to be intuitive at this level of legality. First, judges are obligated in cases like *Kirby* and Fuller's sleeping hypothetical to decide in accordance with "safety-valve" and "spirit" value judgments; second, the laws of such cases are to be identified with these value-laden decisions, not with some supposedly value-free ingredient in them (such as the relevant statutes' "plain meaning"). Functionalism, as we have seen, cannot sufficiently establish either step of the argument. The need to take into account the value or function served by some statute shows that a judge's obligation includes the obligation to make value judgments in his decisions, but cases like *Kirby* remind us that simply serving such a function is an insufficient basis on which to justify a judicial decision. Some general function of all law might support the obligation of a judge to

[61] H. L. A. Hart, "American Jurisprudence through English Eyes: The Nightmare and the Noble Dream," *Georgia Law Review* 11, no. 5 (September 1977): 969–89, reprinted in H. L. A. Hart, *Essays in Jurisprudence and Philosophy* (Oxford: Clarendon Press, 1983).

[62] In Hart's *The Concept of Law*, judges must regard the rule of recognition as obligatory for a legal system to exist.

[63] It is perhaps almost as intuitive that Kirby's legal rights and obligations were the same as those the judge was obligated to discover in his decision. Still, I leave for another day the question of whether the laws of cases necessarily obligate citizens as well as judges. (In this regard, however, see Hurd, *Moral Combat*.) If they do, this stronger first step of the traditional argument for natural law makes the second step easier, since in comparison to judicial obligations, which express just those values defining a discrete role, citizens' obligations are more easily seen as an expression of all the values there are.

decide in accordance with the law of some case, but this obligation seems supportable without reliance on some general function of all law. Functionalism, in short, supports but does not itself generate a natural law theory of the singular propositions of law arising under statutes.

B. *The law of a case after a final judicial decision*

The status of the law of a particular case may seem to change radically after a judge renders a decision. If the time for appeal has expired, or if no appeal can be taken because the court making the decision is the highest court, then the judge's decision is final. This decision, whatever it is, seems to fix the rights and duties of the parties irrevocably; moreover, it seems to do so all by itself.

The irrevocability of such a decision is termed its *"res judicata* effect." Even if the decision is later "strictly confined to its facts," or even overruled in another case, the decision stands with respect to the parties in the original case. For example, even if a judge's conclusion that there is a valid contract between two parties is erroneous, once that decision is final, the parties have the rights and duties of contracting parties.

The seeming sufficiency of the decision to constitute the law of the case may be seen by supposing a completely erroneous decision. If the parties are stuck with such a decision as determinative of their rights and duties, that would show the sufficiency of the decision itself, whatever it is, to constitute the law of their case. Prior to such an erroneous decision, we may suppose that everything (plain meaning, spirit, safety-valve considerations) supported the claim that the truth value of the singular legal proposition "This contract is invalid" was "true"; after the erroneous decision, the truth value of that proposition, nonetheless, seems to be "false." The decision itself seems fully determinative of what the law of this case now is.

Legal positivists should like this account of the law of a case quite a bit. After all, on this account the truth of such singular propositions of law seems to turn on a pure matter of nonmoral fact, namely, the historical fact that the relevant judge decided as she did. The clarity and simplicity of this view, then, inclines the positivist toward the legal realist idea that until the judge makes a decision, there is no law of a particular case.

Unfortunately for the positivist, however, none of this is as it seems. To begin with, we have good reasons, as discussed above, for saying that there is a law for a case prior to some judge deciding it. Furthermore, although a judgment in a case is almost always given *res judicata* effect as the law of the case, that this is so is due to a balancing of values (not solely because of some historical fact), *and,* when that balance tips the other way, it is not so at all.

The doctrine that a legal judgment, once rendered, should conclude the dispute between the parties is justified by important considerations. These include the undesirability of favoring the tireless and the wealthy in disputes, the undesirability of allowing multiple attempts at establishing liability, and the desirability of promoting efficient adjudication by giving litigants incentives to present their best case on the first try. We might think of these considerations as the additional functions served by the law of a case once a decision has been reached ("additional" because the basic function essential to the law of a case, irrespective of whether a judge has actually decided the matter, is the fixing of the legal rights and duties of the parties). Such considerations supporting *res judicata* may well be so strong that they almost always justify both a judge in refusing to "overrule" a prior ruling on the law of a case and a citizen subject to the ruling from disobeying it. The considerations are not so strong, however, as to make *res judicata* into the hard and fast rule many lawyers pretend it to be.

Consider a case in which (1) the mother is declared unfit in a child custody proceeding because the judge concludes, erroneously under the laws of his jurisdiction, that the mother's full-time employment disqualifies her from being a fit parent; (2) the father is erroneously declared fit because the judge does not know that the father has sexually abused the child; and (3) the judge, on the basis of the determinations mentioned in (1) and (2), enters a judgment awarding exclusive custody to the father. It is clear to me that the mother in this case is not obligated to obey the court's judgment. Indeed, her obligation is to do whatever she can to protect her child; this includes secreting the child away from the father at the first opportunity. It is almost as clear that a judge who knows what the mother knows—that is, he knows how erroneous the custody judgment is in both law and fact—is obligated not to enforce it against the mother.[64] This position, of course, raises a procedural worry in that it will encour-

---

[64] In the Anglo-American legal system, we have for centuries tempered the desire for finality in legal judgments with a desire to reopen "final" judgments in order to correct serious substantive or procedural errors. At common law, this was accomplished procedurally by the ancient writs of *coram nobis* and *audita querela*, and in Equity, by bills in equity seeking injunctions against the enforcement of legal judgments. (See J. W. Moore, *Moore's Federal Practice*, 3rd ed. [New York: M. Bender, 1999], secs. 60 App. 105–8.) Even under current federal American law, the old view that courts have inherent power to reopen their own judgments survives; Federal Rule of Civil Procedure 60(b) enumerates five traditional grounds for reopening a judgment and then adds a safety-valve provision specifying that a judgment can also be reopened for "any other reason justifying relief from the operation of the judgment." Under this provision, "[t]he degree of unfairness may properly be considered in determining whether a court is justified in disturbing the finality of a judgment." Moore, *Moore's Federal Practice*, sec. 60 App. 37. As courts recognize, this "catch-all" or safety-valve provision is a "grand reservoir of equitable power to do justice in a particular case." *Compton v. Alton Steamship Co.*, 608 F.2d 96, 106 (5th Cir. 1979).

Currently, the above-referenced procedures for reopening a judgment are available only to the court that rendered the judgment. However, when the degree of injustice caused by an erroneous judgment is serious enough, a "collateral attack" on that judgment can be launched from a different court. See, e.g., *Fay v. Noia*, 372 U.S. 391 (1963), and *Townsend v. Sain*, 372 U.S. 293 (1963), where collateral review of state court factual findings was allowed by the U.S. Supreme Court in order to protect constitutional values. In a civil context, see Feinberg, "The Dilemmas of Judges Who Must Interpret 'Immoral Laws,'" for a discussion of the various techniques used by state court judges in the antebellum North to avoid giving "full faith and credit" to Southern court findings pertaining to escaped slaves.

age litigants to reopen matters of fact and law that are already concluded, but this must be balanced against the worry that severe injustice can be caused if judges are given authority to fix irrevocably the legal rights and obligations of litigants.

What cases like the custody example show us is that when the level of injustice about to be caused by some judgment in a case is quite high, even the strong considerations in favor of *res judicata* yield. Thus, the judgment does not by itself obligate either citizen or judicial obedience. Rather, the content of such obligations is determined by a balance between the considerations behind *res judicata* and the considerations disserved by the judgment. Even when that balance tips in favor of the *res judicata* considerations—as it usually will in a reasonably just legal system— obligation follows this balance of values, not some value-free historical fact.

Here we again face a familiar possibility, that of cleaving obligation from the law of the case. Certainly an idiomatic way of describing the mother's obligation in a case like that above is to say, "She was obligated not to follow the law." We might even say this of the judge—that is, we might say that he was obligated not to enforce the law of that case. It is preferable, however, to keep citizen and judicial obligation in line with the law. If both judge and citizen were obligated to keep the child away from the abusive father before any judgment was entered, and they are similarly obligated after the judgment, then the law of the case did not change when the judgment was entered.

This way of looking at the matter is reinforced by the fact that when we determine that an earlier judgment was erroneous, it is desirable to be able to say that our later determination correcting this judgment is retroactively applicable.[65] Suppose that in the custody case, a later court finds that the initial judgment discussed above was erroneous. Between the time that the initial judgment was entered and the time that it is declared erroneous, what was the law of the case? Was it the erroneous judgment, which therefore both changed the pre-judgment law of the case and was itself changed by the subsequent determination of error? If so, then contempt charges would still be appropriate against the disobedient mother, and disciplinary proceedings would still be appropriate against a judge who had refused to enforce the custody order before the determination of error. Because these consequences are undesirable, it is better to treat the judgment subsequently determined to be erroneous as if it had

---

[65] Anglo-American law, as formally stated, is different from what I am arguing for in this essay. See, e.g., *United States v. United Mine Workers*, 330 U.S. 258, 294 (1947), in which it is stated that "[a]n injunction . . . must be obeyed . . . however erroneous the action of the court may be[.]" If our law really means this, it is bad law. I doubt, however, that our law does mean this. To give the proper incentives to most people, it is doubtlessly useful to utter such categorical, exceptionless pronouncements; in actuality, however, courts merely slap on the wrists actors like Martin Luther King when those actors violate judicial orders (subsequently determined to be erroneous for very good reasons.)

never been the law of the case. On this view, the law of the case never changed, and no one can be punished for doing what he was obligated to do according to that law. Such a view requires us *not* to divorce obligation from legality, and thus *not* to see a judgment as itself constituting the law for its case.

The law of a case after a judgment is entered should thus be a function of exactly the same mixture of value judgments and historical/semantic facts that it was a function of prior to judgment. The difference is that to determine the law of a case after a judgment is entered, the balance of considerations that determined the law of the case prior to judgment must then itself be balanced against the considerations favoring finality of judgments. This view of the law of a case as a complex balance of values is still a natural law view. It is a view partly supported by a functionalist approach to the law of a case; however, just as functionalism is unable to ground the natural law view of cases prior to judgment, it is also insufficient for grounding a natural law view of the law of adjudicated cases.

VI. THE FUNCTIONALIST ACCOUNT OF LAWS

As with the laws of cases, when we speak of the legality of general standards, it is helpful to separate discussion of laws prior to enactment from discussion of laws after positive enactment by some legal institution (i.e., a court, legislature, constitutional convention, administrative agency, etc.). Having used statutes previously in my discussion of the laws of cases, in this section I shall focus on the laws that arise from court decisions—what Anglo-American lawyers call the common law.

A. Common law without controlling precedent

In this subsection, I shall suppose what common law lawyers call a "case of first impression." These are cases where there is no precedent case "on all fours" with the case under consideration, nor is there some entrenched rule of the common law. Of thousands of possible examples in American law, I shall consider *Union Pacific Railway v. Cappier*.[66]

Decided in 1903, *Cappier* put before the Kansas Supreme Court the issue of Good Samaritan duties in tort where the defendant had innocently caused the victim to be in peril. The Union Pacific Railway had nonnegligently run down a trespassing youth named Cappier; the railroad engine severed one of the boy's arms and one of his legs. The railroad's employees stopped its train, ascertained Cappier's injuries, moved him to the side of the track, and went on. Cappier subsequently bled to death, and his mother brought suit.

[66] *Union Pacific Ry. v. Cappier*, 72 Pac. 281 (Kansas 1903).

By 1903, the Kansas courts had not yet spoken on the question of whether strangers who nonculpably place another in peril have a positive duty to rescue the victim from that peril. Prior to 1903, it had been established that in general, strangers owe one another no positive duties of aid in either criminal law or tort; with few exceptions, Kansas tort law held there to be only negative duties not to cause injury to others through our actions. Yet the question of whether those who nonculpably place a stranger in peril might owe that stranger a positive duty of rescue had not been faced by the Kansas courts.

In a situation like this, some legal positivists are tempted by the view that there are no laws governing such cases. They would argue for this view here by noting that no statutory or constitutional rule dealt with this province of the common law, and that no common law rule had been established by prior cases in Kansas. Yet this view runs afoul of Dworkin's well-known arguments that parties to lawsuits such as *Cappier* have legal rights and legal duties even in the absence of any obvious legal rules governing their case.[67] Dworkin's long-held "rights thesis" holds that there are legal rights even in the hardest of cases, and that the generation of such legal rights requires that there be more laws than meet the eye.[68]

Dworkin's argument for the rights thesis was partly derived from observations of Anglo-American legal practice. Litigants like Mrs. Cappier do not appear before judges as suppliants of judicial favor, pleading for a favorable exercise of the judge's discretion to *create* a legal right for them. Rather, such litigants appear as claimants of legal rights, legal rights whose existence must predate any declaration by the judge that they exist. Supplementing this inference from legal practice were Dworkin's arguments from certain ideals about the rule of law. Judges, he noted, do not make law (a job for the legislature); instead, they apply antecedently existing laws to the facts of cases. Furthermore, judges do not retroactively apply laws to transactions that took place before such laws came into existence; they apply laws that existed when the parties acted.

In other work, I have sought to supplement Dworkin's arguments here in two ways.[69] First, no one, to my knowledge, urges that judges should resolve cases of first impression by flipping coins, holding contests of strength between the litigants, using medieval flotation tests, or in any other way utilizing an admittedly arbitrary decision procedure. Hart and the contemporary legal positivists who have followed Hart's lead universally concede that when judges run out of obvious law in hard cases, they should repair to various standards such as utility, efficiency, liberty,

[67] Ronald Dworkin, "The Model of Rules," *University of Chicago Law Review* 35, no. 1 (Autumn 1967): 14–54.
[68] Ronald Dworkin, "Hard Cases," *Harvard Law Review* 88, no. 6 (April 1975): 1057–109.
[69] Michael Moore, "Legal Principles Revisited," *Iowa Law Review* 82, no. 3 (March 1997): 867–91, reprinted as chap. 7 of Moore, *Educating Oneself in Public*.

and the like. However, positivism forces these theorists to urge that such standards are not *legal* standards, and that the rights such standards generate are thus not *legal* rights until the judge makes them so by his decision. Yet notice that judges are obligated to use these standards; they do not have any discretion in the matter. Since this obligation arises for a judge in her role as judge, we have every reason to think of the judge's obligation to decide in favor of one party rather than another as a *legal* obligation, to think of the rights of the winning litigant as *legal* rights, and to think of the standards that justify such legal rights as *legal* standards, that is, laws.[70]

My second argument bolstering Dworkin's rights thesis rests on the observation that the standards judges do and ought to repair to in order to decide hard cases in a nonarbitrary way satisfy certain functional tests for laws. As part of law generally, all laws serve at least the function of making our obligations clearer to us than they would be in the absence of laws. By serving such a certainty-enhancing function, the general standards used by judges in hard cases merit the title "law."[71]

Assuming, then, that there are laws governing hard cases such as *Cappier*, we next need to inquire into the status of these laws under the natural law/legal positivism debate and the degree to which the functionalist approach can support the natural law view of the matter. Prima facie, the natural law account of the laws governing hard cases looks quite plausible. In *Cappier*, the standards at issue included, among others, some principle of liberty that makes it immoral for the state to force us to do some positive action that would prevent harm, even though the state can properly force us to refrain from doing any act that would cause that harm; some principle according to which the causing of a peril that ultimately becomes realized is enough causal involvement in the victim's situation so as to make the creator of the peril obliged to prevent the harm whose risk he has created; and some principle of corrective justice according to which a duty to correct a harm (by paying compensation) arises whenever one is morally obliged to prevent that harm. If one holds that these are all *legal* principles because they are good moral principles, then this is pretty straightforwardly a natural law position about such standards.

There are two maneuvers that legal positivists might use to avoid the unwanted conclusion that the standards that decide hard cases are legal standards only insofar as they are moral standards. I will call these maneuvers the shallow positivist response and the deep positivist response.

A shallow positivist urges that the law contains default rules of the following form: if an act is not clearly prohibited by some law, then that

[70] Ibid., 873 n. 40.
[71] Ibid., 875–76.

act is permitted.[72] In *Cappier*, on this view, there is a standard that pre-exists the judge's decision and which decides the case, but it is not any of the moral principles listed earlier. Rather, the deciding standard is a default rule for torts: if an act is not one described by the existing causes of action for tort, then the law is that there is no tort cause of action. Since there was no common law rule granting Cappier a cause of action against a lapsed Good Samaritan who had caused the victim's condition of peril, the law of Kansas (i.e., the alleged default rule) provided that there was no cause of action against such lapsed Good Samaritans.

This shallow positivist response has both descriptive and normative problems. Descriptively, Anglo-American tort law does not contain such a default rule. As the late William Prosser noted in his famous hornbook on tort law, "There is no magic inherent in the name given to a tort, or in any arbitrary classification[.]" Rather, Prosser urged, Anglo-American tort law had proceeded on the basis that "it is the business of the law to remedy wrongs that deserve it[.]"[73] Normatively, any default rule that would bar novel (and therefore nameless) torts is a bad idea. As J. L. Austin once quipped, "fact is richer than diction."[74] The ways in which a culpable person can injure an innocent person have not all been tried; it being desirable that culpable people pay for the harms they cause innocent people, it is undesirable that the tort causes of action be frozen at the types of wrongdoing hitherto attempted.

The deep positivist response is very different from that of the shallow positivist. The deep positivist admits that there are nonobvious legal standards like the principle of liberty described above, but denies that these standards are part of the law because they are moral standards. Instead, the deep positivist says these standards are laws because they pass a value-free test of pedigree. If such principles are "incorporated by," "implied by," or "exemplified by" the more obvious common law rules, then by this test of logic and history alone, those principles are legal in character.[75]

The deep positivist tenders an extraordinary claim. About the common law, the claim is that in a well-established legal system such as ours, with its multitude of past decisions, even where there seemingly is no common law rule on point for a case of first impression, one unique principle

---

[72] This is Hans Kelsen's view. See Hans Kelsen, "The Pure Theory of Law," *Law Quarterly Review* 51, no. 203 (July 1935): 528. "There is no such thing, of course, as a genuine gap, in the sense that a legal dispute could not be decided according to the valid norms, owing to the omission of a provision directed to the concrete case.... The law says not only that a person is obligated to a certain behavior ... but also that a person is free to do or not to do what he is not obligated to do."

[73] W. Page Keeton, *Prosser and Keeton on Torts*, 5th ed. (St. Paul, MN: West Publishing Co., 1984), 56–57.

[74] Austin, "A Plea for Excuses."

[75] A good example of such deep positivism can be found in Rolph Sartorius, *Individual Conduct and Social Norms* (Encino, CA: Dickenson Publishing, 1975).

adequate to decide that case can nonetheless be extracted from the existing rules by these value-free methods of incorporation, implication, and exemplification.

This claim runs head-on into undetermination worries. For any finite set of decided cases, there are an infinite number of general standards that would cover these cases as instances.[76] Moreover, with respect to any particular novel case to be decided, some of these standards will generate one result, while other standards will generate the opposite result. In other words, value-free extrapolation from past cases is indeterminate with respect to cases of first impression. The upshot of this is that there can be no purely factual pedigree for the legal standards used to decide hard cases. Such standards are in fact what they appear to be on their face: moral standards that are also legal standards because of their moral status.

This is a natural law conclusion about the laws that generate legal rights in hard cases, but the functional approach does little to establish it. True enough, one might conclude that some standard like the principle of liberty is a *legal* standard in part because of the increased certainty in hard cases that use of this principle makes possible. Yet surely judges should pick—and do pick—standards to resolve hard cases more by looking to the all-things-considered moral correctness of these standards than to the enhanced certainty that use of such principles makes possible. This certainty-enhancing function may be common to all legal principles that resolve hard cases, yet their service of this function cannot be the major reason for their selection.

B. Common law with precedent squarely on point

As with singular propositions of law, so here, once courts have issued a rule in prior cases that bears directly on some present case, things seem to be quite different. Except for those who identify law exclusively with either (1) singular propositions of law that decide cases (as did the legal realists), or (2) statutes (as did Bentham), everyone would admit there are laws here. Therefore, we again may put aside any worry that there is no law here to have a natural law theory about.

In the actual *Cappier* case, the Kansas Supreme Court held that the defendant railroad owed the deceased boy no positive duty of aid, despite the railroad's having nonculpably caused the boy's condition of peril. Suppose a similar case arises in Kansas in 1904, one year after the *Cappier* decision. In asking what the law is that governs my hypothesized 1904 case, we need to ask and answer two distinct questions. The first question is about the breadth of the rule laid down in *Cappier*: how similar must the 1904 case be to the facts of *Cappier* for the former to be governed by the common law rule that *Cappier* established? A narrow rule would

[76] See Moore, *Placing Blame*, 14–18.

require a great deal of similarity; a broader rule, less. The second question asks whether it is possible that the rule established in *Cappier* was not the law of Kansas—not in 1904, nor even in 1903. These two questions correspond to the two jurisprudential concerns about common law rules: (1) determining how one fixes the holding (or "*ratio decidendi*") of a precedent case like *Cappier*, and (2) ascertaining the force or "weight" of that holding for future cases. I consider each in turn.

1. *Extracting rules from precedent cases.* The two leading theories of holding are the classical theory and the legal realist theory.[77] According to the classical theory, the general proposition of law for which a precedent stands is the proposition stated as the holding in the precedent court's opinion. According to the legal realist theory of precedent, the holding of a precedent case is to be constructed by describing the facts of the precedent case and by noting what legal action the precedent court took on those facts; the rule, on this view, is one enjoining future judges to take similar action when deciding cases with similar facts. There are variations and mixtures of these two views,[78] but this simple characterization will suffice for our purposes.

Which of these views one adopts depends on what one takes to be the function of giving precedential force to past decisions. To use Dickens's somber phraseology, why is it good that "dead men sit on our benches"? One response to this question is to say that this practice of *stare decisis* increases the predictability of judicial behavior, and that this is good because it makes adjudication more efficient, cuts down on the chilling of liberty that occurs when sanctions are uncertain, and reduces unfair surprise of citizens. Arguably at least, the classical theory serves these values best, because on this theory, to know the common law one need but open the case reports and read the stated rules.

Some, such as myself, have argued that the main value justifying *stare decisis* is equality.[79] The ideal of formal justice is that like cases should be treated alike, and this is achieved only if judges follow the judges who preceded them on some issue. It allows present judges to treat litigants equally (by coordinating around a salient past decision), and it treats present litigants the same way that earlier litigants were treated.

If formal equality is the function served by common law, then this argues against regarding the holding stated by the precedent court in its opinion to be the actual holding of the case. This is because of the fact that on this sort of formal-equality account, judging whether or not a subsequent case is like the precedent case (and thus deserving of like treatment) requires one to judge whether the cases are truly alike in morally relevant respects. Such equality judgments cannot simply adopt the cat-

---

[77] See generally Moore, "Precedent."

[78] Ibid.

[79] Ibid. See also Moore, "Legal Principles Revisited," discussing Dworkin's commitment to seeing equality (rather than integrity) as the function of the common law.

egories stated in the precedent court opinion; instead, equality requires the subsequent court to penetrate the announced reach of the precedent court opinion and decide for itself what makes a relevant difference and what does not. Suppose, for example, that the Kansas Supreme Court had said in its *Cappier* opinion, "We hold that those who innocently cause a condition of peril for another owe that other no positive duty of rescue." By its terms, the stated holding does not apply to *culpable* causers of conditions of peril. Yet suppose a subsequent court deciding the 1904 case sees no relevant difference between innocent and culpable causers of some peril; in the court's view, neither sort of defendant involves himself so much in the victim's plight that he owes that victim a positive duty of rescue. Equality demands that the 1904 court ignore the limits on the holding of *Cappier* stated by the 1903 court, and substitute a broader rule for which *Cappier* stands: "causing a condition of peril, whether culpably or innocently, generates no positive duties of rescue." Only under this broader holding of *Cappier* can we treat the 1904 case like *Cappier* itself, because only under this broader holding can we use a nonarbitrary likeness between the facts of the two cases to judge whether the two cases are deserving of like treatment.

This formal-equality account is a natural law theory of the common law. This is because on this view the general rules that make up the common law are a blend of historical fact (what was decided in prior cases) and moral fact (how far the treatment accorded to litigants in the precedent cases should be projected to other, somewhat different cases, a matter of moral judgment). Such a natural law view, when generated exclusively by the functionalist argument, still presents the worry we have seen before: if precedent decisions are bad enough, there may be little one can do to construct a common law that is sufficiently moral to obligate the obedience of citizens and judges. It is via a doctrine of overruling that the common law surmounts this worry.

2. *Overruling bad precedents.* In addition to being able to broaden the apparent holding of precedent cases like *Cappier*, the common law has always had a variety of devices for *narrowing* the class of future cases to which precedent cases will apply. Precedent cases that have very expansive implications for future cases can nonetheless be narrowed by the time-honored expedient of distinguishing. Cases that are wrongly decided, root and branch, but which still deserve to be followed because of the values served by *stare decisis*, are often severely narrowed in their reach and may even be "confined to their facts," as lawyers often say. These narrowing techniques, along with the broadening techniques discussed above, are part of the common law's insistence on continually rejudging what laws have been established by precedent cases.

Sometimes a precedent case is sufficiently in error such that neither the value it promotes nor the values promoted by *stare decisis* can obligate obedience to it. *Cappier* was such a case. The liberty not to be forced to aid another, which motivated the court's decision, is a real good. Other real goods, like treating others alike and furthering certainty, are served by following precedents generally, and thus would have been served had *Cappier* been followed. Yet the decision flouted values of even greater importance. It was not merely an ought of supererogation that the railroad ignored when it abandoned young Cappier; it was an ought of moral obligation. Moreover, it was not a weak moral obligation such as one owes to any stranger; it was a strong obligation arising out of the fact that it was the railroad's actions that placed Cappier in peril of death. By breaching this strong primary obligation, the railroad had a secondary obligation to correct the injustice it had done in leaving Cappier to die. This good of corrective justice outweighed any liberty interest of the railroad in not being coerced by law to do its duty.

For these reasons, American tort law has by and large overruled cases like *Cappier*. One way to view this is to say that Kansas tort law changed once *Cappier* was overruled. Suppose that this overruling took place via a Kansas Supreme Court opinion issued in 1905. The view that regards overrulings as changing the law would say that cases arising out of facts occurring in 1904—after the 1903 *Cappier* decision, but before the 1905 overruling—would be governed by the "no positive duty" rule laid down in *Cappier*. Yet with occasional exceptions, mostly in criminal procedure, this is not how overruling works in common law systems. What we actually find is that once a precedent is overruled, no pending case, no matter when its facts arose, is treated as being controlled by the original rule. For our example, this implies that the law of Kansas in 1904 was not the no-duty rule of *Cappier*, but rather the 1905 rule that one does have a duty to those one places in peril. *Cappier*, in other words, was never the law of Kansas, not even in 1903. At most, the holding in *Cappier* was only the law of that case—and as we saw in Section V, even that might not be true.

What this shows is that a common law rule, such as that of *Cappier*, is not simply a matter of historical fact. Furthermore, such a rule is also more than just a blend of historical fact, the values that justify the rule, and the values that justify common law in general. Rather, the common law at any given time is a function of all three of these items, and of an all-things-considered value judgment on the rule in question. The rule in cases like *Cappier* is the law only if the values behind the announced rule, together with the values of having common law rules at all, are stronger than the values disserved by continuing such a rule.

This safety-valve function of overruling a precedent court's holding is quite parallel to the safety-valve function of overruling both the letter and spirit of a statute with a similar all-things-considered value judgment, as in cases like *Kirby v. United States* discussed above. In both situations, the function of the rule in question, together with the function of the relevant kind of rules (i.e., the function of statutes or the common law) has to be balanced against all possible competing values. Only rules that reflect such a balance are obligating of judges and citizens—that is, only they are *laws.*

VII. Closing Ruminations

From Aristotle through Aquinas to post–World War II theorists such as Fuller, we have inherited a tradition of natural law that is functionalist (that is, "teleological") in its orientation. So strong is this tradition that many assume that while "one need not be a teleologist about everything in order to be a natural law theorist ... one must be a teleologist about law itself" in order to qualify.[80]

If this were true, natural law would be problematic. As we have seen with respect to both the laws of cases arising under statutes and the laws that consist of common law rules, the functionalist approach is too weak to generate the natural law conclusion by itself. Arguments that proceed from various functions of laws of cases, of particular statutes, of particular common law rules, of the common law in general, of statutes in general, or of law in general do not establish that either laws or laws of cases are necessarily so good that they can obligate obedience. To establish such obligation, functionalism needs to be supplemented by other arguments about how law is best practiced.

These considerations do not settle the question of whether the more ambitious functionalist approach to law in general can sustain a natural law view. In my opinion, neither Fuller's rule-of-law virtues nor Dworkin's notion of "integrity" has much chance of making law good enough to obligate obedience necessarily; both are far too procedural to guarantee substantive justice in systems that conform to them. The common good of Aquinas and Finnis holds more promise here, but perhaps this is only because the common good threatens to collapse into the good of each citizen, and thus into the good *tout court.* Exploration of these matters, however, is beyond the ambitions of this essay.

Law, University of San Diego

---

[80] Susan Dimock, "The Natural Law Theory of St. Thomas Aquinas," in Feinberg and Coleman, eds., *Philosophy of Law*, 31.

THE "LAWS OF REASON" AND THE SURPRISE
OF THE NATURAL LAW

By Hadley Arkes

I. Introduction

The city of Cincinnati, we know, can be an engaging place, but federal judge Arthur Spiegel also found, in the mid-'90s, that it could be quite a vexing place. The city council of Cincinnati had passed what was called the Human Rights Ordinance of 1992, which barred virtually all species of discrimination—including discrimination on the basis of "Appalachian origin." But the bill also encompassed a bar on discrimination based on "sexual orientation." This kind of bill, in other places, had been turned into a club to be used against evangelical Christians who might refuse, on moral grounds, to rent space in their homes to gay or lesbian couples. And so a movement arose in Cincinnati, modeled on a similar movement in Colorado, to override the ordinance passed by the council: this would not be a referendum merely to repeal the law, but a move to amend the charter of the municipal government and remove, from the hands of the local legislature, the authority to pass bills of this kind. In effect, this was an attempt to override an ordinary statute by changing the constitution of the local government. The amendment did not seek to make homosexual acts the grounds for criminal prosecutions; it sought, rather, to bar any attempt to make gay and lesbian orientation the ground for special advantages, quotas, or preferential "minority status" in the law. The framers of the amendment objected to the tendency to treat gays and lesbians on the same plane as groups that have suffered discrimination based on race, religion, or gender. The proposal, known as Issue 3, drew wide support and passed in a referendum in 1993. It was, of course, challenged in the courts, which is why it found its way into the hands of Judge Spiegel.[1]

But to a case amply supplied with philosophic puzzles, Spiegel added a complexity that no one had anticipated: The Human Rights Ordinance passed by the council was rather sweeping in its proclamation of "rights," and in Judge Spiegel's manual of construction, a measure that proclaimed more rights was more authoritative than a measure that proclaimed fewer rights, or refused to grant, to certain claims, the standing of rights. And

---

[1] The policy engaged here, framed as a constitutional amendment, would come to describe a rather strange course: the amendment in Colorado was struck down in the Supreme Court in a rather dazed opinion, while the same policy, in Cincinnati, was upheld by the court of appeals. See *Romer v. Evans*, 517 U.S. 620 (1996).

so, turning on their head the canons of constitutionalism, Spiegel was inclined to regard the *constitutional amendment* in Cincinnati as invalid because it ran counter to a *local ordinance* that was far more liberal. On this matter I speak from direct, personal experience, since I was called in as a consultant on this case precisely for the purpose of addressing this argument.[2] It fell then to the attorneys and professors defending the amendment to remind the judge of the lessons taught by Chief Justice Marshall in *Marbury v. Madison* (1803): Behind the ordinary laws are the "basic laws," the laws that tell us, in effect, just what constitutes a "law." The fundamental law of a constitution bears, then, a *logical precedence* over the statute or the ordinary law.[3]

II. The Logic of a Constitution: The Basic Law and the Ordinary Law

Spiegel seemed to appreciate that the public at large in Cincinnati was far more conservative in its reflexes than were the officials elected in the city. Politicians were far likelier than ordinary citizens to cultivate a sensitivity to virtually any groups with a presence or visibility in the politics of the city. They would be far more averse to measures that promised to irritate any blocs of voters. The judge thought that there was something immanently suspect, then, in appealing to the public in a referendum when it was clear that the public was likely to be far more illiberal in its reluctance to install or confirm new brands of "rights." In taking this line, however, he had to suggest that there was something faintly disreputable, or illegitimate, about a people framing a constitution that puts limits on the use of political power. His understanding, then, would have left the local legislature as the sole legitimate source for shaping or amending the constitution. What seemed to have vanished from the understanding of the judge were the deepest premises of government by consent, premises anchored in the understandings of natural rights. Spiegel seemed to have forgotten the instruction of James Madison, George Mason, and James Wilson: namely, that a legislature is itself the artifact or creation of a constitution; it cannot be its source. As Madison observed, it is a "novel & dangerous doctrine that a Legislature could change the constitution under which it held its existence."[4]

---

[2] At the trial in Cincinnati, I unfolded the arguments that I restate here in the paragraphs to follow. In the transcript of the trial, they can be found in various places, but particularly at 652–60. By the time Judge Spiegel came to write his opinion, he had backed away from his remarkable argument, and there was only a muted reflection of it left in the record. See *Equality Foundation of Greater Cincinnati v. City of Cincinnati*, 838 F. Supp. 1235, 1238 (S.D. Ohio 1993).

[3] *Marbury v. Madison*, 5 U.S. 137 (1803).

[4] James Madison, quoted in Max Farrand, ed., *The Records of the Federal Convention of 1787*, rev. ed. (New Haven, CT: Yale University Press, 1966), 2:92.

John Locke once put the matter this way in his *Second Treatise*, in an instruction that really did run to the root: "the constitution of the legislative being the original and supreme act of the society," it has to be "antecedent to all positive laws." The power to make the positive law is defined by the constitution, *but the constitution itself cannot spring then from the positive law*. It has to find its origins, as Locke said, in that understanding "antecedent to all positive laws," and this authority was "depending wholly on the people," on their natural right to be governed with their own consent.[5]

It is one of the mysteries of our time that many people, even those jurists and writers on the law who are conservative, seem to have forgotten this ancient lesson that the difference between positive law and natural law does not depend simply on a theory, but rather, it is bound up with the canons of propositional logic. Alexander Hamilton drew on this reservoir of understanding to make points quite telling in the Federalist papers. It would appear that these passages have disappeared from the editions of *The Federalist Papers* read by many lawyers, and so they are worth recalling.

In *Federalist No. 78*, Hamilton noted the rule that guides courts in dealing with statutes in conflict: the statute passed later is presumed to have superceded the law enacted earlier. The same rule does not come into play, of course, with the Constitution, for a constitution framed earlier would have to be given a logical precedence over the statute that came later. Were this not the case, that constitution would lose its function, or its logic, as a restraint on the legislative power. But these rules for the interpretation of statutes are nowhere mentioned in the Constitution. As Hamilton remarked, they are "not derived from any positive law, but from the nature and reason of the thing."[6]

Somewhat later, in *Federalist No. 81*, Hamilton went on to point out that the notion of "parliamentary supremacy" in Britain had never been taken to mean that the legislature was empowered to overturn a verdict rendered in a court. The understanding seemed to be settled, then, that a legislature might act instead to "prescribe a new rule for future cases." But here, too, this understanding was not expressed anywhere in the *positive* law of the Constitution. And so what made it valid or authoritative, as an understanding bound up with the Constitution itself? As Hamilton explained, this understanding was simply anchored in "the general principles of law and reason."[7]

In a comment made in passing in one of his opinions, Chief Justice Marshall apologized to his readers for "much time . . . consumed in the

[5] See John Locke, *An Essay Concerning the True Original, Extent, and End of Civil Government*, sec. 157.
[6] *Federalist No. 78* (Hamilton), in *The Federalist Papers* (New York: Random House, n.d.), 507.
[7] *Federalist No. 81* (Hamilton), in *The Federalist Papers*, 526.

attempt to demonstrate propositions which may have been thought axioms."[8] Marshall apparently took it for granted that every literate reader knew that axioms cannot be demonstrated, and that they need not be. Anyone tutored in logic would have understood that "first principles" were indemonstrable in the sense that they depended on certain truths that had to be grasped, as Aquinas said, *per se nota*—as things true in themselves, and true of necessity.

That the Founders understood the matter precisely in this way was nowhere expressed with more elegance and clarity than by Hamilton, in the opening paragraph of his essay in the *Federalist No. 31*. The paper is about taxation, but in setting the ground, Hamilton revealed a mind that ran back, with a strainless grace, to first principles:

> In disquisitions of every kind there are certain primary truths, or first principles, upon which all subsequent reasonings must depend. These contain an internal evidence which, antecedent to all reflection or combination, command the assent of the mind. . . . Of this nature are the maxims in geometry that the whole is greater than its parts; that things equal to the same are equal to one another; that two straight lines cannot enclose a space; and that all right angles are equal to each other. Of the same nature are these other maxims in ethics and politics, that there cannot be an effect without a cause; that the means ought to be proportioned to the end; that every power ought to be commensurate with its object; that there ought to be no limitation of a power destined to effect a purpose which is itself incapable of limitation.[9]

III. KANT AND "THE LAWS OF REASON"

When Hamilton writes of "the nature and reason of the thing," the writing recalls Blackstone, in a similar vein, invoking "the law of nature and reason."[10] When jurists of the founding generation spoke in these accents, it seemed to be understood that they were pointing beyond the positive law to the principles of natural justice. But what seems to have fled from the understanding of jurists in our own day is that the principles of moral judgment, like the principles of natural law, are bound up with the "laws of reason," which Kant referred to in a different way as the "laws of freedom." Just to recall Kant again, the word "ought" marks the intersection of two domains. First, it indicates that we are speaking of the

---

[8] *Gibbons v. Ogden*, 22 U.S. 1, 221 (1824).

[9] *Federalist No. 31* (Hamilton), in *The Federalist Papers*, 188.

[10] William Blackstone, *Commentaries on the Laws of England* (Oxford: Clarendon Press, 1765), 4:67. I am using here the edition published by the University of Chicago Press in 1979, with a copy of the original plates and preserving the same pagination.

world of freedom, not the world of "determinism," governed by the laws of physics. We do not say that it would be "wrong" if the earth did not revolve about the sun, or that the earth is "obliged" to revolve in that way. The use of the word "ought" implies that we are dealing with actors who have some freedom or choice in framing their acts. We are not dealing, then, with causes under the "laws of nature," but with acts motivated by interests and reasons. But in the domain of reason, there are "laws of reason," beginning with the "law of contradiction," the axiom that two contradictory propositions cannot both be true. Of course, these are not like the laws of physics in the sense that people can fall into contradictions, make mistakes, and violate the law of contradiction without the ceiling falling in. The laws of reason will not administer a sanction comparable to the effects visited at once, say, on the person who steps out of a window in a high-rise building, determined to act out his defiance of the laws of gravity. But then what makes these "laws of reason" into "laws"? The direct answer was: they are laws because they have the sovereign attribute, not only of being true, but of being true of necessity. One cannot contradict these laws without falling into contradiction. Therefore, the laws of reason command our respect, or our adherence, simply and solely because they are true, or valid. They therefore hold as laws, as Kant said, for any "rational creature as such."

To take an example I have used before, we might imagine a judge who confronts the accused and says, "Jones, you have been acquitted; therefore, I sentence you to twenty years."[11] The judge has fallen into a serious contradiction. He has recorded the judgment of Jones's acquittal—that Jones was found innocent, undeserving of punishment. And yet the judge goes on to prescribe punishment nevertheless. The ceiling does not come crashing down on the judge for this. But the judge, acting in the domain of freedom, has made a profound mistake: he has violated a law of reason, and on the basis of that mistake he has inflicted a harm. Landslides inflict harms, but we do not hold the landslides responsible or think that we find, in these events, a "moral" fault. Not everything that causes a harm is a matter of moral significance. We locate the moral world in that domain where actors, fueled by motives, tailor means to ends and inflict harms. When we cast judgments, we are appealing to those deeper laws of reason that give us propositions with a necessary force, and a ground then for pronouncing on the things that people ought or ought not do.

Kant once remarked that everything that has standing as a principle in the domain of morals could be derived from the very logic of a rational being as such.[12] We could restate the point in the following way. Every

---

[11] See my "The Right to Die—Again," in Michael M. Uhlmann, ed., *Last Rights: Assisted Suicide and Euthanasia Debated* (Grand Rapids, MI: Eerdmans, 1998), 95–110.

[12] Immanuel Kant, *Groundwork of the Metaphysics of Morals* [1785], trans. H. J. Paton (New York: Harper and Row, 1948), 120 (Academy pp. 452–53).

principle of judgment, in the domain of moral judgment, can be drawn from the conjunction of these two propositions: (1) that in some parts of our lives, at least, we are "free," with the freedom to choose our own course of action; and (2) that in making a practical judgment, we have access to the laws of reason in establishing that the maxim underlying our act is true or false. These ingredients may be considered true *a priori*, in the sense that they are true of necessity: neither of these two can be denied without falling into contradiction. The one who would deny our freedom would assert, by implication, his own freedom to resist our argument. And the man who pronounces our second proposition wrong—the one who denies that we have access to the laws of reason—must himself appeal to standards of judgment outside ourselves, something separate from our subjective feelings, to pronounce this argument right or wrong. He speaks prose, then, without knowing it; he appeals to the laws of reason even as he would deny them.[13]

To restate, then, the sovereign point I would weave into the rest of this essay: What we call the principles of moral judgment are the "laws" that command our reason—that is, our motive for acting—in the domain of freedom, where we are free to choose our own course of action. They are, as Kant said, the "laws of reason," and they command our respect, in our practical judgments, mainly, decisively, because they are true of necessity, and therefore true in all places where the question can be posed. And one of the first axioms, or "first principles," drawn from this understanding was that we cast moral judgments only on "acts," taking place in the domain of freedom: we do not hold people blameworthy or responsible for acts they were powerless to affect. Or as the Scottish philosopher Thomas Reid put it, "what is done from unavoidable necessity . . . cannot be the object either of blame or moral approbation."[14] From this rather simple proposition may spring things as varied as the insanity defense; the ground of our laws on negligence; or the case against racial discrimination. That is to say, from a rather spare collection of axioms, some

---

[13] These two components can be brought together in several different sentences that say essentially the same thing, and so one of Kant's may serve just as well: "Act on that maxim that is fit to be installed as a universal law." The sentence, cast as a form of imperative, has as its subject the implied "you" or "anyone." The subject of the sentence, then, is a person, or rational agent, operating in the domain of freedom. But from that subject we cannot extract, as a necessary implication, a person who is seeking to accord the maxim behind his act with a law of reason, a law fit to be installed as a universal rule. To put it another way, the predicate here cannot be drawn as an implication of the subject in the way that the predicate can in the statement "a triangle has three sides." And so, Kant's statement conjoining the two points does not constitute an "analytic" statement. It is, then, a "synthetic" statement, which brings together things not implied in each other. Therefore, the statement is at once synthetic and *a priori*, for it is a statement about the way in which the world is arranged, and it is rooted in propositions that are true of necessity.

[14] Thomas Reid, *Essays on the Active Powers of the Human Mind* (1788; reprint, Cambridge, MA: MIT Press, 1969), 361. And for a fuller exposition of the understanding sketched out in these pages, see my own book, *First Things* (Princeton, NJ: Princeton University Press, 1986), chaps. 4, 5, 8.

rather momentous implications may flow, explaining large portions of our law.

I bother to make these points in some detail because we find even conservative writers falling into the habit of laying out "theories" of jurisprudence, and placing "natural rights" or natural law within that list of theories. Subtly, the writer may incorporate the premises of relativism: we have a variety of contending moral "theories," each based on premises slightly different, and the implication is that none of them, really, has a clear claim to be regarded as truer than any of the others.

But on the other hand, the presentation of the different theories of jurisprudence may point in a notably different direction. If we are faced with the task of choosing among the contending theories, we are pushed back to some deeper standards of judgment, standards that can tell us just which theory strikes us as more or less persuasive, more or less consistent, more or less afflicted with logical mistakes, and hence more or less true. The problem of choice may merely direct us to the laws of reason, those deeper canons of logic that offer guidance in making choices here or anywhere else. The point that seems to come as a surprise to many people in the law is that once we have reached this deeper stratum, this deeper ground in the principles of judgment, we have finally reached the ground of the natural law, for we have reached those "laws of reason" that anchor all of our practical judgments.

The irony of the problem, then, may be stated in this way: If a writer starts by telling us of theories of natural law, while suggesting that there is no ground of reason for choosing among them, he is not offering us a dispassionate survey; he is beginning by ruling out the very validity, and possibility, of natural law. To the extent that people offer theories with the hope of choosing among them, they seem to lose the recognition that "natural law" is not to be found anywhere in the list they assemble. It is to be found, rather, in those deeper standards of judgment they would draw upon as they seek to make judgments about these rival theories. We might as aptly ask ourselves, Do we use syntax when we order coffee? We cannot seriously talk about the legal judgments that are justified or unjustified without using "the laws of reason," and when we back into the laws of reason, we are "doing" natural law.

IV. FACILE TRAPS: CLICHÉS OF THE LAW AND SELF-REFUTING PROPOSITIONS

As it happens, some of my best friends are positivists, and one of them happens to be a jurist of high standing in this country. For reasons of delicacy, we may simply refer to him here as the Conservative Jurist. He has posted the warning sounded often by positivists: namely, that there are contending moralities, and that the problem with natural law is that it does not elicit a universal acceptance. As the argument then goes, it would be necessary for the law to base itself on premises that enjoy a consensus right away, propositions that are widely accepted even if they may not be strictly true. This argument has been heard among liberals as well as conservatives: it has figured prominently in the writing of John Rawls (e.g., in *A Theory of Justice*[15]), and it has been picked up widely by liberal writers, usually as they stake out arguments against laws on abortion, or laws that impose any serious restriction on styles of sexuality. The premise is announced right away that we ought not legislate when the country is deeply divided, as it is on serious moral questions, and that therefore we should seek some ground of consensus before we legislate. In the meantime, the argument goes, we should be left free to follow our own, personal choices in any matter of moral controversy.

I have pointed out, in other places, that this argument is built on what philosophers would call a self-refuting proposition: namely, that in the absence of a consensus, or in the presence of a disagreement, there is no truth and therefore no valid propositions that would justify legislation.[16] I have made the simple point that I would myself object to *that* proposition, and by its own terms that should be enough to establish its falsity. The United States was deeply divided over slavery, and a hundred years later it was deeply divided over the Civil Rights Act of 1964. Are we to suppose that, under those conditions, it was somehow wrong for any of us to form moral judgments about slavery or racial discrimination, or deeply wrong to have legislated upon those judgments?

But I raise this matter for the sake of taking it from a slightly different angle, one expressed by my friend, the Conservative Jurist: that we do not have tenable grounds on which to legislate in the absence of a consensus. The question that the natural lawyer would raise at this point is, Do we have a consensus on *that* proposition—the proposition that we may not legislate in the absence of a consensus? Had the Conservative Jurist taken a survey and discovered that this rule of construction was itself voted in by the consensus of the public? If this is the claim, I would have to report that I never received my ballot. I would not have voted for this proposition, and it would not, then, have garnered a "consensus." But the question merely points up the fact that the Conservative Jurist himself did not derive this rule from any consensus achieved in any survey of the public. He offers this rule because he apparently thinks it valid on its own terms; that it is true *per se nota*. To borrow language from Hamilton, that proposition may

---

[15] The argument runs, as a strand, throughout Rawls's book, and it is especially prominent in the first chapter, when he sets in place the groundwork for his argument and explains the so-called "original position." See John Rawls, *A Theory of Justice* (Cambridge, MA: Harvard University Press, 1971), 5, 12, 16, 18, 21.

[16] See Arkes, *First Things*, 51, 132–37.

seem to the Jurist to "contain an internal evidence, which antecedent to all reflection or combination, commands the assent of the mind." In other words, the proposition is treated by the Jurist as though it has the properties of an axiom or a first principle. We have backed, once again, into speaking the language of natural law. I happen to think, of course, that my friend's construction of the first principle here cannot be tenable. Still, it is cheery to note that, on his construction, we would have access to certain truths that do not depend in the least on a consensus, or agreement, in the country. And if there is at least one proposition of that kind, which may form the ground of our judgments in the law, there seems to be a lively possibility of discovering others.

The philosopher Russell Hittinger would offer this other criticism of the position staked out by my friend the Jurist. If there is never a consensus on matters of morality, then we must be driven back to the interests or passions that we can count on all men possessing, quite detached from any moral sense. That interest will be, of course, the interest in self-preservation and the avoidance of pain. When the conservative jurists reject, out of hand, the prospect of knowing any "first principles" of a moral character, they too back into the notion of Hobbesian man. That calculating animal, detached from moral reflexes of any kind, becomes for the conservatives, no less than the liberals, the ground and the measure of our jurisprudence. In this way have conservative judges talked themselves out of the premises of natural rights—the premises of the American Founders, the premises underlying the Constitution they are applying— without being quite aware of it.

I have tried to suggest, then, to some of my friends among the judges that they have been speaking prose all their lives. They profess their dubiety about natural law, and yet they keep backing into rules of construction that are true in themselves, true apparently of necessity. They fall back upon the grounds of the natural law without being quite aware of it. But that does not mean that these people become practitioners of natural law. I would offer an account describing a rather more melancholy picture: precisely because some conservative commentators are radically unclear about the meaning of natural law, they may be taken in by arguments that should not claim their credulity, and they may be drawn off in directions that should not be taken by judges who call themselves conservative judges.

V. The Natural Law and the Positive Law

That problem draws us back to that question, at the beginning of the law, as to what exactly should be the relation between the natural law and the positive law. But there is an irony here that seems to have passed by many veterans seasoned in the law. On the one hand, it was understood in the past that the natural law provides the ground of the positive law.[17] We may find a regulation of the positive law posting speed limits on the highway, but what makes that positive law defensible is an antecedent principle that tells us why we may be justified in restraining people who hazard the lives of others through carelessness on the highways. In this construction, the natural law underlies and justifies the positive law, and the corollary is that a positive law that runs counter to the natural law simply cannot claim the name of law.

On the other hand, the tradition of natural law has also embraced an understanding of prudence, which can explain why we would be warranted in putting up with things that fall notably short of what the natural law would enjoin upon us. Aquinas taught us here that we cannot expect human beings to be converted into angels: we cannot expect that humans will be free from all vice, or that the law may reasonably seek to purge us of all moral imperfections. From this perspective, it may be necessary for the law to make an accommodation, say, with the evil of slavery, for the sake of putting it in "the course of ultimate extinction" while avoiding the bloodshed of a civil war.[18]

These two strands in the tradition of the natural law are reconcilable because natural law could tell us why something is in principle wrong, or wrong of necessity, but at the same time offer a certain room for statesmanship to operate in the name of prudence, so that statesmen might find a reasonable path toward achieving ends that are, in principle, rightful. What I want to take up in the balance of this essay, however, is that state of affairs in which the Constitution may incorporate propositions so wrong, so out of accord with the laws of reason themselves, that they present the most straining practical problem for statesmen who are trying to act rightly and yet sustain the Constitution. There are some recent cases, bearing on our politics, that pose this problem well, but I think I could make my way there more clearly if I drew us back to a striking case from earlier in our history.

---

[17] In this vein, see Story's opinion in the case of *United States v. The La Jeune Eugenie*, 2 Mason 409 (Mass. 1822).

[18] This was, of course, the very shape of Lincoln's policy as he sought to reject slavery in principle, while making an accommodation with it as an evil quite hard to dislodge without a civil war. Part of his policy was focused on the fugitive slave clause of the Constitution and on an agreement that he thought was "nominated in the bond" of the Constitution. In this arrangement, the free states agreed to return runaway slaves, while on the other hand, the foreign trade in slaves would be ended, and the expansion of slavery barred from the new territories of the United States. The supply of slaves would be blocked, as much as practicable, from the outside, and the expansion of slavery would be blocked within the country as well. These features marked the compromise, or the settlement, contained within the original Constitution. Lincoln thought that these features formed a design with a clear import to be read by succeeding generations: namely, that the Founders looked upon slavery as something wrong in principle—something to be restrained and discouraged, not something to be celebrated and promoted. Lincoln returned to the logic of that original settlement in his first inaugural address. See Roy P. Basler, ed., *The Collected Works of Abraham Lincoln* (New Brunswick, NJ: Rutgers University Press, 1953), 4:263–64, 268–69.

VI. Syllogisms and the Law I:
Lincoln and the Dred Scott Case

Let us return for a moment to the crisis of our "House divided," and to the senatorial debate between Lincoln and Douglas in 1858. One of the central themes running through these debates was the specter of the *Dred Scott* case.[19] That case, decided in 1857, gave rise to the crisis because it threatened to "nationalize" slavery and overturn the political settlement that had cabined or confined it. In *Dred Scott*, the Court had held that people could not be dispossessed of their property in slaves when they entered a territory of the United States; the Court invoked then the Fifth Amendment and the protections against depriving people of their property "without due process of law." In the course of the debates with Douglas, Lincoln warned that as a result of the *Dred Scott* decision, people in Illinois might go to sleep in a free state and then wake up to discover that they were now living, after all, in a slave state.

From Lincoln's comments we gather that this argument elicited from Douglas some rather disbelieving stares, suggesting contempt: the rejoinder from Douglas was that no serious person—that is to say, no member with real standing in the political class—would take seriously the possibility raised by Lincoln. After all, there were built-in limitations on that holding in *Dred Scott*. The decision applied only to people who traveled with their slaves into territories of the United States, not to people in the entities incorporated as states of the Union. The territories were solely under the governance of the Congress, and that was what had made the due process clause of the Fifth Amendment relevant to the case. For it was the established view at the time, recorded in cases like *Barron v. Baltimore* (1833), that the first eight amendments, or the Bill of Rights, were meant as restraints solely on the federal government.[20] In the understanding of the time, the constraints of those amendments did not apply at all to the states. And so Douglas could affect his deep disbelief when Lincoln suggested that the principle in the *Dred Scott* case could readily be carried over and applied to the states as well. But it was perhaps this affectation of disbelief, this gesture of incredulity, that moved Lincoln to put the problem to Douglas, as he said, "in syllogistic form": "I submit," he said, "to the consideration of men capable of arguing, whether as I state it in syllogistic form the argument has any fault in it."[21] He then set forth the argument in this way:

Major premise: "Nothing in the Constitution or laws of any State can destroy a right distinctly and expressly affirmed

---

[19] *Dred Scott v. Sandford*, 60 U.S. 393 (1857).

[20] *Barron v. Baltimore*, 32 U.S. 243 (1833).

[21] Abraham Lincoln, in the fifth debate with Douglas, at Galesburg, IL, October 7, 1858, in Basler, ed., *Collected Works of Abraham Lincoln*, 3:231.

in the Constitution of the United States." (This is simply a restatement of the supremacy clause of the Constitution, which states that the Constitution, and the laws made under it, shall be "the supreme Law of the Land," nothing in "the Constitution or Laws of any State to the Contrary notwithstanding.")

Minor premise: "The right of property in a slave is distinctly and expressly affirmed in the Constitution of the United States[.]" (This is the holding of the *Dred Scott* case.)

Conclusion: "Therefore, nothing in the Constitution or laws of any State can destroy the right of property in a slave."[22]

Lincoln's argument here may awaken us to the recollection that there were other sources of rights apart from the Fifth Amendment. There was, for example, the original privileges and immunities clause,[23] a clause that Lincoln thought could be the source of protection for Black people apprehended in the North and accused of being runaway slaves. If there really was, as the Court insisted in *Dred Scott*, a right not to be dispossessed of property in slaves, a right secured in the Constitution, then that right could easily be attached to other clauses in the Constitution, which could serve just as well as vehicles for that constitutional right. When Lincoln framed the problem as a syllogism, he knew that he was drawing upon the full logic of the syllogism: if the premises were sound and the reasoning accurate, then the conclusion would flow with the force of logical necessity. As far as I can see, that argument he put to Douglas "in syllogistic form" was in fact unbreakable, unassailable.

Douglas could have testified, in all sincerity, that he and other members of the political class simply did not "see" what the syllogism reveals— and that they would never draw that conclusion. But I take Lincoln's argument to be that the syllogism holds nevertheless: Douglas and his friends might profess not to see what it reveals, but two or three steps later, two or three years later, they may suddenly come to see things in a different way, especially if their interests begin to point in that direction. At that moment, as Lincoln suggested, the people resisting the *Dred Scott* case and the nationalization of slavery would have no tenable ground of objection—if they accepted, without complaint, this first step with the premise planted in the *Dred Scott* case.

For the sake of being fastidious, I should point out that there is a blending here of axioms of our reasoning, along with axioms that arise

---

[22] Each of these quotations can be found at ibid.
[23] U.S. Constitution, art. 4, sec. 2.

only from the character of the American Constitution. In the case of Lincoln, the axioms of reasoning were found in the canons of propositional logic—the canons that confirmed to us that the connections among the propositions were apt, and that the conclusions would apply to all relevant cases. But Lincoln was also weaving in here the logic of the American Constitution. The supremacy clause reflected, after all, the logic of the decision in 1787 to create a genuine national government in place of a confederacy. As Hamilton showed in *Federalist No. 31*—in one of his distinctive flourishes—the logic of the supremacy clause would have been there even if it had not been made explicit in the text of the Constitution.[24] It was simply implicit in the very idea of "law" binding all persons and subsidiary associations within its territory.[25] Lincoln's argument would not have held if the Articles of Confederation had stayed in place; but at the same time, there would have been no prospect of a supreme court or national legislature imposing a policy of slavery on any of the constituent states, whether to abolish slavery or to counter a decision to prohibit slavery. The Supreme Court was able to engage the logic of a *national* government in securing the right to possess slaves even when venturing out of one's home state. Lincoln's argument could not have been countered, then, by calling into question the features of the Constitution that defined a national republic, for any argument of that kind would have worked even more surely against the argument for protecting slavery.

VII. Syllogisms and the Law II: *Chisholm v. George* and the Eleventh Amendment

And so, even though Lincoln's argument mixed the "laws of reason" with the distinct principles of the American Constitution, there was nothing in that mixture that impaired the force of his argument, especially when it was run through the medium of the syllogism. I would suggest that the same things could be said, with the same force, about the blendings we find in the opinions written by Justice James Wilson and Chief Justice John Jay in that classic case of *Chisholm v. Georgia*, in 1793, the first case that elicited a set of opinions from the Supreme Court.[26] It was also the case that was overridden almost at once with the passage of the Eleventh Amendment in 1795, which shored up a certain sovereign im-

[24] In art. 6, sec. 2.
[25] "The intended government would be precisely the same," he wrote, "if these clauses were entirely obliterated. . . . They are only declaratory of a truth which would have resulted by necessary and unavoidable implication from the very act of constituting a federal government, and vesting it with certain specified powers." See *Federalist No. 31* (Hamilton), in *The Federalist Papers*, 198–99.
[26] *Chisholm v. Georgia*, 2 Dallas 419 (1793).

munity for the states.[27] Savvy observers of the Supreme Court have been contending that if there is any legacy of the Rehnquist Court of recent years, or anything that finally connects Justice Anthony Kennedy with Justice Antonin Scalia, it is the interest in firming anew the features of federalism. In this vein, the Court has insisted recently on putting some limitations on the reach of Congress under the commerce clause.[28] But in a recent train of striking cases, the Court seems to have strengthened the grounds of federalism even further by taking seriously again the Eleventh Amendment.[29] For that amendment seems to bolster the authority of the states by setting in place, as an anchoring point, that a state may have a residue of sovereign immunity—that it may not be sued in its own courts, or in a federal court, by a private litigant, without its consent.

That a state may be sued by another state is a condition that seems to be implicit in statehood, in international affairs as well as under the American Constitution. But that the controversy between two states should not be heard in the courts of either state—that it should be heard, rather, in the more impartial tribunal of a *federal* court—*is* a reflection distinctly of the American Constitution. Yet even there, we might add, this arrangement depends on an even deeper principle of the natural law, namely, that no man or state should be a judge in his (or its) own cause. This arrangement of the American Constitution flows so clearly because it seems so eminently fair and reasonable, and it strikes us in that way because our understanding is governed here by principles that are not distinctly American.

From these principles, so seemingly clear on their face, the Supreme Court was able to construct its decision in *Chisholm v. Georgia.* The Court decided on that occasion that there was no such thing as "sovereign immunity" for a state in this sense: a state cannot refuse to make itself responsible for defending its policies in a lawsuit brought by a *private litigant.* The political class received this decision and reacted decisively: within two years, the Eleventh Amendment was passed, and that amendment barred the federal courts from accepting lawsuits brought by private litigants against a state. The recent decisions invoking the Eleventh Amendment have been taken as a singular achievement of the "conservative" justices, but these decisions depend critically on the assumption that there was nothing really compelling, or even mildly interesting, in the opinions brought forth by Wilson or Jay at the beginning, in *Chisholm*

---

[27] The Eleventh Amendment provides that "[t]he Judicial power of the United States shall not be construed to extend to any suit in law or equity, commenced or prosecuted against one of the United States by citizens of another State, or by Citizens or Subjects of any Foreign State."

[28] See, as a notable example, *United States v. Lopez,* 514 U.S. 549 (1995).

[29] The cases were announced to the public in June 1999, to the deep disbelief of liberals and the mild bewilderment of conservatives: *Alden v. Maine,* 527 U.S. 706 (1999), affirming 715 A.2d 172; *College Savings Bank v. Florida Prepaid Postsecondary Education Expense Board,* 527 U.S. 666 (1999), affirming 131 F.3d 353; *Florida Prepaid Postsecondary Education Expense Board v. College Savings Bank,* 527 U.S. 627 (1999), reversing and remanding 148 F.3d 1343.

v. Georgia. But what if Wilson and Jay got it right that day in the same way that Lincoln, in his syllogism, got it right? What if they too produced a judgment in syllogistic form, with the same claim to a necessary force, so that we could truly say here that Wilson and Jay not only got it right, but got it *inescapably* right? If that is the case, then the Eleventh Amendment would stand as an incoherence, as a grand non sequitur, even though it is contained in the positive law of the Constitution. In that event, a grand conservative scheme of jurisprudence that has brought forth, in a prominent place, a revival of the Eleventh Amendment, may show itself before long to be a project freighted with dramaturgy and soaring sentiments, but in the end, entirely barren of substance.

In the legends that surround *Chisholm v. Georgia,* the case is bound up with all of those controversies that arose, quite expectedly, in the aftermath of the revolution in America. Tories or loyalists had to flee; their land was often confiscated, and when peace was restored, the former owners sought to recover their property. Or at least, that was the prospect that worried the political class as its members reacted to the decision in *Chisholm* and sought to gauge the interests of their own that might be imperiled by it. But *Chisholm* itself did not involve these dramas of defection and recovery: it was a far more prosaic case, and far more reflective of the kinds of issues that were bound to recur in our law. Robert Farquhar, a citizen of South Carolina, had furnished supplies to Georgia during the revolution. The authorities of the state had appropriated the funds necessary to pay its vendors, but the commissaries in Georgia had failed to pay for the purchases. Farquhar died, but his heirs simply pressed a suit quite familiar: a person seeks the honoring of a contract on the part of a state, and he goes to court for the sake of vindicating the real interests and injuries he has at stake. The Supreme Court found this to be an eminently plausible—and even compelling—claim, and had no difficulty in deciding in favor of Farquhar's heir, Chisholm. And that was the decision that the political class moved immediately to override, in a sentiment that swept far too easily among that first union of states, clustered on the eastern seaboard.

In the recent run of cases dealing with the Eleventh Amendment, the conservative justices took it as a settled fact that the amendment had overridden *Chisholm v. Georgia,* and so they treated the opinions in that case as discredited. Apparently, nothing had flagged to them that Wilson and Jay had been doing anything in their opinions that ran to the root—to the principles that would be necessary for anything that called itself "jurisprudence." Yet the signs were all about. For one thing, as noted earlier, this was the first case that elicited a full array of opinions by members of the Court. Wilson expressed the awareness that was evidently present among his colleagues, that they were at the beginning here of the American law. They could draw upon no precedents that had sprung from the experience of law under the Constitution. As Wilson explained then, it was necessary to set some first principles into place. Before Wilson would speak about the text of the Constitution, he would speak about "the principles of general jurisprudence." But even before that, something else had to be set in order: before the Court would begin expounding the principles of legal judgment, Wilson found it necessary to acknowledge something of the laws of reason and "the philosophy of mind." And so, before Wilson invoked the authority of any case at law or any commentator on matters jural, he invoked the authority of "Dr. [Thomas] Reid, in his excellent inquiry into the human mind, on the principles of *common sense*, speaking of the sceptical and illiberal philosophy, which under bold, but false pretensions to liberality, prevailed in many parts of Europe before he wrote."[30]

Wilson began, then, by rejecting "scepticism" as the fount of all forms of relativism in morality and law. In that vein, he took the occasion to point out that the law in America would be planted on an entirely different ground from that of the law in England. That law in England, made familiar by Blackstone, began with the notion of a sovereign issuing commands. But the law in America, wrote Wilson, would begin "with another principle, very different in its nature and operations":

> [L]aws derived from the pure source of equality and justice must be founded on the consent of those, whose obedience they require. The sovereign, when traced to his source, must be found in the *man*.[31]

In his slightly earlier lectures on jurisprudence (in 1790), Wilson had already made it clear why the rejection of positivism, or the rule of a superior, was bound up with the premises of natural right. Wilson had pointed out that there were circumstances under which the rule of a superior was eminently justified, most notably, with the rule of "Him who is supreme." But among the sublunary beings, those beings somewhere between the angels and beasts, there could be, said Wilson, "neither superiority nor dependence."[32]

Wilson observed that the very term "sovereignty" was bound up with feudalism and the notion of a lord or sovereign. But that notion had little application to a polity founded on the consent of those ordinary men who constitute the political community. And indeed, once that understanding was put into place, the notions of "sovereign" and "state" were transformed. What we now call a state is a political association, an association of "sovereign" persons, sovereign in the sense of bearing the right to govern themselves. If one asks how a state, or an association of persons,

---

[30] *Chisholm*, 2 Dallas at 453–54.
[31] Ibid., at 458, italics mine.
[32] James Wilson, "Of the Law of Nature," in James DeWitt Andrews, ed., *The Works of James Wilson* (Chicago: Callaghan and Co., 1896), 1:96.

can bind itself, the answer is: on the same ground that any one person can bind himself, can recognize a law beyond himself, and understand the possibility that he may be called to account by this law in a court. And so, as Wilson wrote, "if one free man, an original sovereign, may do all of this"—may bind himself to the law—then "why may not an aggregate of free men, a collection of original sovereigns, do this likewise?"[33]

Chief Justice Jay took the same problem from another angle, but applying the same premises: namely, that there was not, in the United States, a natural superior and a natural "subject," or "one citizen inferior to another."[34] In that event, it was plain that "one free citizen may sue another" who is the source of injuries. But on that ground, he may sue "any number on whom process can be conveniently executed"—if that aggregation of men may be charged with an offense. Conceivably, then, said Jay, he may sue "forty thousand; for where a corporation is sued, all the members of it are *actually* sued, though not *personally*, sued."[35] In other words, a single person could sue the forty thousand persons who composed the city of Philadelphia. The state of Delaware, next door, had a population of fifty thousand. Did it make sense that a person, a citizen of the United States, could sue Philadelphia but not Delaware? As Jay asked, tellingly, "Can the difference between forty odd thousand, and fifty odd thousand make any distinction as to right?"[36]

Jay found, in the Constitution, or in logic, no such incompatibility between the right to sue the forty thousand who constituted Philadelphia and the right to sue the fifty thousand who constituted the polity of Delaware. And from that point, he sought to deepen his argument in this way:

> There is at least one strong undeniable fact against this incompatibility, and that is this, any one State in the Union may sue another State, in this Court, that is, all the people of one State may sue all the people of another State. It is plain then, that a State may be sued, and hence it plainly follows, that suability and State sovereignty are not incompatible.... But why it should be more incompatible, that all the people of a State should be sued by one citizen, than by one hundred thousand, I cannot perceive, the process in both cases being alike; and the consequences of a judgment alike.[37]

From this perspective, the notion of one state suing another was altered dramatically as it was read through the premises of a government founded

[33] *Chisholm*, 2 Dallas at 456.
[34] Ibid., at 472.
[35] Ibid.
[36] Ibid.
[37] Ibid., at 473.

on the consent of the governed. For to say then that one state may sue another—that Delaware may sue Pennsylvania—was to say that "all" of the citizens who constitute Delaware may sue "all" of those citizens who make up Pennsylvania. And if "all" may sue "all," then Jay suggested, in the style of a syllogism, that "one" of those members comprehended in the "all" may then sue the "all" who constitute the other state.

Well, not quite. Jay might have been right most of the way, but he may have slipped here into a problem of misplaced quantifiers or categories. If the forty thousand who make up Philadelphia may sue the fifty thousand who make up Delaware, why may not the several hundred thousand who make up the city of Haifa sue the state of Delaware, or a citizen of Haifa sue Delaware? As a colleague of mine puts it, it does not follow that if the United States may declare war on Germany that any one citizen, helping to form the polity of the United States, could be free, on his own, to declare war on Germany.[38] But here we run again into the problem mentioned earlier in regard to Lincoln: the argument must build in a recognition of the way in which the problem is affected by the principles and arrangements of the Constitution, or by the presence of different polities, that is, distinct jural entities. Jay himself recognized that his argument would have to be modified for these reasons, for he was not apparently persuaded that it would sustain the right of a citizen to sue the United States. And that was not because there was anything defective in the moral argument, but because of the practical constraints he found in the arrangement of the constitutional order:

> [I]n all cases of actions against States or individual citizens, the National Courts are supported in all their legal and Constitutional proceedings and judgments, by the arm of the Executive power of the United States; but in cases of actions against the United States, there is no power which the Courts can call to their aid. From this distinc-

---

[38] My friend Daniel Robinson offered me this further word of caution in a piece of personal correspondence: "Kripke's *Naming and Necessity* made out a strong and famous case for proper names being *rigid designators* in ways that descriptions are not. They are 'rigid' in that they are unaffected by radical alterations in the context of their use. Thus, what is picked out by 'Napoleon' is rigid in a way that descriptions of the sort, 'was born in Corsica' is not. The argument underlying this requires a logical status for 'Philadelphia' radically different from the status of 'all now living within the following lines of longitude and latitude.'"

In the case of political entities, these kinds of confusions may be deepened. Robinson put it with his usual succinctness, and comic genius:

> Suppose we advance the proposition that a and b are identities, where a = "Delaware" and b = "everyone now alive and living in the territorial space designated as "Delaware." ... Just in case those comprising the set b pick up one night and *en masse* relocate in the territorial space previously designated as "Paris"—whose occupants, for some reason, now think it best to pick up and relocate in Belgium—then $p = a$ where p once was the place-designator "Paris." Surely this doesn't work.

tion important conclusions are deducible, and they place the case of a State, and the case of the United States, in very different points of view.[39]

The structure of the American Constitution had to constrain or impair the working of Jay's syllogism. But even within that structure, his argument could still retain a syllogistic force, much in the style of Lincoln's argument about the logic of the *Dred Scott* decision. For as Jay pointed out, it was clear beyond cavil that under the Constitution, one state may sue another. And it was utterly clear from the logic of the Constitution that in a controversy of that kind, the cause could not be heard in the courts of one of the contending states. The dispute would therefore have to fall within the jurisdiction of the national courts.

The Constitution itself spoke of instances in which a state may be a "party" to a lawsuit in the federal courts. The attorney general, Edmund Randolph, acting here privately on behalf of Chisholm, observed that the term "party" contains the possibility that a state may be a defendant as well as a plaintiff. If not, why use an expression such as "party" instead of saying, persistently, "plaintiff"? As the Chief Justice then pointed out, a state could indeed be a *defendant* in a federal court by the very terms of the Constitution. If that was the case, why could a state not be a defendant in an action brought by an ordinary citizen? In pressing this argument, Jay could draw again—and draw persuasively—on those deeper premises that underlay the whole construction of a constitution built on the right of the people to govern themselves. And so, Jay could summon a certain moral leverage in noting that

> it would be strange, indeed, that the joint and equal sovereigns of this country, should, in the very Constitution by which they professed to establish justice, so far deviate from the plain path of equality and impartiality, as to give to the collective citizens of one State, a right of suing individual citizens of another State, and yet deny to those citizens a right of suing them.[40]

As the attorney general observed, the Constitution contained many guarantees of rights secured against the states: there was a ban on ex post facto laws and bills of attainder, there were provisions for habeas corpus and prohibitions on acts that impaired the obligation of contracts. But those provisions in the Constitution could be rendered into nullities if they could not be vindicated, in a court, by persons who were directly injured through the operation of these unconstitutional acts. To raise these points anew was to remind ourselves that the very logic of the

[39] *Chisholm*, 2 Dallas at 478.
[40] Ibid., at 477.

movement to a national government marked a shift away from the notion of a confederacy, in which the "citizens" were the states that composed the confederacy. As the writers of the Federalist papers made clear, the move to create, at the national level, a real government manifested itself in a government that could act directly on individuals.[41] And a government that could bypass the states in this way could also vindicate the injuries inflicted on individuals by the laws in any state. Madison had famously remarked during the Constitutional Convention that the movement to a new constitution was fueled by the assaults on private rights that were taking place within the separate states, at the hands of local governments, or with the acquiescence of the local authorities. "Interference[s] with these [private rights]," he said, "were the evils which had more perhaps than anything else, produced this convention."[42] In the first years of the new republic, the powers of the national government to intervene in the states had not been filled out, for they had barely been flexed. Yet they were contained in the logic of the Constitution, and time would bring out more fully what had been there from the beginning. From the beginning, that is, the Constitution comprehended the possibility that the national power would be engaged on the side of vindicating the rights of individuals against the breaches of justice within the separate states. That power was not exercised widely in this period by the legislative branch; it would be found mainly in the power of the federal courts. The doctrine of sovereign immunity had indeed been long planted, but it was hardly an unthinkable reach, or a move out of character with this new Constitution, to come to the judgment that was reached by Wilson, Jay, and their colleagues: the federal courts can vindicate the rights of individuals against states; the states may be parties to suit in federal courts, and individuals should therefore be able to vindicate their rights in federal courts when they suffer injuries, even at the hands of states other than their own.

I would argue, then, that in this classic first case, Wilson and Jay offered an exemplary lesson in tracing matters back to first principles; and even if one built in a proper limitation for the framework of the Constitution, their arguments, within that framework, had a syllogistic force that could

---

[41] In the *Federalist No. 39*, Madison had taken care to explain the distinctions engaged here:

> The difference between a federal and national government, as it relates to the *operation of the government*, is supposed to consist in this, that in the former the powers operate on the political bodies composing the Confederacy, in their political capacities; in the latter, on the individual citizens composing the nation, in their individual capacities. . . . [This] operation of the government on the people, in their individual capacities, in its ordinary and most essential proceedings, may, on the whole, designate it, in this relation, a *national* government.

Federalist No. 39 (Madison), in *The Federalist Papers*, 248.

[42] See Madison's notes for June 6, 1787, in Farrand, ed., *Records of the Federal Convention of 1787*, 1:133–34.

not simply be evaded or waved aside. Yet the political class looked at this decision and recoiled. They would have none of it, for they certainly wished to have no vexing business of their states being sued by former loyalists. The response was not merely to say "No, we don't accept that judgment"; the recoil was carried all the way into a constitutional amendment. The Eleventh Amendment would provide that "the Judicial power of the United States shall not be construed to extend to any suit in law or equity, commenced or prosecuted against one of the United States by Citizens of another State, or by Citizens or Subjects of any Foreign State."

VIII. THE ENIGMA OF THE ELEVENTH AMENDMENT

It must stand as one of the deep ironies in the recent cases on the Eleventh Amendment that among the justices, only David Souter has bothered to recall the reasoning of the judges and advocates in *Chisholm* — and not because he wishes us all to appreciate again the natural law reasoning that made those opinions compelling. Souter, as a devotee of Justice Holmes, does not have the slightest respect for natural law, and he uses these cases rather as an occasion to twit his colleagues. With as much merriment as his soul can summon, he has accused his colleagues of conjuring up a "natural law" argument in support of the "sovereign immunity" of states, running well beyond anything in the Eleventh Amendment.[43] This was a charge his colleagues seemed to find baffling, since most of them have little truck with natural law. As far as they are concerned, the Eleventh Amendment is part of the positive law of the Constitution, and they are trying to make sense of it. They assume that the opinions of Jay and Wilson have been displaced, and they seem remarkably inattentive then to the possibility that anything in the natural law reasoning of those opinions might still be valid.

But if my reading is accurate, the arguments set down by Wilson and Jay were not only plausible at the time or plausible generally, but inescapably right under the logic of the Constitution—and their judgment would be as right today as it was when it was handed down. What then would we make of the Eleventh Amendment—and its revival, to the applause of conservatives, in our own day? If my own judgment is right, then the attempts of the justices in subsequent years to construe the Eleventh Amendment were destined to exhibit a pattern of bewilderment and futility. In one notable aside, in a case in 1890, Justice Harlan seemed to lift his head from the puzzle and opine that he thought the Court had

---

[43] See, most notably, his dissenting opinion in *Alden*, 527 U.S. at 760. I surmise that it is Souter's accounts reviewing the winding jurisprudence of the Eleventh Amendment that inspired a remarkably tart rejoinder from Scalia: in *College Savings Bank* he complained of "the now-fashionable revisionist accounts of the Eleventh Amendment set forth in other opinions in a degree of repetitive detail that has despoiled our northern woods." *College Savings Bank*, 527 U.S. at 688.

actually gotten it right in the first place in *Chisholm*.[44] But if the judges found themselves straining their wit trying to make sense of the Eleventh Amendment, the project became even more maddening—it became immanently implausible—in the aftermath of the Fourteenth Amendment.

For with the Fourteenth Amendment, the national government was empowered, even more explicitly, to counter the policies of a state that denied the due process or equal protection of the laws. In our own time, the controversy over the extension of federal power would come to center on the problem of how the national government would reach directly to the wrongs committed by private persons. As students of the law constantly reminded themselves, the Fourteenth Amendment was concentrated on the actions of states ("No State shall . . ."), and so it could not reach to the problem of racial discrimination in private establishments, such as Ollie's Barbecue in Birmingham, Alabama. But no one doubted that the Fourteenth Amendment readily reached, with the Civil Rights Act of 1866, those offenses committed "under color of law." These offenses might be lawless acts performed by sheriffs, but the federal law could reach them because they involved harms that people were distinctly placed to commit because they were acting with the authority of the law, as agents of the state.[45]

In that event, the federal government would enforce the Fourteenth Amendment by directing prosecutions at officers of the states who were acting improperly under the cover of authority, or enforcing the policies of the state. Clearly, the aim of these prosecutions or lawsuits was not to hold these officials responsible as private persons for the wrongs they committed in pursuing their own, private ends. For many years, those kinds of concerns were obviated as the common law accumulated understandings of personal immunity, at first for executives, then for judges, and then a kind of parliamentary immunity for legislators. If people in office could be held personally liable for the injuries that may be cast up in the workings of the law, then almost no one could afford to serve. As Justice Robert Jackson observed in one of his notable aphorisms, "it is not a tort for the government to govern."[46]

Hence, a federal judge in Ohio in the early 1970s had good reason to conclude that a lawsuit brought against Governor Rhodes of that state, for a violation of civil rights, could not have been an action for *personal* damages. Rhodes had called in the Ohio National Guard during the troubles at Kent State University in that "Cambodian spring" of 1970. In the en-

---

[44] *Hans v. Louisiana*, 134 U.S. 1, 38–39 (1890).

[45] But even this was a stretch. Jurists like Felix Frankfurter held for many years to the narrowest reading of the Fourteenth Amendment, expressed by Lyman Trumbull. On this reading, the Civil Rights Act of 1866 was directed against those "who were not punishable by state law precisely because they acted in obedience to unconstitutional State law and by State law justified their action." Trumbull, quoted by Frankfurter in *Screws v. United States*, 314 U.S. 160, 182 (1946).

[46] *Dalehite v. United States*, 346 U.S. 15, 57 (1953).

counter between the students and the guardsmen, tempers flared, vio-
lence erupted, and several students were killed. The governor was then sued
by parents of some of the students, who claimed that the governor bore
responsibility for the incontinent acts of guardsmen, because he had called
them forth. The judge in the federal district court thought that the case was
really a complaint then about the decisions made by men in authority in
Ohio. But in that case, the judge thought that the suit had to be dismissed
at the threshold, because it ran against the Eleventh Amendment.

A somewhat surprised Supreme Court overrode this dismissal in the case
of *Scheuer v. Rhodes* (1974), and Chief Justice Burger made what should have
been the obvious point, that a reading of that kind would make a nullity
of the Fourteenth Amendment. Under the rationale of the district court, federal courts would be barred from entertaining civil suits brought by private litigants claiming that their civil rights had been violated by people
armed with official authority, acting as agents of the state.[47]

It might be said, then, on one commonsense reading of the problem,
that the Fourteenth Amendment had essentially superceded the Eleventh.
And that may explain, as much as anything else, why the Eleventh Amendment went into a kind of eclipse after the Fourteenth Amendment was
ratified: it was still on the books, but rarely mentioned and rarely a factor
in the judgments of the Court. But I would be inclined myself to suggest,
in addition, that on this point the Fourteenth Amendment simply made
explicit what had been implicit in the logic of the national government all
along. The opinions of Wilson and Jay in the *Chisholm* case might by seen,
by some, to become plausible again with the Fourteenth Amendment; but
what made them seem *compelling* again were the reasons that should have
made them compelling the day they were written.

Still, in *Scheuer v. Rhodes*, the Chief Justice had been reluctant to conclude that the Eleventh Amendment had been overridden by the Fourteenth. He sought to recall then the ways in which the Court had tried to
reconcile the two amendments in the past. The precedent that sprang
most readily to mind for him was *Ex parte Young* (1908), and the opinion
written by Justice Rufus Peckham.[48] That case involved regulation of
railroads and rates in Minnesota, and it offered some juicy questions of
this kind: Were the rates set so low that they were virtually confiscatory?
Did the regulation, ostensibly focused on intrastate commerce, overflow
into an interference with interstate commerce? The Court found a field
rich in possible violations of the Constitution,[49] and it refused to shelter
the officers of the state from a legal challenge by bringing down the

---

[47] See *Scheuer v. Rhodes*, 416 U.S. 232, 237, 243 (1974).

[48] *Ex parte Young*, 209 U.S. 123 (1908).

[49] The case also raised these other questions with a constitutional edge: Did the state
attach such penalties to a challenge in the courts that they virtually removed the equal
protection of the laws and the right to seek access to the courts? And could a stockholder get
an injunction to enjoin an officer of the state from enforcing such a ruinous policy?

screen of the Eleventh Amendment. Sixty-six years later, Chief Justice Burger would draw this lesson, quoting from Peckham:

> [W]hen a state officer acts under state law in a manner violative of the Federal Constitution, he comes into conflict with the superior authority of that Constitution, and he is in that case stripped of his official or representative character and is subjected in his person to the consequences of his individual conduct. The State has no power to impart to him any immunity from responsibility to the supreme authority of the United States.[50]

What Peckham had done was to restate that critical axiom of moral judgment, used tellingly by Aquinas, Lincoln, and James Wilson: that there cannot be a "right to do a wrong." In the hands of Wilson, that axiom brought home to us that, when the government restrained our freedom to murder, steal, or rape, it restricted us in nothing that we ever had the rightful freedom to do. For not even in the state of nature did we ever have the "right to do a wrong."[51] In the same way, Peckham suggested that the Eleventh Amendment could not possibly insulate officials in the state from charges, quite plausible, that they had violated the federal Constitution. The persons faced with real injuries as a result of those unconstitutional acts must have the freedom to use the courts to protect their rights. And when their rights are vindicated, there is not the slightest infringement on the sovereignty of a state, for *the state would not be restricted in anything it ever really had the right to do.*

This construction makes, I think, eminent sense, but it also makes a shambles of the Eleventh Amendment. For the assumption, deeply installed, is that these challenges against officials of a state may be brought into a federal court, where federal judges can ponder the merits of the claims and decide whether the Eleventh Amendment is being invoked aptly or improperly. But this is to say, in effect, that the federal courts are receiving suits brought by private litigants against a state. If the Eleventh Amendment were taken seriously, however, the suit would be cut off at the threshold, dismissed for want of jurisdiction. The decisive authority would then rest in the hands of the state as it ponders whether to invoke or waive its sovereign immunity.[52]

---

[50] *Ex parte Young*, 209 U.S. at 159–60, quoted by Burger in *Scheuer*, 416 U.S. at 237.

[51] Blackstone had remarked, in Book I of his *Commentaries*, that "the law, which restrains a man from doing mischief to his fellow citizens, though it diminishes the natural, increases the civil liberty of mankind[.]" To that observation, Wilson responded with a simple question: "Is it part of natural liberty," he asked, "to do mischief to anyone?" James Wilson, "Of the Natural Rights of Individuals," in *The Works of James Wilson*, ed. Robert Green McCloskey (Cambridge, MA: Harvard University Press, 1967), 2:587.

[52] In a counterpoint to this argument, Chief Justice Marshall had held that it was no violation of the Eleventh Amendment for a federal court to inquire into the merits of a lawsuit in the first place, in judging whether there is a ground to sustain the action. See *Cohens v. Virginia*, 6 Wheaton 264, 410 (1821).

Whether Peckham meant it or not, I take his judgment in *Ex parte Young* to mean nothing other than the fact that the Court takes a certain notice of the Eleventh Amendment, but treats it as a non sequitur: the amendment remains on the books as a kind of relic, but it would no longer have any practical or defensible application. And yet, to come to this recognition is to come back essentially to the original way that John Marshall, with his own genius, managed to construe—and finesse—the amendment in 1824. The case was *Osborn v. President and Directors of the Bank of the United States.*[53] Ralph Osborn was the auditor of Ohio, who had sought to enforce a policy of the state, imposing taxes on all banks and corporations. In line with that policy, the state insisted on taxing the Bank of the United States. But as the Supreme Court had held much earlier, instrumentalities of the federal government could not be taxed by the states, for they could then be countered or even destroyed by the states. Still, it was contended by the state that the rights engaged here, on the part of the Bank and its directors, could not be vindicated in a lawsuit directed against the state or its officers, for that would be a violation of the Eleventh Amendment.

As Marshall reflected on the problem, he observed that this kind of reasoning could undo every function of the federal government: "The carrier of the mail, the collector of the revenue, the marshal of a district . . . may all be inhibited, under ruinous penalties, from the performance of their respective duties."[54] As Marshall noted, there were disputes between states over their boundaries, and those disputes came within the jurisdiction of the Supreme Court. But suppose, said Marshall, that "the collecting officer of one State should seize property for taxes belonging to a man who suppose himself to reside in the other State, and who seeks redress in the federal Court of that State in which the officer resides."[55] The powers set forth in the Constitution would be nullified if this person could not have access to the federal courts in vindicating his claims.

Then how could all of this be reconciled with the Eleventh Amendment? The amendment was an exercise of the positive law, and Marshall was disposed to honor it with the narrowest reading of the positive law: a state would not be considered a party to a suit unless the state were the party of record. In the case at hand, the suit was directed at Osborn as an agent of the state. But if anything could be clear in this world, it should have been clear that this lawsuit was not a personal action, directed against Osborn as a private person. Yet Marshall reasoned in this way:

> [I]f the person who is the real principal, the person who is the true source of the mischief, by whose power and for whose advantage it

[53] *Osborn v. President and Directors of the Bank of the United States,* 22 U.S. 738 (1824).
[54] Ibid., at 847–48.
[55] Ibid., at 854.

is done, be himself above the law, be exempt from all judicial process, it would be subversive of the best-established principles to say that the laws could not afford the same remedies against the agent employed in doing the wrong which they would afford against him could his principal be joined in the suit.[56]

Marshall's colleague, Justice Story, would famously teach the dictum that what may not be done directly, may not be done indirectly. If it were truly wrong to hold the state responsible for its policies, it should have been just as wrong to launch an action against the officers who were the agents of those policies. Marshall's posture here made sense only on the assumption that the Eleventh Amendment stated no real principle, which deserved to be taken seriously. With that reading, the amendment would do nothing to dislodge what Marshall understood as the deeper principles of the law—namely, that a wrong deserved a remedy, and that rights under the Constitution could be vindicated in federal courts. If there were rights to be vindicated, and the state could not be made a party in a lawsuit, then the only plausible thing to do was to sue the officers who enforced the policy. But as I have pointed out, it was long understood that officers, as persons, could not be held personally liable for any injuries resulting from their official acts. Marshall had to understand that officers were being sued as agents of the state, and therefore, if he nevertheless insisted that the suits could be maintained, he was offering another one of his telling lessons. In a muted way, he was saying, in effect, that the Eleventh Amendment was a non sequitur. Whatever else it meant, it could not mean the dismantling of the national government or the refusal to vindicate rights that were protected by the Constitution.

IX. The Revival of the Eleventh Amendment

These problems, running to the logic of the Eleventh Amendment, might be disguised, or covered over, in lawyer-talk about writs of assumpsit or detinue; but Marshall had seen the core of the matter, and for the balance of the nineteenth century, the justices would strain their wits as they sought artful ways to talk around the problem. The justices preserved their piety about the Constitution, but they seemed to regard the Eleventh Amendment as part of the jural furniture, an heirloom not quite fitting, and best ignored. Wonder of wonders, then, that in our own day, conservative jurists would discover a new romance in the Eleventh Amendment and seek to recruit a new reverence for it. And yet, the practical implications of this move, even in the cases at hand, seem rather bizarre. Consider, for example, this thought experiment: A Clintonesque candidate for governor in one of the states proclaims his interest in reducing

---

[56] Ibid., at 842.

medical costs by having the state sell "off-label" drugs, starting with Viagra. As a result of the recent round of decisions by the Supreme Court, Pfizer, the manufacturer of Viagra, would not be able to sue to protect its patent under federal law. For the state would now be insulated by "sovereign immunity."

The case in the recent series that corresponds with this hypothetical example is *College Savings Bank v. Florida Prepaid Expense Board* (1999). The state of Florida entered into the business of arranging packages for the payment of tuition in college. These packages allowed parents to buy several years of tuition at a reduced cost. But the policy also trespassed on a "methodology" that was patented by the College Savings Bank in Princeton, New Jersey. A deep axiom of the law holds that the power to establish must entail the power to preserve: if the federal government can establish post offices, for example, it must have the authority to secure the mails against theft. For compelling reasons, the authority to issue patents was assigned, under the Constitution, to the federal government. This constitutional authority could be made a nullity, though, if the holders of patents could not vindicate their rights in federal courts when the patents were infringed—and the infringer happened to be a state gone into business. As a federal judge remarked, in a lower court, "[t]here is no sound reason to hold that Congress cannot subject a state to the same civil consequences that face a private party infringer."[57]

The liberals on the Court offered this distinction: they were prepared to recognize sovereign immunity when a state engages in functions typically performed by a state, but not when it enters upon activities undertaken, usually for profit, by private persons or corporations. The distinction is beguiling, but Justice Scalia pointed out that it is nowhere contained in the Constitution. That is, if we think that states have, under the Constitution, a sovereign immunity, then we leave it precisely to the states, or their political processes, to determine what states happen to do.

From this perspective, with the focus placed by Scalia, the accent would be on the power assigned to institutions, and the Court would not arrogate to itself the authority to ration or refine the powers of a state with distinctions struck from its own genius. But the curious point is that Justice Scalia and his colleagues did not seem to apply the same principles of construction to themselves in their relations with the Congress. Take again the issue of patents that emerged in *College Savings Bank*. The authority to issue patents is clearly assigned to Congress under Article I of the Constitution. In recent years, however, the Court has argued that the powers of Congress under Article I may not be used to override the "sovereign immunity" of the states.[58] The Court has sought to confine

---

[57] *College Savings Bank*, 148 F.3d at 1355.
[58] See, most notably, the decision of the Court in *Seminole Tribe v. Florida*, 517 U.S. 44 (1996).

that power of Congress to the Fourteenth Amendment, which has the national government directly countering the laws of the states. Yet, even there, the Court has insisted that Congress may formulate remedies only when *the courts* find that constitutional rights have been denied. In the case of patents, the justices did not agree that there was a constitutional violation to be remedied because there were only a handful of cases involving patents. But why should the number of cases matter? Surely, Congress has the authority to *protect patents lawfully granted*, and the Court concedes that in this field, there can be no immunity to lawsuits brought by individuals. After all, that is what the law must involve: individuals and companies defending their patents. In other words, the Court has conceded that both the ends and the means are legitimate. On what ground, then, would the justices displace the legislators in mulling over the question of whether it is politic, or fitting, at any moment to legislate?

The argument might be made, though, from a different angle, that Congress is free to protect patents, but not through the device of authorizing private lawsuits brought against a state.[59] From this perspective, the honoring of the Eleventh Amendment need not imply any impairment of the powers of Congress or the national government: if Congress wishes to enforce its policy, it may authorize the attorney general to bring suits against the officers of a state. There may be some lingering arguments over sovereign immunity, but they would no longer be arguments under the Eleventh Amendment, for they would not involve private litigants using the courts. What could be at work, then, with the Eleventh Amendment, is a restriction mainly on the powers of the *courts*: the amendment might prevent judges from colluding with private litigants to hamstring the policies of the state. As Justice Kennedy suggested in *Alden v. Maine* (the companion case to *College Savings Bank*), the object of the Eleventh Amendment may be to preserve the integrity of the *political process* in the separate states. If the voters and their representatives settle upon a policy, that policy should be overturned only by a political process at a higher level. As Kennedy points out, "suits brought by the United States itself require the exercise of political responsibility for each suit prosecuted against a State, a control which is absent from a broad delegation to private persons to sue nonconsenting States."[60]

Yet this argument against the power of the courts is not the argument that the justices have concentrated their wit in explaining, and indeed, their

[59] Justice Breyer, as a "realist," thought that the Constitution required a certain "flexibility" in dealing with a modern economy with computers, and that flexibility could be served by allowing private citizens to police the borders of regulation with private suits, directed against any players, including the state, when it becomes a player. But "flexibility" could also be served by removing that vexing power of Congress to assent to the executive orders of the President. As Scalia remarked, "Congressional flexibility is desirable ... but only within the bounds of federal power established by the Constitution."

[60] *Alden*, 527 U.S. at 756.

arguments have pointed quite dramatically in a different direction.[61] On the surface, the Court claims to be shoring up the authority of the states against the national government. But the real import of these cases on the Eleventh Amendment is that the judiciary is again cutting back on the power of Congress in relation to the courts. In a telling sign, the Court leans on its precedent in *City of Boerne v. Flores* (1997), when the Court struck down the Religious Freedom Restoration Act (RFRA).[62] The concern in that case was that Congress had gone beyond the Court's interpretation of the Fourteenth Amendment and upended many local laws touching on religious practice. But in striking contrast, there was not a trace of such concern twenty-four years earlier, when the Court itself, in *Roe v. Wade*, overturned in a single stroke all of the laws banning abortion in all of the states.[63] Nor was there the slightest inhibition, most recently, from "sovereign immunity" when the Court decided that the states would be held accountable for acts of sexual harassment carried out by fifth-graders.[64]

The sober political truth may begin to emerge as soon as we recognize that no Congress would ever have acted in the style of the Court in *Roe v. Wade*, in sweeping away all the laws on abortion in all of the states.[65] From the beginning, Congress has been constituted in a way that makes it sensitive to local interests, and so it has been the most reliable protector of federalism in the national government. Under the banner, then, of protecting the states, the Court has really weakened the main counterweight to the Court itself in imposing policies on the states. And the result that dare not speak its name is this: beyond the distraction of labels, the Court has now assigned to itself a legislative power ever more sovereign. That brute fact can be read in two simple measures: the authority that determines when Congress is permitted to legislate is a legislative power even higher than that of Congress; and when the Court "legislates," it is

[61] Even apart from this, the argument would not strictly be consistent with the understanding of the rule of law and "government by consent." For even when a person is part of the minority in this country, he is understood to have the right to withdraw his consent to the policies of the government by removing himself from the territory. But well short of this extreme, he would have the right, simply as one person, to come into a court of law and challenge the ground of law on which the government claims to commit him to its policies. We recall that one establishment of kosher butchers managed to bring down the National Recovery Act in the days of the New Deal; see *Schechter Poultry Corp. v. United States*, 295 U.S. 495 (1935). We would hardly think of ourselves in the same country or regime if we said that individuals can seek to vindicate the wrongs they are suffering, but only if they can act politically as part of a majority.

[62] *City of Boerne v. Flores*, 521 U.S. 507 (1997). The Religious Freedom Restoration Act had sought to cast an added layer of protection around conduct that was bound up with religious practice. The act would have required local laws to cite a "compelling interest" before they could interfere with activities that grew out of religious rituals.

[63] *Roe v. Wade*, 410 U.S. 113 (1973).

[64] See *Davis v. Monroe County Board of Education*, 526 U.S. 629 (1999), reversing and remanding 107 F.3d 1390.

[65] The case for this proposition was assembled in a compelling way by the late Morton Grodzins in his *The American System: A New View of Government in the United States*, ed. Daniel J. Elazar (Chicago: Rand McNally, 1966).

majestically freer than Congress, for it will never be inhibited by the "sovereign immunity" of the states. Behind the slogans of limited government, the limits have been dismantled even further.

X. CONCLUSION

What we may have here is another chapter in the unfolding, improbable story of "conservative jurisprudence": once again the conservative justices may have talked themselves into an inversion of their ends, to the bafflement of their enemies and the astonishment of their friends. I began here with an account of the laws of reason as the ground of the natural law, in part to show the kinds of things we may see as even more firmly anchored and compelling when we become alert again to the ground of their truth. But I offered this account in part because it comes as news to many jurists and writers in our own day.[66] If we could recover the understanding held by our first generation of jurists about the axioms of the law and the laws of reason, we might be able to see again more clearly, or avoid the kinds of mistakes that promise to be grievous. In these recent cases on the Eleventh Amendment, we might have avoided a haze of false sentiment that promises to distract us. And when that haze dissolves, we may find not a new movement in our jurisprudence to strengthen the states, but rather a shift that strengthens the legislative power of the courts. Whatever contributes to that end, threatens to advance a trend that has been, I think, baneful for our own time: the withdrawal of more and more subjects of moral consequence from the domain of politics, where they had been subject to arguments among ordinary people speaking ordinary language. Those issues have been removed now to a rather closed domain, ruled by judges, and carried on in a language shaped in the schools of law. In short, it would never be out of season to give ourselves a refresher course in the ground of the natural law in the "laws of reason." But with the recall of the Eleventh Amendment, and its effect over the years in befuddling our judges, we would set the ground for a more notable ending, in the inverting of Justice Holmes. Holmes has often been quoted, in that aphorism of his in the *Eisner* case, that "a volume of history is worth a page of logic."[67] After what we have seen, I think we are in the position to install instead a rival maxim: that an ounce of logic may be worth several generations of misspent history.

Political Science, Amherst College

---

[66] Even jurists as advanced in their careers as Richard Posner or David Souter have confounded natural law with empirical theories about the incorrigible tendencies of human beings, or with the ways of life that are thought acceptable by most people. See Posner, in mid-career, in *The Problems of Jurisprudence* (Cambridge, MA: Harvard University Press, 1990); and Souter, in his early years, in "Holmes' Legal Positivism and the Criticism from a Current Position of Natural Law" (senior honors thesis, Harvard University [1961]).

[67] *New York Trust Co. v. Eisner*, 256 U.S. 345, 349 (1921).

NATURAL LAW AS PROFESSIONAL ETHICS:
A READING OF FULLER*

By David Luban

I. Introduction

In Plato's *Laws*, the Athenian Stranger claims that the gods will smile only on a city where the law "is despot over the rulers and the rulers are slaves of the law."[1] This passage is the origin of the slogan "the rule of law not of men," an abbreviation of which forms our phrase "the rule of law." From Plato and Aristotle, through John Adams and John Marshall, down to us, no idea has proven more central to Western political and legal culture.[2] Yet the slogan turns on a very dubious metaphor. Laws do not rule, and the "rule of law not of men" is actually a specific form of rule by men (including, nowadays, a few women). These rulers are not slaves to anything. Furthermore, the construction of the slogan—rule of law and *not* of men—has unfortunate connotations. It suggests that the personal qualities of the human rulers required to secure the rule of law are nothing more than forbearance and disinterestedness—a resolution to stay out of law's way.

What if the rule of law is more demanding than this? What if it turns out to be a particularly elaborate and technically ingenious form of the rule of (let me say) men and women? What if the rule of law establishes a moral relationship between those who govern and those whom they govern? Furthermore, what if sustaining this relationship requires certain moral attitudes and virtues on the part of the governors that are not simply disinterested forbearance, and not simply the moral attitudes and virtues required of everyone?

* I have received helpful comments and criticisms from a number of readers, including the other contributors to this volume and participants in the Georgetown University Law Center faculty workshop. In addition, I should like to thank Brian Bix, Ellen Frankel Paul, Fred Schauer, and Wibren van der Burg for extensive written comments on an earlier draft of this essay.

[1] Plato, *The Laws of Plato*, trans. Thomas L. Pangle (New York: Basic Books, 1980), 715d.

[2] Aristotle offers a similar phrase in the *Politics*, at 1287a1–b1. Jonathan Barnes, ed., *The Complete Works of Aristotle* (Princeton, NJ: Princeton University Press, 1984), 2:2042. John Adams introduced the phrase "government of laws, and not of men" into America in his 1774 "Novanglus Paper" (no. 7), reprinted in Charles Francis Adams, ed., *The Works of John Adams* (Freeport, NY: Books for Libraries Press, 1969), 4:106. From there it migrated into the Massachusetts constitution of 1780 and eventually into Justice Marshall's opinion in *Marbury v. Madison*, 5 U.S. 137 (1803). Fred R. Shapiro, *The Oxford Dictionary of American Legal Quotations* (New York: Oxford University Press, 1993), 319.

In that case, the rule of law would turn out to rely on the specifically professional ethics of the lawmakers. One might be tempted to call this "political ethics," the ethics of rulers. But that is not quite right. Rulers are not identical with lawmakers. Rulers make decisions and devise policies, but decisions and policies are not yet laws. Embodying decisions and policies in the form of laws is a tricky business, technically difficult in exactly the same way that embodying private parties' intentions in a legal contract is difficult—and the people who carry out each of these lawmaking tasks are (what else?) *lawyers*. Thus, the rule of law relies on the professional ethics of lawyers (even if they do not call themselves lawyers or belong to the bar).

Finally, what if the professional ethics of lawyer-lawmakers—the moral relationship and attitudes and virtues required by the rule of law—cohere better with laws enhancing human dignity than with laws assaulting it, because enacting laws that assault human dignity tends to undermine the moral relationship that sustains the rule of law? If this were the case, we would be entitled to assert that the rule of law morally constrains the content of laws. This sounds like a natural law theory. We could call it a theory of the "morality of law," provided we understood that the phrase refers to the morality of *lawmakers*, and only derivatively to the morality of laws. We would have a theory of natural law as professional ethics.

What I have just described is the unfamiliar argument of a very familiar book, Lon Fuller's *The Morality of Law* (hereafter *ML*), first published in 1964.[3] (Note that in what follows, my page references to *ML* refer to the revised edition, published in 1969.) I call the argument unfamiliar because readers have typically treated *ML* as a book on general jurisprudence, not on professional ethics, and have neglected its moral theory to focus on what they regard as analytical claims about "the concept of law." But "the concept of law" is H. L. A. Hart's title, not Fuller's.[4]

As Fuller himself observed in 1969 (*ML* 188), this misunderstanding is perfectly natural given the state of play in legal theory when he first published *ML*. For several years, he had been engaged in a debate with Hart, beginning with their famous exchange in the *Harvard Law Review*.[5] Hart weighed in next in *The Concept of Law*, which Fuller criticized in

---

[3] I will use the following abbreviations for works of Fuller to which I cite repeatedly: *ML* = *The Morality of Law*, rev. ed. (New Haven, CT: Yale University Press, 1969); *LQI* = *The Law in Quest of Itself* (Evanston, IL: Northwestern University Press, 1940); *PSO* = *The Principles of Social Order: Selected Essays of Lon L. Fuller*, ed. Kenneth I. Winston (Durham, NC: Duke University Press, 1981); *PFL* = "Positivism and Fidelity to Law—A Reply to Professor Hart," *Harvard Law Review* 71, no. 4 (February 1958): 630–72; *RFCL* = "Reason and Fiat in Case Law," *Harvard Law Review* 59, no. 3 (February 1946): 376–95; *RN* = "A Rejoinder to Professor Nagel," *Natural Law Forum* 3, no. 1 (1958): 83–104.

The present essay examines, from a different perspective, themes I discuss in "Rediscovering Fuller's Legal Ethics," published concurrently in *Georgetown Journal of Legal Ethics* 11, no. 4 (Summer 1998): 801–29; and Willem J. Witteveen and Wibren van der Burg, eds., *Rediscovering Fuller: Essays on Implicit Law and Institutional Design* (Amsterdam, The Netherlands: University of Amsterdam Press, 1999), 193–225.

[4] H. L. A. Hart, *The Concept of Law* (Oxford: Clarendon Press, 1961).

[5] H. L. A. Hart, "Positivism and the Separation of Law and Morals," *Harvard Law Review* 71, no. 4 (February 1958): 593–629. Fuller's reply is *PFL*, cited in full in note 3 above.

chapter 3 of *ML*. Hart returned the compliment when he reviewed *ML*,[6] and Fuller responded in the new appendix he wrote for the revised edition of *ML*. Subsequent readers have naturally assumed that Fuller and Hart were still debating the same issue of whether legal norms are logically distinct from moral norms—an issue framed by Hart in his own terms at the beginning of the debate.

On this assumption, *ML* gets read approximately as follows. The central argument of *ML* begins with the famous parable "Eight Ways to Fail to Make Law," found in chapter 2. The parable does two things. First, it provides an analysis of the rule of law into the eight familiar canons that Fuller calls "principles of legality." These hold that laws should exhibit (1) generality (i.e., legislating through rules rather than case-by-case directives), (2) publicity, (3) nonretroactivity, (4) clarity, (5) noncontradictoriness, (6) obeyability in practice, (7) constancy through time, and (8) congruence between the rules as announced and their actual administration (*ML* 39). Second, the parable argues that when these canons are violated, the result is not bad law, but no law at all. The canons, then, are necessary conditions on the concept of law. They are also, or so Fuller claims, an "inner morality of law"; because they have to do with the promulgation of laws, not with their content, this inner morality is a "procedural natural law." There is also a substantive natural law, but Fuller leaves the connection between the procedural and substantive branches of natural law obscure. And that's about it.

How do those who read Fuller this way react to his argument? They generally like his analysis of the rule of law, which ranks alongside comparable efforts by John Rawls and Joseph Raz.[7] Many accept the idea that without these canons there can be no law at all; however, most reject the claim that the canons represent principles of morality, inner or otherwise. It is this latter claim that forms the crux of the issue between Fuller and Hart, and the dominant view seems to be that Fuller was wrong.

Undoubtedly, that latter claim is important. But reading Fuller in the manner described above slides over his treatment of substantive natural law, and treats the first chapter of *ML*, on ethical theory, as if it does not exist. As a result, the argument about professional ethics with which I began simply disappears from the reading entirely. And that is too bad, because in important ways (not every way) Fuller's argument is right.

II. "The Word 'Law' Means the Life Work of the Lawyer"

Fuller never disguises his intentions. He says in *ML* that he will offer only one definition of law: "the enterprise of subjecting human conduct

---

[6] H. L. A. Hart, "Book Review—*The Morality of Law*," *Harvard Law Review* 78, no. 6 (April 1965): 1281–96.

[7] John Rawls, *A Theory of Justice* (Cambridge, MA: Harvard University Press, 1971), 235–43; Joseph Raz, "The Rule of Law and Its Virtue," *Law Quarterly Review* 93, no. 2 (April 1977): 195–211.

to the governance of rules" (*ML* 106). His title, *The Morality of Law*, then, must be paraphrased thus: "the morality of the enterprise of subjecting human conduct to the governance of rules." Fuller explicitly calls attention to the fact that his definition classifies law as an activity rather than, say, a set of propositions of law, or a distinctive kind of social norm. The activity of *subjecting* human conduct to rules, unlike the activity of governing one's own conduct in accordance with rules, is performed specifically by the rule-designer. "So when I speak of legal morality, I mean just that. I mean that special morality that attaches to the office of law-giver and law-applier."[8] He labels this a "role morality," and likens it to the distinctive ethics of lawyers—it is "no mere restatement of the moral principles governing human conduct generally, but . . . special standards applicable to the discharge of a distinctive social function" (*ML* 193; see also *PSO* 201). In the second edition of *ML*, Fuller complains that "no modern positivist elevates to a central position in his thinking any limitations contained in 'the law job' itself" (*ML* 192). The "law job" is performed by the lawyer, whom he elsewhere calls the "architect of social structure" (*PSO* 50-52, 253, 264-70). This makes clear that *ML* is a book about professional ethics—specifically, the professional ethics of those lawyers Fuller refers to as lawgivers and law-appliers.[9]

This way of thinking about law was already evident in 1940, when Fuller first discussed natural law and positivism in *The Law in Quest of Itself*. After rehearsing the definitions of law offered by several philosophical schools, he considers the obvious concern that debates among them amount to little more than terminological hairsplitting. Here is how he responds:

> Yet if in these definitions the word "law" means the life work of the lawyer, it is apparent that something more vital than a verbal dispute hinges on the choice between them. Surely the man who conceives

---

[8] Lon L. Fuller, "A Reply to Professors Cohen and Dworkin," *Villanova Law Review* 10, no. 4 (Summer 1965): 660. He employs similar phrasing at *ML* 206.

[9] I do not mean that Fuller literally thought all legislators are professional lawyers. He understood, of course, that nonlawyer legislators decide on what should become law before turning it over to lawyers for drafting. He emphasized that the lawmaking job has a technical side, because embodying policies in effective rules is difficult in exactly the way that embodying parties' intentions in a well-wrought contract is difficult. Negotiating these difficulties is precisely the special craft of lawyers. Fuller also argued that the technical aspect of lawmaking imposes substantive constraints on what policies can be embodied in laws, because human activity "always involves a reciprocal adjustment between ends and means." Lon L. Fuller, "The Philosophy of Codes of Ethics," *Electrical Engineering* 74, no. 5 (October 1955): 916. See Fuller's "Means and Ends," in *PSO*, 52-58. Not every conceivable end can be turned into workable law. In this sense, all legislation requires the exercise of lawyerly skills, even when the legislator is not a lawyer. The reciprocal adjustment of ends and means likewise implies that a transactional lawyer papering a deal shapes it rather than serving as a mere scrivener: lawyering requires the exercise of legislative skills, even when the lawyer is not a legislator. It follows that the roles of legislators and lawyers are closer than appears at first sight, and this overlap matters to Fuller—it is one of the points of his King Rex parable. Hence my talk of lawyers in the text.

his task as that of reducing the relations of men to a reasoned harmony will be a different kind of lawyer from one who regards his
task as that of charting the behavior of certain elderly state officials.
(*LQI* 3–4)

"The word 'law' means the life work of the lawyer." This is not just a rhetorical
hook to capture the interest of the law school audience to which he was
lecturing. It is, in paraphrase, the very definition he employs in *ML*.

In the second sentence of the quotation from *LQI*, Fuller offers his own
characterization of natural law, or rather, of the activity of the natural law
lawyer: "reducing the relations of men to a reasoned harmony." On its
face, this is strikingly different from the most common understanding of
natural law in analytic jurisprudence. Analytic philosophers of law tend
to regard natural law and positivism as competing theses about the relation between legal and moral propositions. Jules Coleman's careful definition is a good example: on his account, *positivism* is the "proposition
that there exists at least one conceivable legal system in which the rule of
recognition does not specify being a principle of morality among the truth
conditions for any proposition of law."[10] *Natural law*, then, is the view
that in *every* conceivable legal system, the rule of recognition (the rule by
which we recognize valid laws) specifies that being a principle of morality is among the truth conditions for any proposition of law.

Fuller characterizes natural law as a way of conducting a practical
activity—"reducing the relations of men to a reasoned harmony"—
rather than as a philosophical thesis about the truth conditions of propositions of law. For Fuller, there is not really a thesis associated with
natural law at all (*RN* 84). Of course, Fuller believes that there is a
characteristic morality associated with the "law job" (*ML* 192). But this
marks an important shift in emphasis. Where other writers on all sides
of the positivism/natural law debate understand the phrase "the morality of law" to refer to the morality of *laws*, for Fuller it refers to the
morality of *lawmaking*.

This usage, which is quite consistent in Fuller's work, is bound to
create confusions for those who assume that the phrase "the morality of
law" refers not to the moral code of the rule-designer but rather to the
moral content of legal rules. In particular, it means that when positivists
deny that the law has any necessary moral content, Fuller tends to hear
them asserting that no moral code governs lawgiving, a claim that he
finds preposterous. Positivists, however, do not really intend to make this
claim. Similarly, when Fuller insists that there is a morality to law, his
critics assume that he is making a conceptual claim about the necessary

---

[10] Jules L. Coleman, "Negative and Positive Positivism," in Marshall Cohen, ed., *Ronald
Dworkin and Contemporary Jurisprudence* (Totowa, NJ: Rowman and Allenheld, 1983), 31. This
is Coleman's definition of "negative" (that is, minimal) positivism.

connection between legal rules and morality, rather than arguing that lawmaking is a profession with a distinctive professional ethics. But it is the latter that Fuller means.

I said earlier that Fuller classifies lawgivers and law-appliers (legislators and judges) together with lawyers.[11] This will seem puzzling until we realize that Fuller invariably has in mind transactional lawyers, not litigators (who, he observes, are a small minority of the legal profession [*PSO* 252-53]). As noted above, Fuller views the lawyer as an "architect of social structure"; he regards litigation, the recourse when social structure fails, as a poor—even perverse—focus for understanding what makes lawyers' work important. It would be like trying to understand an educator's work by focusing on the process of disciplining classroom troublemakers, or trying to understand marriage by examining divorce.[12]

Three characteristics of the transactional lawyer make him the paradigm jurist in Fuller's eyes. First, his job is to facilitate interaction between two or more private parties—and facilitating interaction is, for Fuller, the principal aim of law. Second, although the transactional lawyer advises his client, sometimes quite forcefully—he is not merely a mouthpiece or a scrivener—he understands that the client, not the lawyer, is the person who has to do the interacting after the deal is made. This is the fundamental moral fact about the relationship. Third, the transactional lawyer facilitates the interaction by drawing up a framework of rules—a contract, the transactional equivalent of a piece of legislation.[13]

III. Excellences as Powers: "Sin Is a Sinking into Nothingness"

When we fully appreciate that *The Morality of Law* is a book about professional ethics rather than a traditional treatise on jurisprudence, we can better understand why Fuller begins the book with a chapter on ethical theory, and why the chapter opens with contrasting definitions of 'sin', rather than, say, justice or injustice. Talk about sin would be strange

---

[11] On this point, see also Kenneth I. Winston, "Legislators and Liberty," *Law and Philosophy* 13, no. 3 (August 1994): 393-96.

[12] These analogies are mine, not Fuller's. Although transactional lawyers must anticipate possible litigation, "battening down the hatches against possible future litigation" (*PSO* 253) cannot be their principal job as they draft contracts. The clients are trying to get something done, not merely avoid losses when their projects shipwreck. Fuller more than once quotes Aquinas's dictum that if the highest duty of a captain were to preserve his ship, he would keep it in port forever. Aquinas, *Summa Theologiae*, I-II, q. 2, a. 5, quoted at *PSO* 56, *ML* 185.

I discuss Fuller's conception of lawyers' work more fully in "Rediscovering Fuller's Legal Ethics," 810-19.

[13] Fuller argues, strikingly, that the terms contained *in* a contract are just as much law as the rules governing the formation of contracts. *PSO* 174-75. He is a *legal pluralist*—someone who believes that there are many legal systems in a society, not just the big legal system administered by the state: on this account, both private actors and the state can make law. Fuller argues explicitly for legal pluralism at *ML* 123-29.

if the subject were the morality of laws, rather than the morality of law-making. Because Fuller is focusing on the latter, however, he is interested in the ways lawyers can sin against the enterprise in which they are engaged. To an unusual extent, Fuller personalizes jurisprudence: he sees acts of legislation and interpretation as products of lawgivers and law-appliers, products whose quality depends crucially on the people who make them.

Fuller's moral theory turns on a distinction between the *morality of duty*—"the most obvious demands of social living" (*ML* 9)—and the *morality of aspiration*—"the morality of the Good Life, of excellence, of the fullest realization of human powers" (*ML* 5). Several points stand out.

1. There is, first of all, the idea that aspiration has a morality. This is hardly an obvious point. Many of our aspirations fall under the general heading of things that it would be nice to do, but there is nothing especially moral about the category of the 'that-would-be-nice'. It would be nice if I could play the piano, speak German, and work the exercises in the old mathematics textbooks that have been hibernating on my shelf since college. All these things being among my interests, it is natural to think of them as aspirations. But it would be odd for anyone to take me to task for my failings at piano, German, and mathematics, and equally odd for me to feel ashamed about them. In contrast, speaking of moral failings implies, at the minimum, a dimension of blame and shame: moral failings are among those failings that do deserve criticism (from both oneself and others). Otherwise, why call them *moral* failings? From a moral outlook centered on rights and duties, "mere" aspiration is a non-moral phenomenon; Fuller's claim to the contrary marks out a distinctive moral position.

2. Kant believed that we lie under a duty to improve ourselves; this and the duty to promote others' happiness are the principal obligations he elaborates in the "Doctrine of Virtue."[14] These two duties roughly correspond with Fuller's categories, but Fuller rejects the reduction of aspiration to duty (*ML* 5). Instead, he finds that criticism appropriate to the morality of aspiration involves terms like "failure" and "shortcoming, not . . . wrongdoing," as well as assertions that one has not engaged in "conduct such as beseems a human being functioning at his best" (*ML* 5; see also *ML* 3). In other words, the morality of aspiration employs the vocabulary of human excellence—what philosophers call 'aretaic' concepts—rather than 'deontic' concepts, the vocabulary of right or wrong action. In that sense, the morality of aspirations lies very close to contemporary

---

[14] See generally Immanuel Kant, "The Doctrine of Virtue," in Kant, *The Metaphysics of Morals*, trans. Mary Gregor (Cambridge: Cambridge University Press, 1991). The treatise is divided into two principal sections: "On Duties to Oneself as Such" and "Duties of Virtue to Others." See also Marcia Baron, "Kantian Ethics," in Marcia Baron, Philip Pettit, and Michael Slote, *Three Methods of Ethics: A Debate* (Malden, MA: Blackwell, 1997), 13–21.

virtue ethics, the view that places aretaic concepts at the heart of moral theory.[15]

3. When is it appropriate to treat aspirations morally, rather than merely as things it would be nice to do? Fuller never explicitly addresses this question, but the use to which he puts the distinction suggests one important answer: *our aspirations have a moral dimension whenever other people's well-being depends on them.* Paradigmatically, this will be true in the sphere of work, and specifically in the professions. It is hardly coincidental that aretaic concepts evolved in Greek thought to characterize warriors, whose excellences and failures meant the difference between prosperity and disaster for those who relied on them.[16] In more peaceable societies, we continue to think "aretaically" when we choose a surgeon or a lawyer. We want something more than dutifulness, which after all is merely the requirement for avoiding malpractice liability. We want someone who strives for professional excellence and attains it. We criticize professionals who fail for want of excellence, along with those who do not even strive for it. This is moral criticism, and it is based in the morality of aspiration.

Even when no one else's well-being depends directly on our work (as is true, for example, in the writing of philosophy), the morality of aspiration applies in a derivative way. It would (merely) be nice if I could play the piano; playing the piano is, for me, a nonmoral aspiration. But, as a writer on philosophical topics, it is a more serious failing that my German is not good enough to read Kant or Hegel. If my philosophizing is slipshod, that is an even more serious failing. Here, the morality of aspiration applies.

In general, it seems, aspiration "goes moral" when our aspirations tie in to serious commitments, when they move from the amateur to the professional. Fuller is in love with the idea of professionalism. He celebrates the virtues of excellence in work; in this respect, his nearest literary counterpart is Primo Levi in *The Monkey's Wrench* and *The Periodic Table.*[17] Thus, the third point that emerges from Fuller's "two moralities"

[15] For an alternative approach to Fuller's theory, see Wibren van der Burg, "The Morality of Aspiration: A Neglected Dimension of Law and Morality," in Witteveen and van der Burg, eds., *Rediscovering Fuller*, 174–80. Van der Burg focuses on Fuller's claim that the moralities of duty and aspiration lie on a single continuum (ML 9–10), but I believe that this was a mistake on Fuller's part. The continuum image implies that there will be some point above which everything is aspiration and below which everything is duty. However, ideals such as always doing my duty, never being negligent or unfair for even a single second, or leading a perfectly blameless life belong simultaneously to the morality of duty and the morality of aspiration: to deviate from these ideals violates the morality of aspiration, but by definition each deviation also violates a duty. Hence, the continuum metaphor must be incorrect. For this reason, I emphasize the categorical differences between aspiration and duty.
[16] A. W. H. Adkins, *Merit and Responsibility: A Study in Greek Values* (Oxford: Clarendon Press, 1960), 30–60.
[17] Primo Levi, *The Monkey's Wrench*, trans. William Weaver (New York: Penguin, 1987); Primo Levi, *The Periodic Table*, trans. Raymond Rosenthal (New York: Schocken, 1984).

discussion—alongside the ideas that aspiration has a morality, and that its morality is a kind of virtue ethics—is the thought that professional ethics includes the morality of aspiration as one of its central features.

4. Next, consider the quotation with which Fuller begins the first chapter of *ML*: "Sin is a sinking into nothingness" (*ML* 3).[18] The absence of excellence, of virtue, is not badness so much as nonbeing. This is a familiar Platonic and Augustinian idea, and I think it is quite false as a general account of evil. It makes a great deal of sense, however, when applied to aretaic concepts such as "virtue" (a word that for Fuller has the "original sense of power, efficacy, skill, and courage" [*ML* 15]). If a lawyer is not doing any of the things a good lawyer does, she is not merely practicing law badly. She is not practicing law at all. Virtues are functional excellences, and a professional role is defined by its functions; take away enough of the professional virtues, and the result is simply not recognizable as the professional role.

It should be clear why these four major points are important to understanding Fuller's jurisprudential argument. I have been claiming that Fuller's morality of law is a set of excellences that belong to the professional ethics—the role-morality—of lawmakers. This is specifically true of the inner morality of law: Fuller's eight canons of lawmaking. It is significant, after all, that Fuller introduces the canons with the parable of King Rex, who aimed "to make his name in history as a great lawgiver" (*ML* 34)—an entirely aretaic ambition. As Fuller tells the story, moreover, Rex's failures led him repeatedly to reflect not on the concept of law, but on his own personal failings—further evidence that Fuller's focus is on the legislator, not the legislation.[19] If sin is a sinking into nothingness, then we can understand Fuller's famous conclusion that Rex "never even succeeded in creating any law at all, good or bad" (*ML* 34) in a somewhat nonstandard light. It becomes an observation about the role-morality of law-giving rather than an analytical claim about necessary conditions on the very concept of law. Fuller is simply pointing out that whatever King Rex did when he issued directives in a fashion that entirely lacked the characteristic excellences of the lawgiver's craft, he was not subjecting human conduct to the governance of rules. He was not making law.

These observations derive from a more general point about what I will call *purposive concepts*—concepts that define objects by the functions they serve in fulfilling purposes. For example, 'light switch' is a purposive con-

---

[18] "Der Sünde ist ein Versinken in das Nichts." Significantly, Fuller says he may have imagined this quotation, an admission that suggests how central it is to his outlook.

[19] Consider, for example, these statements found in the parable: "His first move was to subscribe to a course of lessons in generalization" (*ML* 34); "Rex undertook an earnest inventory of his personal strengths and weaknesses" (*ML* 35); "Continuing his lessons in generalization, Rex worked diligently. . . ." (*ML* 35); "Recognizing for the first time that he needed assistance. . . ." (*ML* 36); "By now, however, Rex had lost his patience with his subjects" (*ML* 36); "Reflecting on the misadventures of his reign, he concluded. . ." (*ML* 37).

cept: it defines objects by their function of turning lights on and off.[20] Fuller's fundamental insight into purposive concepts is that to identify an object purposively is implicitly to specify a standard of success and failure. Fuller puts this strikingly when he writes that the concept of a steam engine "overlaps mightily" with the concept of a good steam engine (*LQI* 10–11). 'Steam engine' is a purposive concept: what makes devices steam engines is their ability to convert steam power to usable mechanical energy. What a steam engine *is good for* and what a steam engine *is* "overlap mightily."

This point carries the important consequence that when we use purposive concepts in descriptions, we are automatically evaluating as well as describing. Take a simple example. Touring a house, I notice an odd-looking bump on the wall. It can be wiggled from side to side, but wiggling it does nothing whatsoever. I'm puzzled. Suddenly I recognize that the bump is a broken light switch. This is one single recognition, not two: to identify the bump as a light switch is simultaneously to identify it as a defective light switch. If I have no idea that a light switch that does not turn the lights on or off is defective, I lack the concept 'light switch' altogether.[21]

The way that Fuller usually phrases this point is to say that the *is* and the *ought* cannot be sharply distinguished, or that they merge. This is a maddeningly elusive way of putting things, and even Fuller recognized that "phrases like 'a merger of fact and value' are unsatisfactory" (*RN* 83). The reason such phrases are unsatisfactory is that they wrongly suggest that to describe something as a steam engine is already to describe it as a good steam engine. This is certainly not what Fuller means to say. Substitute the word 'law' for 'steam engine' and this sort of misinterpretation is disastrous.

As I interpret them, such phrases instead assert that to recognize something as a steam engine or a light switch is already to recognize what it ought to do, to recognize a built-in standard of success or failure. Success or failure at what? At being a steam engine or a light switch—at being what it is, one might say. Purposive concepts are *aspirational* concepts—and now we recognize that Fuller's morality of aspiration is intimately connected with his analysis of purposive concepts, and hence with the is/ought distinction.

This point can be turned around. If an object is so bad at converting steam power to mechanical energy or turning lights on and off that we cannot even recognize it as *unsuccessfully* doing these things, then we will be unable to recognize the object as a steam engine or light switch at all. The worse things get at fulfilling the purposes of steam engines and light switches, the closer they get to the threshold between being a bad steam

---

[20] Defining objects purposively is a special case of functional definition; it is not the only case, of course, because there are also functional concepts defining objects by the roles they play in nonpurposive processes. For chemists, 'catalyst' is a functional concept, but it is not purposive, because chemical reactions are not purposes.

[21] Fuller argues that omitting the purpose in descriptions of purposive objects makes them misdescriptions. Lon L. Fuller, "Human Purpose and Natural Law," *Natural Law Forum* 3, no. 1 (1958): 68–70.

engine or light switch and not being a steam engine or light switch at all. Sin is a sinking into nothingness.

One more point about the evaluative dimension of purposive concepts turns out to be crucial to Fuller's understanding of the morality of law. There is nothing distinctively moral about converting steam power to usable mechanical energy or turning lights on and off—so the "merger of *is* and *ought*" in these examples is not quite a merger of fact and value. Matters are different, however, when the purposively defined entity is a person defined through her social or occupational role ('parent', 'physician', 'lawyer', 'lawmaker'), and the means by which she fulfills the role's purposes create a long-term moral relationship with other people. In such cases, the standard of success implicit in the purposive concept is not just fulfillment of the occupation's ends narrowly conceived. Instead, the standard of success is fulfillment of these ends in a manner consistent with the moral relationship, for if the role-occupier chronically betrays the moral relationship, the other parties will dissolve it. Under this standard, a relationship that originates only as a means to an end becomes incorporated into the end itself.

IV. "THE CITIZEN'S ROLE AS A SELF-DETERMINING AGENT"

According to Fuller, when a lawmaker systematically violates any of the canons of the internal morality of law—the role-morality of his or her job—the result is not law (*ML* 39). What, then, if not law, is it? Fuller seems to think that there are two characteristic answers to this question. His first answer emerges when he discusses the Nazi legal system or other criminal legal systems. In this discussion, he leaves little doubt that he considers these systems as nothing more than Hart's illegitimate "gunman writ large"—examples of raw power disguised as law.

However, violating the eight canons need not be illegitimate in the way that the gunman writ large is illegitimate. Fuller's second answer is that law must be distinguished from "managerial direction" (*ML* 207)—a form of governance that is perfectly legitimate in many everyday contexts, but that involves no commitment to the canons of generality or congruence between official action and declared rule.[22] Managerial direction is a form of governance, but it is not the enterprise of subjecting human conduct to the governance of rules, because managerial directives are not necessarily rules: a manager can deviate from his own general directives whenever circumstances require.

[22] Fuller mistakenly asserts that the issue of nonretroactivity never arises in managerial direction, because no manager would ever order someone today to do something yesterday (*ML* 209). However, a manager might find it quite expedient to change a policy retroactively. For example, a manager might decide to deduct the costs of tools that workers damage from their pay, and it is easy to imagine circumstances in which the manager might wish to make this policy retroactive. If the terms of employment do not protect workers from policies like this, and if there is no labor union to fight the policy, we can readily imagine that the manager will be successful. Thus, Fuller's point should have been that in a managerial context, there is no necessary moral commitment to nonretroactivity.

Usually, when Fuller asserts that governance that systematically violates the eight canons is not law, the way to understand the phrase "not law" is as an abbreviation for "not law but tyranny" or "not law but managerial direction."[23] (The distinction between tyranny and managerial direction is that in the latter, but not the former, subordinates share their superiors' aims.) For Fuller, the "identification of law with every conceivable kind of official act" (*ML* 169) is a conceptual mistake that leads to misunderstandings about the morality of law.[24]

In particular, Fuller argues that governing the conduct of others through law rather than managerial direction is itself a morally freighted choice. According to Fuller, it implies "a certain built-in respect for [the] human dignity" of those subject to the law ("the governed," as I shall call them for short), in a way that managerial direction does not.[25] This is the case for several reasons.

First, it recognizes that the form of governance will not be by moment-by-moment direct supervision. Governance through general rules, unlike managerial direction, presumes a measure of respect for the moral powers of the governed. "To embark on the enterprise of subjecting human conduct to the governance of rules involves of necessity a commitment to the view that man is, or can become, a responsible agent, capable of understanding and following rules, and answerable for his defaults" (*ML* 162). Elsewhere, Fuller makes the Wittgensteinian point that legal rules cannot explicitly exclude all aberrant interpretations in advance, and concludes that relying on the governed to follow rules presupposes shared "notions of the limits of legal decency and sanity."[26] Governance through rules implies that the governed and the governors belong to the same interpretive community and have roughly equivalent powers of intellect and will.

Second, governance through general rules, unlike specific directives, presupposes the autonomy of the governed. "The law does not tell a man what he should do to accomplish specific ends set by the lawgiver; it furnishes him with baselines against which to organize his life with his fellows. . . . Law provides a framework for the citizen within which to live his own life" (*PSO* 234).[27] Elsewhere, Fuller describes "the view of man implicit in legal morality" (*ML* 162) as "the citizen's role as a self-

---

[23] The one notable exception is the King Rex parable itself. There, the hapless king is neither a manager nor a tyrant—he is merely an incompetent.

[24] Here (and in other places) my reading is influenced by Jeremy Waldron, "Why Law—Efficacy, Freedom, or Fidelity?" *Law and Philosophy* 13, no. 3 (August 1994): 259–84.

[25] Fuller, "A Reply to Professors Cohen and Dworkin," 665.

[26] Lon L. Fuller, *Anatomy of the Law* (New York: Praeger, 1968), 63.

[27] Fuller makes the same point in *ML*: "[L]aw furnishes a baseline for self-directed action, not a detailed set of instructions for accomplishing specific objectives." *ML* 210. He also uses the "baseline" terminology to make the converse point, namely, that not only does law presuppose the goal-setting freedom of the governed, but that the goal-setting freedom of the governed requires law. "To live the good life . . . requires the support of firm base lines for human interaction, something that—in modern society at least—only a sound legal system can supply." *ML* 205. He elaborates this latter point in "Freedom—A Suggested Analysis," *Harvard Law Review* 68, no. 8 (June 1955): 1305–25.

determining agent" (*ML* 166). To be a lawgiver rather than a command-giver is to treat the citizen as a self-determining agent.

Governing through general rules also implies a certain impersonality in the relationship between governors and governed. Each individual falls under a rule only as a member of a general class, and each action is likewise judged only on the basis of general characteristics. What matters is *what* we are and do, not *who* we are—our deeper identity remains outside law's purview. Government through general rules contrasts starkly with the patrimonial familiarity that breeds contempt; law treats us as '*Sie*' rather than '*du*', as '*vous*' rather than '*tu*'.

Third, governance through rules, unlike the gunman writ large, assumes a measure of self-enforcement and self-monitoring on the part of the governed. Governance through rules, which is relatively cumbersome, would be unnecessary if an enforcer were always present. Although a tyrant can dominate a hostile population using a surprisingly small number of police—by making it extremely dangerous to even attempt to organize resistance that could overwhelm the police force—governance through rules presumes at least the passive cooperation of the governed (*ML* 216).[28]

Respect for the governed, respect for the autonomy of the governed, and trust in the governed—these are the three overlapping moral values underlying a governor's choice of law, rather than managerial direction, as the specific form of governance. Fuller's point, then, seems to be that embarking on the enterprise of subjecting human conduct to the governance of rules creates a certain kind of moral relationship between governor and governed. It is, specifically, a relationship in which a governor abjures the streamlined efficiency of managerial direction in favor of trusting the governed to understand and follow general rules on their own.

Once we see this point, a puzzling passage from *The Morality of Law* begins to make sense. Many of Fuller's critics complain that Fuller's eight principles of legality are merely conditions of efficacy, not moral principles. They accept that Fuller's King Rex parable demonstrates that governors must follow the eight canons if they want people to obey their laws. These critics argue, however, that this is true whether the laws in question are good or evil, and thus that the canons themselves have nothing to do with morality. To illustrate the point, Hart observes that there are also rules of effective poisoning. Dworkin makes the same point with blackmail and genocide; Marshall Cohen, with murder; and Schauer, more recently, with lynching.[29]

---

[28] For an illuminating explanation of how even widely hated police states can maintain their dominance using a surprisingly small number of enforcers, see Russell Hardin, *One for All: The Logic of Group Conflict* (Princeton, NJ: Princeton University Press, 1995), 29–32.

[29] Hart, "Book Review—*The Morality of Law*," 1286; Ronald Dworkin, "Philosophy, Morality, and Law—Observations Prompted by Professor Fuller's Novel Claim," *University of Pennsylvania Law Review* 113, no. 5 (March 1965): 676; Ronald Dworkin, "The Elusive Morality of Law," *Villanova Law Review* 10, no. 4 (Summer 1965): 634; Marshall Cohen, "Law, Morality, and Purpose," *Villanova Law Review* 10, no. 4 (Summer 1965): 651; Frederick Schauer, "Fuller's Internal Point of View," *Law and Philosophy* 13, no. 3 (August 1994): 302–4.

Fuller responds strangely: "I must confess that this line of argument struck me at first as being so bizarre, and even perverse, as not to deserve an answer" (*ML* 201). But what is so bizarre and perverse about it? Fuller himself insists that his eight canons are principles of efficacy (*ML* 155–56); indeed, when he introduced the idea of an internal morality of law in his 1958 reply to Hart, he argued for its canons solely on grounds of efficacy (*PFL* 644–45).

What strikes Fuller as perverse about the accusation that he has confused morality with efficacy is that he regards the choice to govern through law rather than managerial direction as a *sacrifice* of efficacy for moral ends (*ML* 202–3). To put the point another way: while Fuller agrees that the principles of legality are instrumentally necessary to make governance by law effective (*ML* 155–56), he thinks that governing by law rather than managerial direction represents a sacrifice of expediency in the name of principle. The ultimate justification of the principles of legality is therefore moral, not instrumental. Fuller finds the poisoning and blackmail analogies perverse because they assume that an evildoer would for some mysterious reason choose as an instrument of evil a relatively ineffective tool—a tool, moreover, that is relatively ineffective because it displays precisely the kind of moral regard for its victim that an evildoer lacks.[30]

Consider, by analogy, a professor's decision to teach a large class through the Socratic method of eliciting the classroom material by questioning students rather than by straight lecture. (The analogy is mine, not Fuller's.) The Socratic method is much less efficient than lecturing, and much harder to do well. It sacrifices coverage of material, it frequently frustrates and puzzles students, and it makes classroom progress hostage to the commitment and capabilities of the class. Why, then, would a teacher choose the Socratic method? The principal reason is that teachers wish to train their students in the art of analyzing issues for themselves, along with the art of explaining their own thinking, in public, on their feet. The point of Socratic teaching is to cultivate the students' active powers, even at the cost of efficiency. This is very similar to what Fuller takes to be the point of governance through law: to cultivate activity rather than passivity, to enhance rather than restrict the citizens' powers of self-determination, even though self-determination is unruly and therefore inefficient.

---

[30] As I read Fuller's argument, it is precisely the argument offered by John Finnis in his exposition of Fuller: "Adherence to the Rule of Law (especially the eighth requirement, of conformity by officials to pre-announced and stable general rules) is always liable to reduce the efficiency for evil of an evil government, since it systematically restricts the government's freedom of maneuver." Finnis, *Natural Law and Natural Rights* (Oxford: Clarendon Press, 1980), 274. Thus, "[a] tyranny devoted to pernicious ends has no self-sufficient *reason* to submit itself to the discipline of operating consistently through the demanding processes of law, granted that the rational point of such self-discipline is the very value of reciprocity, fairness, and respect for persons which the tyrant, *ex hypothesi*, holds in contempt." Ibid., 273.

Socratic teaching is also subject to characteristic abuses that are quite
analogous to the abuse of law by tyrants. When a teacher really has a
lecture idea in mind, but tries to elicit it through Socratic questioning, she
will find herself compelled to deal brusquely with student answers that
do not take the discussion where she wants it to go. She will cut corners
to guide the discussion, and students will quickly perceive that they are
involved in a Socratic shell game of guessing what the teacher has in
mind, not in cultivating their own powers. They will rightly view this as
a betrayal of the teacher-student relationship: the teacher here is merely
pretending to respect the students' intellectual autonomy and cultivate
their powers; in reality, she is dominating them.[31]

Does Fuller mean to deny, then, that a lawmaker may have domination
on his mind? Not at all.[32] His conclusion is substantially more interesting
than that. Fuller argues that *every* exercise of social power requires some
reciprocity. Even a blackmailer has to exercise some restraint; otherwise,
his victim might elect to reveal his own shameful secret in order to bring
the bite to an end. Here, Fuller observes, we can imagine the blackmailer
pleading with the victim not to do this, and promising to be less greedy
in the future (*PSO* 195–96). Elsewhere, Fuller suggests that a tyrant will
find that domination will be easier if he enlists his subjects' cooperation
by enhancing their freedom and happiness.[33] If a lawmaker persistently
abuses his relationship with the governed, he will be unable to count on
the governed to interpret and follow rules; therefore, a decision to govern
through rules rather than orders, perhaps undertaken initially because
the order-giver cannot be everywhere at once, imposes moral constraints
on the order-giver. The more that the power-holder turns tasks over to the
subordinate for his own convenience, the more he makes himself dependent on the agency and independence of the subordinate. In that case,
reciprocity tends toward at least rough equality, and one-way projection
of authority becomes two-way interaction.[34]

---

[31] A famous philosophy professor (no names, please) was a legendary practitioner of the
Socratic shell game, and generations of students parodied his teaching with the following
dialogue. *Professor*: I'm thinking of a number between 1 and 500. Mr. A, please tell me the
number. *Student A*: 15? *Professor*: No. Ms. B? *Student B*: Um, is it 96? *Professor* (fiercely): Ms.
B, I asked you to name the number between 1 and 500 I am thinking of. Do you really think
you've answered my question? Mr. C, tell us the number. *Student C*: 216. *Professor*: That is
correct. Ms. B, now do you see your mistake?
   The professor was widely regarded as an unforgivable intellectual bully.
[32] "I have never asserted that there is any logical contradiction in the notion of achieving
evil, at least some kinds of evil, through means that fully respect all the demands of
legality." Fuller, "A Reply to Professors Cohen and Dworkin," 664.
[33] See Lon Fuller, "Freedom as a Problem of Allocating Choice," *Proceedings of the American Philosophical Society* 112, no. 2 (April 1968): 105–6.
[34] Although this is not the place to discuss this point in any detail, Fuller has offered a
version of Hegel's master/slave argument from the *Phenomenology of Spirit*. There, Hegel
describes the evolution of relationships of *pure dependency* (of the slave on the master, who
holds the power of life and death over him) to relationships of *reverse dependency* (as the
master comes to rely on the slave, who takes over the active role, playing Jeeves to the

Fuller describes his theory as an *interactional* view of law (*ML* 221), because in his view the choice of law over managerial direction implies a moral relationship between governors and the governed based on mutuality (*ML* 209, 216).

> Government says to the citizen in effect, "These are the rules we expect you to follow. If you follow them, you have our assurance that they are the rules that will be applied to your conduct." When this bond of reciprocity is finally and completely ruptured by government, nothing is left on which to ground the citizen's duty to observe the rules. (*ML* 39–40)

This is an entirely different moral relationship than that of managerial direction—"the basic relation of order-giver and order-executor" (*ML* 209)—although even managerial direction creates *some* reciprocity. Interestingly, Fuller insists that within the managerial context, the canons of clarity, noncontradictoriness, obeyability, constancy through time, and publicity really are principles of efficacy and nothing more (*ML* 208–9); the clear implication of this point is that he believes that these canons have a different status in the context of law. There, they are professional virtues of the lawgiver, part and parcel of the mutual respect that Fuller believes is at the heart of the relationship between a lawmaker and those whom she governs.

In what sense are canons like clarity, noncontradictoriness, or constancy through time professional virtues of the lawgiver? Consider a group of people who wish to go into business together, and who retain a lawyer to draw up a partnership agreement that reconciles the divergences that inevitably exist among their interests. The partners are entrusting their joint venture to the lawyer; they are counting on the lawyer's professional ability to craft an agreement that will provide a workable architecture for their enterprise. If the partnership agreement turns out to be unclear, self-contradictory, or incapable of execution, this is betrayal, not just incoherence or "inefficacy."[35] The partners will suffer for the

---

master's increasingly infantile and incompetent Bertie Wooster) and, later, to relationships of *reciprocity*. G. W. F. Hegel, *The Phenomenology of Spirit*, trans. A. V. Miller (Oxford: Oxford University Press, 1977), 111–19.

[35] Indeed, all of these infirmities are breach-of-contract defenses at common law: they void at least the afflicted clauses of the instrument. When we notice this, and recall that Fuller was a contracts scholar, it is tempting to argue that Fuller derived the canons by asking himself what conditions are necessary for a valid social contract between governors and the governed. Recall in this connection the passage quoted above, in which government "makes an offer" to citizens: "These are the rules we expect you to follow. If you follow them, you have our assurance that they are the rules that will be applied to your conduct." This sounds a great deal like a social contract. It is noteworthy as well that when Fuller discusses total failure to abide by the canons, he writes, "[i]t results in something that is not properly called a legal system at all, *except perhaps in the Pickwickian sense in which a void contract can still be said to be one kind of contract*." *ML* 39, emphasis added.

lawyer's fecklessness. Those who claim that Fuller's canons merely represent conditions of efficacy appear to overlook this point when they emphasize that a ruler who violates the canons will be unable to accomplish his aim, as though the point of the ruler's activity is only to accomplish his own aim, rather than the aims of those he rules. It is this, perhaps, that leads Fuller repeatedly to accuse his critics of viewing government "as a one-way projection of authority" (*ML* 204).

We can be more specific about how the eight canons are virtues of lawmaking. The two most fundamental—the canons that distinguish the law-giving enterprise from managerial control—are the canons of generality and congruence between rules and their enforcement. The former insists that governors give directions in the form of general rules; the latter demands that they treat those rules as binding on themselves as well as on the governed, in the sense that they will not depart from the rules they have announced.[36] The commitment to bind the governed only through general rules that also bind the lawmaker establishes the moral relationship of reciprocity between governors and the governed. These two canons are moral commitments that define the enterprise as law-giving rather than something else.

The remaining six canons fall into two natural groupings: precepts of *clear communication* and precepts of *reasonable expectation*. Once the lawmaker has undertaken to govern through general rules binding on both her and the governed, she must announce the rules to the governed, and she must ensure that her rules are ones that the governed may reasonably be expected to follow. Rather obviously, the canons of clarity and publicity are aspects of clear communication, while the canons of constancy and obeyability are aspects of reasonable expectation. The remaining canons—nonretroactivity and noncontradictoriness—may be regarded as aspects of both clear communication and reasonable expectation. A rule requiring me to do something today is not adequately communicated if it is not issued until tomorrow, nor is it reasonable to expect me to abide by it; likewise, a self-contradictory rule conveys nothing (because anything follows from a contradiction), and cannot be obeyed.

The burden of understanding and complying with rules falls on those whom the rules govern; the reciprocal relationship between governors and the governed places a corresponding burden on the governor to make the rules understood and capable of being complied with. That, ultimately, is why clear communication and reasonableness are moral virtues of the lawmaker.

---

[36] A manager may also issue orders in the form of general directives—rules—but remains at liberty to depart from the directives when circumstances require. In the terminology of Rawls's "Two Concepts of Rules," the manager adopts a "summary conception" of rules, whereas the lawmaker adopts a "practice conception." John Rawls, "Two Concepts of Rules," in Rawls, *Collected Papers*, ed. Samuel Freeman (Cambridge, MA: Harvard University Press, 1999), 34–39.

V. "'DISCOVERY' IN THE MORAL REALM"

Why does Fuller call his view "natural law"? Fuller energetically rejects the traditional idea that natural law represents "higher law" (*RFCL* 379, *ML* 96, *RN* 84), and indeed he suspects that the appeal to higher law is an unfortunate residue from positivism (*PFL* 656, 659–60). Strikingly, he attributes *no* authority to laws as such: like a good legal realist, he argues that judges should treat statutes and precedents simply as "one [more] of the realities the judge must respect in making his decisions" (*RFCL* 380)—in other words, as constraints within which judicial problem-solving must maneuver, not as authorities to which judges must defer. If Fuller had never employed the term "natural law" in connection with his views, we might be hard-pressed to guess that his *is* a natural law jurisprudence.

Fuller's pronouncements about natural law do not help much. "I discern . . . one central aim common to all the schools of natural law, that of discovering those principles of social order which will enable men to attain a satisfactory life in common. It is an acceptance of the possibility of 'discovery' in the moral realm that seems to me to distinguish all the theories of natural law from opposing views" (*RN* 84). Talk of the possibility of discovery in the moral realm makes it sound as if Fuller equates natural law theory with moral realism. But *moral realism*, the thesis that moral judgments are objective and referential, is not distinctive to natural law. Positivists, who believe that law can and should be open to moral criticism, can accept the realist thesis without difficulty. Indeed, many of the positivists were utilitarians, and utilitarians hold that judgments of right and wrong—claims about which actions are utility-maximizing and which are not—are objective and referential.

Elsewhere, Fuller cautions that "for many the term 'natural law' still has about it a rich, deep odor of the witches' cauldron" (*RFCL* 379). But all it really signifies, he says, is

> that there are external criteria, found in the conditions required for successful group living, that furnish some standard against which the rightness of . . . decisions should be measured. . . . Certainly it would never occur to him [the natural lawyer] to describe the natural law he sought to discover, and felt bound to respect, as a "brooding omnipresence in the skies." Rather for him it would be a hard and earthy reality that challenged his best intellectual efforts to capture it. The emotional attitude . . . would not be that of one doing obeisance before an altar, but more like that of a cook trying to find the secret of a flaky pie crust. . . . (*RFCL* 379)

Once again, there is nothing here that a utilitarian positivist could not enthusiastically embrace. Like Fuller, the utilitarian positivist is an ethical naturalist, who believes that deciding what the law ought to be is hard intellectual work, with external standards of success determined in large part by empirical facts about nature and human nature.

I believe, however, that once we think of Fuller's theory as the professional ethics of lawmaking, we find a coherent answer to the question of what makes it a natural law theory: it derives moral requirements of the lawmaker's job from features unique to the lawmaking enterprise. Unlike other natural law theories, however, the morality implicit in Fuller's concept of law is the morality of lawmaking, not of the law made.

Fuller complains that positivists neglect the distinctive role-morality of lawmaking: "If the lawgiver enacts what Hart calls 'iniquitous' laws, he sins of course against general morality, but there is no special morality applicable to his job itself" (ML 193). This description is plainly true of utilitarianism, which regards a job as nothing more than a causal path connecting an agent's input to output in the form of utility, the way that a transmission connects an auto's engine to its wheels. The utilitarian would regard the role-morality of a job as nothing more than an application or instantiation of the principle of utility. For Fuller, however, it is a fallacy "to assume that moral precepts retain the same meaning regardless of the social context into which they are projected" (ML 207); he accuses both utilitarians and Kantians of this fallacy (PSO 201). What both overlook, Fuller argues, is that when you take on a job, intending to pursue it in a way that respects general morality, you discover that the job creates moral expectations of its own (PSO 200–201). Fuller's arguments about the morality of law are meant to show that lawmaking has its own distinctive virtues (conformity to the eight canons) and its own distinctive moral outlook (respect for the self-determining agency of the governed), both of which follow from the nature of the lawmaking enterprise and not directly from general morality.

This is what Fuller has in mind when he writes about discovery in the moral realm. He is not tendering a general commitment to moral realism, but rather making the more specific claim that institutions, particularly legal institutions, although they are entirely human creations, have moral properties of their own—properties that their designers may never have intended or even thought about, and that are connected only indirectly to general morality. Identifying the morality of institutions, the virtues and vices of participating in them, is a matter of discovery, not invention—a matter of reason rather than fiat.

I think Fuller is right. We can observe these phenomena in the evolution of games like baseball. Games are in one sense an entirely positivist creation: the rules define the game, and presumably, if the rules permit a practice, engaging in it cannot be cheating. One might argue that the game would be better if the rules forbade certain practices—in positivist terms, that the game as it is isn't the game as it ought to be. But as long as the rules do not favor one team over the other, abiding by these rules cannot be criticized on the ground that it is not a fair way to play baseball. So goes the positivist argument.

Yet in actuality, the rules of baseball have been modified repeatedly over the years because as the game develops, it becomes clear that some behavior permitted by the rules really is cheating. Fielders intentionally miss infield pop-ups when there are runners on first and second base, in order to get an easy double play; pitchers make the ball curve by spitting on it; base runners block batted balls with their bodies to prevent fielders from making a play; hitters peek at the catcher to see whether he is setting up for an inside or outside pitch; batters with two strikes against them intentionally swing and miss at wild pitches so they can run safely to first base when the ball flies past the catcher. All of these practices were at one time permitted by the rules, and the first three were banned—not because the game would be better if they were banned (though this is true), but because it became clear that missing infield flies to get the cheap double play, throwing the spitter, and interfering with batted balls were forms of cheating. These were moral discoveries about baseball-playing, of just the kind that Fuller claims to have made about lawmaking. They are part of the natural law of an artificial institution. Interestingly, no rule currently forbids batters from peeking at the catcher to see where he is setting up. However, if the opposing players catch him in the act, the batter will be hit by a pitch his next time up, and no one will complain, because even the batter knows he deserves it. He has violated the natural law of baseball.[37] The same goes for the batter with two strikes against him who swings at a wild pitch: one writer recalls that when he did this in high school, his own teammates shunned him afterward.[38]

One might object that these practices are cheating not because they violate the "natural law of baseball," but merely because the written rules did not do a good enough job of codifying the game as it was supposed to be played. But no one knew *a priori* how baseball was supposed to be played; refining the rules was not merely a means to the end of preserving the original intent of baseball's framers. The discovery that throwing the spitball is a form of cheating was simultaneously a discovery about the point of the contest between batter and pitcher. The relationship is dialectical, not hierarchical.

[37] See Keith Hernandez and Mike Bryan, *Pure Baseball: Pitch by Pitch for the Advanced Fan* (New York: HarperCollins, 1995), 125-27. Interestingly, Hernandez (an all-star first baseman) states both that the peeker deserves to be hit by a pitch *and* that peeking is neither cheating nor bad sportsmanship. That is because Hernandez believes that nothing, not even practices forbidden by the rules, is unfair if the other team or the umpires have a fair opportunity to catch and punish the players who engage in it. His is a *legal realist* view of cheating, desert, and self-help, quite distinct from both natural law and positivism.
[38] Ted Cohen, "There Are No Ties at First Base," *Yale Review* 79, no. 2 (October 1990): 321-22. "[My teammates] did not care for what I had done. . . . They regarded me as someone who did not really grasp the nature of the game. I thought that in knowing the rules I knew the game; they knew the game in some other way." Ibid., 322. I am grateful to David Brink for calling Cohen's hilarious essay to my attention.

VI. The Progressive Positivists' Critique of Natural Law

I now turn to criticisms of Fuller's view. In his review of *The Morality of Law*, Hart wonders whether he and Fuller are perhaps "fated never to understand each other's work,"[39] and on one central issue it seems clearly true that Fuller and his positivist critics talk past each other. This is the curious issue of which theory provides its adherents with the morally superior point of view on the law. The issue is curious, of course, because ordinarily we think that theories should be chosen on the basis of whether they are correct, not whether they morally improve their adherents. Nevertheless, the argument turns out to be an important one both for Fuller and his critics.[40]

Let us put it most directly. Fuller repeatedly accuses positivists of being statists, "overprimed with power" (*PSO* 277); theirs, he says, is "the view that identifies the lawyer's work with established state power" (*PSO* 252). And repeatedly, progressive positivists like Fred Schauer, Neil MacCormick, and Robin West level the identical accusation of statism against natural lawyers.[41] (By *progressive positivists*, I mean positivists who deny per se moral authority to the legal status quo and therefore to the state.) According to Schauer, "the classical natural law theorist" believes "that the very existence of a legal system ... provides ... assurance that the legal system has been designed either to incorporate moral criteria or to produce morally desirable ends."[42]

This argument between natural lawyers and progressive positivists originates in one of the most important passages in Hart's half of the debate with Fuller. In "Positivism and the Separation of Law and Morals," Hart accuses natural lawyers of having only "half digested the spiritual message of liberalism."[43] Natural lawyers understand that in the face of evil enactments by the state, individual conscience prevails over the duty to obey. This is the spiritual message of liberalism. But natural lawyers have only half-digested it, because it seems that the only way

[39] Hart, "Book Review—*The Morality of Law*," 1281.

[40] See Philip Soper, "Choosing a Legal Theory on Moral Grounds," in Jules Coleman and Ellen Frankel Paul, eds., *Philosophy and Law* (Oxford: Basil Blackwell, 1987), 31–48.

[41] See Frederick Schauer, "Positivism Through Thick and Thin," in Brian Bix, ed., *Analyzing Law: New Essays in Legal Theory* (Oxford: Clarendon Press, 1998), 65–78; Schauer, "Fuller's Internal Point of View," 305–12; Frederick Schauer, "Constitutional Positivism," *Connecticut Law Review* 25, no. 3 (Spring 1993): 805–7; Frederick Schauer, "Positivism as Pariah," in Robert P. George, ed., *The Autonomy of Law: Essays on Legal Positivism* (Oxford: Oxford University Press, 1996), 31–55; Neil MacCormick, "A Moralistic Case for A-Moralistic Law," *Valparaiso Law Review* 20, no. 1 (Fall 1985): 10–11; Robin West, "Three Positivisms," *Boston University Law Review* 78, no. 3 (June 1998): 791–812; and Robin West, "Natural Law Ambiguities," *Connecticut Law Review* 25, no. 3 (Spring 1993): 831–41. West, it should be noted, expounds the progressive positivist view sympathetically without wholly endorsing it.

[42] Schauer, "Positivism Through Thick and Thin," 70.

[43] Hart, "Positivism and the Separation of Law and Morals," 618; Hart, *The Concept of Law*, 205–6.

they can license disobedience is by denying that evil enactments are law. Apparently, they cannot shake off the idea that law must be obeyed. In legal philosopher Donald Regan's felicitous phrase, they still think that law has a halo.[44] This is the illiberal side of natural law.

Positivists, according to Hart, are morally more clear-headed. They understand that law has no necessary moral content, no halo. They labor under one less illusion about where their moral duty lies, and are less likely to accede to bad law merely because it is law. Quoting Schauer once again, "in insisting that the concept of law does no moral work the [progressive positivist] is taking the irreducibly moral position that we ought not to expect our understanding of law and legal institutions to carry any of the moral water when we engage in personal decision-making or institutional design."[45]

It is very curious to find a natural lawyer like Fuller and progressive positivists like Hart and Schauer each accusing the other side of being too statist—in effect, each is trying to outflank the other on the left (which of course leads battlefield adversaries to revolve in a perpetual circle around a point of engagement that neither ever reaches). At least one side in this debate is failing to grasp something about the other's position. In this case, I think, both are.

Let us begin with Fuller's accusation that positivists identify law with "a one-way projection of authority, originating with government and imposing itself upon the citizen" (ML 204). This is only half-true, because positivists argue only that legal systems *may* be one-way projections of state authority, not that they *must* be. Even if the accusation were true, though, Fuller wrongly supposes that positivists approve of one-way projections of state authority. Hart's argument, of course, is that when the law authorizes something evil, a liberal positivist will disapprove and disobey.

Next, look at the progressive positivists' moral critique of natural law. Schauer, recall, argues that for classical natural law theorists, the very existence of a legal system ensures its morality. Why should that be? Schauer offers no argument, but evidently he believes that the classical theorists contrapose the natural law maxim "unjust law is not law" into the claim that law is just. However, natural lawyers do not actually make this mistake in contraposition. The natural law maxim is shorthand for "unjust *positive* law is not *genuine* law." This is logically equivalent not to the claim that (all) law is just, but to the claim that positive law that is also genuine law is just.[46] The mere existence of positive law leads to no conclusion whatever about its justice or injustice.

---

[44] Donald H. Regan, "Law's Halo," in Coleman and Paul, eds., *Philosophy and Law*, 15–30.
[45] Schauer, "Positivism Through Thick and Thin," 70.
[46] Among the progressive positivists, West is clear about this. She regards these two ways of reading the natural law maxim as an ambiguity in natural law theory, whereas I regard them as a positivist misunderstanding of natural law.

Let me rephrase all this in a more polemical and less logic-chopping manner. Progressive positivists like Hart, MacCormick, and Schauer think that the natural law maxim will confuse its adherents and make them too impressed with law, too complacent with the status quo, and too likely to obey. But of course, "unjust law is not law" is the traditional argument for disobedience, not obedience—so who exactly is it who is confused? In its most famous contemporary American incarnation, the natural law maxim figures prominently in Martin Luther King's "Letter from Birmingham City Jail," where King invoked it to explain, in the most stirring terms, why he was right to disobey a court order forbidding a 1963 civil rights march.[47] If the progressive positivists think that the natural law maxim is an invitation to complacency and obedience, then they must believe that King misunderstood the maxim, because he was neither complacent nor obedient. King misunderstood the maxim, apparently, by failing to draw the wrong conclusion from it. Isn't it more likely that the progressive positivists have misunderstood why natural lawyers like King insist that unjust law is not law?

The positivist moral critique of classical natural law misfires in a slightly different way against Fuller's version. The progressive positivists fear that anyone who believes in "the morality of law" will illicitly regard legal enactments as having already passed a preliminary threshold toward moral acceptability. As we have seen, Fuller thinks just the opposite. For Fuller, to call something law entails that it has *extra* moral demands placed on it by virtue of the "morality of law"—the role-morality of law-giving. Law's halo, on Fuller's account, provides additional grounds for criticizing law, not for obeying it.

In this respect, at any rate, Hart and Fuller were talking past one another. Notice, for example, that when Fuller speaks of "fidelity to law" (in *PFL*) he is generally talking about officials' professional obligation to maintain the legal system in good order, not about the citizen's obligation to obey the law, which is Hart's topic. Fuller asks how German judges, not ordinary Germans, should have responded to the Third Reich, and he answers that fidelity to law—which is *not* the same as obedience to law—should have led them to resist.

In a recent essay, Schauer offers a different criticism of Fuller, one which presents an interesting twist on the progressive positivist argument. Schauer focuses on the fact that Fuller's is "insider jurisprudence," designed and built to help conscientious legal professionals become better lawyers. In the terms I have been urging, it is jurisprudence in the service of professional ethics. Schauer accurately remarks that "Fuller's perspective flows smoothly from *his* role as a legal theo-

[47] Martin Luther King, Jr., "Letter from Birmingham County Jail," reprinted in King, *Why We Can't Wait* (New York: Mentor, 1964), 76–95.

rist explicitly seeing himself located in a law school and speaking to actual or would-be lawyers."[48] Insider jurisprudence presupposes that the professional project has worth, and is worth the efforts of conscientious people to improve it.

Suppose, however, that one is an outsider, whose question is not "What kind of lawyer shall I be?" but "Why should anyone be a lawyer?"[49] An outsider need not begin by supposing that the legal system has any worth at all, but she does need to understand what the legal system is. For the outsider, then, positivism is the superior starting point, for only positivism facilitates the project of "first . . . characterizing the legal system, and then . . . morally evaluating it."[50]

To illustrate Schauer's point, let our outsider be a visitor newly arrived in a foreign country, who asks someone, "What is the legal system like?" (Perhaps she is thinking about emigrating to the foreign country and going to law school.) And suppose the answer is this: "The judges do whatever the regime tells them to, the regime is repressive, the lawyers are not allowed to disagree with the judges, the laws are vague and change all the time, and the schedule of criminal penalties is a state secret." If a Fullerian overhearing the conversation chimes in, "You see, it isn't a legal system at all!" the outsider will reply, "Call it whatever you like—but the person I just talked with answered the question I am interested in." The outsider has rightfully asked a positivist question and gotten a positivist answer. If the outsider had instead approached the Fullerian to ask "What is the legal system like?" and received the answer, "There is no legal system here," this answer would be misleadingly coy, and in no way more truthful.

Nor is "There is no legal system here" a caricature of Fuller's way of talking. In his reply to Hart, Fuller quotes a Hitler-era statute against slandering the Nazi Party, deems it a "legislative monstrosity," and then embraces the view of postwar German courts that "saw fit to declare this thing not a law" (*PFL* 654, 655). Schauer's point, I take it, is that there is a straightforward "positivist" sense, glossed over by Fuller, in which the statute *is* a law (and not, say, a poem). Otherwise, how could Fuller call it a "statute" and declare it a *legislative* monstrosity?

Embedded in Schauer's argument we find a claim that Fuller denies: that the insider's concept of law, which Schauer agrees is and should be a moralized one, is unnecessary to describe a society's legal institutions—a "positivist" description is available. The examples just presented make

---

[48] Schauer, "Fuller's Internal Point of View," 305.

[49] Ibid., 308.

[50] Ibid., 309-10. In "Positivism Through Thick and Thin," Schauer remarks that he finds it no coincidence that among three of the austerest positivists—himself, Jules Coleman, and David Lyons—"two do not possess law degrees and the third no longer teaches primarily in a law school." Schauer, "Positivism Through Thick and Thin," 70 n. 1.

this seem plausible, but Fuller would not be without a response. It would go, I take it, as follows.[51]

'Lawmaking' is a purposive concept, and the purpose of lawmaking is to subject human conduct to the governance of rules (*ML* 146). Like all purposive concepts, it contains implicit criteria of success and failure. As we have seen, lawmaking creates a moral relationship between governors and the governed, and successfully carrying out the terms of that relationship is part of what succeeding at lawmaking means. It follows that if our outsider can recognize what her informant has described as a legal system at all, she can, and indeed must, recognize it as a deviant legal system. Its servile judges, repressive rulers, gagged lawyers, vague and inconstant rules, and secret punishments represent a gross deviation from the aspirations inherent in the lawmaking enterprise.

Could the positivist resist this conclusion by declining to describe legal systems purposively? This is easier said than done. When the outsider asks "What is the legal system like?" she must have in mind some concept of what a legal system is, for not just anything can count as a legal system. If the informant answers the outsider's question by saying, "People wander through the countryside gathering grapefruit, which they sell in the marketplace," the outsider would not think, "My, what an unusual legal system." She would instead draw the Davidsonian conclusion that she and her interlocutor are not understanding each other's words properly.[52] And she would draw that conclusion because what the informant has described does not do, badly or otherwise, what legal systems do—thus, her informant cannot be talking about a legal system.

An outsider's description of an alien legal system is implicitly a comparison of that system with her, and our, concept of what a legal system is and is for. Such a concept is an insider's purposive concept. The idea that one can dispense with the internal perspective on legal systems turns out to be untrue, because we need the internal perspective—our understanding of the point of a legal system—in order to recognize a legal system when we encounter one. Even the outsider's viewpoint on a legal system presupposes the priority of the purposive point of view.

It may be thought, however, that all these arguments overlook the progressive positivists' most basic concern, which is simply that insider jurisprudence lacks critical bite. For a critique of human sacrifice you do not turn to the priest—not even the ethical priest who treats the victim

---

[51] In the arguments that follow, I am drawing freely from (and modifying in part) *LQI* and *RN*. Interestingly, Ernest Nagel offered an argument very similar to Schauer's thirty-five years earlier. Ernest Nagel, "On the Fusion of Fact and Value: A Reply to Professor Fuller," *Natural Law Forum* 3, no. 1 (1958): 79.

[52] Donald Davidson has for many years defended the so-called "principle of charity" in linguistics, a rule of thumb which states that if your translation of a foreigner's utterances implies that the foreigner has crazy beliefs, the fault lies in your translation. Donald Davidson, *Inquiries into Truth and Interpretation* (New York: Oxford University Press, 1984), xvii, 196–97.

with impeccable concern and respect, at least until the altar is ready. Lawyers, it might be feared, are like these priests. They have too much invested in their system to seriously contemplate major revisions. Furthermore, lawyers' knowledge is system-specific local knowledge, and the sheer desire for epistemic comfort, the fear of the unknown, may well block lawyers from grasping that entire continents of their legal system are unjust or dysfunctional.

This may be so, but precisely the same things might be said of nonlawyers. Unjust laws are seldom *only* legal injustices. They typically represent the moral views of dominant or once-dominant groups in the larger society—what King, in his Birmingham letter, accurately described as the "numerical or power majority group." Nonlawyers who belong to a system's numerical or power majority group are beneficiaries of the system just as lawyers are, and they are no less likely to confront epistemic vertigo at the prospect of abandoning the familiar evils and the moral beliefs that ratify them.

Perhaps, then, the authentic outsider's standpoint is that of the victims of unjust laws. However, victims are usually cut off from access to information about how their oppressive legal system operates, and in many cases are also denied the basic goods of education. Historically, the great social and legal critics have been insiders or semi-insiders whose lively sense of critical morality allows them to pass beyond their own self-interest and identify with the victims of bad law. I see no reason to suppose that legal insiders will have a weaker sense of critical morality than outsiders. Are legal professionals like Thurgood Marshall or Catharine MacKinnon really at a disadvantage in diagnosing bad law? Worse at it than Malcolm X or Andrea Dworkin? There is no reason to suppose anything of the kind.

VII. "A BRUTAL INDIFFERENCE TO JUSTICE AND HUMAN WELFARE"

And yet there does seem to be something amiss in Fuller's theory, something too quick and easy in the way it concludes that an immoral lawmaker is not just letting down his subjects, but is also betraying the very idea of law. As we have seen, Fuller argues that the enterprise of subjecting human conduct to the governance of rules presupposes a moral relationship between governors and the governed—a moral relationship aimed at promoting the self-determining agency of the governed. From this relationship, it follows that the eight canons are moral excellences, not just rules of efficacy. All this seems like an awful lot to derive from the bare concept of people governing other people through rules. Fuller has pulled a very large rabbit out of a very small hat. His theory seems too good to be true.

I wish to suggest that it *is* too good to be true. Like Schauer, I trace Fuller's overoptimism about the law to his insider perspective. This is not, however, because of the generalized worry about insiders that I have just discussed. The problem is not with insider jurisprudence as such, but with the fact that Fuller's insiders are *lawyers*. Quite simply, the lawyer's role is more problematic than Fuller admits.

At one point, Fuller throws out a challenge to his doubters, rhetorically asking whether "history does in fact afford significant examples of regimes that have combined a faithful adherence to the internal morality of law with a brutal indifference to justice and human welfare" (*ML* 154). He plainly believes that the answer is "no," but I begin my argument by suggesting that the answer is "yes" *in almost every regime that has ever existed*. This is because almost every regime that has ever existed has legislated expressly to *deny* the self-determining agency of women, and has thereby denied what Fuller claims is the substantive morality imminent in law. Until the most recent times in a bare handful of nations, women have enjoyed few or no political rights, have been classified as property or quasi property, and have been subjected by law to the tutelage of their husbands and fathers. One might offer analogous examples drawn from the histories of slavery or legally explicit ethnic subjugation. (Would Fuller deny that the American law of slavery adhered rather well to the internal morality of law? On what grounds?) However, I think that the for-all-practical-purposes-universal legal subjugation of women offers the most striking example of what goes wrong in Fuller's theory.[53]

The important point, it seems to me, is this. Fuller maintains that any legal regime that abides by the eight canons will respect the self-determining agency of those to whom its rules are addressed; so far as it goes, his argument is profound and correct. But it does not go as far as Fuller hoped, because he overlooks an important qualification: those whose self-determining agency law aims to further need not include the entire population subject to the law, because the rules may really be addressed only to a numerical or power majority (to borrow King's words once again). That is, it may well be that the legal edifice of patriarchy aims to enhance the self-determining agency of men. But it does so at the expense of women, who are subject to the tyranny (or, at best, the managerial direction) of their husbands and fathers. Justice for the guys coexists with injustice for women.

The crucial condition under which this form of mixed justice and injustice can exist is that the dominant group is able to exert direct control over the subordinate group by virtue of living side-by-side with them. To take a straightforward illustration, legal regulation of slaveholders, es-

---

[53] One might object that regimes of slavery or ethnic/gender subordination violate the canon of generality, and hence they are not genuine rule-of-law regimes. However, generality does not mean that identical laws apply to everyone. It means only that when a rule classifies people, it applies equally to everyone in the specified class. For example, a rule forbidding married women from forming binding contracts without their husbands' permission would satisfy the generality requirement if it applied to all married women.

tablishing a framework of general rules that advances and respects their self-determining agency, turns out to be wholly consistent with tyrannical or managerial regulation of slaves. In just the same way, patriarchal legal orders enhance the self-determining agency of men in part by enhancing their license to exert unfettered authority over women. The problem, it seems, is that even though both men and women fall under the law's jurisdiction, the law excludes women from the community whose freedom it aims to enhance.

I can find no evidence that Fuller ever considered the catastrophic asymmetry between whom the law binds and whom the law helps, nor the implications for his jurisprudence of the law's exclusion of women from the community of freedom. He was certainly aware, though, of the "basic question": "Who is embraced in the moral community?"—that is, "Who shall count as a member of the in-group?" (*ML* 181). He was, after all, writing during the heyday of the civil rights movement.

> Within a given political society there are men commonly described as being of different races. These men have lived together for many years. . . . They have together produced a common culture. Is there no moral principle that can imperatively condemn drawing a line between them, and denying to one group access to the essentials on which a satisfactory and dignified life can be built? (*ML* 183)

Fuller recognizes that he needs an affirmative answer to this question, but the one he provides is unsatisfying, except perhaps as rhetoric. He cites the parable of the Good Samaritan and a famous Talmudic aphorism to argue "that we should aspire to enlarge that community [the moral community] at every opportunity" (*ML* 183), because the morality of aspiration "cannot refuse the human quality to human beings without repudiating itself" (*ML* 183). Confusingly, Fuller asserts that these are propositions from the morality of aspiration that are fully as imperative as duties. So far as I can tell, Fuller provides no reason for supposing that the scriptures he cites truly set out the morality of aspiration, or for thinking that cosmopolitan aspirations have the force of duties, or for assuming that cosmopolitanism belongs to the morality of law as Fuller understands it—namely, the professional ethics of lawgivers and law-appliers. Fuller seems to have forgotten his own distinction between criticizing bad laws on general moral grounds, which he disfavors, and criticizing them as violations of the distinctive role-morality of the legislator, a practice of which he approves.

He cannot, for example, really mean that any lawmaker who enacts sexist or racist legislation has violated the role-morality of the legislator's craft. The legislative role-morality surely does not contain an equal protection clause built in *a priori*. If anything, the argument seems more plausible going the other way: perhaps legislators have a role-obligation to enact laws that they find morally objectionable if those laws truly codify the dominant morality of the society.[54] Tennyson's ultracosmopolitan Ulysses ("I am a part of all that I have met"), having returned from his wanderings to govern the cultural backwater of Ithaca, understands that only "slow prudence" will be able "to make mild a rugged people, and thro' soft degrees subdue them to the useful and the good." In the meantime, "I mete and dole unequal laws unto a savage race."[55] Unequal laws, apparently, are all that a savage race can handle, and a conscientious lawmaker will not jump the gun. This argument may be wrong: there is a genuine question about whether a professional's role-morality can override the demands of universal morality.[56] But even if the answer is no, the reason that it is no is because of the priority of the universal over the particular, not because the demands of universal morality are built into the structure of role-morality *a priori*, for legislators or anyone else.

Fuller is indulging in wishful thinking. He wishes that lawmaking were inherently cosmopolitan, because his argument requires a cosmopolitan solution to the problem of defining the moral community. He confronts a familiar problem in legal ethics. His lawmakers, we have seen, are like transactional lawyers, aiming to facilitate their clients' interactions with a well-crafted structure of rules. But transactional lawyers have clients, and there are limits to how far lawyers can take into account the interests of nonclients. Even when transactions require reciprocity between clients and other parties, each lawyer's primary loyalty runs to her own client — and none of the lawyers may pay attention to the interests of parties who are not part of the transaction at all, regardless of whether the transaction affects those parties' vital interests. The Fullerian legislator is like a transactional lawyer whose "client" is the numerical or power majority in the community; and, as in the case of the lawyer, there is a tension between legislating on behalf of the client's interest and legislating on behalf of everyone's interest.

In his many writings on the adversarial ethics of the legal profession, Fuller made it clear that he was aware of the problem that advancing client interests may not be in the public interest; but he never found a successful solution to it.[57] That is because no successful solution can be found. Proving that the pursuit of special interests is identical to the

---

[54] That, at any rate, was Oliver Wendell Holmes's conclusion. "[T]he proximate test of good government is that the dominant power has its way," he wrote, and "legislation . . . should modify itself in accordance with the will of the *de facto* supreme power in the community." The first quotation comes from "Montesquieu," in Oliver Wendell Holmes, *Collected Legal Papers* (New York: Peter Smith, 1952), 258; the second, from Oliver Wendell Holmes, "The Gas-Stokers' Strike," *Harvard Law Review* 44, no. 5 (March 1931): 796.

[55] Alfred, Lord Tennyson, "Ulysses," in Robert Penn Warren and Albert Erskine, eds., *Six Centuries of Great Poetry* (New York: Dell, 1955), pp. 411–12, 11.3–4, 18, 36–38.

[56] I have offered an extended treatment of this question in my *Lawyers and Justice: An Ethical Study* (Princeton, NJ: Princeton University Press, 1988), chaps. 6 and 7.

[57] I argue this in detail in "Rediscovering Fuller's Legal Ethics," 819–29.

pursuit of general interests is like squaring the circle. It is a problem that political philosophers have always wrestled with—Kant argued that the interests of male property-holders are suitably universal, Hegel entered the same claim for bureaucrats, Marx for the proletariat, György Lukács for the Communist Party, and innumerable patriarchs for the menfolk. History has been unusually generous in providing counterexamples to their theories. Civic republican constitutional theorists have in recent years made the claim of universality on behalf of judges.[58] But Fuller is perhaps the only philosopher to do so on behalf of lawyers.[59] That is one of his great strengths; no one, it seems to me, has thought more deeply or perceptively about the services of lawyers in the liberalization of societies. But (let's face it) lawyers aren't *that* good.

Law and Philosophy, Georgetown University Law Center

[58] See, for example, Frank I. Michelman, "Foreword: Traces of Self-Government," *Harvard Law Review* 100, no. 1 (November 1986): 4-77; and Cass R. Sunstein, "Interest Groups in American Public Law," *Stanford Law Review* 38, no. 1 (November 1985): 29-87.

[59] Talcott Parsons, however, argued that lawyers play a central role in mediating between public interests (represented by the law) and private interests (those of clients). See Talcott Parsons, "A Sociologist Looks at the Legal Profession," in his *Essays in Sociological Theory*, rev. ed. (New York: Free Press, 1954), 370-85. In some ways, his structural-functionalist argument was anticipated by Tocqueville in his famous chapter on lawyers as the American aristocracy in *Democracy in America*. Alexis de Tocqueville, *Democracy in America*, ed. J. P. Meyer, trans. George Lawrence (Garden City, NY: Anchor Books, 1969), chap. 8, 1:263-70. For discussion of the Tocqueville-Parsons tradition, see my "The *Noblesse Oblige* Tradition in the Practice of Law," *Vanderbilt Law Review* 41, no. 4 (May 1988): 717-40.

FAIRNESS IN HOLDINGS: A NATURAL LAW ACCOUNT OF PROPERTY AND WELFARE RIGHTS*

By Joseph Boyle

I. Introduction

In this essay I will try to develop a natural law justification of welfare rights. The justification I will undertake is from the perspective of Catholic natural law, that is, the strand of natural law that has been developed theoretically by Roman Catholic canonists, theologians, and philosophers since Aquinas, and affirmed by Catholic teachers as the basis for most moral obligations. Catholic natural law is, therefore, natural law as developed and understood by Catholics or others respecting Catholic traditions of inquiry. It is not, however, primarily or exclusively natural law *for* Catholics, since the very idea of natural law includes the conviction that it is accessible in principle to anyone.

By welfare rights, I mean a species of political rights. I understand rights to be the grounding of duties in the interest or welfare of other people. I understand political rights to be legally recognized and established claims by members of a political society on that society as a community, whose leaders and members have duties based upon the interests of those who have the rights in question. Welfare rights are not simply the claims of some and the duties of others to forbearance, but claims and duties to provide or guarantee the provision of a fair share of those instrumentalities or empowerments important for living good human lives: these include things like education, housing, health care, and welfare support for the elderly, the unemployed, and the underemployed. There are various ways for a political society to guarantee that such needs are met, and various ways to organize the provision of assistance to the needy. These ways of giving legal form and social reality to the welfare rights of the needy are themselves, of course, subject to moral scrutiny. However, the thrust of this essay is to establish the moral grounds for the political establishment of welfare rights themselves, not for any particular social arrangement that implements these rights. In particular, I am not arguing that government should presumptively be the provider of assistance for the needy; Catholic natural law suggests that voluntary associ-

* I wish to thank the other contributors to this volume for their helpful comments on a presentation of an earlier draft of this essay. I am also grateful to John Finnis, Germain Grisez, James Murphy, Ellen Frankel Paul, and Michael Vertin for written comments on the earlier draft, which revealed many errors and suggested significant improvements.

ations should play this role whenever possible. My argument is, therefore, for the conclusion that political society should use its legal authority to guarantee that the welfare rights of its needy members are recognized.

A political society cannot guarantee such support for people in need without some form of taxation, particularly of those not in need. Thus, taxation that is redistributive of wealth in at least this sense is required for welfare rights. The justification of political welfare rights, therefore, must be grounded in moral considerations sufficiently weighty to justify some redistributive taxation.

I undertake this justification of welfare rights because some within the tradition of Catholic natural law reasoning, particularly twentieth-century Catholic moralists and teachers, have affirmed significant welfare rights and have, in effect, held them to be *natural* by claiming that they are required for human dignity.[1] Yet these statements and the body of theoretical literature supporting them do not appear to contain a philosophical explanation of precisely how such rights are justified. Lacking such an explanation, one might be led to suppose that such talk on the part of Catholic exponents of natural law is overstated, or simply an arresting way of restating traditionally held obligations that are really social rather than political.

This supposition appears to be supported by the tradition's classic sources. Catholic exponents of natural law, at least since Thomas Aquinas (1224–1274), have emphasized the common obligation of every person, as his or her capacity allows, to assist those in need. This obligation, however, is a responsibility, at least initially, of individuals, and perhaps of small communities like families, neighborhoods, or parishes—it is not a responsibility of political society. There are warrants within Catholic natural law thought for transferring individual and small group responsi-

---

[1] The classic statement is Pope John XXIII, *Pacem in Terris* (Peace on Earth), trans. National Catholic Welfare Conference (Washington, DC: National Catholic Welfare Conference, 1963), par. 11: "Beginning our discussion of the rights of man, we see that every man has the right to life, to bodily integrity and to the means which are suitable for the proper development of life; these are primarily food, clothing, shelter, rest, medical care, and finally the necessary social services. Therefore, a human being also has the right to security in cases of sickness, inability to work, widowhood, old age, unemployment, or in any other case in which he is deprived of the means of subsistence through no fault of his own." This teaching is continued in Vatican Council II and in subsequent papal teaching; for the most recent statement of this, see Pope John Paul II, *Centesimus Annus: On the Hundredth Anniversary of Rerum Novarum* (Boston: Daughters of St. Paul, 1991), par. 48. John Paul rejects what he calls the "welfare state," but his reasoning makes plain that this position is meant to be consistent with welfare rights. Papal teaching does not stipulate the specific forms or organizational structures that respecting welfare rights requires; it affirms welfare rights as social responsibilities that political society has the responsibility to enforce, and rejects socialist remedies that either deny private property or remove individual and nonpolitical group initiative.

For earlier defenses of welfare rights by Catholic moralists in the natural law tradition, see John A. Ryan, *Distributive Justice: The Right and Wrong of Our Present Distribution of Wealth*, new rev. ed. (New York: Macmillan, 1939), 87–113, 268–81; and Johannes Messner, *Social Ethics: Natural Law in the Western World*, trans. J. J. Doherty, rev. ed. (St. Louis, MO: B. Herder, 1965), 646–55.

bilities to the ambit of political communities; notable among these warrants is what is nowadays dubbed "the principle of subsidiarity" (to be explained in Section IV below). But I am not aware of any detailed application of such warrants to the specific case of welfare rights.

Within the Catholic strand of natural law thinking, then, there is a lack of developed analysis showing how welfare rights emerge from more fundamental moral principles, and there are perhaps even some significant tensions between a characteristic natural law affirmation of property rights and a willingness to allow redistributive taxation. I will take a few steps toward filling in this lacuna and reducing the apparent tensions. I propose to do this by (1) recounting Aquinas's account of property rights and their limits; (2) considering whether and to what extent this account is compatible with welfare rights; and (3) arguing that very basic natural law principles, applied to certain conditions of modern social life, imply social obligations that are properly coordinated by political authority. This political action has the effect of making actual, in the form of enforceable entitlements, the right to assistance from the better off that the needy already have. I believe that this implication secures welfare rights that are natural in a limited but important sense.

II. The Thomistic Account of Property

Aquinas presents his fullest account of property and its justification in his most thorough and systematic discussion of stealing. The account he presents is consistent with and complements other things that he says about property rights.[2] It begins with an argument that the human possession of nonhuman realities or "exterior things" is natural. The sense of "natural" in this context is indicated by the Aristotelian and biblically based arguments Aquinas presents for his conclusion: "natural" does not mean anything like "biologically inevitable" or "in accord with laws of nature"; rather, it means "appropriate or morally justified." The human possession that Aquinas holds to be natural is said to be such because (1) humans, as rational creatures, are capable of the use of nonhuman realities for human benefit; (2) such use is not, as such, an affront to God's dominion over the universe; and (3) such use is no affront to nonhuman things themselves, which, as less perfect, are properly ordered to human benefit.[3] The second and third of these reasons are likely to be controver-

---

[2] For a discussion of all the relevant texts, see John Finnis, *Aquinas: Moral, Political, and Legal Theory* (Oxford: Oxford University Press, 1998), 189-96. Finnis explains the textual nuances and complexities that my shorter recounting slights.

[3] Thomas Aquinas, *Summa Theologiae*, II–II, q. 66, a. 1. The second part of the second part of the *Summa Theologiae* contains Aquinas's mature doctrine on specific moral issues. The first part of the second part contains his ethical theory and moral psychology, including his general treatment of natural law. Question 66 of the second part of the second part is his question on stealing; it is part of the discussion of injustice. Because the *Summa Theologiae* appears in many editions and translations, most of which can be followed through use of the

sial, and I cannot defend them here. However controversial, they provide
an idea of what Aquinas means by saying that the possession of or dominion over what he calls "exterior things" is natural for humans: the
possession he has in mind is use for human benefit, and that use is
natural, that is, morally justified.[4]

This analysis does no more than normatively situate humans before the
array of nonpersonal realities by arguing for the legitimacy of human use,
for human purposes, of all such things. It does not address questions
concerning the fair distribution of such things or of the fair distribution,
among humans, of the benefits of using these things. Aquinas does not
say here, nor does he provide premises for concluding, that the superper-
sonal realities he calls "exterior things" (which I will simply call "things"
in the remainder of this essay) are limited to things undeveloped by
human initiative. The plain sense of his arguments is that all things—
whether straight from the hand of God, such as trees and rocks, or developed by humans, such as farmlands and artifacts—are to be used by
humans. If human improvement affects things in a way relevant to fairness, it is not at this level of natural possession.

Nor does Aquinas say or suggest that things are in some way the
common property of all. His analysis does not concern the relationships
between humans that arise because of the common human need to use
things; instead, it concerns the relationships between humans as such, on
the one hand, and God and things on the other. If his analysis implies
anything at all about *common* possession of such things, it is simply that,
as things, they are to be used to serve needs that are characterized only
generically as human needs.

Questions about the relationships among humans that arise because of
their common need to use things are addressed by Aquinas in his discussion of whether it is permissible for anyone to possess something as
his or her own (*quasi proprium*). In Aquinas's terminology, "*proprium*" (or
"proper") is simply the contrary of "common." Hence, this discussion
is not concerned solely with individual or private possession, but with
any assignment of things to smaller groups or individuals within a
community—to a corporation or religious community within a polity as
well as to individuals within a family or region. However, Aquinas's
language and argumentation both suggest that his focal case for this
discussion is individual ownership.

To answer the question he poses, Aquinas distinguishes two aspects of
the human possession of things: the authority to take care of and distribute things, and their actual use. He maintains that in respect to the

---

standard method of referring to the work, I will use the standard method, exhibited in the
first sentence of this note.

[4] The English word "possess" does not seem to capture precisely the relationship to things
that Aquinas is after here. Nevertheless, he uses the Latin noun "*possessio*" and the Latin
verb "*possidere*." I do not know why he did not use the word "*usus*."

first aspect, possession may be—and in some situations needs to be—proper and not common; in respect to the second aspect, he says that possession should be common. Both elements of this position require some explanation.

Aquinas holds that it is licit for some individuals to have the authority to take care of and distribute (*potestas procurandi et dispensandi*) things, by which Aquinas means the authority over how they are to be used; I will refer to this authority as "ownership."[5] He appears to think that this claim is uncontroversial once it is distinguished from his thesis that things, in respect to their actual use, should be held in common. The limited character of Aquinas's claim about ownership is taken by him as sufficient to remove objections that this norm is egoist. Moreover, the considerations of the kind that he thinks show that there is *necessity* for individual authority over useful things also plausibly establish, *a fortiori*, its permissibility.

Aquinas lists three reasons for the claim that ownership authority over things is necessary. The first reason is that a person is more careful with things that he alone is expected to care for than he is with things that are held in common. Supporting this is the observation that when dealing with things that are commonly held, people avoid labor and leave things to others; we see this happen when a multitude of officials supervises the same activity. The second reason is that human affairs are conducted in a more orderly way when different people are in charge of different things; confusion arises if all are in charge of everything. The third reason is that social life is more peaceful if the authority over things is divided among people. A cause of quarreling is avoided if people are satisfied with their own things.[6]

The first of these reasons seems to be based on the purpose of possession—to use things for human benefit. This purpose will be significantly compromised, at least among humans likely to flee labor, if holdings are common. The third reason seems to be based on the requirements for harmony among people: as long as people are tempted to quarrel about things held commonly, harmony requires a division of ownership of things. The second reason seems to hover between these considerations, for the confusion that arises when all are in charge of everything could be considered objectionable because it impedes the effective use of things or because it inhibits harmony among people. Whichever considerations support the second reason, however, the result

---

[5] Aquinas, *Summa Theologiae*, II–II, q. 66, a. 2. The verb "*dispensare*" also means "to weigh out or pay out" and "to manage." Having the power or authority both to take care of something and to distribute it or its benefits seems very close to the idea of being in charge of something and being responsible for its use. Ownership may suggest a stronger claim on a thing, so my usage has a stipulative component.

[6] See ibid., II–II, q. 66, a. 2c.

is the same: the second reason, like the first and third reasons, supports giving people ownership authority over things.

Aquinas does not explain precisely how strongly these considerations are meant to support the necessity of ownership, nor does he specify the exact moral significance of that necessity. His reasoning suggests that the necessity in question is that of a necessary means to the morally defined ends of human utility and harmony. This would seem to make a division of things into those owned by some and those owned by others an implication of moral principle—of the natural law. Yet Aquinas nowhere affirms precisely this, and several times he denies that any particular ownership arrangement is required by the natural law.[7] No doubt he was concerned to allow for the early Christian practice of common life, as well as the practice of consecrated poverty in which the vowed religious, like himself, owned nothing. He was also taking note of the possibility that circumstances could arise in which humans would not be tempted to shirk work or quarrel over things—circumstances that he thought existed before the fall of Adam.[8] Therefore, he likely regarded the necessity of dividing things by ownership as characterizing most, but not all, situations of human life. Whenever the factors requiring such a division do not obtain, the obligation to establish a regime including private ownership does not exist. As a practical matter, however, this condition is rarely fulfilled. Thus, some sort of property arrangement is morally required in most societies.

The character of the necessity that makes ownership a moral requirement does not, of course, settle the details of a regime of property. These details are settled by custom and legislation, which determine, in the light of principles of fairness, such things as the protocols for the acquisition and disposal of property, the limits of owners' authority over their property, and so on. Aquinas has little to say on such matters. More fundamentally, neither the character of this necessity nor the set of powers, permissions, and proscriptions that define a property regime implementing this necessity has, by itself, a fixed moral position in relation to other normative considerations. Aquinas's discussion of the second aspect of possession—use—establishes this position.

Aquinas introduces the statement that use should be common as if it were unproblematic. He simply says that "with respect to this [use] a human being should not have exterior things as his or her own, but as common, that is, so that someone may readily share them for the neces-

----

[7] Among other places in Aquinas's discussion of *possessio quasi proprium*, see ibid., II–II, q. 66, a. 2, ad 1. See Alan Donagan, *The Theory of Morality* (Chicago: University of Chicago Press, 1977), 99, for a generalization from this text to the effect that Aquinas represents the Hebrew-Christian moral tradition here in denying that there is any natural right to private property. However, I do not think that this Thomistic text or any other denies that *some* division of property among groups or individuals—as opposed to a detailed, specific division—is a requirement of moral considerations prior to human decision, and therefore a matter of the natural law.

[8] See Aquinas, *Summa Theologiae*, I, q. 98, a. 1, ad 1.

sities of others," and then cites St. Paul's letter to Timothy as support.[9] This suggests a sense of "common" that is more robust and morally specified than that which was present in Aquinas's earlier discussion of the natural status of human possession. In the context of possession, "common" was merely a reference to who has ownership authority over the things in question; deciding who was to receive the benefits derived from the use of things had not yet been addressed. When Aquinas specifically addresses use, we find him using "common" to refer to the particular *beneficiary* of the thing being used—that is, the term indicates a contrast between the "common" beneficiary and the "proper" owner. Owners—that is, those who are in charge of something—should make it (or its fruits) available to relieve the necessities of others.

This norm regulating the relationships between human beings with respect to things is clearly meant to serve the welfare of all humans, not just the welfare of those who happen to be in special relationships toward things. Consequently, this norm falls within the domain of justice. Aquinas's claim here is that things are to be used in a fair way to serve human utility, and that a regime of property rights can be, and usually is, required to serve that moral end. This goal implies the requirement of common use. Aquinas and the wider Christian moral tradition have focused on a specific implication of the requirement of common use, namely, the obligation to help those in need. So, common use does not deny the legitimacy of ownership, but indicates the scope of owners' responsibilities. Consequently, an owner's use of her things to serve her own needs or to carry out familial obligations does not violate the requirement of common use unless her use of her things is in some way unfair to others.

This becomes more explicit in Aquinas's discussion of taking others' property in cases of extreme necessity, in which he says that such takings can be permissible and that permissible takings of this sort are not examples of stealing. In discussing the extreme necessity cases, he begins to spell out his account of the relationship between the natural and the conventional aspects of the human use of things. The natural aspects imply that things should be used to relieve human necessity; this seems to be a specification of the requirement of common use. The conventional aspects are the basis for dividing and apportioning things among various owners. This division of things by human law need not prevent their use for relieving human need. Quite the opposite: the natural law requires owners to use anything residual or superfluous to help the needy.[10] This

---

[9] Ibid., II-II, q. 66, a. 2. The translation is mine. Aquinas's Latin for what I translate as the last clause reads *ut scilicet de facili aliquis eas communicet in necessitates aliorum.*

[10] See also ibid., II-II, q. 32, a. 5. Here, Aquinas treats giving alms as a moral obligation. That is, he maintains that giving alms falls under a precept, not a counsel of perfection, when one has more than one needs. He goes on to define what is superfluous and makes clear that taking care of one's own necessities and providing for those in one's care is not superfluous and is ordinarily the prior responsibility. Finnis, *Aquinas*, 190–93 details the nuances of Aquinas's understanding of what is superfluous.

norm is to be distinguished from the charitable counsel that people should consider nonobligatory generosity from resources needed for their own good purposes. That counsel surely is part of Christian tradition, but the norm here states a distinct *obligation* to use what is extra for others. The context of this norm suggests the beginning of an implicit definition of what is surplus or extra: this definition includes permission for owners to use their property initially to meet their own needs, as well as the requirement that they carry out basic vocational responsibilities, such as taking care of their families, before attending to others in need. Additionally, owners retain discretion over how to use their property to help the needy, since, as Aquinas observes, many people are in need, and this need cannot be met from a single thing.

It is only in cases of extreme and immediate need that Aquinas believes that necessity overrides ownership. In discussing this issue, Aquinas seems to accept the dictum that in cases of necessity, all is common.[11] This is not a general declaration that in extreme circumstances moral norms do not apply, but a claim that in conditions of urgent necessity, the requirement of common use—that is, fair use of things for human benefit—overrides the reasons and conventions that support claims of ownership. In these circumstances, a person in need or one helping him or her may justly take what law assigns as the property of another, if that legal condition is the only moral bar to taking it.[12] The reasons why common use overrides ownership in these cases are morally decisive considerations of fair and rational utility. Ordinarily, these considerations are served by ownership, but not in extreme circumstances.

This very brief recounting of Aquinas's treatment of property indicates that several characteristic features of Thomistic moral theory combine to ground an account of property that sees it as an instrument for securing aspects of the human good. Ownership of useful things ordinarily facilitates the good use of those things. Initially, the owner and those for whom the owner is responsible benefit, and then, if utility remains and the owner acts responsibly, others in need benefit. The effect of the Thom-

[11] See Aquinas, *Summa Theologiae*, II-II, q. 66, a. 7, *sed contra*. At least in the *Summa*, this part of a Thomistic article is usually an authority with whom Aquinas largely agrees. Here, however, no authority is cited—there is simply the dictum—*in necessitate sunt omnia communia*. This dictum was likely a canonical commonplace. Aquinas affirms this sentence unambiguously elsewhere; see, for example, II-II, q. 32, a. 7, ad 3. But here at II-II, q. 66, a. 7, ad 3, he qualifies the dictum by saying that necessity renders the thing taken the property, not of everyone, but of the person in need.

[12] Finnis, *Aquinas*, 191–93 provides the details of Aquinas's position on this matter. Although Aquinas's discussion appears to emphasize the duties of owners rather than the rights of the needy in these situations, it seems to me that because these duties are chiefly grounded in the needs of the needy, it is reasonable to refer to these duties as rights that the needy possess; see note 16 below. For the canonical background of Aquinas's discussion, which suggests that some canonists recognized the existence of the rights of the needy in these situations (and that some canonists considered the possibility of enforcing these rights via ecclesiastical authority), see Brian Tierney, *The Idea of Natural Rights* (Atlanta, GA: Scholars Press, 1997), 73–75.

istic analysis is to give to those who have charge of some useful things considerable discretion over how these things or their fruits will be used. This discretion, however, exists within a framework of strict moral obligations.

Within this normative framework, this combination of discretion and obligation is not a surprise. The Thomistic version of natural law is perfectionist: a good life is one that reason shows to be perfective of persons. The reach of a good person's reason into his or her life goes very far, farther than general moral considerations, because right reason should shape the whole of a person's life into that of a virtuous character. Thus, although there is little or no room within this perfectionist morality for valuing autonomy (that is, merely doing just as one pleases), the discretion of individuals with respect to property (and other aspects of life) is justified for the reasons Aquinas adduced.

However, as later natural law theorists have held, it appears that on a natural law conception of human life, this discretion is not simply an effect of social arrangements based on other considerations, but is itself a necessary means to or component of several aspects of the human good.[13] Without some discretion over property and other aspects of life, a person's ability to maintain life and health, to work creatively, to respond to others generously, to worship God appropriately, and to create a morally good character are seriously limited. If discretion with respect to property is a necessary means to or an element of the human good, then that is another reason, besides those presented by Aquinas, why natural law grounds the judgment that a person should own some things. I will assume in what follows that the natural law account of property includes the idea that ownership not only facilitates the proper use of things and promotes harmony, but also provides a form of discretion that is a component of many dimensions of a good life, including virtuous living itself. I believe that this element of the natural law account is important in thinking about welfare rights and their limits.[14]

---

[13] Catholic social teaching since Pope Leo XIII (1810-1903) emphasizes this element of value in private property: it is the ground for Catholic judgments that property should be widely held and not concentrated in the holdings of a few. See my "Natural Law, Ownership, and the World's Natural Resources," *Journal of Value Inquiry* 23 (1989): 196, and the sources cited there.

[14] I am not supposing that all natural law accounts of property and political society would be consistent with welfare rights. Stoic natural law theory—at least as represented by Cicero, whom Aquinas read—would likely have rejected welfare rights as incompatible with the importance of political society's respect for private property. See Cicero, *De Officiis*, trans. Walter Miller (Cambridge, MA: Harvard University Press, 1913), bk. II, chap. 73: "For the chief purpose of constitutional state and municipal governments was that individual property rights might be secured. For although it was by Nature's guidance that men were drawn together in communities, it was in the hope of safeguarding their possessions that they sought the protection of cities." See also chap. 79. For Aquinas, political society is natural in a way that property—and certainly ownership—is not. Yet even modern natural law theorists whose normative views are more like Aquinas's than Cicero's reject welfare rights; see Henry B. Veatch, *Human Rights: Fact or Fancy?* (Baton Rouge: Louisiana State

III. PROPERTY AND WELFARE RIGHTS

There are several ways in which one might think that Aquinas's account of property is incompatible with welfare rights. One global form of this argument is the claim that the Thomistic account of property, like natural law positions generally, is formulated in terms of the authority and responsibilities of various people in social situations, and that this normative outlook is so different from modern conceptions of rights as to make them conceptually incommensurable. According to this claim, even though Aquinas's language might be understood as implying the defeasible property rights of owners, the far more important thrust of his analysis is to elucidate the responsibilities of owners and others.

I think it is true that most modern conceptions of rights are in some deep ways opposed to premodern theories of natural law. However, the point of opposition is not, I think, in the very concept of rights and its relations to more traditional deontic conceptions, but in several distinctively modern values associated with rights—in particular, with the connection between rights and autonomy understood as doing what one pleases.[15] The concept of rights itself is not incommensurable with deontic concepts of obligation or responsibility. As I indicated in Section I, rights, including welfare rights, can be reasonably understood as grounds of certain obligations, that is, as grounds of duties that people have toward others because of these others' needs or welfare. The issue at hand is a good example: if those capable of helping a needy person have a duty to help that is grounded in the welfare of the needy person, then the needy person has a right to that help grounded in need.[16] I am not suggesting here that the idea of welfare rights as political rights existed in the thought of a medieval writer such as Aquinas. As I will argue below, the very possibility of political welfare rights presupposes a modern organization of society. But as Aquinas's discussion of the responsibilities of owners and the rights of those in extreme need makes plain, he does have the essential idea that some duties of individuals are based upon the needs of others.

The differences between political welfare rights and Aquinas's conception of the duty to help the needy remain very clear. The requirements of

University Press, 1985), 177–97; and Douglas Rasmussen, "Economic Rights Versus Human Dignity: The Flawed Moral Vision of the United States Catholic Bishops," in Douglas Rasmussen and James Sterba, *The Catholic Bishops and the Economy: A Debate* (New Brunswick, NJ: Transaction Books, 1987), 45–84.

[15] For evidence that Aquinas had a conception of human rights, see Finnis, *Aquinas*, 132–38.

[16] See Joseph Raz, *The Morality of Freedom* (Oxford: Oxford University Press, 1987), 166: "*Definition:* 'X has a right' if and only if X can have rights, and, other things being equal, an aspect of X's well-being (his interest) is a sufficient reason for holding some other person(s) to be under a duty." Raz deals here with the general concept of a right, not with specific issues created by the legal establishment of rights. I assume that Raz's general account of rights is silent about the moral principles needed to move from a person's need to others' duties.

common use, including the requirement that things a person owns should be shared to relieve the needs of others, is plainly a distinct moral proposition from those involved in the affirmation of modern, political welfare rights. As articulated by Aquinas, this requirement is a responsibility of individual owners, one generally to be carried out at their discretion even when the requirement is a strict obligation. The duties that exist under modern, political welfare rights are carried out in ways that are not similarly individualized and discretionary. The duties are not simply those of individuals but of the polity as a community, and they are carried out by taxation, which is not discretionary for the taxed—paying one's taxes is ordinarily morally obligatory and enforced by public authority. Nevertheless, political welfare rights are logically and practically compatible with ownership; indeed, fairly widespread private ownership ordinarily provides the tax base needed to finance welfare rights. Other systems of ownership may be less able to accommodate both welfare rights and ownership rights. For example, more thoroughly socialist arrangements— even if they could fund welfare rights from publicly owned resources— would, to whatever extent they deny people significant rights of ownership, run afoul of the natural law considerations that support ownership.

The tensions between political welfare rights and property as justified by Aquinas's arguments are between welfare rights and some values (such as owners' discretion and effective use of things) secured by ownership conventions. They are not tensions between welfare rights and common use as such, for political welfare rights are a way of securing one aspect of common use—sharing resources with the needy. Even as a way of implementing the moral responsibility of common use, a system of political welfare rights will fail morally if it ignores Aquinas's reasons favoring ownership, for these reasons indicate that ownership ordinarily serves common use. Thus, if the establishment of welfare rights undercuts the effectiveness that ownership provides in securing human benefit from things, causes disharmony among people, or deprives people of the discretion needed for living a creative and morally good life, then establishing these rights will be morally questionable.

However, a society's program to implement welfare rights need not run afoul of the reasons supporting ownership. I shall offer three arguments by way of explanation. First, as noted above, such a program should not seek to replace ownership as the basic way humans make good use of things. Rather, a program should provide a way of sharing resources and the benefits from their use with those in need. Their use of the resources provided to assist them in meeting their necessities is a good use of resources, and in some cases, at least, puts them in a position to act as productively as they can. Of course, some of the needy will abuse the help that they are given and squander the resources or irresponsibly wait for another handout—this outcome of a program of welfare rights is probably an unavoidable side effect of any undertaking of this kind. This bad side effect can be minimized by those designing and administering the programs implementing these rights. Even if a program is ineffective at stopping such side effects, however, one can ordinarily undertake important initiatives having bad side effects if accepting those bad side effects is not excessively harmful to those affected by the initiative. Therefore, unless the abuse of welfare rights by some is very harmful to either the abusers or to others, the welfare of the needy prevails and it is reasonable to tolerate this side effect.

Second, the use of a system of welfare rights to carry out the responsibility of sharing surplus with those in need is not inherently a cause of disharmony. The specific source of quarrels that Aquinas thought common holdings caused does not exist, for under systems of welfare rights, goods are not treated as common but as the property of owners or of the needy to whom they are provided as a matter of right. Welfare rights are not a form of access to a commons—rather, they are grounds of duties, held by those controlling resources, to use those resources fairly to benefit the needy. A system of welfare rights can contribute to resentments of various kinds—enforced support makes owners resent the needy, and their own dependency makes the needy resent the owners. However, unless we assume the moral rectitude of such resentments, they can hardly be decisive factors as we set up social forms that facilitate the moral use of things. Furthermore, if these resentments are not taken as decisive, then they are really just side effects of welfare rights, and therefore can be minimized and accepted unless they are so great as to make social cooperation impossible.

Third, a system of welfare rights is compatible with providing people a level of discretion over their lives that is needed for developing a virtuous and creative life. Indeed, it provides the needy with some of the resources that are necessary for exercising discretion in the same way as better-off owners.

Surely, however, there is a danger, when administering plans of welfare rights, of reducing the taxpaying part of the citizenry to a kind of moralistically based servility. There is no bright line that indicates when this has happened, but there are some relevant considerations. For example, if many of the ordinarily law-abiding citizens begin to feel morally justified in cheating on their taxes because they think that an excessive amount goes to help others, then the line has probably been crossed. When this line is crossed, the other values at stake in ownership—the good use of things and social harmony—are also likely to be compromised.[17] This is because resentment at unreasonable levels of taxation and the government's apparent indifference to whether the recipient used the funds

---

[17] Cicero, in *De Officiis*, bk. II, chap. 79, details the moral and social effects of unjustified expropriation and redistribution of property. Any regime of welfare rights requiring the sort of expropriation Cicero describes would run afoul not only of Cicero's theory of property, but also Aquinas's more limited and circumspect approach.

productively will affect taxpayers, while recipients will suffer demoralization caused by servility.

Therefore, there is a significant limit on the extent to which a polity can provide welfare rights. A regime that impoverishes its citizens to maintain welfare rights beyond levels that the society can afford would likely be unstable. Such a regime would also violate the requirement of common use, since it would undercut the capacity of owners to fulfill their obligations, including that of sharing their holdings or the fruits thereof with the needy.[18] Still, the experience of modern polities indicates that it is possible for societies to tax at levels that provide significant help to the needy without removing from taxpayers' lives the discretion that they need for virtuous living. This, of course, presupposes that such societies are wealthy enough that many of their members can reasonably be taxed for welfare purposes; this makes sense morally only if (1) many members of these societies have surpluses that they can share, and (2) doing so will not compromise members' discretion over their lives.

IV. Welfare Rights and Social Conditions

The requirement of common use—that things are to be used to serve human utility in a fair way—is a very basic principle of the natural law. Common use includes the prescription that things are to be used for human benefit, that is, as instruments for the individual and communal action by which people perfect themselves by choosing to live good lives. Common use also presupposes that people are facilitated in living good lives when those capable of exercising responsibility for their own lives (and for those too immature or infirm) have a level of authority sufficient to allow them to carry out their responsibility. Ownership makes this kind of authority possible, and for this and other reasons, ownership implements common use, with the rider that any excess of goods must be shared with those in need.

A mature person's responsibility to take care of himself or herself and those near and dear expands over time to include more people. This happens as one comes to identify with others (neighbors and coworkers, for example), and to include their welfare as part of one's own good. It can also happen in a more straightforwardly moralistic way whenever a person recognizes that, solely because of his feelings of indifference or hostility, he is denying others the benefits that he secures for those in his circle of affection or responsibility. Furthermore, one's circle of affection or responsibility can also enlarge when application of the Golden Rule causes one to adjust one's feelings as reason demands—at the very least,

---

[18] For an earlier statement of mine of this limitation on welfare rights, see Joseph Boyle, "Catholic Social Justice and Health Care Entitlement Packages," *Christian Bioethics* 2, no. 3 (December 1996): 284-86.

such application of the rule may cause one to choose to set aside unreasonable emotional limits when deciding how to act.[19]

This dynamic of expanding affection and moral concern has no natural limit short of including everyone. Yet, a reasonable way of identifying a limit is to focus on feasibility. One might formulate a moral norm for dealing with neighbors: that all are obliged to provide assistance to those in need whom they are capable of helping. This capacity to help is limited in two major dimensions. First, when one can provide aid, there are limits as to what one may permissibly do. One goes beyond neighborly assistance when one tries to meddle in or take over responsibility for someone's life. Assisting someone in need by providing encouragement, advice, and the means for that person to solve his own problems is helpful. Doing more than this is likely to be futile and morally problematic.

The second limit on the capacity to help involves proximity, but is more carefully stated as capacity. The relevant consideration here is that the needy are within reach of one's assistance. Yet a person or community's capacity to help those in need is not just a matter of physical proximity. The capacity to help is more complicated than that. For example, one might be *morally* incapable of giving neighborly assistance even to someone close at hand, if one's other obligations preclude such aid. Because of this, obligations of neighborly assistance necessarily allow for significant discretion over how one should respond to the needy whom one encounters. But this justifiable discretion does not release us from providing assistance when we have surplus funds, even when those in need are at some distance. We should try to help if we can reach these people and if our assistance might be productive.

The dynamics of the expansion of the obligation to assist others in need and the limits of this obligation are each affected by technology and the character of a community's social organization. These dynamics require using available methods to embrace more people and to serve them better when that is possible; technology and social organization can change the de facto limitations on one's capacity to help. Therefore, one's responsibility for others reaches farther to the extent that technology and social organization expand one's capacity to help without bringing other limits to capacity into play. When those conditions obtain, one's duty to help becomes a duty to make use of the technology and social organization at hand.

It is recalling a truism to note that modern society is based on a division of labor unheard of in earlier agricultural and urban societies. Functionally differentiated professions and occupations make possible a far more

---

[19] The Golden Rule has historically been taken as a principle, or as closely related to principle, in natural law; I cannot defend the status of the Golden Rule here. For a brief exploration of some of the historical and conceptual issues, see Donagan, *The Theory of Morality*, 57-66. For an account of the logic of the Golden Rule, see Germain Grisez, *The Way of The Lord Jesus*, vol. 3, *Difficult Moral Questions* (Quincy, IL: Franciscan Press, 1997), 861-70.

effective and efficient pursuit of various human goods, including easier provision of very elementary empowerments such as food, health care, shelter, and education—the things the needy most often lack, and which others can provide. Within this differentiated and technologically developed condition of society, people can pay specialists to do many of the things that they formerly did for themselves, thus freeing them for other pursuits. Similarly, people today can assist others by providing funds to charitable organizations. Thus, the full use of the resources of modern society can help the needy in ways not dreamed of in earlier centuries. Moreover, modern social organization can extend the reach of helpers to many who were formerly beyond reach. Modern communications and the fungibility and mobility of money also allow us to reach many needy individuals who were formerly out of sight.

The preceding two points lead one to the conclusion that the obligation of neighborly assistance is transformed and extended by the conditions that define modern society. Modern owners routinely fulfill their own personal and familial responsibilities by making use of the resources that society provides, and they ordinarily judge themselves duty-bound to do so. Since these resources are the very same instruments that are needed to assist the needy, and because the Golden Rule plays a major role in determining the extent of the responsibility, it follows that those who have these resources and use them for their own benefit are also required to use them to fulfill their duty to share with the needy.

Therefore, the requirement of neighborly assistance cannot, in modern societies, be limited to the direct and face-to-face help of those in need. Moreover, it is hard to imagine the resources of a modern society being used rationally and efficiently without both significant common action by cooperating groups and some level of regulatory action by various authorities. Plainly, voluntary associations, such as the United Way or Catholic Charities (both based in the United States), do much to create and channel common action for the sake of the needy.

The social organization of voluntary groups to help the needy appears to be common in most societies. Moreover, on natural law grounds, an individual's cooperation with such organizations by joining them and giving them resources is frequently more than a voluntary and charitable action—it is an obligation. Such an obligation exists when a person is obliged to provide assistance, but cannot do it (or do it well) without cooperating with others. Thus, although the underlying obligation is, and remains, an obligation of each owner, common action is often the most efficacious course in modern society.

Consider a voluntary charitable association of owners in a region who are dedicated to meeting the needs of the poor living among them. Suppose that this organization frees the owners to do other good things with their time and resources, allows them to reach many more of the poor, lets them secure the needs of the poor more fully, and yet does not have such a high subscription fee that owners cannot pay without failing in their other responsibilities. It seems to me wrong for an owner not to join, particularly if one's refusal is based on the ground that one favors other ways of serving the poor that are less beneficial.

Such favored ways of helping the needy may, of course, have side benefits that are not included within the category of "things." Sometimes, for example, face-to-face help is valuable, not only because of the material help it provides the needy person, but also because it makes possible a kind of community and even friendship between the needy person and the owner. These human goods are not embraced by a consideration of what means will best provide the material necessities of life to the needy with the least negative impact on other things that owners should be doing. But focusing too much on individual acts of charity in the condition of modern society would leave far too many needy people unattended. Also, it would overlook the social and personal benefit of anonymous charity. While personally engaged solidarity with the needy can be good, it is above all necessary to see to the needs of people, especially those whom one cannot personally and directly befriend but still can help. The responsibility to provide the necessities of life for those who lack them is not trumped by the propriety and goodness of seeking a personal relationship with those whom one helps. Most of us will have a responsibility to help the needy both in directly personal ways and in less personal but more far-reaching and effective ways.

This natural law picture of people using their resources as a part of their efforts to live virtuous lives requires a robust sense of responsibility to assist the needy on the part of each person capable of providing that assistance. The reach of this responsibility is extended by the technological opportunities available within a society and by the possibilities of cooperating with others in common action to relieve need. But I am assuming that welfare rights are entitlements established by political society, and the argument I have developed so far does not show that there is a ground for establishing politically the social obligation for which I have argued. The Golden Rule considerations on which my argument has depended show that the duty to assist the needy is an extensive social responsibility, but not that it is the responsibility of political society.

Therefore, I must address a further question: how can we justify not simply the move from individual to social obligation, but the additional move from morally required nonpolitical group action to political action? I believe that this second move is justified because in modern developed societies, conditions exist in which carrying out the individual and social obligation to assist the needy requires the specific form of social coordination provided by political action.[20]

---

[20] My earlier formulation of this argument did not attend sufficiently to the role of voluntary associations in fulfilling the responsibility of common use; see Joseph Boyle,

There are two major reasons why the needy in modern politics need the action of political society in order to secure the assistance to which they have a prepolitical right. First, political society properly has regulatory powers over much of the complex organization that characterizes modern life. Voluntary organizations normally lack regulatory power unless it is mandated by government recognition and backed by government enforcement. Such regulatory power makes a unique contribution to aiding the needy; for example, the municipal regulation of rents and the regulation of the pharmaceutical industry to allow the marketing of generic drugs each provide benefits to the needy that voluntary organizations could match only with great expense.

The second reason that the needy require the action of political society is that political society has the capacity to compel public support through taxation. Even if limited to providing tax deductions or credits for charitable donations to organizations such as United Way, taxation would be redistributive. Such deductions or credits have two important benefits. First, enacting such tax breaks guarantees a higher level of predictable support. Second, with tax breaks as an incentive, the morally responsible are less likely to be the only contributors to the needy, for the greedy now have an incentive that they lacked in a purely discretionary system. Tax breaks motivate both the virtuous and the weak-willed to provide the help that they should, and to guarantee to the needy at least some of what is due them.

If political action (1) regulates for the sake of facilitating assistance to the needy, (2) subsidizes other social organizations, or (3) directly supports the needy through tax support, then there exists a system of political welfare rights in the sense that I am defending. That is, legally enforceable entitlements exist, not just duties of owners based on the welfare of the needy. The precise form and extent of such an entitlement system depends on such factors as the wealth and organization of a society and the capacity of its voluntary associations to assist the needy. But whatever the precise form of the system of welfare rights, the duty of owners to use their surplus to assist the needy—a duty grounded in their need—is politically enforced through taxation and regulation. These are the minimum conditions for establishing welfare rights in the sense that I am defending.

I do not believe that all societies are equally able to use political action to help secure welfare rights. The requirements of capacity—including moral capacity—that limit the extent of one's personal responsibility to assist others also apply to common responsibility, including political responsibility. In societies without money or significant division of labor, an

---

"Catholic Social Justice," 286. Here I recognize that voluntary associations are presumptively the proper vehicle for providing social assistance to the needy, but argue that the specific coordination of common action, which only the authoritative action of political society can provide, is also necessary.

organized social effort supported by political action would likely serve the needy no better than could individuals or informally organized groups. Such societies would likely lack professional organizations, the ability to enact significant regulation, and the resources to tax its members or to distribute the funding needed for assisting those in need. More importantly, some societies may not be able to actively assist the needy without violating other grave political responsibilities. For example, some societies could not support the needed taxation without reducing taxpayers to servility. As noted above in Section III, this provides a real moral limit to this form of government action.

In advanced societies, the existence of political welfare rights does not change the nature of the underlying human obligation: this remains an obligation of individual owners in the society to use their surplus for the needy. When a society engages in political action to create a public entitlement, it does this to assist its property-owning members in carrying out part of this underlying obligation and to help the needy receive what is their due.

This political action in support of individuals' carrying out their prepolitical obligations is justified in twentieth-century Catholic natural law theorizing by reference to what is called the "principle of subsidiarity." This so-called "principle" is really a gathering of several elements of the normative outlook of natural law theory to illuminate the relationships that should obtain among interlocking communities and between any community and its members. The principle can be understood as comprising two moral norms and their rationale. The first of these norms precludes larger and more powerful communities (in particular political societies) from taking over from individuals and less powerful communities activities that individuals can do on their own. The second norm allows and sometimes requires assistance from larger and more powerful communities for the needed actions of individuals and small groups, when individuals and small groups alone are incapable of doing what is required.

The rationale for both the norms comprising the principle of subsidiarity is the perfectionism of natural law: the aforementioned claim that people live good lives by carrying out, in their freely chosen actions, the projects and commitments in which they find their personal and communal fulfillment as human beings. On this view, the purpose of organized communities, such as political society, is to facilitate the flourishing of individuals.

The first of the norms of subsidiarity is perhaps the better known. It blocks actions of political society that threaten to take over or usurp, rather than assist, individuals and voluntary associations in carrying out their proper responsibilities. One violates this norm when one seeks to take over people's lives. For example, political ownership of productive property is usually judged by natural law theorists as violating this norm.

The second norm justifies the political action involved in establishing welfare rights. This norm holds that activities of political society affecting matters initially within individual or small group responsibility are permissible and sometimes required when those activities provide needed help for the proper functioning of individuals and voluntary associations.[21]

Generally, political society can offer its members an irreplaceable form of assistance by establishing authoritative and legally enforceable coordination of actions that allow its members to live responsible lives and to cooperate with others within and without the polity. In the specific case of welfare rights, political society uses its specific legal authority to set up social conditions, primarily regulations and redistributive tax laws, in which owners are facilitated in carrying out a basic social responsibility that could not otherwise be carried out so effectively.

This is a proper application of subsidiarity, for here the individual responsibility that political action facilitates is connected in the proper way with the common good of political society. The proper use of things and the fair distribution of resources is initially the responsibility of individuals, families, and voluntary associations, but their actions in dealing with these matters are appropriately directed by the actions of political society, which alone has the impartial and legal standing to settle authoritatively the disputes that emerge when individuals and associations have discretionary power over their own actions. Thus, political society has the responsibility to protect owners' rights and to adjudicate property disputes. Likewise, it has the responsibility to see to it that the requirement of common use is not systematically subverted by the conventions that protect owners' discretion.

The social responsibility of owners, I have noted, is rooted in their having a surplus and in the welfare of the needy; even before there are any voluntary or political initiatives to assist them, the needy have a moral right to the help that can be given to them. By requiring owners to pay taxes, political society enforces this right of the needy against owners who might otherwise refuse to act responsibly; in this way, political society vindicates the rights of the needy and gives their entitlements legal form. Thus, political society does no wrong to irresponsible owners who resent or seek to evade the tax, since their pre-political duty to the needy already included giving what reasonable taxation requires (and probably then some). Nor does it wrong the law-abiding, who accept this political action as a needed way of coordinating the administration of an important responsibility connected to their membership in political society. Indeed, the need to coerce the irresponsible, in order to vindicate the rights of those harmed by their irresponsibility and to secure for the law-abiding the benefits of their own social responsibility, is an important reason why the development of welfare rights is a proper political action.

---

[21] See John Finnis, *Natural Law and Natural Rights* (Oxford: Oxford University Press, 1980), 146–47, 159; and Germain Grisez, *The Way of the Lord Jesus*, vol. 2, *Living a Christian Life* (Quincy, IL: Franciscan Press, 1993), 356–59.

Legal coercion is a form of the coordination of social action that only political society can properly perform.[22]

As we have seen, there is an important moral limit to what a polity can require from its citizens: since political society is not entitled to enforce obligations that a person might not have, and because it cannot know the extent of each individual's various moral obligations, it must respect the discretion needed for responsible living. In a fair regime of redistributive taxation, then, considerable discretion will remain. Many people, however, have a responsibility to help the needy that is not completely fulfilled once they have paid their taxes. In other words, while there are limits on what political society can reasonably do to establish legal welfare rights, this political limit is not a moral limit on what any given owner may owe to his or her neighbors. Political welfare rights implement the underlying moral responsibility—they do not exhaust it. Regardless of whatever policies political society imposes, one is morally obligated to do what one can to help one's needy neighbor, and this will be a function of one's capacity to help as determined by one's resources and one's other responsibilities. Thus, wealthier owners have a greater obligation to help the needy than do the less well off, and this greater obligation is usually not met merely by paying higher taxes. We can generalize this point to the larger society, too: the level of assistance that a political society is obligated to provide its needy members is higher in a wealthy society than it is in a less wealthy society. Thus, just as there is no universal standard for what an individual owes another, there is also no universal standard for what a society owes its needy.

Finally, it should be noted that political welfare rights, as something a society can organize itself to provide, are significantly limited to political society. The underlying obligation to neighborly assistance and the moral right that underlies this obligation are natural and thus exist in all human societies. However, the authority of a polity is limited in many ways by its borders, so that it cannot collect taxes or establish meaningful entitlements beyond them. Worldwide versions of the United Way and Catholic Charities probably deserve the support of owners in wealthy countries, and perhaps the support of those countries as well. But without a worldwide polity, there cannot be the political coordination of action that is needed to make the welfare rights served by these groups into legally established rights for all human beings.

V. Conclusion

In this essay, I have developed a natural law argument, based on Catholic tradition, for welfare rights. The argument may be summarized as

---

[22] For Aquinas's account of the common good of political society and of the specific form of coordination provided by its legal actions, see Finnis, *Aquinas*, 247–52.

follows: The importance of the ownership of things within Aquinas's conception of social life does not compromise his characteristically Christian concern for helping those in need. This concern is generally met when owners have responsibility for things. Yet this same concern, when formulated as a norm of neighborly assistance and applied in modern social conditions, requires a system of welfare rights if society can support such a system without rendering its members servile by depriving them of discretion over their lives. In the conditions of modern life, prosperity, advanced technology, and social differentiation expand the number of people who can be benefited by neighborly assistance and increase the quality of the benefits that people can provide for themselves and others. Political society has the competence to guarantee welfare rights because the fair use of things is an element of society's common good that can only be obtained through the use of political society's legal authority.

Philosophy, University of Toronto

NATURAL LAW, NATURAL RIGHTS, AND CLASSICAL LIBERALISM: ON MONTESQUIEU'S CRITIQUE OF HOBBES

By Michael Zuckert

I. Montesquieu as a Natural Law Thinker

Montesquieu is not often thought of as a significant natural law thinker. The article on natural law in the *International Encyclopedia of the Social Sciences* discusses many theorists of the natural law, but Montesquieu is not among them.[1] A valuable older survey of natural law theorizing by legal philosopher A. P. d'Entrèves cites the Frenchman but once, as a very minor character in a story with far more significant actors—Thomas Aquinas, Hugo Grotius, even Georg Hegel.[2] A yet more comprehensive survey of the topic, *Natural Law and Human Dignity*, by French philosopher and social theorist Ernst Bloch, does not mention Montesquieu at all.[3]

More significantly, Montesquieu is often seen, along with other eighteenth-century thinkers like Hume and Bentham, to be among the executioners of natural law/natural rights thinking. He is the originator, so it is said, of a new way of thinking about law, later to be dubbed "sociology of law," which contributed importantly to the perception that natural law was at least dispensable and perhaps even quite misguided.

Although he does not have a reputation as a natural law thinker, Montesquieu does make a clear appeal to that venerable concept in his masterwork, *The Spirit of the Laws*. He identifies natural law (or natural right—*droit naturel*) as one of nine different sorts of laws by which "men are governed," and he devotes the entirety of Book I, chapter 2 to the laws of nature (*loix de la nature*).[4] Despite these important occasions of thematic address to the law of nature, however, the concept frequently drops out of sight for such long stretches of time that one can easily forget it is

---

[1] Leo Strauss, "Natural Law," in David L. Sills, ed., *International Encyclopedia of the Social Sciences* (New York: Macmillan, 1968), reprinted as Leo Strauss, "On Natural Law," in Strauss, *Studies in Platonic Political Philosophy* (Chicago: University of Chicago Press, 1983), 137.

[2] A. P. d'Entrèves, *Natural Law: An Historical Survey* (New York: Harper and Row, 1951), 54.

[3] Ernst Bloch, *Natural Law and Human Dignity* (Cambridge, MA: MIT Press, 1986).

[4] Charles Louis de Secondat, Baron de la Brède et de Montesquieu, *The Spirit of the Laws*, ed. Anne M. Cohler, Basia Carolyn Miller, and Harold Samuel Stone (Cambridge: Cambridge University Press, 1989), I₂, XXVI. Unless otherwise indicated, references to *Spirit* will be given in the text by Book and chapter numbers and will be taken from this translation. Occasionally I silently revise the translation; when I have done so, I have used the French text as presented in Montesquieu, *De l'Esprit des Loix*, ed. Jean Brethe de la Gressaye (Paris: Societé les Belles Lettres, 1950).

mentioned in this very large text. Political theorist Thomas Pangle's careful tally of references in *Spirit* to the law of nature reveals the concept's
strong, though far from overwhelming, presence, concentrated in only a
few (seven) of the work's thirty-one books.[5]

Perusal of what Montesquieu says in *Spirit* and in related places suggests a quite specific way of characterizing his efforts in the sphere of
natural law thinking. The chapter called "On the Laws of Nature" contains only one proper name, that of Hobbes, who is mentioned twice right
in the chapter's center. Hobbes is brought in here in order to be refuted.
Indeed, Montesquieu says that his intent in *Spirit* is "to attack the system
of Hobbes, a terrible system which [makes] all virtues and all vices depend on the establishment of laws made by men."[6] Philosopher Simone
Goyard-Fabre goes so far as to identify Montesquieu as an "anti-Hobbes,"
exactly as Aristotle was an "anti-sophist."[7] Montesquieu "attacks" Hobbes
primarily, if not exclusively, on the issue of the law of nature, for he fights
most fiercely against Hobbes's conventionalism, that is, his notion that
there are no public binding standards but those established through positive law or human agreement. Montesquieu means to vindicate natural
standards—natural law—in the face of Hobbes's rejection of the same. In
this, Montesquieu joins a vibrant post-Hobbesian tradition, for Hobbes
triggered such a stream of refuters as almost by himself to keep the
printers in work. Some of the most important political philosophy in the
century after *Leviathan* was part of this literature of refutation, which
includes Samuel von Pufendorf's various writings on natural law, Locke's
philosophy, Richard Cumberland's splendid (though now neglected) *Treatise on the Laws of Nature*, and a large number of works by even lesser
known figures.[8] Montesquieu clearly locates himself within this movement.

It was not, however, a uniform movement. Some, like Pufendorf, responded to Hobbes by recurring to Grotius; others, like Locke, by devel-

[5] Thomas Pangle, *Montesquieu's Philosophy of Liberalism* (Chicago: University of Chicago
Press, 1973), 309–10. Natural law (either *droit* or *loi*) appears in $I_{1,2}$; $VI_{13,20}$; $X_{2,3}$; XIV_{12};
$XV_{7,12,17}$; XXIV_6; and $XXVI_{3-7,14}$.
    [6] Montesquieu, *Defense de l'Esprit des Loix*, in Montesquieu, *Oeuvres Complètes*, ed. Daniel
Oster (Paris: Editions du Seuil, 1964), 809. The translation is mine.
    [7] Simone Goyard-Fabre, *La Philosophie du Droit de Montesquieu* (Paris: Librairie C. Klincks-
ieck, 1973), 103. The anti-Hobbes theme is strong throughout her book and most of the rest
of the scholarly literature. See Mark H. Waddicor, *Montesquieu and the Philosophy of Natural
Law* (The Hague, The Netherlands: Nijhoff, 1970), 37, 65, 73, 75; Robert Shackleton, *Montesquieu: A Critical Biography* (Oxford: Oxford University Press, 1961), 248; and Sheila Mary
Mason, *Montesquieu's Idea of Justice* (The Hague, The Netherlands: Nijhoff, 1975), 207–8, 211,
243. There are dissenting voices, however, who see some deep affinities between Hobbes
and Montesquieu on natural law. See, for example, Pangle, *Montesquieu's Philosophy*; and
Pierre Manent, *The City of Man* (Princeton, NJ: Princeton University Press, 1998), 19.
    [8] See Samuel I. Mintz, *The Hunting of Leviathan* (Cambridge: Cambridge University Press,
1962). For the works themselves, see Samuel Pufendorf, *De Jure Naturae et Gentium Libri Octo*
(Oxford: Oxford University Press, 1934); John Locke, *Two Treatises of Government*, ed. Peter
Laslett (Cambridge: Cambridge University Press, 1988); and Richard Cumberland, *De Leg-
ibus Naturae* (London: 1672).

oping quite novel theories of natural law; still others, by returning to more traditional notions. It has not proven easy, however, to locate Montesquieu on the map of known and cartographed natural law theories. Almost all the commentators on this subject feel obliged to speak of their own and, of course, others' puzzlement over Montesquieu's position. The most thorough survey of the various efforts to make sense of Montesquieu on natural law not only "finds [the] critics sharply divided on this issue," but also that they are either themselves confused about Montesquieu's position or are certain that Montesquieu himself was confused. The same survey says that Montesquieu's definition of law, apparently essential to understanding his version of the law of nature, "was received [at his time] with hostility or bewilderment, and it has generally met with the same reception from later critics."[9]

The blame for this hostility and bewilderment lies to a large extent on Montesquieu's own head, for his treatment of natural law has many odd features that cannot but contribute to a reader's frustration with his text. For the sake of economy, let me merely mention three such features of *Spirit*. First, Montesquieu regularly positions natural law within larger contexts of laws, but these contexts are in themselves complex as well as consistently underexplained and underdefined. To make matters worse, they differ from one place to another in *Spirit*. Thus in Book I, Montesquieu presents natural law in the context of a general theory of law as "the necessary relations deriving from the nature of things"; in this sense, he notes, "all beings have their laws" (I_1). Which of these laws are natural laws, however, Montesquieu does not specify, although he does indicate that lower animals "have natural laws" (I_1) and that human beings do also (I_2).[10] There are a variety of other laws that Montesquieu invokes in I_1—laws of religion, laws of morality, political and civil laws—but whether any of these is identical with natural law he does not say.

In X_3, Montesquieu lists natural law along with three other laws, all of which seem to be different from it: the law of the natural light, the law that forms political societies, and the law drawn from the nature of conquest. (The topic at issue in X_3 is the law of conquest.) Montesquieu makes the issue far more complex in Book XXVI, where he identifies "[t]he various sorts of laws, [by which] men are governed." There are, it turns out, nine sorts of law: natural law (*droit naturel*), divine law (*droit divin*), ecclesiastical or canon law, the law of nations (*droit de gens*), general political law (*droit politique géneral*), particular political law, the law of conquest, the civil law of each society, and domestic law. Book I was comprehensive in one sense, in that it set natural law into the context of the laws that govern "all beings." Book XXVI is comprehensive in another

[9] Waddicor, *Natural Law*, 19, 181. See also Shackleton, *Montesquieu*, 244–45.

[10] See David Lowenthal, "Book I of Montesquieu's *Spirit of the Laws*," *American Political Science Review* 53, no. 2 (June 1959): 493.

sense, in that it sets natural law into the context of all the laws that govern humanity. Montesquieu does not deign to explain how these two contexts relate to each other, nor, for that matter, whether his shift in terminology from I_1, where he uses the French word *loi* for law, to XXVI_1, where he uses the word *droit* instead, has any significance. Montesquieu's fecundity in identifying types of law surely is admirable in its way, but it does not help his overloaded readers follow him, especially when he says so little about the plethora of laws and beings he invokes. Montesquieu combined a remarkable concision of expression with his rich conceptual jungle. Some attribute this mode of expression to haste or sloppiness in composition, but Robert Shackleton, Montesquieu's leading biographer, rejects such speculations on the basis of extensive study of manuscript evidence. Shackleton argues instead that

> Montesquieu's finished product was the result of continued and deliberate transference of sentences from one place to another, of intentional polishing, of conscious pursuit of the epigram and the paradox, of the constant suppression of the redundant and of the intermediate link between two ideas, of the rearranging of a sequence of ideas so that the consequence precedes the cause.[11]

Shackleton's is as good a description of the peculiarities of Montesquieu's method of exposition as I have seen. Though Montesquieu's style has many virtues, it nevertheless contributes to the difficulty of nailing down his thought on the law of nature.

A related and widely noted source of confusion about Montesquieu's natural law doctrine derives from his vacillation between a purely descriptive notion, the law of nature as analogue to or illustrated by, for example, the law of gravitation, and a normative notion, the law of nature as a rule and standard to guide the behavior of moral beings, as in traditional law of nature doctrines.[12]

A final source of frustration for the reader and of difficulty for those trying to place Montesquieu's doctrine is that he teasingly evokes a number of familiar positions but fails to conform consistently to any of them. He is always reminding us of someone we know without ever quite being that someone. Like many other post-Hobbesian natural lawyers, Montesquieu at times gives the impression that he reverts to the most traditional and well-established natural law doctrine, an unsurprising move in those who oppose Hobbes, who had himself opposed that very same doctrine. Montesquieu reminds us, for example, of Thomas Aquinas. They both invoke a complex set of laws within which lies natural law. The two agree

[11] Shackleton, *Montesquieu*, 238.
[12] This ambiguity is remarked upon by nearly every commentator on *Spirit*. Again, Waddicor supplies a helpful survey of the literature in his *Natural Law*, 16–21.

in presenting a doctrine of law covering "all beings," up to and including God. Montesquieu's system has five types of beings, each with its own set of laws: God, the material world, the intelligences superior to humanity, beasts, and humans. Aquinas gives us a world populated with those classes of beings, and a wonderful plethora of kinds of laws to govern them: the eternal law, the natural law, the human law, the divine law, even a law of "the fomes of sin." Montesquieu no more than puts us in mind of Aquinas's position, however, for comparing the definition of law supplied by each makes clear how much the two philosophers differ. According to Aquinas, law is "an ordinance of reason for the common good, made by him who has care of the community and promulgated."[13] Montesquieu's definition of law hits quite different notes: as noted above, he says that laws are "the necessary relations deriving from the nature of things." This definition is not only different from Aquinas's, but is obscure in itself and little clarified in subsequent discussion.[14]

The Montesquieuian emphasis on "necessary relations" in turn makes us think of Grotius, who, a little more than a century before Montesquieu, had identified a law of nature as "a rule that [can] be deduced from fixed principles by a sure process of reasoning."[15] If this is correct, then natural law would appear to have the kind of rational necessity Montesquieu affirms in his definition of law. Yet here again Montesquieu's resemblance to another thinker is only superficial, for Montesquieu and Grotius differ greatly in that Grotius never viewed law as such (as opposed to the natural law) as a set of "necessary relations." Indeed, he emphasizes that laws other than natural law are constituted precisely by their lack of such necessity and deducibility.[16] Moreover, Grotius silently passes over the main point of Montesquieu's I_1: Grotius does not place natural law into a context of laws governing "all beings." He is concerned only with laws governing human beings and (very occasionally) animals. The laws of the broader universe (if he recognizes such laws) are irrelevant to his enterprise. Montesquieu thus reminds us of Aquinas in the comprehensiveness and complexity of his theory of law; he reminds us of Grotius in his emphasis on necessity. He combines these two emphases, however, in a novel but very murky manner.[17]

The murkiness dissipates a bit if we look more carefully at the details of Montesquieu's discussion of the kinds of beings. He lists, as we have

---

[13] Thomas Aquinas, *Summa Theologiae*, trans. Fathers of the English Dominican Province (New York: Benziger Brothers, 1947), I–II, q. 90, a. 4.

[14] Cf. Lowenthal, "Book I of *Spirit*," 493.

[15] Hugo Grotius, *On the Law of War and Peace* (Oxford: Oxford University Press, 1913–1925), Proleg. 40.

[16] Ibid.

[17] Thus I partly agree and partly disagree with Mark Hulliung's assessment that "Montesquieu was still entrapped in the philosophical rationalism and modernized natural law of Grotius or Spinoza." Mark Hulliung, *Montesquieu and the Old Regime* (Berkeley: University of California Press, 1976), 112.

already noted, five kinds of beings; his tally is nearly identical to that of Descartes in Meditation III, where the latter speaks of God, corporeal and inanimate things, angels, animals, and men.[18] Although Montesquieu speaks of "intelligences superior to men" rather than angels, he apparently has in mind much the same cosmos as Descartes. The context of the list in Meditation III is a proof for the existence of God, and that too is the immediate topic of Montesquieu's discussion when he presents his enumeration. Montesquieu's proof is directed against those who "have said that blind fatality has produced all the effects that we see in the world" (I_1); by Montesquieu's testimony, Spinoza is the target here.[19] Montesquieu's proof is different from Descartes's, but it is nonetheless broadly Cartesian. It is a simple proof: "[A] blind fatality" cannot produce "intelligent beings." There must be a "primitive" intelligence or reason, for "the world, formed by the movement of matter and devoid of intelligence," cannot be the source of intelligence. There are thus, according to Montesquieu, two radically different kinds of being: matter and intelligence. These are obviously Montesquieu's versions of Descartes's two substances, *res extensa* and *res cogitans*. Montesquieu thus begins with Descartes's dualist ontology. Once we recognize this, many of the themes in I_1 appear comfortably Cartesian: the emphasis on necessary relations, the appeal to mathematics as a model, the emphasis on human errancy as a constitutive character of the being that mysteriously combines the two substances, the same obscurity as to the nature and possibility of that combination. Montesquieu's discussion not only closely tracks Descartes's; on occasion, he nearly quotes from the latter's works without attribution. According to Montesquieu, "the laws according to which God created are those according to which he preserves" (I_1). According to Descartes, "the act by which God now preserves the world is just the same as that by which he created it."[20] Although Descartes was not himself a natural law thinker except in his belief that "the laws of mechanics ... are identical with the laws of nature,"[21] we can tentatively characterize Montesquieu's project as the attempt to develop a natural law theory on the basis of Cartesian ontology. Herein lies the novelty of Montesquieu. Given Montesquieu's project, we can appreciate, even more literally than was intended, d'Alembert's appraisal of Montesquieu in his 1755 elegy upon the latter's death: "Montesquieu was to the study of laws what Descartes was to philosophy."[22]

---

[18] Descartes, *Meditations on First Philosophy*, in John Cottingham, Robert Stoothoff, and Duglad Murdoch, trans., *The Philosophical Writings of Descartes* (Cambridge: Cambridge University Press, 1985), Meditation III. All subsequent references to Descartes's works refer to the translations provided in this Cambridge edition.

[19] See Montesquieu, *Defense*, 809.

[20] Descartes, *Discourse on Method*, V, p. 133; see also Descartes, *Principles of Philosophy*, II_{12}.

[21] Descartes, *Discourse on Method*, V, p. 139; Descartes, *The World*, pp. 92–93; Descartes, *Principles of Philosophy*, Part II.

[22] Montesquieu, *Oeuvres Complètes*, 26.

II. The First Critique of Hobbes

Montesquieu attempts to refute Hobbes with a new philosophy of law, including natural law, apparently constructed on the basis of Cartesian ontology. He takes his task seriously, for he launches two critiques of his English predecessor within the first five pages of *Spirit*. The two critiques are quite different, however, and they need to be reconciled or have their differences explained. The first critique occurs in I_1, in the context of Montesquieu's very quick sketch of the laws that govern the different classes of beings. Without comment, Montesquieu revises his original list of beings when he comes to actually discuss them, for he drops out the class of "intelligences superior to man" and replaces it with "particular intelligent beings"; this latter phrase, he makes clear, refers to humans.[23] Thus in his discussion of the types of beings and their laws, his list of the types of beings includes men twice: God, the material world, humans, beasts, humans.

Our ability to grasp Montesquieu's first critique of Hobbes, which occurs as Montesquieu discusses the "particular intelligent beings," depends, it would seem, on our ability to make sense of (1) the silent replacement of "superior intelligences" (i.e., angels) with phrasing that refers to men, and (2) the subsequent relationship between Montesquieu's two treatments of men. The first is, I think, a large question, but perhaps a relatively simple answer can be given to it. The affirmation of "superior intelligences" or angels (i.e., thinking beings uncompounded with body) occurs within the context of Cartesian dualism, and perhaps even more within the context of Descartes's desire to prove to the ecclesiastical authorities that his new philosophy is helpful rather than harmful to the church.[24] If intelligence, *res cogitans*, is a substance, as Descartes claims it is, then by definition it is capable of separate existence. "By *substance* we can understand no other than a thing which exists in such a way as to depend on no other thing for its existence."[25] This is in turn Descartes's basis for concluding that the soul (that is, the thinking substance) can exist without the body and therefore survives its demise.[26]

Descartes is nonetheless reluctant to speak of angels or separated thinking beings other than God. In Descartes's work, as in Montesquieu's, these beings drop out of every discussion and are normally replaced by human intelligences. This Cartesian practice reflects a difficulty in Descartes's own thinking that was no doubt greatly intensified and made more manifest in Montesquieu's time, for Montesquieu wrote in a post-

[23] Cf. Lowenthal, "Book I of *Spirit*," 489: "The standpoint chosen is that of human rather than angelic societies." For a brief discussion of Montesquieu's references to "intelligences superior to man," see Lowenthal, "Book I of *Spirit*," 489 n. 14.

[24] Descartes, *Meditations*, Dedication. On angels as incorporeal substances, see Descartes, *Objections and Replies to the "Meditations,"* reply to the sixth set of objections, item 3.

[25] Descartes, *Principles*, I_{51}.

[26] Descartes, *Meditations*, Dedication.

Spinozistic, post-Lockean era. Both Spinoza and Locke had forcefully argued against that form of Cartesian dualism that might have supported the positing of particular disembodied intelligences;[27] the difficulty with this dualism concerns the particularizability of *res cogitans*. Human intelligences are particularized in their attachment or relation to separate human bodies, which in effect supplies a basis for mind to be somewhere, to be local and separate, that is, particular. We cannot—and I think this is Spinoza's main point in denying separate and particular substances— conceive clearly and distinctly of *particular* intellectual substances (or, says Spinoza, material ones, either). Locke, for his part, challenges Descartes's claim that thinking cannot be an attribute of matter. Locke's position on this issue was taken up by many leading intellectuals in Montesquieu's France, perhaps including Montesquieu himself. His tendency to side with Locke in these battles over metaphysics has been oft-noted.[28]

When Montesquieu quietly drops superior intelligences, perhaps he understands himself to be following what may be Descartes's more considered view, or the views of the later critics who were more unequivocal in rejecting separated intelligences. In any case, the initial positing and then retraction of these nondivine, nonhuman intelligences points to the problematic character of the metaphysical dualism Montesquieu seems to endorse in I_1.[29] As we shall see, there are quite a few other indications of Montesquieu's reservations about this dualism.

In any case, Montesquieu's first critique of Hobbes occurs in the very place where he drops the superior intelligences. His discussion is meant to do double-duty: it not only begins the refutation of Hobbes, but it

---

[27] Both accepted the implications regarding personal immortality that follow from rejecting such a dualism. Spinoza more or less denies that such immortality exists; Locke concedes that reason is unable to demonstrate it. See Edwin Curley, *Behind the Geometrical Method: A Reading of Spinoza's "Ethics"* (Princeton, NJ: Princeton University Press, 1988), 85–86; Spinoza, *Ethics*, in Edwin Curley, ed. and trans., *A Spinoza Reader* (Princeton, NJ: Princeton University Press, 1994), V, prop. 21; and John Locke, *On the Reasonableness of Christianity*, ed. George W. Ewing (Chicago: H. Regnery, 1965), paragraphs 243, 245.

[28] See, for example, Hulliung, *Montesquieu*, 108–9 and the citations to Montesquieu therein.

[29] Other indications abound of a subterranean Montesquieuian unease with the Cartesian dualism he invokes in I_1. His proof of God, for instance, contains a logical flaw so evident as to make us wonder how serious he can be about the argument itself. He infers from the fact that unintelligent matter cannot be the source of intelligence that there must be a "primitive" intelligence; he then concludes that this intelligence is the source of everything, that is, it is the source of the intelligent beings and "matter devoid of intelligence." Furthermore, Montesquieu challenges the doctrine of creation when he affirms both that God is unchangeable and that the laws by which the world is governed are the same as those by which God created the world. If God must be eternally the same, as Montesquieu argues, then the act of creation cannot be made intelligible. The laws that govern the universe (by which Montesquieu clearly has in mind the mechanical laws of physics) cannot be at work in creation because among other things, those laws guarantee that in the physical universe we never have a case of creation *ex nihilo*. For a version of this problem, see Descartes, *Discourse on Method*, V. See also Montesquieu's intriguing appraisal of Descartes in Montesquieu, *Mes Pensees 1720-1755*, in Montesquieu, *Oeuvres Complètes*, nos. 1283, 2070, 2072, 2077-78, 2104-5. On Montesquieu's proof for God's existence, see the very helpful discussion in Lowenthal, "Book I of *Spirit*," 487; and Pangle, *Montesquieu's Philosophy*, 27.

illustrates Montesquieu's opening claims about laws being "necessary relations deriving from the nature of things." As noted above, Montesquieu identifies *Spirit* as a counter to the "terrible" doctrine of Hobbes, according to which "all virtues and all vices depend on" positive law. In I_1, Montesquieu, without naming Hobbes, responds to the claim "that there is nothing just or unjust but what positive laws ordain." Hobbes had indeed clearly stated that in the state of nature, prior to the establishment of a sovereign authority and therewith positive law, "nothing can be unjust."[30] Compared, say, to the response to Hobbes by Samuel Clarke, from whose theory of law Montesquieu's own theory is often thought to be derived, Montesquieu's reply is very restrained.[31] Clarke was outraged by Hobbes's supposition that "right and wrong, just and unjust . . . have no foundation in the nature of things, but . . . depend entirely on positive laws; that the rules or distinctions of good and evil, honest and dishonest are mere civil constitutions; and whatever the chief magistrate commands, is to be accounted good; whatever he forbids, evil."[32] Clarke's reply certainly has something in common with Montesquieu's, for he finds Hobbes "guilty of the grossest absurdity and inconsistency that can be."[33] The "greatest and strongest of all our obligations," Clarke says, "depend not at all on any human constitution, but must of necessity . . . be confessed to arise originally from and be founded in, the eternal reason and unalterable nature and relations of things themselves."[34] Men, says Clarke, are "obliged" always by the laws of nature.[35] The Hobbesian state of nature has no normative standing because "it is not in any sense a natural state; but a state of the greatest, most unnatural and most intolerable *corruption*."[36]

According to Clarke, then, the laws of nature are actual laws, binding always and necessarily in the same way, whether in a so-called state of nature or in society. Montesquieu differs from Clarke on these issues in several understated but highly significant ways. First, though Montesquieu affirms, against Hobbes, that there are "relations of fairness prior to the positive law that establishes them," he pointedly does not call these relations natural law (I_1). His failure to do so is more than inadvertent, it seems, for two paragraphs later he explicitly speaks of the beasts and the "natural laws" that govern them, and these laws are altogether different

[30] Thomas Hobbes, *Leviathan*, ed. Richard Tuck (Cambridge: Cambridge University Press, 1991), chap. 13.

[31] On Clarke as a possible influence on Montesquieu's discussion of law in general, see Goyard-Fabre, *La Philosophie*, 95; Shackleton, *Montesquieu*, 71, 73, 152, 246; and Waddicor, *Natural Law*, 189. For evidence that Montesquieu knew Clarke, see Montesquieu, *Mes Pensees*, no. 73.

[32] Samuel Clarke, *A Discourse of Natural Religion*, reprinted in D. D. Raphael, ed., *British Moralists: 1650–1800* (Oxford: Oxford University Press, 1969), 1:222.

[33] Ibid., 1:221.

[34] Ibid.

[35] Ibid., 1:220.

[36] Ibid., 1:222.

in character from the rational or necessary relations he speaks of in his anti-Hobbesian passage. Similarly, in I₂ Montesquieu will speak of laws of nature that apply to human beings, and these are far more similar to those laws he finds imposed on the beasts than to the relations of fairness applicable to "particular intelligent beings."

A second difference between Montesquieu and Clarke lies in Montesquieu's precise way of describing these relations: they are not actual, but "possible laws," or "possible relations of justice." In at least one decisive respect, he seems to agree with Hobbes over and against Clarke: the positive law makes these relations actual. In Montesquieu's words, "the positive law *establishes* them." Montesquieu speaks of these relations in this way for two apparent reasons. First, he has just made an argument to the effect that "a primitive reason," which he names God, is "creator and preserver" of the universe, and most especially of the particular intelligences—that is, human beings—within it. If the argument is correct, then these human beings need not exist for there to be law: "Before there were intelligent beings, they were possible; they had then possible relations and consequently possible laws." Montesquieu draws a precise parallel to the world of mathematical objects: "To say there is nothing just or unjust but what positive laws ordain or prohibit is to say that before a circle was drawn, all its radii were not equal."

One wishes Montesquieu had said more here, for this parallel does not seem in all ways apt. Is a circle we draw an actual circle in the way that an existing human being is an actual human being? Are mathematical objects similar to human beings in that we would say there were only "possible circles" before there were constructed circles? Moreover, do the relations that Montesquieu identifies as "possible laws" and "possible relations of justice" have the same sort of necessary interconnection that the equality of a circle's radii has with that circle's being? Does it follow with such necessity, for example, that "if there were intelligent beings that had received some kindness from another being, they ought to be grateful for it"? Montesquieu seems to suggest that it does, but at the very least he needs to argue this out more fully, for as his argument stands, the effect it has is almost the opposite of what he seems to intend. Using the circle analogy highlights the differences between the necessary relations in the circle and the alleged relations regarding human beings. Montesquieu's pre-positive laws are perhaps neither actual nor necessary.

The second reason why Montesquieu holds back from endorsing Clarke's actual natural laws is hinted at in Montesquieu's first example of a "possible relation of justice": "assuming that there were societies of men," the example reads, "it would be just to conform to their laws." Apart from the fact (again) that it is by no means evident that Montesquieu's syllogism is correct (or why it would be), Montesquieu here affirms what Clarke refuses to affirm, that is, that society is no more natural or necessary than human existence itself. As Montesquieu confirms in the next chapter, "the constitution of our being" is most visible in man "before the establish-ment of societies" (I$_2$). Montesquieu thus accepts what Clarke unequiv-ocally rejects: the state of nature. Montesquieu holds, then, that justice, involving relations among men, cannot be primitive or natural, for hu-man beings are not primitively or naturally social (see I$_2$).

It is clear, then, that the "possible laws" Montesquieu holds up against Hobbes are not the sort of naturally binding "actual laws" posited by Clarke. In fact, Montesquieu's "possible laws" seem to be more like ra-tional rules that, if recognized and followed, could serve as necessary supports for society. They have the character, one might say, of hypothet-ical imperatives: if you are to have a society, you must obey these laws. The "possible laws" are in this sense necessary to social life, but since social life is not strictly necessary, or at least is not natural, neither are these hypothetical rules. This is why Montesquieu does not call these rules natural laws, and why he quietly concedes that positive laws actu-ally establish these "possible relations of justice."

Ironically, except for terminology, Montesquieu is actually far closer to Hobbes than he is to Clarke. Hobbes had presented, under the rubric "laws of nature," a series of "generall rules, found out by reason," which conduce to general self-preservation by making society possible. These natural laws have the character of moral precepts. For example, Hobbes's fourth law of nature, the law of gratitude, reads: "That a man which receiveth Benefit from another of mere grace, endeavour that he which giveth it, have no reasonable cause to repent him of his good will."[37] Hobbes is willing to use the language of the law of nature to refer to these rules—more willing to do so than is Montesquieu. However, he explicitly says that "these dictates of Reason, men use to call by the name of Lawes, but improperly: for they are but conclusions, or Theoremes concerning what conduceth to the conservation and defence of themselves; whereas Law, properly is the word of him, that by right hath command over others."[38] The position that Montesquieu takes as he allegedly refutes Hobbes from the platform of Cartesian ontology is thus nearly indistin-guishable from Hobbes's own position. Like Montesquieu with his "pos-sible laws," Hobbes has no difficulty affirming that his "Lawes of Nature" are "Immutable and Eternall."[39] The sort of "laws" each theorist is pos-iting here, however, are not really laws, nor are they natural.

To discern that Montesquieu is much closer to Hobbes than he first appears is not to say, of course, that he is a Hobbesian. It is to say that he wishes to leave his readers with the impression that the distance sepa-rating him from Hobbes is greater than it actually is. Hobbes was a renowned materialist and a much-suspected atheist; the Cartesian dual-

[37] Hobbes, *Leviathan*, chap. 15.
[38] Ibid.
[39] Ibid.

ism that Montesquieu deploys, whatever else it may mean to him, allows him to establish his distance from both these positions.

As noted above, Montesquieu takes up man twice in I_1. We have just considered the first of these discussions; here, humans are discussed as "particular intelligent beings," where that classification is itself a substitute for the class of "superior" or perhaps separate finite intelligences. Montesquieu returns to man at the end of the chapter, this time explicitly emphasizing humans' composite character as beings that are both physical and intellectual. No more than Descartes does Montesquieu clarify how matter and intelligence can combine in this way, but the fact that the two substances do combine is nonetheless much emphasized by both theorists. At the conclusion of his treatment of human beings as "particular intelligences," Montesquieu had conceded that human beings were "limited by their nature." By "their nature" here he seems to mean humans' particular or finite nature as intelligences rather than their composite character, because at this point he continues to refer to the human world as "the intelligent world" as opposed to "the physical world." The finite nature of human intelligences, Montesquieu says, subjects them to "error"; when this errancy is combined with the "freedom" that intelligent beings possess, the result is that humans as "particular intelligences" "do not consistently follow their primitive laws," presumably meaning the "possible laws" he has just discussed.

When Montesquieu returns to humanity at the end of I_1 and emphasizes its composite character, he also extends the theme of its errancy: man, he says, "*constantly* violates the laws God has established" (I_1, emphasis added). The increased errancy results from the fact that a human is a physical being and can therefore "feel": "As a feeling creature," Montesquieu says, a human "falls subject to a thousand passions" (I_1). The rational "possible laws" do not suffice to govern human beings because these passions play too important a role in motivating human action. The passions are stronger and more effective than reason, and thus are, in that sense, more natural.

This may explain why Montesquieu's first use in *Spirit* of the term "natural laws" (*loix naturelles*) occurs in the discussion of the beasts that intervenes between the two discussions of humankind. The animals, Montesquieu says, are driven "only by feeling"; for them, knowledge plays no role in motivating action. As they are "united by feeling" alone, Montesquieu concludes that the beasts have "natural laws"; without knowledge, however, "they lack positive laws."[40] Their feelings, especially their pleasures, express natural law either in them or to them; this natural law is therefore nothing rational. It is apparently nothing normative either, but rather is the actual motivating force that drives animals to behave as they

[40] See Lowenthal, "Book I of *Spirit*," 494: "By nature, then, man is a being of sentiment and passion rather than reason, and primarily selfish."

do. The natural law is thus very different from the "possible laws" Montesquieu discusses earlier in I_1, for those laws are both rational and normative in character.

Nature for Montesquieu is that which is effectual; like Machiavelli before him, he takes his bearings from "the effectual truth of things." Nature suffices to govern the lower animals, but not men. The passions and feelings that animals have effectively guide them to "preserve their particular being" and "their species." The lower animals, Montesquieu observes, "even preserve themselves better than we do and do not make such bad use of their passions." Humankind is neither governed as effectively by reason as disembodied particular intelligences might be, nor governed by nature as the beasts are. Montesquieu's point is not merely to bemoan the human condition, but to reveal to us the necessity of positive laws, three different sorts of which—laws of religion, laws of morality, and civil and political laws—he mentions at the end of I_1. It turns out that Montesquieu's goal in presenting the various sorts of beings governed by "necessary relations" is to make clear why humanity is governed not by such necessary and invariable laws, but rather by positive and variable legislation. The latter, not the former, is his subject in *Spirit*.

III. THE SECOND CRITIQUE OF HOBBES

The analysis to this point shows that when one probes slightly beneath the surface, Montesquieu's understanding is rather like Hobbes's, and that therefore the first critique is in fact not telling. However, Montesquieu returns to the attack in I_2, this time with an explicit mention of Hobbes. Here Montesquieu makes clear that there are genuine differences between him and Hobbes. I_1 implicitly establishes that despite the impressions some readers may get, Montesquieu's anti-Hobbesianism is not of the same kind as that espoused by Hobbes's traditionalist critics. Montesquieu is closer to Hobbes than to Aquinas and his followers, Grotius and his followers, or Clarke and his rationalist natural law. Having established this, Montesquieu proceeds in I_2 to clarify the genuine and important basis for his rejection of Hobbes's "terrible system."

Montesquieu does not maintain in I_1 that human beings have no natural law to govern them; he merely asserts that the natural law is less effective in humans than it is in the nonrational beings. I_2 clarifies both what the human natural law is and why it is so much less effective. The natural law in human beings is identical in kind to the natural law in beasts. It is the same both in being a matter of "feeling" and in terms of sorts of feelings involved: fear, hunger, sexual desire, and finally, the "desire to live in society." All except perhaps the last clearly operate like the natural law of beasts in that preservation of the individual and the species seems to be the natural law's aim or result. As Montesquieu later says more explicitly, "the law of nature makes everything tend toward the preservation of the species" (X_3).[41]

The last law of nature moves beyond the laws of the beasts: the knowledge human beings gain gives humans a "second bond, which other animals do not have." Montesquieu means that humans come to know the advantages that society provides with respect to preservation of self and species. (For example, men may learn that hunting in groups is more effective than hunting alone.) The subsequent "desire to live in society" is a slight but obviously significant modification of more primordial desires that are quite independent of any knowledge.[42]

Montesquieu holds that human beings are by nature—that is, in terms of the effective forces that naturally move them—very much like the animals. Montesquieu explicitly distinguishes his conclusions here from those of Hobbes, but it is worth noting that in this matter Montesquieu disagrees just as much as Hobbes does with the whole (or nearly the whole) of the aforementioned corps of natural law thinkers. In fact, however much Montesquieu differs here from Hobbes, he is closer to the Englishman than to most other natural law thinkers, for Montesquieu agrees with Hobbes that one must posit a state of nature, the human situation "before the establishment of societies" (I_2). In contrast, the pre-Hobbesian natural law thinkers and the later anti-Hobbesians like Clarke almost uniformly rejected the state of nature.

Montesquieu agrees with Hobbes about the necessity of thinking about a state of nature, but he does so in order to attack Hobbes's account of the naturally effective forces in humanity. Montesquieu's general point here is much like the point Rousseau makes in his later and better-known critique of Hobbes.[43] The claim is that Hobbes has attributed to primordial human nature motives and ideas that are not natural, but are rather the products of the experience of society and the learning that occurs there. Montesquieu does not deny that human beings become more or less as Hobbes describes them, that is, that they come to desire to subjugate one another, and that they are dominated by "motives for attacking others and for defending themselves." Montesquieu would deny Hobbes's identification of the state of nature with a state of war, but he does not deny that the human condition does at some point degenerate into a state of war, one similar to but more complex than that which Hobbes posits (I_3).

Since Montesquieu argues that it is part of the human condition for man to pass through a "state of war" phase, it is not easy to understand why he is so insistent that this state of war is a derivative condition rather than one that is natural. Whatever the answer to this question, Montes-

---

[41] Cf. Pangle, *Montesquieu's Philosophy*, 31.

[42] See ibid., 32; and Lowenthal, "Book I of *Spirit*," 494.

[43] Jean-Jacques Rousseau, *Discourse on the Origins of Inequality Among Men*, in Rousseau, *Basic Political Writings*, ed. and trans. Donald A. Cress (Indianapolis, IN: Hackett, 1987), 53.

quieu's analysis helps make clear why the law of nature is much better at governing beasts than it is at governing humans. Montesquieu argues that the human natural law, natural forces that effectively motivate human beings, does not mandate war and dissociation, as Hobbes argued, but rather peace and society. Montesquieu knows this because he knows that human beings are animals and that they consequently have the same survival requirements that other animals have. They must eat, they must reproduce. Dominating one another is not a necessary part of the human biological repertoire. Furthermore, Montesquieu rejects the Hobbesian psychological construct that sets human beings against each other. The desire to subjugate others is not only not biologically primitive, but, unlike at least the first three natural laws, it can only motivate individuals who possess certain ideas. "The idea of empire and domination is so complex and depends on so many other ideas, that it would not be the one they [men] would first have" (I_2). Montesquieu leaves it at this brief hint, but he seems to be referring here to Hobbes's own analysis of the "principal causes of quarrell":[44] competition, diffidence, and glory. Montesquieu is correct in noticing the complexity of the ideational substructure of the desire to subjugate others. At the very least, an agent moved by this desire must have firm ideas of the self, of the other, of power, of the future, and of resources and their possible scarcity. Montesquieu notes that in the state of nature, human beings would not think of God: "A man in the state of nature would have the faculty of knowing rather than knowledge. It is clear that his first ideas would not be speculative ones; he would think of the preservation of his being before seeking the origin of his being" (I_2). It is for these same reasons that humans in the state of nature would not think of dominating others.

Montesquieu opposes Hobbes here by appealing to the Lockean "way of ideas," not to Cartesian innate ideas or to Cartesian dualism. Montesquieu's adoption of the Lockean methodology has two elements: (1) the recognition that many of our actions are "idea-dependent," that is, they depend on our having certain thoughts or ideas; and (2) the insight that we cannot assume that the human mind is automatically furnished with the full inventory of possible ideas. One must, in effect, construct a "history of ideas," or as Locke said, one must investigate ideas through use of "the plain historical method." Montesquieu shows himself to be a good Lockean in his second critique of Hobbes, even as he uses Lockean methods to revise, to some degree, conclusions that are themselves Lockean.

Montesquieu follows Hobbes and Locke in positing a state of nature, but does so for reasons different from both. For Locke, the essential issue is legitimacy—if human beings are natively free and equal, that is, not legitimately subordinate to one another, how can we understand the genesis and nature of legitimate authority? Hobbes shares this concern

---

[44] Hobbes, *Leviathan*, chap. 13.

with legitimacy, but his larger concern is to show what can be inferred about the natural condition of mankind given the nature of the passions. Montesquieu is neither so concerned with legitimacy as Locke, nor so persuaded as Hobbes that one can infer things about the natural condition of humanity by extrapolating from the passions of social men. Indeed, this is just the point where he and (a few years later) Rousseau agree in rejecting Hobbes's account of the state of nature. The state of nature is extremely important for Montesquieu precisely because he posits social life as a condition in which human beings wonderfully transform themselves in such a way that the original natural laws are nearly effaced.[45] As particularly fearful animals, human beings are naturally timid and standoffish. Desires, however, sexual and otherwise, drive them together with their fellows, and in society they lose that feeling of weakness that is natural to them. They come to "feel their strength," and only then does the Hobbesian state of war commence. The desire to dominate others is hence derivative, a transformation, an erasure (almost) of the original laws of nature. This is, no doubt, the main basis for the following claim that Montesquieu makes in the Preface to *Spirit*:

> Man, that flexible being who adapts himself in society to the thoughts and impressions of others, is equally capable of knowing his own nature when it is shown to him, and of losing even the feeling of it when it is concealed from him. (Preface, xliv–xlv)

In drawing his picture of the state of nature, and more generally in writing his book, Montesquieu is showing human beings their "own nature" and thereby causing them to recall the "feeling of it." In doing so, Montesquieu discovers what Hobbes failed to understand—that man is a most "flexible being." Perhaps this is Montesquieu's way of announcing deep reservations not only against the purely mechanistic human nature posited by Hobbes, but against the substance metaphysics presented by Descartes. As flexible beings, humans are capable of great variety in how they actually live. Montesquieu's doctrine of the weakness of natural law in humanity is the prerequisite for his new science of laws. For the most part, Hobbes and Locke leap over actual human historical experience; both move from discussing the state of nature to discussing the rational, legitimate, or best political order. In contrast, Montesquieu moves from discussing the state of nature to considering the historical variety of laws and polities, and leaves his readers somewhat uncertain as to whether he has a model of the rational, legitimate, or best regime. The political science of Hobbes and Locke culminates in a kind of universal natural constitutional law; Montesquieu's produces a comparative soci-

---

[45] See Pangle, *Montesquieu's Philosophy*, 28.

ology of law as well as a broader study of comparative politics.[46] Montesquieu's predominant goal is to show that "amidst the infinite diversity of laws and mores, [men] were not led by their fancies alone" (Preface, xliii).

Despite Montesquieu's concession that the Hobbesian state of war is indeed a moment in human development, it is now apparent that much turns on Montesquieu's critique of the Hobbesian state of nature. In fact, it would not be an overstatement to say that everything of significance in Montesquieu's political philosophy flows from this critique. As noted above, Montesquieu's new kind of science of laws (or of the "spirit of laws") flows from his new theory of natural law, and this theory emerges during the critique of Hobbes. The new theory also provides a foundation for Montesquieu's novel version of the rational, legitimate, or best regime—as we shall see, Montesquieu does in fact present such a thing.

Montesquieu's critique of Hobbes is both deep-going and fertile; it produces a richer political science, a more liberal and humane political prescription, and a more nuanced understanding of the relation between nature and human experience. For Hobbes, this relationship is relatively straightforward. Nature dissociates men, and men associate themselves by overcoming or counteracting nature. For Montesquieu, however, nature works in a more complex fashion: it first associates natural isolates, but in the process produces the conditions that dissociate men in a more problematical way, a situation to which human beings must then react further. Montesquieu's thought on this point is far more dialectical than Hobbes's thought is; one can discern here a glimmering of the kind of process that Hegel and his German successors will develop yet more fully. At the same time, Montesquieu's vision is also more tragic than Hobbes's, or at least it is more ironic and bittersweet. In the very movement that men make to preserve themselves and their species, they produce a psychological condition, the feeling of strength; it is this very feeling, however, that produces the social condition, the state of war, which threatens mankind's preservation. Montesquieu begins, then, with a view of the deeply paradoxical character of human social life. His task in *Spirit* is to find a way beyond this paradox.

IV. Positive Law and Natural Right: The Third Critique of Hobbes

Human beings become social before they become political; they become social when obeying the law of nature, they become political in response to the near effacement of this same law. Social bonds overcome that natural feeling of weakness that induces human beings to seek peace. The

---

[46] Leo Strauss, *Natural Right and History* (Chicago: University of Chicago Press, 1954).

result is war between and within societies, as "the individuals within each society . . . seek to turn to their favor the principal advantages of the society" (I_3). After the beginnings of war, and with them the return of a feeling of vulnerability if not exactly the primordial weakness, we find "the establishment of laws among men."

In the context of describing these positive laws, Montesquieu quietly draws a conclusion to which the whole preceding discussion has been leading: "Law in general is human reason insofar as it governs all the peoples of the earth" (I_3). The phrase Montesquieu uses here, "law in general," is significant, for it is nearly the very phrase that serves as the title to Book I as a whole: "On Laws in General" (*Des Loix en Général*). The definition of law that Book I is seeking is hence not that definition provided at the opening of Book I, but rather the definition provided here in this sentence in I_3. From the vantage point of I_3, one can see this easily enough: Montesquieu had described his definition of laws in I_1, namely, law as "necessary relations deriving from the nature of things," to be a description of laws "in the broadest" or "most extended meaning" ("*dans la signification la plus étendue*"). In French, *étendue* can mean "extended" to the point of dilution, as when we speak of bread crumbs as an "extender" for meat loaf. Hence, of the two definitions, the first is of law in a "*most* extended" or perhaps metaphorical sense, while the second is of law in the proper sense, the sense in which Montesquieu is concerned with it in *Spirit*.[47]

The differences between the two definitions are numerous and significant. The two most obvious differences concern the subject and source of each sort of law. Under the first definition, the subject of law is "all beings"; under the second, it is "the peoples of the earth." The source of the first law is "the nature of things" and derives from "their necessary relations." The ultimate source of this sort of law is perhaps God. The source of laws under the second definition is "human reason" engaged in "governing." Law in this proper sense does not express "necessary relations deriving from the nature of things," but rather the efforts of human reason attempting to meet the needs of biological survival in the context of both the psychic dislocations produced by social life and the states of war initiated by and within society. In particular, human law must cope with the odd combination of human feelings of weakness and vulnerability, on the one hand, and human feelings of strength and bellicosity, on the other. Another important difference between the two sorts of laws is that law in the first or "most extended meaning" is "invariable," "uniform," and "consistent" (I_1), whereas law in the proper sense is marked by "infinite diversity" (Preface). Human laws do not derive from the nature of human beings per se, but "relate to" a great variety of factors,

---

[47] For a similar conclusion reached by a very different route, see Lowenthal, "Book I of *Spirit*," 490–91.

none of which has the rationalist necessity that Montesquieu speaks of in his first definition. This is not to say that laws vary in random and merely arbitrary ways, for then Montesquieu could have no science of laws. Whatever regularities there are, however, cannot be discovered via any sort of essentialist metaphysics.

According to the definition of "law in general" in I_3, the law of nature as Montesquieu has discussed it is not a law. (In this, Montesquieu again verbally agrees with Hobbes.) On Montesquieu's account, then, the law of nature is only in the metaphorical sense of the aforementioned first definition a law. The only "real" law is positive law.[48] At bottom, Montesquieu agrees with those like Hobbes who see law as the will of the lawgiver, although, as it turns out, Montesquieu has a much broader and more flexible conception of law-giving than Hobbes does.

When speaking of the laws that human beings institute in response to the state of war, Montesquieu identifies three sorts of laws: laws "bearing on the relations . . . peoples have with one another," "laws concerning the relation between those who govern and those who are governed," and "laws concerning the relation that all citizens have with one another" (I_3). In speaking of these three sorts of laws, Montesquieu for the first time uses the term *droit* rather than *loi* (*droit de gens*, *droit politique*, and *droit civil*, respectively).[49] Law proper is *droit*, human reason addressing human reason. *Droit* has a necessarily normative element that *loi* lacks. *Loi* can be used to describe the regular relations among physical bodies, such as the laws of motion, whereas *droit* cannot. In accord with his new terminology, when Montesquieu lists the great variety of laws by which "men are governed" in Book XXVI, he labels them all as *droit*.

The establishment of positive laws represents some sort of reassertion of the law of nature, for these laws are a response to the state of war unleashed by human forgetfulness of their original nature in society. The coming of law and governments does not imply the full return of the law of nature, however. As Montesquieu makes clear in the next sequence of *Spirit* (Books II–VIII), the three main types of government all involve major breaches of the law of nature.

Despotism is a form of government in which fear rules, and with it a false sort of peace: "While the principle of despotic government is fear, its end is tranquility; but this is not a peace, it is the silence of the towns that the enemy is ready to occupy" (V_{14}). As this passage implies, the fear under a despotism only imperfectly secures what the law of nature provides—namely, preservation of the individual and the species.

In some ways, monarchies and republics violate the law of nature even more deeply than does despotism, for at least depotism displays the natural motive power (fear based in a feeling of weakness) that Montes-

---

[48] Lowenthal draws a similar conclusion in his "Book I of *Spirit*," 496.
[49] Ibid., 494.

quieu sees in the state of nature. In republics, the citizens act on the basis of virtue, a feeling of solidarity and love for the community; this leads them to risk their lives willingly for the republic. In monarchies, the chief subjects are motivated by honor, a sentiment that leads them to despise the fear of death and which makes them willing to risk death in order to achieve distinction. After the institution of positive law or right, society resists (or controls and regularizes) the state of war that was introduced through the formation of society and the subsequent near erasure of the law of nature. Yet society does not do this through a restoration of the law of nature. Contrary to Hobbes and even (to some degree) Locke, Montesquieu thinks that one cannot understand political life predominantly in terms of nature and natural law. The chief task, almost, of Montesquieu's treatment of actual governments is to explore how they operate *against* nature and the law of nature. The great disparity between actual human history and natural principles sets Montesquieu on the path to his new political science.

Partly because natural law comes so close to being erased in society, it cannot serve as a standard for political life in the way posited by so much of the pre-Montesquieu natural law tradition. Even if it could, it is not clear that the sort of natural law Montesquieu discusses would be a suitable normative guide to political life. Unlike both the "possible laws" and the forms of *droit*, the law of nature is not normative in its own terms, although it might have some normative implications (see XXVI_{3-5}). It is not clear how strong these implications are. We can use slavery as an example here: does the natural law condemn slavery in a clear and unequivocal way, or would it accept slavery if slaveholders could engage in it without risk to themselves? To put the problem another way, if the natural law is merely the motivating passion that is effective in the state of nature, what force, normative or actual, does it have when it is no longer the motivating passion? What force does it have, for example, when it is replaced by the passions that serve as the "principles" of the several kinds of government?

So little does Montesquieu insist on natural law as a standard for positive law that many readers wonder whether he has a standard of political right at all. Readers of *Spirit* break into two major camps—those who think he is more or less a complete relativist (or who think that to be consistent, he should be), and those who see him favoring one or another of the forms of government that he depicts. Within the latter class, one finds those who see Montesquieu as a supporter of monarchy, others who consider him an advocate of republics, and still others who believe, as I do, that Montesquieu is a proponent of the hybrid and unique "free constitution" that he describes in Books XI–XII. One reason readers disagree about where Montesquieu stands, apart from his sly efforts to confuse and confound us, is the elusiveness of the ultimate standards in terms of which he judges politics.

It is not possible to enter into a complete (or even close to adequate) discussion here, but despite the failure of some readers to see it, Montesquieu is not in the least a moral or political relativist, as his fierce opposition to despotism and slavery should make clear. He does possess a standard of political right. This standard is that of natural right (as opposed to natural law). Montesquieu speaks most clearly of natural right in Book X as he prepares to turn his attention in Books XI and XII to the kind of political order most in accord with that standard. "Men," Montesquieu reveals, "have the right to kill in the case of natural defense" (X_1). Like natural law, natural right prescribes preservation. The laws of nature tend toward preservation (equivocally, as it turns out). This is not merely a natural fact; it is a moral fact as well, for preservation is also something to which human beings have a right. Montesquieu does not ground this right in a Hobbesian or Spinozistic manner, that is, the right is not grounded in the fact that men are (sometimes) irresistibly driven to act so as to preserve themselves. Montesquieu notes instead that "in the case of natural defense I have the right to kill, because my life is mine" (X_2). The idea here is that I have a right to my life, and others do not; because it is mine, it belongs to me. It is an injustice for others to take from me what is mine, and therefore I may rightly act to protect and preserve what is mine. On this basis, Montesquieu argues that conquerors do not have a general right to enslave the conquered, and concludes more generally that slavery, despotism, and the like are great travesties. Because of these aspects of Montesquieu's thought, I mostly disagree with political scientist David Lowenthal's conclusion that Montesquieu "refuses to take the natural rights of man . . . as the new basis of orientation."[50] Montesquieu, like Locke, finds the bedrock ground of political morality not in natural law, but in right understood as self-ownership.[51]

Given the agreement between Montesquieu and Locke in regard to the ultimate standard of right, it is not surprising that Montesquieu's account of the just or rational political order is recognizably a development of Locke's account of the same. Books XI and XII, probably the best known parts of *Spirit*, depict the "constitution" that "has political liberty for its direct purpose" (XI_6). In these books, Montesquieu provides both his account of the rational order and his translation of the natural standard of self-ownership into political terms; in each instance, Montesquieu can be

---

[50] Ibid., 495.

[51] I partially agree with Hulliung's conclusion that "[b]oth the Christian deity and the law of nature were expendable as methods of condemning evil. Of and by itself, historiography was equal to the task of condemning injustice." Hulliung, *Montesquieu*, 141. Hulliung means by this that historical investigation can reveal the self-defeating character of unjust actions and policies. This may be correct for Rome (Hulliung's example here), but Montesquieu is clear that despotisms have quite impressive survival power. Besides, one needs a standard of what makes for a good or bad outcome. For a discussion of Locke on self-ownership, see my *Natural Rights and the New Republicanism* (Princeton, NJ: Princeton University Press, 1994), chap. 9.

seen as revising Locke's positions on the relevant matters. For Locke, self-ownership flowers into the rights of life, liberty, and estate, and the proper or legitimate end of government is the preservation of the objects of these rights. For Montesquieu, self-ownership leads to the standard of liberty: the rational or good order is the one that is free.

Montesquieu's revision of Locke is twofold. First, unlike Locke, Montesquieu does not unequivocally identify the rational order with the legitimate order. Montesquieu's examination of the various forms of government has convinced him that no one standard of legitimacy can be affirmed. Even a despotism, abhorrent as such a system is, may be the best option available in certain sorts of circumstances. Because of this, Montesquieu refuses to lay down a standard of legitimacy that would deny such a government some claim on the allegiance of its citizens (Preface). It is not the case here that Montesquieu has replaced Locke's relatively stringent standard of legitimacy with some other standard that is more lenient. Rather, Montesquieu has merely set the question of legitimacy aside.

In his second revision of Locke, Montesquieu defines the standard of right or good government in terms of "liberty," where that term is understood as "that tranquility of spirit which comes from the opinion each one has of his security" (XI_6). Put more simply, liberty "consists in security or in one's opinion of one's security" ($XII_{1,2}$). The security Montesquieu has in mind is the assurance an individual has that neither he nor his possessions will be infringed upon by the ruling authorities or other citizens. Interactions with authorities and interactions with other citizens are, as noted above, the two types of relations that can lead to war within societies once members of these societies "feel their strength" as a result of social bonding. Liberty, then, is the true pacification of society with respect to these two dimensions of war. Locke and Montesquieu agree that only a free society supplies this true pacification. Despotisms by their very nature cannot supply it, for under such systems the body of the society is laid open to the use of force (or of threats of force) by the ruler. Even the ancient republic, that government marked by virtue and capable of such prodigious human actions as takes away Montesquieu's breath at times, does not succeed at providing the solution to the state of war. This is because republics "are not free states by their nature" (XI_4):

> Observe the possible situation of a citizen in these republics. The body of the magistracy, as executor of the laws, retains all the power it has given itself as legislator. It can plunder the state by using its general will; and, as it also has the power of judging, it can destroy each citizen by using its particular will. (XI_6)

Monarchies are better at providing liberty, but they are still very imperfect compared to the free constitution proper. They "do not have liberty for their direct purpose ... ; they aim only for the glory of the citizens, the state, and the prince" (XI$_7$). Montesquieu concedes, even insists, that "this glory results in a spirit of liberty that *can* ... produce equally great things [as are seen in the free state, per se] and *can perhaps* contribute as much to happiness as liberty itself" (XI$_7$, emphases added). Monarchies are good only to the extent that they mimic and approximate a free regime; notice how qualified Montesquieu's judgment is on how likely they are to do so. Moreover, even when a monarchy does mimic a free regime, the achievement is fragile, for it depends not so much on fixed structures, but rather on the will of the monarch. This is because it is the monarch who must see the wisdom and goodness of the division of authority between himself and his nobles, especially with regard to the placement of the judicial authority. Montesquieu is keenly aware of a tendency of monarchies to "degenerate into despotism" (XI$_7$).

Montesquieu's views are quite close to those expressed by Locke, although Montesquieu spends much more time examining the types of government attempted throughout human history. He differs somewhat from Locke in that he emphasizes liberty rather than the securing of rights, and because he speaks of liberty in terms of security or the opinion of security. On the whole, Montesquieu subjectivizes the criteria of political right. For him, the good order is not so much a certain kind of order per se, but the order that produces a certain subjective state in citizens. This shift leads in turn to several modifications in the Lockean model of the rational constitution. Since Montesquieu considers the *opinion* of security to be of primary importance, he concludes that the rational order requires a separate judicial power in which authority remains centrally in the hands of the people (or at least some of them) in the form of institutions like juries. Locke, in contrast, had left the judiciary as part of the executive power. In Montesquieu's scheme, the concern for opinion of security also produces a more unequivocal requirement that there be popular representation in the legislature. Locke had required representation of the property-owners for the sake of taxation, but Montesquieu extends this in a markedly republican direction.

Montesquieu's emphasis on the opinion of security rather than on actual security derives in part from his taking seriously the Hobbesian/ Lockean analysis of the causes of war on the one hand, and the Lockean analysis of labor on the other. Hobbes especially had emphasized the "subjective causes" of war: people, he said, make war out of "diffidence," that is, fear they will be at risk if they do not act first. They also make war when they believe they can get away with dominating others. Montesquieu's emphasis on the opinion of security is meant to address these subjective elements in the genesis of the state of war, and thus contribute to the pacification that the right order produces.

Montesquieu's positing of the opinion of security as the standard of liberty also appears to be an embodiment of the Lockean insights into

labor. Locke demonstrated the political significance of time: the blessings
of civil life depend to a very great extent on human labor, the procurement of which requires securing to the laborer the fruits of that labor, for
labor is painful and therefore costly. Given the nature of things, most
labor must be expended for the promise of reward, for the fruits appear
only in the future. A society organized around labor is thus a futural
society, one where present protection of one's rights is by no means one's
sole interest: one desires an assurance of continuing protection, that is, of
security. One wishes for "the opinion of security." If one has that, then one
is satisfied. Montesquieu's emphasis on the opinion of security is indeed
a modification of Locke, but, as can be seen, it is not a major modification,
or one that requires any fundamental reformulation of Lockean principles.

V. Some Conclusions

In Montesquieu we see a phenomenon visible in many other places
in the early liberal tradition—an amazingly ambiguous stance toward
Hobbes. Montesquieu, like Locke, Pufendorf, and Hume, is much less
anti-Hobbesian than he seems. As is the case with these other theorists,
the thought that Montesquieu stands in stark opposition to Hobbes is
partly due to conscious deception on Montesquieu's part and partly due
to the subtleties of Montesquieu's actual position. Montesquieu most
agrees with Hobbes in a critique of traditional natural law doctrines.
Montesquieu, like Hobbes, rejects these doctrines on the ground that they
contain an inadequate understanding of nature; in both thinkers, this
rejection is clearly associated with the rejection of teleology that occurred
as a result of the scientific philosophical discoveries of the seventeenth
century.[52] Hobbes loudly and openly embraces materialism and pure
mechanism, and loudly and openly challenges any lingering vestiges of
the authority of Aristotle. Montesquieu is neither loud nor open, and
appeals to Cartesian dualism rather than simple materialism. The result,
as far as nature goes, is the same for both theorists—teleology is rejected,
mechanism is affirmed. Montesquieu, at least in *Spirit*, seems more interested in getting this result than in how he establishes it, and thus one
finds him generally willing to almost indiscriminately combine his dualism with appeals to Lockean monism. Montesquieu takes a more imma-
nent view of nature than did those thinkers who represent the classical
natural law tradition. He is concerned with "the effectual truth" of nature,
and thus he seeks to understand nature as the array of forces that move
the material and human worlds.

At the same time, however, Montesquieu is not a Hobbesian. When we
look back over the trajectory of Montesquieu's rejection of Hobbes, two
main points seem particularly important. The first of these points is that,

---

[52] Hulliung, *Montesquieu*, 115, 241–42, 242 n. 33.

ironically, Hobbes misunderstands nature (at least human nature) as much as the ancients did, for he is led into grave error through his failure to appreciate the "flexible" or, as we might say today, the "historical" character of humanity. Montesquieu builds on the Lockean "way of ideas" to open up this insight that Hobbes, in his more naive way, missed.

Montesquieu also disagrees with Hobbes by saying that the true normative foundation is that of natural right. He does not see natural right as Hobbes does, as "a right of every man to everything, including one another's body," or as a simple liberty. Rather, Montesquieu follows Locke in grasping natural right as self-ownership and thus as containing within it limitations such that no one has a natural right to "another's body" or another's goods.

Montesquieu uses these insights to build a new practical science of politics as well as a more sophisticated normative science. One might say that with Montesquieu the liberal tradition reached a level of maturity it has not surpassed since. This achievement was made possible by Montesquieu's discovery of human "flexibility," a concept that Rousseau will later refer to as "malleability." Montesquieu resists the antiliberal effect this insight had in the hands of Rousseau and his nineteenth-century German successors by holding firmly to the idea of natural right. This idea is one fruit of the critique of traditional natural law doctrines that was initiated by Montesquieu's predecessors in the liberal tradition and extended by Montesquieu himself.

Government, University of Notre Dame

INDEX

For EU product safety concerns, contact us at Calle de José Abascal, 56–1°, 28003 Madrid, Spain or eugpsr@cambridge.org.

www.ingramcontent.com/pod-product-compliance
Ingram Content Group UK Ltd.
Pitfield, Milton Keynes, MK11 3LW, UK
UKHW020334140625
459647UK00018B/2137